gh conway '72

D1060569

Principles of His Physical Education

HAROLD M. BARROW, P.E.D.

Chairman and Professor
Department of
Physical Education,
Wake Forest University
Winston-Salem, North Carolina

Lea & Febiger 1971 PHILADELPHIA

Health Education, Physical Education, and Recreation Series

Ruth Abernathy, Ph.D., Editorial Advisor
Chairman, Department for Women, School of Physical and Health Education,
University of Washington, Seattle, Washington 98105

Copyright © 1971 by Lea & Febiger. Copyright under the International
Copyright Union. All rights reserved. This book is protected by copyright.
*No part of it may be reproduced in any manner or by any means, without written
permission from the publisher.*

ISBN 0-8121-0330-0
Library of Congress Catalog Card Number: 72-135678
Printed in the United States of America
Published in Great Britain by Henry Kimpton, London

Dedicated to the memory of my wife

GRACE

whose patient understanding and constant encouragement in life and inspiration in death have made this book possible

Foreword

A book designed to present concepts of human movement and to discuss their application in education obviously draws from many sources. Harold Barrow has reviewed many fields and a number of subspecialties in developing this broad study of the scope of physical education with particular reference to the school setting. From the mass of data, he has developed guidelines for action by teachers in planning for teaching and in deciding *what* and *how* to teach.

The nature of physical education is currently the focus of much heated discussion. Yet, when intent is examined, it would appear that semantic differences are one source of misinterpretation. The idea that a field of inquiry dealing with one or more aspects of human movement must underlie physical education is gaining general acceptance. This in turn has led to the use of the term "physical education" to designate the applied or school program.

Recognition that planning for the application of data from the field of inquiry to programs of physical education must be based upon some systematic valuing is relatively widespread. The actual relation of program outcomes to the breadth or the limited view of goals has been repeatedly cited in the literature of the field for at least half a century. Some of the exciting idea conflicts among our professional forebears exemplify this as do the persistence of some problems and issues. One current evidence is the view of physical fitness as an objective or valued outcome as contrasted with the view of physical fitness as a program. A thoughtful appraisal of the difference, when planning for behavioral objectives, leads to an increased appreciation of the practical necessity for a clearly enunciated value system. The practitioner inevitably must view his growth toward professional maturity in terms of lifetime learning of new knowledges, of a continuing synthesis of beliefs, of challenging established plans and methods, and of ongoing replanning and restructuring of value hierarchies.

Barrow briefly explores the role and the structure of traditional systems. In addition to a simple yet clear presentation of views, the student may enjoy comparing differences in observable practice with beliefs that may underlie such differences. The direct relation between a constellation of beliefs about one's field and one's actions in that field is examined all too infrequently. In this book, interesting examples of beliefs and outcomes are presented.

In a period of emphasis on the relevant *now*, the review of activity patterns, forms, and programs may prove to be particularly helpful. In spite of brevity, the variability in beliefs and values underlying physical activity *in* and *through time* may stimulate some questioning as to current diversity in programs and in pros and cons of some professional issues. Some fundamental beliefs about the body, about dance, and about athletics, for example, can be classified more readily when re-examined in the light of value variables observed in different countries at different times.

Personally, the emphasis on the profession, on the promotion of the profession, and on the professional leader could serve simply as an addendum. Yet the clarification of the differences between a trade and a profession or a technician and a master teacher or leader may be important for physical educators. Of all fields in education, we appear to be the most worried and at the same time to have a real cause for worry. In part, this reaction may stem from a confusion as to the nature of physical education. Is *the* profession the *professional* athlete, the prize fighter, the grand prix driver, or the dramatic wrestler? We say not, but apparently are rarely sure what our relationship or responsibility really may or should be. In fact, only now are we *beginning* to resolve or at least appreciate the problems associated with role prescriptions in planning for physical education or the related programs of intra- and extra-murals, not to mention athletics as preparations for professional sports.

If the potential teacher or coach comes to the field with only an emotionalized conception of the nature and scope of physical education, the early emphasis on *the profession* may help to set the stage for a more analytical and cognitive appreciation of the breadth of responsibility required. Such awareness must be the basis for substantive change. On the other hand, such a review might be more comprehensible following the trauma of an initial exposure to the field of inquiry. This exposure would require an exploration of data essential to understanding or at least some appreciation of the import of such basic problems as a description of human movement, an identification of major sources of movement variability, or a discrimination between the meaning and the significance of moving. Preference as to which comes first may well arise from institutional or college goals and the consequent perceptions of priorities by faculty members.

Barrow effectively sets the stage for an examination of selected sources of information by describing the nature, consistency, relative permanence and use of principles. The extrapolation of guidelines from data regarding biological structure and function is relatively common to the field of physical education. For many years this represented one of the few widely adopted substantive areas in programs of teacher preparation. Facts underlying principles of physical conditioning and performance and related guidelines should be helpful.

The forthright attempt to deal with complex data derived from the behavioral sciences is admirable. As more specific research is reported in these areas of motor learning, sensorimotor development, and individual and group interaction, the identifiable principles will lead to major changes in programs and significant shifts in methodology. Some of the exciting developments in programs for elementary school age children reflect possible re-directions.

It is even more difficult to examine some of the implications of the more obvious cultural and social cues such as sex or class and activity interests and choices, or role prescriptions, or perception and performance level. Could we generally accept the guidelines that might be derived if we understood why some people need the security of a structured multiperson sport while others may seek a patterned yet individual-group activity such as contemporary dance? What similarities and differences exist in the meaning of the experience to those who participate in ballet, in gymnastics, or even in weight-lifting or wrestling? Other timely questions in this area might arise from an examination of the possible implications of sex-linked physical fitness problems that may arise from the increasing number of hours per week of major sport TV broadcasts. Are there other implications for cohesion in the nuclear family in sex-linked sports interests? What are implications for specificity as contrasted with generality of *social* learning in activities requiring high cohesion and group loyalty, as contrasted with activities requiring highly internalized reinforcement and limited reliance on external cues? It is interesting to speculate on physical education content and progression in school programs when "prescription" is as clear and obvious in this area as for a given level of skill or muscle fitness.

Curriculum revision is under way in many schools as well as in teacher preparation. The major difficulty will be to insist on basic understanding and thoughtful progress rather than partial, limited and ultimately indefensible developments. It would be most unfortunate if essential revisions were delayed by attention to objectives stated in traditional ways to meet stereotyped goals for tomorrow's youngsters.

Evaluation of the process and the product are important and clearly stated. It is hoped that the student will review Part III and ponder the possibility *and* the necessity for rigorous evaluation of proposed goals and stated objectives. Such evaluation should also include questioning the validity of the *hierarchy* of objectives.

Much of the content in this book documents and supports new directions in physical education. Some chapters are more restricted to common practices and undoubtedly will be revised as new data become available.

Ruth Abernathy

University of Washington
Seattle, Washington

Preface

This book is designed as an introduction to the profession of physical education for the student major. It provides an orientation to the field and is aimed at developing a philosophy of physical education that will enable the student to conduct himself as a knowledgeable and concerned professional.

The book is organized into four parts. The *first* section provides an introduction to the principles to follow. In this section the need for physical education is emphasized. The relationship between education and physical education is explored. Since the student must build a philosophy of education and physical education for himself, the traditional and educational philosophies are presented, and because goals grow out of philosophy, aims and objectives are discussed. The *second* unit provides an orientation to the profession itself. It includes a study of leadership and professionalism, professional training, and professional opportunities. The *third* part contains the heart and core of the manuscript. It encompasses the principles of physical education and for sake of expediency has been categorized into the following subunits: (1) the principles involving the biological aspects of man and his quest for fitness; (2) principles involving sociological and anthropological man culminating in the study of human values and a value system; and (3) principles involving the psychological aspects of man with special emphasis on motor learning and performance. The *fourth* unit involves application of principles and is concerned with the curriculum and its evaluation.

The content has been structured as a sort of continuum, not in importance, but more with reference to an evolving understanding. The student is first exposed to the introductory aspects which are necessary tools for an understanding of education in general and the specialized field of physical education. He learns about his profession and how he, as a professional, may fit into the professional cycle. He next becomes acquainted with the historical, biological, sociological, anthropological, and psychological principles of his discipline. At the end of the continuum he is provided an opportunity to learn how his philosophy and principles may be applied as his acquired knowledges and comprehensions are crystalized through his thinking into a program. This program together with its evaluation completes the various facets of the educational and professional cycles.

Any work of this nature owes its origin and fulfillment to many sources. A particular debt of gratitude is expressed to my many professional students who taught me much more than I taught them. A special appreciation is expressed to Mrs. Grace Krug and Mrs. T. M. McClelland for their assistance in reading and editing the manuscript and to Mrs. Mary Petty for preparing it in its final form.

HAROLD M. BARROW
Winston-Salem, North Carolina

Contents

v. good
capsule

good chart overview

PART I

Introduction to Physical Education

Chapter 1

Physical Education— Its Meaning and Relationship

INTRODUCTION

This is a book on the introduction and principles of physical education. In the complex technological world of today physical education can be understood only when it is looked upon in a frame of reference of the larger domain of education and society itself. Therefore, the student using it must understand that physical education is an integral part of the total educational spectrum and that education plays a dominant role in society. Ulrich suggests that education has three primary responsibilities to society (14–4).

First, the ultimate purpose of education in a society is the perpetuation of that society's social and cultural heritage. This is done through the educated individual. Each new generation is born into society with a biological inheritance but without the benefit of inheriting its culture genetically. This simply means that while biological traits are passed on to the offspring through the genes, cultural traits are not. Man only inherits a sufficiency to take on cultural traits. The culture of mankind must be learned

by each separate individual and everyone, culturally speaking, must start from scratch at birth. Education thus becomes society's primary means of enculturation. If this purpose is achieved even in part, it becomes incumbent on those who have been educated to live more effectively not only within their society but also within themselves.

Society does not entrust the responsibility of perpetuating its culture and socializing its youth to unorganized groups nor is it left to chance. Historically, educational institutions have been chartered for this purpose (14).

Education has a second primary responsibility. As its institutions perpetuate culture and society by transmitting the sociocultural heritage to each new generation, they are also charged with the responsibility of helping these new generations to adjust to the demands of this sociocultural heritage (14–4). This problem of adjustment of the individual to his culture is the second major responsibility of education. In the processes of education, youth must be trained for future occupations, their values and character must be instilled, their health, fitness and welfare must be promoted, and their modes of thinking, judgment, and behavior must be cultivated. These processes are based on values and each society must establish its own values—values which it considers desirable and essential for its welfare and survival. Then, in the educational spectrum, it selects those educational experiences which best seem to reflect the established values. Thus, those being educated become both a means and an end. They become an end of the educational processes but they also become the means through which the future of society is safeguarded and transmitted.

The educational processes which are the means to this end comprise the formal educational curricula (see Chapter 17), which are structured to acquaint the young with their culture, then to teach them how to live happily and effectively in their society by adjusting to its demands. Tests reveal that education has done a fair job in passing on the knowledge of culture but empirical observation reveals it has failed in the latter charge of adjustment—its responsibility of teaching for a happy and effective life. It has been assumed that these knowledges will result in behavior that will enable the individual to live more effectively in the present as well as the future and to make acceptable adjustments. It is doubtful, however, if education can ever be measured in terms of transmitted knowledges alone because it is behavior rather than knowledge that makes the real difference and knowledge does not necessarily lead to desirable behavior. Thus, the job of education is ultimately to bring about desirable modes of behavior. Therefore, one of the challenges of education is to teach for transfer. In addition to passing on knowledge of one's culture, education must aid the individual in adjusting his behavior to the demands of these

knowledges. Education must, therefore, transmit both knowledge and behavior since the ultimate test is not knowledge but life performance. This has always been a challenge in education.

This challenge today, however, is becoming more difficult as man's complex way of life becomes increasingly less effective in promoting this transmission. Today is truly a critical period for tomorrow with all its apocalyptic threats to survival. Culture has become so complex and society so demanding that more and more is required of the individual than ever before in the way of learning and powers to adjust. These complexities are constantly being accelerated. As the future begins to unfold, it becomes increasingly clear that some guidelines must be established in order to meet the demands of what may be a total new order brought on in some cases by a militant minority but chiefly by peaceful revolutions in a wide area of human concern. Relevance is a difficult but vital matter in these times. Some age-old problems which have plagued man are now being solved, but others still persist and in all too many instances seem little closer to solution now than in the past. However, to these age-old problems are added a multitude of new ones brought on by technology and the explosion of population and knowledge. These problems along with other aspects that are a residue of a burgeoning culture act, react and interact to make our times the most complex of any era in history. It is paradoxical that modern culture presents two ends of the spectrum. It not only has in it the potential for the ultimate in living, but also the potential for man's destruction. Modern society is characterized by a constellation of these interacting processes and the challenge of solving problems growing out of them is further complicated by more problems growing out of solutions. For example, there is the paradox of exercise in a democratic technological society. On the one hand it seems a technological culture has taken the drudgery out of man's work and has freed him from his need to exercise and to struggle in order to be physically strong and fit. Man has always strived for comfort and ease. On the other hand a democratic society permits him to discipline himself. The paradox is, of course, that the biological necessity for exercise is still there. Thus, it may well be that survival in the future will depend more on a society's value system and how well that system is implemented toward a self-disciplined citizenry than any other aspect of culture.

Therefore, a third paramount responsibility of education is to discover new relationships and knowledges along with values which will guide man away from the path of destruction which he has created for himself. This places education directly and unequivocally in the role of an effector of social change.

CONCEPTS BASIC TO THE NATURE AND MEANING OF PHYSICAL EDUCATION

There are some basic aspects to the rationale presented above which must be recognized in education as it establishes its processes and selects its values. There are numerous implications for physical education too. Some of these are significant and involve concepts which must become the concern of both general education and physical education. An explanation of five of these concepts seems relevant at this time if the professional student of physical education is to understand what is to follow in this text. It would be foolish, indeed, in an introductory chapter of a book designed to introduce the physical education student to the underlying principles and guidelines of his profession to provide answers to all of these problems.

The problems of society are not that simple nor is education for that matter. However, it would be of help for the student to be made aware at the beginning of his training career of the significant reasons why physical education must occupy a place of importance in society, and why the physical educators must play an important role in education. These five concepts will be briefly presented at this point so that the student may be made fully cognizant of the nature and meaning of physical education, of the status it has as a profession, and the importance of his role as a professional. These concepts will only be touched upon briefly here but will be more fully developed at a later point in this book. These concepts are not new and no one discipline has a monopoly on them. However, while they may not be new, they have not always been applied fully to educational practices to date. The professional student in physical education needs an early exposure to them. Then, as he forms his basic beliefs, these issues will serve as guidelines for him in his thinking and actions. He should understand their full import as the rationale for these could well be the capstones of his profession.

The Unitary Aspects of Man

The first concept has to do with the unitary aspect of the individual and the interdependence of all his parts. This interrelationship involves the mental, social, spiritual, and physical aspects and should force educators to take cognizance of all these facets as they operate in educational experience. This is commonly referred to as the *organismic theory* or the *whole student* point of view where in any given act of learning, the whole student reacts and learning takes place in all these areas simultaneously. Learning is never a singular process. This concept, as expounded by Plato over two thousand years ago, has only recently become a widely accepted principle in education. It still has not been put into practice in many instances in spite of its acceptance in theory. The deification of the mind and the dogmas of formal discipline are still lethal in some phases of education; only complacency rivals them as deterrent to educational progress.

This issue has several points of departure which should help in developing a philosophy of educational thought. Among the first things a physical education student should learn is the significance of this concept. It is a fundamental proposition of science and philosophy that no part can be understood aside from the whole and by the same token the whole man cannot be perceived fully until there is specialized knowledge of his parts. Thus, the student must recognize that movement and its related play, games, sports, exercise and dance are not just means of sweat, fun, and weight reduction, but they are basic to all types of learning, intellectual as well as physical. He should know that the parameters of learning encompass far more than traditional education implies. There is no learning that is purely physical or intellectual. Learning is a continuum along a linear scale. At one end of this continuum may be classified that learning which is more physical than mental but both are involved to degrees. At the other end the reverse is true and while learning may be more mental than physical, the physical is ever present. The difference between mental and physical learning is in degree rather than kind (3). The spectrum of learning has many shades, but they are all related. Lawther states that hypothetically no part of the whole reaches zero activity when other parts are engaged in learning (9).

When learning is accepted in this context of a multidimensional process, some new dimensions face education. There has already been a breaking down of barriers or divisions between disciplines as has never before been experienced. This dissolving of barriers and the integrative processes which draw the areas together are a result of both philosophy and research broadening the vistas of all disciplines and cutting across the lines of self-interest and isolationism. Both science and philosophy recognize that the individual is a whole. As they delve farther into the mysteries of this holistic concept, they can see no definite boundaries between the different aspects where in the past tradition has separated them. This wholeness can be understood only to the extent that the many commonalities are understood, and each of these can be understood only as a part of the whole and not as entities.

Learning must take place in a setting governed by this holistic concept— where the total person is involved. However, it must be admitted that the complex interrelationships of this process are not always clearly understood. As President Kennedy said, "The relationship between the soundness of the body and the activities of the mind is subtle and complex. Much is not yet understood." (6) There is much which is still cloaked in darkness, and it is, as the psychologist Penfield said, like men at the foot of a mountain. They stand in the clearings they have made on the foothills, looking up at the mountains they hope to scale. While in many aspects the peaks are hidden in the clouds of misunderstanding and lack of knowledge, extensive research in these areas is widening the "clearings" and the boundaries between the known and the unknown are being pushed back continually.

Permanence of the Nature of Man

The second concept concerns the permanence of the nature of the individual in the light of his evolution. The muscular system of man came first in the processes of evolution and all other systems of the body arose in response to its needs. In a sense today these systems still depend on exercise for their growth and development. The needs, characteristics, and qualities which are basic to biological life have changed relatively little in the last thirty thousand years. It is reasonable to expect no appreciable change in man's biologic nature during the next several thousand years since the processes of evolution operate slowly and only over long periods of time. However, due to the demands of the modern world, more and more is being required of the individual in the way of mental and emotional stresses and less and less in the way of physical activity. This biological need for exercise is permanent and while man's culture no longer requires it for survival, his biologic nature does. Man must choose to engage in some form of strenuous physical movement since his environment no longer forces him into activity. If he does not choose to exercise, he faces degenerative effects biologically since this biological basis of life is inexorably operative and nature brooks no interference in its developmental design.

While it is reasonable to expect no change in man's biological nature in the immediate future, perhaps changes will occur in the sociological area (15). The demands of the social environment have grown in far greater proportions than have man's adjustment powers. There is considerable agreement that unless changes for the better do occur, the species of man may grow extinct as so many other species have in the past. Adaptations which failed to occur rapidly enough to meet changing environments, or evolution which got out of control in the past, has generally led to degeneracy with the result of species extinction. Man's sociocultural evolution must narrow the gap. His biological

evolution for all practical purposes is no longer operative.

Changed Way of Life

A third issue or fact concerns the changed condition of man's nurture—of his way of life and his physical universe. While his nature has not changed in the last two thousand years, and this includes the powers of his intellect if not the amount of knowledge, his environment has changed greatly. While he evolved to live in an environment characterized by a great deal of big-muscle activity, outdoor living, coarse foods, and uncomplicated social relationships, he now finds himself living a life characterized by automation, mechanization, sedentarianism, increased leisure, and complex social interaction. Each of these in its own way contributes to soft living. Technological progress, atomic power, and space travel are realities and in the ensuing years will open new vistas heretofore undreamed of in daily living. In general, all of these changed conditions began with the advent of the Industrial Revolution. It was the catalyst which changed man's existence and which catapulted him into the age of electronics, atomic energy, space exploration, and increasing control of the universe. At the same time, however, it has exacted a toll on the other end of the continuum. In the past, changes in the environment have come about slowly in terms of time and, until recently, man had time to adjust to whatever these changes were. The great renaissance bridging the last century with its remarkable technical changes has resulted in "easy living" on the one hand but on the other has resulted in many stresses and strains particularly in the mental and emotional areas. Education must face up to the residue inherent in an evolving culture such as prevalence of degenerative diseases, lower levels of fitness, obesity, nervous disorders, alcoholism, along with numerous social ills.

In the last few decades sociocultural changes have come about quite rapidly, and it seems inevitable that they will proceed at a more accelerated pace in the future. In fact the only constant in the present seems to be change. Man in the past has always had great adjustment powers and through the ages he has always been able to make adjustments when they are needed. However, such changes in the past came about slowly and the evolutionary processes were inexorably operative through his biological heritage and his culture. Until the last few decades man's mode of living and his environment furnished the needed conditions for biologic survival. In the last half century, however, changes have occurred at such a rapid pace within such a comparatively short span of time that man simply has not had time to adjust to the new conditions. There has not been sufficient time for his biologic nature to change even accepting the premise that further biologic evolution is possible.

Modern society requires more of the individual than ever before and these demands are increasing each year. However, there is a paradox here. While civilization has rapidly accelerated its demands on the individual for adaptive behavior, particularly mentally and emotionally, it has, at the same time, limited his opportunities for developing such behavior by taking away both the necessity and the opportunity for normal amounts of movement.

It would seem that there is a paradox here. While man was originally intended to live his life in one kind of an environment, and the set of his whole being was oriented in this direction for thousands of years, he now finds himself in the short span of a century committed to a different life. He must exist in a setting for which he is poorly equipped by his heritage. A study of anthropology will show that man has only partially adjusted to his new role (see Chapter 13). Since he is experiencing difficulty in making the necessary biologic and sociological adjustments which are appropriate for a good life in a fast changing culture, some safeguards must be taken by society. Returning to nature and the uncomplicated life of a bygone era might solve some of these problems in part. Since this solution is out of the question, it is the job of education along with physical education to cope with the dilemma in other ways. Education along with other socializing agencies must take man's original nature as it has evolved and now exists and will continue to exist in the foreseeable future and make it compatible with a dynamic culture which is changing rapidly and will continue to change more rapidly and dramatically with each new marvel. Since these changes in man's life created conditions which make it increasingly more difficult for him to make adaptations, and since culture grows more complex with the passage of time and with explosions of population, techniques, and knowledges, education faces a great challenge and must, by the very nature of its functions, become more complex and inclusive, and at the same time more selective. But there is a warning lesson here, too. On the one hand education must deal with a new order and project itself into the new and sometimes unprecedented, and on the other it must also return to some of the basic patterns of living (8).

This is especially true with reference to the biological needs for exercise and movement and the psychological needs for releases from the stresses, strains, and drains brought on by the complexities of modern pressures. The problems growing out of the complexities as well as the simplicities of education are multifaceted, and they inevitably create great challenges for educators. The individual must be guarded against overexposure to the complexities of society, while at the same time his opportunity for contact with the simplicities must be protected. The solutions to these problems must be found not only in the sciences but also the humanities. To this extent education must be eclectic since its philosophy, practices, processes, and methodology are drawn from all of these sources.

Physical education can meet its share of the challenge, in part at least, in this area of responsibility by teaching not only the movement skills of games, sports, dance, and exercise, but also the necessary knowledge and values which will motivate people to choose to perform them.

Continuity of Social Experience

Another issue of the first three is the continuity of social experience. Dr. Delbert Oberteuffer has stated, "This country is not going to be saved—or destroyed—by muscle. But by the quality of its moral fibre." (11) Basically, moral fiber has the connotation of one standing up for what is considered to be right by a society and ability to overcome the hostile tendencies of primal nature and get along with people. As man evolved biologically and psychologically, he was also evolving sociologically. Thus, sociological aspects are as much a part of the physical education experience and the educational problem as are the biological and psychological. In the process of evolution, man moved from a state where his original nature was animal to one where he took on human traits. His evolutionary processes produced not only significant biological and psychological changes but also sociological as well. While all of these changes together brought about salutary results, they came about in a subtle way, spread over millions of years. There was no moment of truth when man crossed the threshold between animal and man and emerged as a human being. The process was a long one growing out of a continued interaction of pre-man with a changeable and demanding environment.

Human nature can be measured in a sense by man's ability to relate to others and get along with them. While much remains to be learned about original nature and man's origin, it is reasoned that his relation to the group developed out of his indisputable need for safety. The continuity of experience tended to evolve into something much more complex. As man scaled higher on the evolutionary ladder, these relationships became increasingly more complex. The need to relate to others evolved into as much a part of man's heritage as the shape of his head or the integration of his thought processes. This need to relate begins at birth and continues throughout life.

It may be the biological and psychological which are the core of life and life's processes, but it is the ability of man to relate to others through interaction and get along with them which makes that life worth living. It is the social relationship which gives meaning to life and which gives it depth, variety, and content. As man was evolving biologically, his ability to relate to others was also evolving. Man's original nature interacting with environmental conditions led to increasingly more complex experiences. When his activities with others were interwoven in experience, more complex social relationships and patterns were initiated. These experiences evolved into needs which are now basic and deep-seated. These needs, rooted in his relationship with others for survival, grew out of a harsh environment. As man now matures, his needs to relate can be met only on a higher and higher level. He can meet them only by being exposed in ever widening circles to the social milieu. In the modern and dramatically changing world these needs become even more complex.

While man's biological evolution is, for practical purposes, completed, his social and cultural evolution are ongoing continuing processes (15). He must learn to relate on a much higher level than he is currently operating if he is to survive. His biological evolution took place in response to the challenge for survival. His ability to survive in the next centuries encounters new problems which will have to be solved. While his survival in the past was more biological, his survival in the future may well be more in the nature of the sociological. While he probably had little to say about his biologic evolution, he has the potential to guide his socio-cultural evolution. Thus, whether he does survive in the future or not will depend not so much on his biological and psychological heritage, but rather on how well or how adequately his social make-up can evolve and adjust to the demanding requirements of the times.

This must become one of the primary challenges in education in the years ahead. Just as technology has revolutionized industry and the economy of nations, social organization has itself been revolutionized. It has been ordered into something highly developed and complex. Youth today are challenged to reflect this organization. If they are to meet the challenge, they must become more adept at adjusting and relating socially. These social skills are rooted in the processes of evolution and are related to the basic skills and concepts growing out of movement in the same manner that all other types of learning are.

Man's social experience is inexorably related to his political experiences. In fact it is said that a democracy is essentially a social system. If this be true, it could well be that man has not yet evolved socially to the extent that his democracy is workable. In view of the recent events growing out of the social morasses created by racial strife and the attack by youth on old standards and values, the democratic social processes are challenged. With the attitude of the judiciary and the reluctance of the courts to deal strictly with offenders of the law along with the attitude of most people to overlook justice and law and their tacit sanctions of wrongdoing, it may be that democracy can no longer deal forcefully with the disintegrating factors which would destroy it. One wonders perhaps what form of government could deal effectively with the forces which would destroy it. It is the nature of the democratic way of life that its efficiency and strength are incumbent on the citizen's integrity and willingness to accept sacrifice for the common good. When this democratic and social value erodes beyond a reasonable limit, the foundation on which a democratic society rests becomes unstable.

Movement as a Process of Integration

Everything a child knows and can do had to be learned. Certainly at the early stages of his life, all learning has a physical basis. The basic mechanics for learning are present in his genes at conception and in his body at birth, but knowing and doing are learned processes. Man literally learns his way through life. Racially speaking, in a sense, all accumulated knowledges and learnings which are now embodied in civilization are a result of movement and its ensuing process of integration. The processes of evolution got under way only when the organism started to move about and the need for locomotion arose. The development of the muscular system started the wheels spinning inexorably along the path of evolution and the eventual emergence of man. Thus, the muscular system is the oldest of the body systems and all the other systems arose and finally developed in response to its needs. Through cell division and specialization of function, the muscular system evolved and as it grew in complexity, it was followed by other systems including the nervous system. As the nervous system was elaborated upon in evolution in order to meet the needs of the muscular system and its accompanying organic systems, an inextricable relationship was set up between the two. In a sense, the nervous system and its elaboration is a product of the muscular system and its movement.

In organized patterns of motion, three movement components are recognized: postural, transport, and manipulative. In the integrative process the child develops and learns through all three of these avenues. The first two involve patterns of movement which are used to overcome the force of gravity. They involve muscles and nerves which are older in the evolutionary cycle and which are more durable and less complex than muscles which govern manipulative movements. They are generally regarded as fundamental muscles and their movements are called *gross motor activity* or *big-muscle activity*. These muscles are phylogenetically older and tougher than the manipulative type, and their vigorous movements enable man to develop the nervous stability needed to offset the stresses and strains of modern civilization. His neurological organization begins with these movements. The postural adjustments are the bases of all movements and together with the transport type provide the movement patterns for dealing with the force of gravity. All transport and most manipulative patterns of movement must originate with posture.

In the integrative processes the child must first learn to hold up his head and later to manipulate tension in his mus-cles in order to sit up. As he gains in the necessary adjustments for posture, he is also learning patterns of locomotion. Postural-transport movements start with crawling which resembles the movements of the amphibian. It is done with the body in contact with the floor, the arms and legs working in a homolateral pattern. By homolateral is meant the arm and leg on one side are extended while the arm and leg on the other are flexed. The next stage in development is creeping with the child's body off the floor with his weight supported on the hands and knees, the limbs moving in a cross-pattern motion denoting the principle of opposition (see Chapter 11) with the opposite hand and knee alternating in flexion and extension.

Delacato states that these stages must be experienced in this order if proper neurological organization is to occur in the child (4). He emphasizes that nature brooks no interference in the evolving processes, and the development of the child must not be accelerated so as to bypass these stages since in the processes of ontogeny these forms of movement occur. His theory is based on the principle that ontogenic must repeat phylogenic development. His theory implies that if these earlier transport movements of crawling and creeping are not exercised in a normal way over a normal time span, nature will be thwarted and the child may later suffer problems of mobility and communication or both.

The next stage of postural-transport activity is the child's venture into the biped position followed by walking. Unless he has mastered the cross-pattern activity of creeping, he may have difficulty not only in walking but later in his mental learnings, particularly reading. Delacato's theory states that the child's neurological organization is incomplete because he has bypassed the proper stages in development. These theories have not been shown to be true yet through scientific evidence. However, in his clinic Delacato has shown that the slow learner can be improved dramatically when he participates in a program of movement.

There does appear to be a pattern of life from embryonic beginning to maturity marked by a series of stages in development. The stages must of necessity overlap but they are nevertheless clearly identified. While postural and transport movements come first in the scheme of development and the specialized movements of the accessory systems come later, they should not be thought of as separate systems or entities. The individual is segmented at this point partly for better understanding and partly for convenience in description. Getman lists six sequential and interrelated areas in the developmental processes which account for the totality of the child (5). He points out that a child's development is a combination of all of these areas as they are interwoven through the child's own experience. The development of "general movement patterns for action" is placed first in the sequence because, as Getman points out, chronologically this process develops first. These are the same as the postural-transport patterns discussed on the preceding pages. Getman believes them to be the primary process and that they form the basis for all performance and learning. This theory is borne out by the theme in a recent physical education convention: "Learning to move and moving to learn." While this is not an entirely new idea in education, it has only recently taken on new meaning and emphasis. There is an emerging concept that movement is a modality for the basic integration of man's totality, especially the mind.

Getman's second area concerns the development of "special movements patterns." In this instance, the child de-velops and learns as he uses his movements to control and manipulate objects and matters in space around him. In phylogeny these smaller muscles involving the extremities of the arms and legs and the speech mechanisms are referred to as the accessory muscles. They came later in the evolutionary cycle and as a result are younger, more complex, and less efficient in developing the endurance and stability of the nervous system than the older fundamental group. Their conditioning must not be rushed ahead of the fundamental muscles in the educative process.

One of the first specialized movement patterns learned by the child is the hand-eye coordinations where the hands and eyes work in combinations. This relationship between the hands and eyes in movement patterns is extremely complicated and requires an extended period of time to perfect. Such learnings are not a result of maturation, although there is little doubt that time in the child's development is of essence since such coordinations are a product of many months and perhaps years of doing and practicing. This hand-eye combination is one of the first complex learnings the child achieves, and his ability to integrate such action patterns contributes immeasurably to other learnings including intellectual. The development of man's brain is highly correlated with the delicate refinements of manipulative movements in his hands and the accompanying perceptual integration which follows. In the process of evolution the eyes and hands were situated to furnish a double action system which became inextricably and intimately related with perception. Psychologists now agree that the evolution of the brain is highly related to the progressive refinement of perceptual motor integration. Perception and motion are no longer looked upon as separate aspects of learning and behavior. Together they are regarded as one entity, a mechanism which adapts movements of the body with respect to time and space (12). The child is a sensory-perceptual motor organism. Forces from his surroundings are constantly impinging on him. He must convert these forces into something that has meaning and significance for him (2). These forces from his universe consist of energies such as heat, light, mechanical things, and the like. If he is to survive, grow and develop in this environment of impingements, he must process the information which is brought to him through his sense organs. In the first place he must move in order to overcome these forces and subsequently process the information they bring to him. However, he is able to do this only to the extent that his movement patterns have been developed properly. Thus, he must move in order to learn and he learns to move because of stimuli—external stimuli from the energies which surround him and internal stimuli furnished by feedback from his own unique nature (see Chapter 15 on Feedback).

Movement is adjusted to perception and in a like manner, perception depends on movement. Through this process of interaction the child gains perceptions as he obtains meaning from the stimuli. Kephart calls the process of combining the perceptual information and motor information into a meaningful whole the "perceptual motor match" (7). When specific perceptions are generalized, conceptualization takes place; thus, the child goes from the specific to the general. It is a succession of such generalizations which comprise thinking. Is it possible that the thinking process is triggered by movement?

Getman points out that "As the child learns to combine and integrate the movements of the eyes with the movements of the hands, he is setting the patterns for the integration of all other combinations which are possible in all perceptual systems of the body" (5). The interrelationship is so marked that the better he is in one category, the more likely will be his improvement in another. Research evidence now indicates that the child's motor patterns which are involved with hand-eye coordination are highly integrated with his ability to discriminate and differentiate sounds and his ability to form words (13). Barsch suggests that while communication potential is dependent on how well the child has been able to process visual, auditory, tactual, and kinesthetic stimuli, communicative efficiency is dependent on efficient patterns of movement (2). All learning, abstract as well as motor, is a result of "doing" followed by feedback (see Chapter 15). These abstract processes including speaking, reading, writing, and thinking are either in themselves motor activities or are based on motor activities. Psychologists claim that those movements concerned with writing are closely related to the child's early movements components of posture, transport, and manipulation. Special education people are now cognizant of the relationship between postural-transport as well as hand-eye activities and the processes of speech and reading.

Thus, the delicate coordinated movement patterns of the hands were movements of a higher order and eventually in the process of evolution led to precise articulations of speech and the symbolic operations of reading and writing (10) (13). This movement in a special interrelationship with present and stored perceptual motor experiences leads to the formation of concepts and in turn these concepts lead to the thought process. The significance of this concept to physical education and to education is colossal and a bit staggering. Movement first led to a more advanced organization of man's behavior and this advance paralleled his hand-eye coordinations, his use of tools, and his corresponding explorations in the area of abstractions and symbolic behavior. Therefore, it may be theorized that basic to all intellectual behavior is the development, control, and coordination first of the fundamental and later the accessory muscles of the body. Intellectual development must be preceded by movement and efficient movement is caused by the coordination of muscle groups into fundamental and special type skills.

THE EDUCATION CYCLE (1-15)

Education is the process of getting man to adjust to the society in which he finds himself and at the same time giving him the impetus to help improve that society. This implies, first of all, that there must come about a change or a modification in the individual as a result of educational experience. This change must not be regarded in too narrow a sense. It certainly must encompass the holistic concept. Traditionally, education has been characterized by the intellectual approach without due regard for other aspects of life. Modern education must take cognizance of the importance of the physiologic and psychologic approaches as well. This change or modification, even when governed by the holistic concept, still is limited by two things. First, it is limited by man's own nature. While behavior is never predetermined and growth and development can never be predicted exactly, there are certain limits within the frame of reference of man's original nature. Many of these limitations are obvious. Some are called physiological limits, some are psychological and still others are sociological. The second limitation is concerned with the type of environment or society itself. A certain type of society tends to propagate itself. This does not negate the fact that social order

cannot improve or be improved, but over the long haul, improvement does come about gradually and rather slowly. The change or modification in the individual as a result of experience will be made within the limits of man's nature and in accordance with the demands of the society of which he is a part. The customs, traditions, and mores of a people have great impact on the education of the young. Educators must be aware of these influences and the part they play. In fact, if they are not cognizant of their full import, society will soon make them aware. Educators must be willing to press for social change when the need is indicated, but in the same vein, they must accept in part, at least, an attitude of sensitivity to present social order and its resistance to sudden change.

Formal education itself follows a rather definite pattern and there is a continuity of its parts. These parts form a continuous dynamic cycle (1-24). *First*, there is the establishment of values, the defining of purposes, formulation of goals, and establishment of directions. This step should be the initial one in educational endeavor and is a product of philosophy. In fact, it is the supreme problem of philosophy. The *second* step concerns the planning of an approach, and it can be defined as the educational process since it is made up of many procedural factors. These are procedures to implement goals. The *third* step consists of the implementation of the process through techniques and methods of teaching, and the *final* step is the judgment and appraisal of results. These steps follow each other logically in an ordered sequential pattern. After appraisal, the entire cycle is repeated. In the light of facts shown from the appraisal, the values may be restudied, the goals and purposes re-stated, the program re-planned, new methods and techniques established and the whole cycle repeated. Thus, education is a continuous ongoing cycle. It can never be static any more than it can be a short-term process.

Before goals can be established, however, it is necessary to know where those goals are to lead eventually. In education the end result is the educated individual. He is the product, the type of person needed by society to perpetuate and improve itself. Then, in the light of this value, goals are set. These goals are dictated by philosophy and generally represent ideals which are set up as a result of frontier thinking followed by experience. Practices generally fall short of these ideals, but nevertheless they furnish the horizons to explore and the frontiers to conquer. The dynamic nature of education must have relevancy to its product as well as primacy to these goals. Formal education historically has narrowed its parameters as to what constitutes a liberally educated person. There has always been the tendency to restrict culture to verbalization and the fine arts. Concepts of culture and the liberally educated person must be broadened to be consistent with the issues and concepts which have just been discussed in this chapter. A liberally educated person would connote freedom—freedom from bias and ignorance. The concept that the child is a sensory-perceptual motor organism, while not entirely new, is a relatively new approach in educational procedure (2). In the future, culture and the educated man must be broadened to encompass the holistic concept.

After values have been determined and goals have been formulated in terms of the parameters which have been set for education, it is necessary in the education cycle to establish procedures. These have been called the *process*, and they include all the procedures which have been used in implementing the objectives and achieving the end prod-

uct. The process is a means, and education should prevent any of these procedures from becoming ends in themselves. Among educational procedures are facilities, administration, program, instruction, and personnel. Administrative policies must be determined, programs established, facilities and leadership made available and methods and materials of instruction developed. The last step in process involves the appraisal and judgment of results. This is accomplished in two ways. First, through evaluation of the product which is an indirect approach, and second, through the more direct approach of measuring the process itself. Neither approach has primacy over the other, but both may be used in abetting the continuity of the educational cycle. In the light of evaluation data, goals are re-stated, programs re-planned, and methods and materials altered. These in turn are followed by re-evaluation and the education cycle continues.

THE NATURE OF PHYSICAL EDUCATION

Physical education may be defined as education through big-muscle play activity such as sports, exercise, and dance where education's objectives may be achieved in part. By big-muscle activity is meant activities which involve the large muscles of the trunk, upper torso, and legs as opposed to muscles of the extremities. It is frequently referred to as gross motor activity. Like education, the physical education product must be determined. This product is a physically educated person. This value should be one of many values of the liberally educated person, and it has meaning only when it is related to the totality of the individual's life. However, the parameters of this aspect are somewhat more difficult to establish than other aspects and are not as clearly defined. This will become more apparent in Chapter 3 when aims and objectives will be discussed in more detail. This value means one who has attained a reasonably high level of skill in a variety of physical activities, who has an acceptable source of knowledges in sports and physical activities, who has achieved a high level of fitness, and who has developed attitudes and appreciations in social conduct to make him a socially acceptable partner or opponent. Perhaps the one overriding attitude on the part of the student is the desire to participate and make a creative approach to his leisure time. In other words, the student will choose to participate in some worthwhile activity which will contribute not only to his biological but also his psychological well-being. Each aspect is related to the other and neither can stand alone.

Then, physical education must establish its process which includes the usual factors of program, administration, leadership, facilities, method and materials and evaluation. Effective instruction is an important part of process because it is through teaching that the total curriculum is implemented and integrated. There should be a significant relationship between the process and the product, and the product is always dependent on the objectives. In fact, when physical education is effectively organized, administered, and conducted, it offers one of the best media for education and development of the total individual.

THE RELATIONSHIP OF PHYSICAL EDUCATION TO EDUCATION

It should now be needless to point out that physical education is an integral part of the total process of education. The issues that have been discussed and the evidence presented in the unit "movement as a process of integration" can lead to no other conclusion. There should be no conflict between physical education and education in matters per-

taining to either the product or the process.

In the matter of the product, the values sought in a well-oriented and organized program of physical education do not in any sense conflict with the values which are expounded for a liberally educated person. Since a liberally educated person is the value sought by education in general and since physical education can make its contribution to this liberal education through its physically educated person, the values should be compatible. The goals of general education have been accepted and recognized throughout education disciplines, although in some instances the glib jargon of the educationist may not be used. Physical education has these same goals, although since it is but one aspect of education, it makes a contribution to them in somewhat different degrees and dimensions. In Chapter 3 on aims and objectives it will be shown that physical education serves all of education's objectives either directly or indirectly.

Since the individual is an entity and his education cannot be entirely separated and segmented, the end result sought is a unified integrated and effective individual whose biological and physiological needs are inextricably related to the psychological and sociological. Thus, the physical must take its place in the education process along with the other aspects of the mental, social, and spiritual. It is unfortunate that this education involving movement and motor skills has been called "physical education." This is a misnomer; there can be no such thing as physical education if the evidences expounded by science and philosophy concerning the unity of man is accepted. Since movement does not take place without something happening to the whole individual as well as his interrelated parts, the ultimate end of this so-called physical education is not the "physical" but the good of the whole individual.

REFERENCES

1. Barrow, Harold M., and Rosemary McGee: *A Practical Approach To Measurement in Physical Education.* Philadelphia, Lea & Febiger, 1964.

2. Barsch, R. H.: *A Movigenic Curriculum.* Bulletin No. 25, Bureau for the Handicapped, State Department of Public Instruction, Wisconsin, 1965.

3. Brackenbury, R. L.: Physical Education, An Intellectual Emphasis? Quest, Vol. I., 3–6, December, 1963.

4. Delacato, C. H.: *The Diagnosis and Treatment of Speech and Reading Problems.* Springfield, Illinois, Charles C Thomas, 1963.

5. Getman, G. N.: *How To Develop Your Child's Intelligence.* A research publication. Luverne, Minnesota, 1962.

6. Kennedy, John F.: The Soft American. Sports Illustrated, Vol. 13, No. 26, December, 1960.

7. Kephart, N. C.: *The Slow Learner in the Classroom.* Columbus, Ohio, Charles E. Merrill Books, Inc., 1960.

8. Langton, Clair V.: Man and His Environment. Quest, Vol. III, 15–18, December, 1964.

9. Lawther, John D.: Directing Motor Skill Learning. Quest, Vol. VI, 68–76, May, 1966.

10. Nash, Jay B.: Those Hands. Quest, Vol. II, 53–59, April, 1964.

11. Obertueffer, Delbert: On Learning Values through Sports. Quest, Vol. I, 23–29, December, 1963.

12. Smith, K. U., and W. M. Smith: *Perception and Motion.* Philadelphia, W. B. Saunders Company, 1962.

13. Steinhaus, A. H.: Your Muscles See More Than Your Eyes. Journal of Health, Physical Education and Recreation, Vol. 37, No. 7, 38–40, September, 1966.

14. Ulrich Celeste: *The Social Matrix of Physical Education.* Englewood Cliffs, Prentice-Hall, Inc., 1968.

15. Williams, J. F.: The Destiny of Man. Quest, Vol. IV, 17–21, April, 1965.

Chapter 2

Physical Education— Its Philosophical Bases

INTRODUCTION

Education has been partially defined in Chapter 1 as a "change or modification in the individual as a result of educational experience." This educational experience concerns *process*, but subsequent to process in the education cycle is the establishment of direction of the change or modification. This concerns first the establishment of values or the defining of purposes followed by the formulation of *goals*. These goals concern aims and objectives as well as outcomes and should reflect the primary values of society, its philosophers and educators. This step in the education cycle is a product of philosophy since philosophy determines ends. Thus, goals are established by philosophy. In fact, ultimate goals become the supreme purpose and problem of philosophy. The next chapter is concerned with direction, values and goals, and since philosophy is unequivocally the sources of these, it seems expedient for the professional student to have some knowledge of philosophy and its various systems. In any walk of life a person must have a philosophy of his own to clarify issues and define problems. Education is no excep-

tion. A teacher who has a philosophy of education as well as life is better than one who has none. An educator or a physical educator without some systematic philosophy is superficial, aimless and unscientific in his educational processes.

Philosophy is variously defined in the dictionary as a study of the truth or the principles underlying all knowledge; or a study of the most general causes and principles of the universe, or a system for guiding life. In this unit of study, it is both a product and a process. As a product it is a system of values. As a process it is a means of establishing that system of values. Thus, it becomes both a means and an end. Historically it has consisted of a search for goodness, truth and beauty, but in more modern times its role is to find meanings in all things.

Ultimately all values are established by philosophy and come from knowledge. The word philosophy itself is derived from the Greek words meaning *love of wisdom*. This knowledge or wisdom comes from many sources: facts inherent in scientific evidence, facts revealed by history, and facts revealed by reflective thinking which in turn is based upon best held opinion at the time. Best held opinion may be based on scientific facts, or on tradition or common sense. In the past where scientific evidence was non-existent or difficult to come by, common sense had to suffice. Many beliefs and common practices today have been handed down from generation to generation. While we may say they are based on tradition, their origin may have been rooted in superstition or taboos. Common sense when used as a basis for action may serve as a catalyst for scientific experimentation or philosophical reflection. However, it may be rationalized into complacency, expediency, or conformity rather than high standards through study and experimentation. It is through the extension of knowledge, facts, and wisdom that philosophy emerges and is further validated. In formal education these knowledges, facts, and wisdom add up to scholarship. Thus, philosophy emerges from basic beliefs and principles which were revealed through scholarship. However, it will be pointed out in the chapter on principles (Chapter 8) that philosophy also is a means of establishing principles and thus produces knowledge and scholarship as well as being dependent on them.

The subject matter of philosophy concerns truths, reality and values and it deals with such concepts as aims, objectives, purposes, outcomes, principles, assumptions, hypotheses, and the like (14). As was previously stated, knowledge is basic to philosophy since these concepts listed above are based on high level scholarship. Without knowledge one's beliefs can become no more than biases. Knowledge, when it is organized, analyzed, and generalized, reveals truths and from these truths, ultimate references and values are established and basic beliefs formed. It is these basic beliefs which make up one's philosophy and which influence and dic-

tate behavior. An individual's philosophy is the most significant aspect about him, since it dictates his patterns of thought, his direction in life, and ultimately his behavior.

Two of the more salient purposes of philosophy have to do with the frontier thinking which is necessary for establishment of direction and goals, and then the interpretation of these ultimates after they have been set in terms so they can be understood by the educator. Also, it is no doubt true that in many facets of education, philosophy is used to analyze and evaluate some goals already existing. Since knowledge is so basic to philosophy, it is inevitable that it become a part of a cycle that includes *scholarship, philosophy* and the *scientific process.* Bookwalter suggests that this cycle starts with scholarship (1). However, scholarship has reverberations. When knowledge is understood, when it has become functional, and when it "hath power," it inevitably leads to a sounder philosophy and a richer sense of values. Philosophy and scholarship are germane; they are inexorably related. Excellence in scholarship will lead to a more acceptable philosophy and a sounder philosophy will reveal problems and uncover gaps in the field of learning (1). These problems and gaps in knowledge stimulate intellectual curiosity which in turn will lead to inquiry and inquiry will culminate in research. Through scientific research, problems are solved and the gaps are filled in leading to more knowledge and better scholarship. The better scholarship in turn helps to further validate and clarify philosophy and then the cycle is completed. This entire cycle is repeated over and over in any discipline. Each part of the cycle is related to the other as the total operates in a sequential pattern. This cycle also may run in the reverse direction. For example, philosophy can, through reflective thinking, add to knowledge and scholarship and this step in turn may lead to inquiry (see Chapter 8 on principles). In any event this trilogy of values forms the very basis of any discipline. Philosophy sets the boundaries for both scholarship and research without regard for the direction the cycle moves. Philosophy and science supplement and at the same time complement each other. Philosophy is an end and attempts to answer the question "why," while science is a means and answers the question "how."

An unsound philosophy or no philosophy at all is inimical to progress in any discipline or for that matter any walk of life. When educational practices are based on a paucity of ideas and knowledges, the opinions, beliefs, and values held to by society become biased and warped. When either high level scholarship or sound philosophy is lacking, bigotry and dogmatism frequently prevail and what may be even more condemning, complacency and lethargy may take over in educational process. Kneller has said, "An educator who does not use philosophy is inevitably superficial. A superficial educator may be good or bad—but, if good, less good than he could be, and, if bad, worse than he need be." (10–128)

In physical education, philosophy is pre-eminently the source of all goals, aims, objectives, criteria and standards. Out of the principles of physical education which have evolved from scientific facts and reasoned judgments, philosophy emerges, values are molded, and references are made. The physical educator's philosophy becomes deeply rooted in his life as it dictates his behavior because since philosophy determines his values, it also determines his practices—what he teaches, what he does, how he acts, and to what he gives his attention. All his practices are triggered by his basic beliefs, and his decisions are colored by his system of values.

As a system of values, philosophy is the key in selecting alternatives. Therefore, for the educator, it must represent mature judgment and sound appraisal based on reflective thinking.

The source of philosophy in physical education includes many areas. The past is an important conveyor of knowledge, so history becomes one of the most important sources (7). The sciences with special emphasis on human biology, anatomy, physiology, psychology and hygiene furnish principles out of which basic beliefs are formed. Sociology and anthropology are equally rich in thought and experience which affect basic beliefs. Since physical education also qualifies as a humanity, many concepts from social sciences influence its philosophy.

COMPONENTS OF PHILOSOPHY

In this chapter it is not the purpose of the author to give the student a deep discourse into philosophy. There is neither space nor time for such an in-depth study. However, the student would profit greatly from a course in general philosophy as a part of his liberal arts education and at the graduate level in physical education he should be given an opportunity to become more involved in the philosophic processes. Since philosophy colors every act or concept of the teacher as he plays the various roles required of the physical education professional, he can profit by a better understanding of the classical philosophies as they relate to the various facets of the educational processes. Also, he should be familiar with the educational philosophies which arose from the traditional philosophies.

Before considering the major schools of philosophy or the traditional ones and their counterparts in educational philosophy, it is essential that the students know something about the basic fields of study in philosophy. These are as follows:

Metaphysics

This position is associated with "being" and studies the ultimate nature of things. It takes a speculative approach and raises questions about everything concerning man and his universe. It seeks answers to what is reality? What is real? Does the universe have meaning? Is reality monism, dualism, or pluralism? Is there a spirit? Does God exist? What is the nature of God? These questions and many like them cannot be answered by science and must be pondered by each new generation. Each person has to consider these at some time in his life and, thus, man is a metaphysical being with an inordinate desire to find meaning in the ultimate nature of himself and his universe (10–7).

Epistemology

Epistemology is the theory of knowledge and its acquisition. It is concerned with the nature and kind of knowledge that can be obtained and the methods of obtaining it. It deals with truth, its origin, nature and limits. There are different types of truth or knowledge: knowledge revealed by God, authoritative knowledge by experts, intuitive knowledge by one's inner apprehensiveness, rational knowledge through reasoning and valid judgments, and empirical knowledge through observation by means of the senses (10–8).

Axiology

Axiology is that branch of philosophy which studies values. It culminates in the development of a system of values. Values may be objective such as goodness, truth or beauty and are ends in and of themselves, or they may be subjective when they are means to an end—in most cases characterized by personal desire (10–13). Values can be fixed and permanent or they can be dynamic and changing. Also, values may differ in worth, and they may be viewed in terms of a hierarchy where some have a higher status than others.

Logic

Since metaphysics deals with reality, epistemology with truth, and axiology with values, there must be some sound and intelligent method of reasoning concerning questions about them. This is the concern of *logic*, which describes the exact steps in relating ideas. It essentially deals with the methods of induction and deduction. However, these have been expanded into experimental reasoning and problem solving in leading to accurate thinking. Logic attempts to validate standards by which accuracy of ideas can be evaluated.

Ethics

Ethics is actually a subdivision of axiology and is concerned with moral and ethical standards. It is a study of the nature of good conduct and the outcome of such study is a moral philosophy. From this moral philosophy comes a knowledge of right-and-wrong and codes of ethics and moral behavior. It attempts to answer the question "What is the good life?" for man (see Chapter 14). An ethical system may or may not be associated with religion. If it is, its standards are generally fixed and unchanging. If not religiously oriented, they may be viewed as having originated from man and determined by his needs, interests, and desires.

Esthetics

Esthetics is also a subdivision of axiology and is a study of the nature of beauty in the arts such as painting, sculpture, music, drama, dance and the like. It studies values in relation to the ways the artist may express himself and seeks answers to the question "What is beauty?"

These six fundamental categories are the basic aspects in developing a philosophy. The traditional philosophies of life as well as the educational philosophies can be understood more fully when they are viewed through this structural framework. These same components are needed in the formulation of a philosophy for any particular field like physical education, or for one's own personal philosophy.

TRADITIONAL PHILOSOPHIES

There are different systems of philosophy. Historically proponents of different beliefs have been categorically divided into three groups dependent on how they viewed the nature of such concepts as *truth, value,* and *reality* (2–20). The traditional philosophical systems are *idealism, realism* and *pragmatism.*

A more modern approach to reality and truth is *existentialism.* How one views life in general and physical education in particular will depend on the philosophy one holds. There are basic differences among philosophies, and because of these basic differences, there follows divergencies in beliefs and practices. One only has to attend a meeting of professional people and observe how they differ on many issues which appear basic. However, it is through philosophic means that such discussions and examinations of alternatives provide understanding and some measure of uniformity.

There is no part of education which is unaffected by philosophies. One's philosophy will determine what educational problems are uncovered and how these problems are solved. Also, it will determine what knowledge and skills are considered important and first order, and what information and activities are secondary. Thus, it will dictate what curricular experiences that youth will have since the curriculum translates philosophy into actual experiences. Methods of teaching and techniques of leadership are colored by one's basic be-

liefs; policies and procedures in administration will vary, and even the way principles are interpreted may be affected to some degree. In a day and time when human values are significantly important, one's value system is dictated by his philosophy.

However, educators or physical educators rarely fit into a pattern in these traditional philosophies of idealism, realism and pragmatism, or the newer existentialism. Society in general and education in particular have been undergoing dramatic and sometimes traumatic changes in the last few decades. The walls of the traditionalist have been attacked again and again, and the turbulence which followed has led to much self-reflection and self-criticism ending in a search for more workable philosophies. There is no denying the fact, however, that most thinking at the present is influenced by all the philosophies of the past and the present. In a sense, the philosophy to which any one person holds is a composite of many beliefs and selected from many doctrines. To this extent one's philosophy is eclectic, which means choosing those beliefs which seem best from various sources rather than following any one system (6–5).

Proponents of various philosophies are loosely categorized in relation to how they view or arrive at conclusions about the nature of *reality, truth* and *value* (12). Obviously the proponents of the various schools of philosophy are vitally influenced in their thinking and actions by how they view these entities. Since philosophy speaks in terms of ultimates, and as it is the source from which all practices and actions spring, it will influence one's aims, objectives, program, methods of teaching and procedures of evaluation. It will determine how the teacher views the nature of the student and at the same time determine how the teacher views his own role in the teacher-pupil relationship.

In this chapter once again it is not the intention to present an in-depth discussion of traditional philosophies. However, since philosophy is pre-eminently the source of our aims, objectives and outcomes, since these goals are based on established values, and as the parameters of these values must be set by philosophy, some understanding of basic systems is needed by the professional student in physical education.

Idealism

Idealism has a long heritage extending back beyond the time of the Greeks. Plato was its recognized Hellenic leader and expounded over 2000 years ago some of the key concepts of idealism. The idealist thinks that *reality* depends on the mind for existence and is spiritual in nature rather than physical. He believes that ideas are ultimate reality, and that reality resides not in the physical individual and his environment but in the thinking and spiritual individual. The physical world exists only in the mind. Therefore man lives in a world characterized by ideas which are eternal, unchanging and perfect, and are the only real things of the universe. Thus, the universe can be known only through the thinking process—through the senses by perception and conception. Examples of eternal and perfect ideas are goodness, truth and beauty.

The idealist looks on *truth* as ideas and knowledge which are universal and absolute. Such truth has to be discovered through mental processes of reflective thinking, reasoning, and evaluating, and to the idealist intuitive thinking is as good as scientific thinking. Truth has always been truth and will not change even if man does change (6–6). It has a purpose—to be used for the self-development of the individual.

The idealist looks on *value* as those essentials of life which are fixed and unchanging. Value originates as a function of ideas through intellectual activity. Values may be imperfectly or wrongly conceived or interpreted by the individual, but this has no effect on the true values themselves since these are absolute and permanent (13).

The idealist's aim in education is to discover these fundamental ideas and to interpret the universe in terms of the conclusions he draws about reality, truth and value. His aim for the individual is the development of the personality and the attainment of a full life physically, intellectually, socially, and morally. The mind and the spirit are the paramount issues here where all good education might be termed character education and search for the good life (6–7).

The idealist's objectives grow out of his aim which affirms personality as the ultimate worth, along with such verities as truth, good and beauty (9–60). While the emphasis of the direction is the development of the individual's creative capacities, idealistic objectives direct one to search for truths and information so that the body, mind, and spirit may develop to their fullest. Such objectives are more generally met in an atmosphere where the liberal arts prevail, and where culture, knowledge and refinement are achieved through the exercise of the mind and the use of creative powers for reasoning and reflective thinking. The development of the physical, while it is a part of the hierarchy of values, is nevertheless usually placed at the bottom of the totem pole of objectives (12).

The program for the idealist might be termed a traditional one where fixed ideas, knowledges and truths mentioned earlier are basic. It would be a fairly stable system, because it is based on learning which has been tried and is true, and needs little change. Therefore, subject matter is of the utmost importance and it is planned by teachers. The content of the program must lead to the development of self through the culture and accumulated wisdom of the ages. This self-development emphasis should be directed toward the good, the true and the beautiful in all aspects of the individual—the intellect, emotional, social, and the physical. The program content is more qualitative than quantitative.

The methodology for the idealist may vary depending somewhat on the situation. No one method can be said to characterize idealism as opposed to other schools of thought. The teacher is more important than other aspects of the process; methodology is less important than what is taught in the curriculum. Such methods as lecture, question and answer, assigned readings and discussion, project, and even the scientific are employed. Thus, the method itself is not as important as the way it is used. The purpose of the method is to achieve the aims and objectives for the student through the positive influences of the instructor who teaches by means of both precept and example. Exemplary action of leadership is important (6–8).

The idealist believes in evaluation. However, while he uses both quantitative and qualitative techniques, he is most concerned with the subjective aspects because these are the qualities of the individual on which he places most emphasis. Since the idealist is more concerned with the development of self—the personality, mind, character, citizenship, and behavior in general, and since these qualities do not lend themselves to objective measurements, he is not afraid to use the subjective approach to measurement, evaluation and grading.

Realism

Realism, too, is a heritage from the Greeks and is relatively as old as idealism. Aristotle was its first proponent followed over the centuries by Thomas Aquinas and John Locke and later on by Rousseau and Pestalozzi. It is a broad system of belief in its scope and is characterized by many differences within itself. Proponents of realism view *reality* in terms of the physical world and scientific facts. In fact the physical world is reality to them. It is concrete and it exists independent and apart from human experience. As a theory of fact, it is objective and depersonalized to the extent that the objects and matters of the universe have an independent existence and exist outside of the mind of the knower (14–45). However, while the physical world is made known to the mind through the senses and perception, it does not depend on the mind for its existence as claimed by idealists. However, it does exist as it appears to man through his perceptual processes.

The realist accepts *truth* as the real object of the universe. Truth is knowledge that has its origin in the physical world but is obtained through experimentation. This experimentation involves scientific investigation and deals with the objective as opposed to the subjective approach. Truth is found in the material things of the world which speak for themselves rather than having to be perceived to become real. It deals with nature—its rules, laws, order, principles and tenets.

The realist sees *value* as something objective which has been shown to be good or true or beautiful through scientific reasoning and procedures. Whereas the idealist sees value only as it exists in the mind, the realist sees value only as it conforms to the laws, principles, and order of the physical world as revealed by science and he sees them as they really exist. An object or thing has value to the extent it actually exists in nature.

The realist's aim of education is to

provide for the student the type of training necessary for him to meet the realities of life as a successfully participating member. This aim depends on the basic sciences and sense perception to discover and interpret the real things of life. The emphasis is on the whole individual—physical, mental, social, and moral—for a full life in the world as it exists—the real world independent of the mind. The realist's objectives also emerge from this aim. Since reality exists in the objective world and the aim is the development of the whole individual to function in this world, the realist sets his objectives so as to develop the competences of youth. Youth must be taught the laws and order of nature and to live his life fully in relation to them and at the same time the utilization of scientific method and procedures.

The program of the realist is based on content that is quantitative and is developed through scientific means. It is both traditional and modern in content and sequence. It is traditional because it uses the best of the old; it is modern because it uses the new knowledge which has been arrived at through the scientific process. The program is systematically organized, with the emphasis being on the scientific facts and principles, which are presented in an orderly and logical manner (14–59).

The methodology of the realist is as varied as the idealist but for a different reason. The realist teacher educates through the real world and will use demonstration, field trips, audio-visual aids, drill technique as well as the more time-honored methods of lecture, discussion and project. Since his methods vary, his approach will also vary somewhat. However, he will generally be systematic, firm, orderly and logical in his teaching. His courses will present outlines and syllabi. He is more impersonal than the idealist teacher and can be more of a disciplinarian particu-

larly if he uses traditional methods. The realist teacher does not play the central role the idealist teacher does chiefly because, for the realist, learning is subject-centered rather than teacher-centered. However, he decides what knowledge the students learn.

The realist employs evaluation, but the emphasis is on measurements where the results can be recorded in objective scores. His emphasis is on the quantitative approach and he tries to steer away from the more qualitative aspects where he has to measure and grade intangibles. His tests are the objective type as opposed to subjective and are indicative of the realist's use of scientific method for more objective evidence. He may emphasize the subjective qualities in his teaching but avoids them in his grading (9–90).

Pragmatism

Pragmatism predates both idealism and realism and began with the Sophists under Heraclitus. It may be called *experimentalism* or *instrumentalism* by some and is a derivative of a Greek word implying "Practice." Along the way to modern times, Francis Bacon, William James, and John Dewey appeared. Dewey's instrumental theory of education has had great impact on democratic educational practices. The pragmatist views ultimate *reality* as something which is experienced (16–13). Unlike the idealist who views reality as fixed and unchanging, the pragmatist sees no absolutes. To him reality cannot be static because it results from experience and experience changes according to circumstances and situations. Thus, reality is dynamic and is constantly changing—the sum total of experience. Reality changes because both man and his environment are changing.

Truth to the pragmatist is that which is discovered through experience. Just as reality is not an absolute, neither is truth. Truth is relative and tentative, and changes when the situation dictates. The validity of truth is inherent in whether or not it works (6–17). If it works, it is true. If it does not work, it is open to question. Truth will vary with times and places. As situations and circumstances change, so will truth (12). As new knowledge comes about through scientific experimentation and philosophical insight, these experiences will dictate revision of old hypotheses and perhaps even discard them entirely. Truth must be functional, it must explain, it must provide answers, and it is a matter of consequences.

Values to the pragmatist once again are relative and not the fixed and unchanging ideas of the idealist. They are based on man's judgment as a result of his experiences. Values to him are not irrefutable, since they are based on experiences which differ with each set of circumstances. Values, then, are established by the individual as a result of his experience and are judged by him not in terms of his own selfish interest but in terms of the social good of the group (12).

The pragmatist establishes his aims and objectives to encompass the whole of the individual with emphasis on the social efficiency. His aim is to provide the student with the opportunities through experience to solve the problems he is confronted with in life and to become a better functioning member of society as a result of this experience.

The program of the pragmatist is based on the "doing" approach (9–124). The program is student-centered since it is based on the needs and interests of the individual. It is not systematically organized in a rigid manner but is based on the problem-solving approach. The student is given an opportunity to apply the scientific method and gain experience in a wide variety of activities. In these activities the emphasis is on working together and cooperation is the keynote.

In education this philosophy has been called by various terms such as instrumentalism, functionalism, and experimentalism. In the main, pragmatism would teach for relevance and lifelike situations.

The pragmatic approach to methods is the problem-solving technique. The teacher works with students in an effort to guide them in defining problems, then using the scientific method in solving them. Just as there is little emphasis on a systematized program, there is even less emphasis on formal methodology such as the traditional methods of lecture, drill, and recitation. The socialized approach is used where it is more important for the student to learn how to think instead of what to think (12). The response-to-command method of teaching should be replaced by the command-to-discovery approach.

The pragmatist believes in evaluation in its broadest sense and sees it as an integral part of the education cycle. He looks beyond such things as scores and norms and appraises the students in terms of behavioral changes. He is primarily concerned with the student's ability to solve problems and adjust to change. Since these aspects do not lend themselves to exact measurements, the pragmatist uses the subjective approach. Self-evaluation on the part of the student is encouraged.

Existentialism

Existentialism is a much newer mode of thinking than the three traditional philosophies. Its basic ideas are expressed by Kierkegaard, Nietzsche and Sartre. The existentialists believe that *reality* is something that lies within man —his experience of being. Also, with existence man has a freedom of choice, but he exercises this choice with the knowledge of his unalterable responsibility of his moral self. Reality is something fashioned out of his choice that will determine his essence (12). Sartre, leading thinker for existentialism, wrote that "existence precedes essence" (10–54), which means the real is there before meaning can be attached to it. Man is there before he reads meaning into himself.

For the existentialist, *truth* is something arrived at by the individual from within himself through his own experience. It is not an ideal that is eternal nor a result of the objective outside world. Knowledge in the form of truth comes from free choice of man and exists in his feelings. To the existentialist truth is personal because it is his choice, and he accepts the responsibility for his choice.

The existentialist contends that *values* are a result of his freedom of choice and that man, while he is an intellectual creature, is also a creature which values and has feelings. However, he does not accept without question the time-tested moral values which have been established by social and religious thinkers because if he does accept them uncritically, he loses his contention that his existence precedes his essence and that he has the right to choose. His value system is one that he has arrived at by looking within himself and then by making his own choices and being responsible for those choices not only in terms of his own self but for society in general. Since the individual has freedom of choice and since he must bear the consequence of his choice, he must understand the burden of the responsibility. He alone is responsible for what happens to him. He must be guided toward self-realization, self-determination, originality, and self-acceptance, and to an awareness of his moral self. The freedom of choice demanded by young militants and certain other elements today must not be construed in this light because their freedom of choice in action is not followed by an assumption of responsibility. Also, many of them choose to be different as a matter of principle. This is a type of conformity and therefore negates the very basis of the authenticity and freedom they seek. The true existentialist would to his own self be true.

The aim of existentialism is to place the focus on the student and his self-actualizing independent self. The student is encouraged to make his choices in his freedom with a responsibility for moral behavior and consequences of his action. Self-determination and self-actualization are the objectives of the teacher as well as the educational processes.

The program of the existentialist would not be a prescribed cut-and-dried systematized curriculum (11). It would be a break from tradition and would tend toward nonconformity. While emphasis is placed on a great deal of traditional program content, the curriculum builders are less concerned with what is in the program than for what purpose it is to be used (9–156). The purpose of a program is to present a wide selection of alternatives in the content, and then to help each individual fulfill his unique, self-actualizing independent self through them. Since emphasis is on the realization of individual essence, individual type activities would probably be selected over group type. However, if the individual chooses to find his essence in group activities, he might select them as a part of his program but under no pressure and of his own free will.

The methodology of the existentialist is the Socratic approach. The teacher does not serve as an image or model as in the case of idealism, nor does he use the problem-solving technique of the pragmatist, nor is he the dispenser of knowledge as the realist. He raises questions, he provokes thought, but at the same time he attempts to make the student aware of his moral responsibilities. He uses the subjective approach in such ways that the student will search for alternatives and weigh consequences. The teacher does not come up with ultimate answers for the student must find these for himself as he moves up the social continuum toward self-realization. The teacher's job is to encourage the student to do reflective thinking about possible consequences before choices are made and then to become aware of his responsibility in accepting consequences as a result of his choice. He provokes the student and then leaves him free to take his own course of action. The student learns to develop his own principles and probably takes pride in not following the crowd except when the crowd is going in his direction as revealed by his own self-actualizing self.

The existentialist does not believe in testing in the traditional sense. He has no interest in such things as either local or national norms and he is not interested in measuring progress in program content since what is taught is relatively unimportant when compared with the deeper underlying purpose for which it is taught. These ends would be difficult to evaluate.

EDUCATIONAL PHILOSOPHIES

In the last unit the three traditional philosophies of idealism, pragmatism, and realism were discussed briefly along with one of the newer modes of thinking, existentialism. The traditional three are systematically structured and have played a major role in educational thought and practice as they have also done for other institutions and human endeavors. The newer mode of thinking, existentialism, is now beginning to exert some influence along with the traditional modes. It would seem pertinent at this point to look at not only what the philosophers have had to say about education but also what the

educators themselves have said. There are several of these philosophies of education which have attempted to bring reform to education. Kneller suggests that these may actually be theories which seek solutions to educational problems by referring to the basic philosophies (10). It is true that the educational philosophies discussed here are dependent to a large extent on the general philosophies since these pretty well span the waterfront in studying the various facets of human behavior. However, educational philosophies are characterized by experience growing out of education and unique to it.

The general philosophies differ basically in the way they view and interpret reality, truth and value. Metaphysics is concerned with reality; epistemology deals with truth; and axiology studies and establishes values. While no hierarchy of importance has been assigned these branches of philosophy by philosophers for the field of education, axiology must become the center around which the others revolve because it gives man his system of values. It is the system of values based on reality and truth and arrived at through logic that gives tone, meaning, and character to educational processes and practices and, of course, to the final product. Therefore, it is axiology which is the main girder of support between the traditional and the newer educational philosophies. The contemporary educational philosophies that will be briefly discussed here are: *progressivism, perennialism, essentialism,* and *reconstructionism.* While there are other contemporary views, this constellation of beliefs covers the main issues—the ones that have led to educational reforms.

Progressivism

Progressivism, sometimes identified as instrumentalism, is a philosophy which basically applies pragmatism to education. John Dewey, the great philosopher of education, was the instigator of progressive education and bridged the gap between pragmatism and the new approach. Dewey's definition of education as "that reconstruction or reorganization of experience which adds to the meaning of experience and which increases the ability to direct the course of subsequent experience" sets the tenor of the progressive movement (8–89). It brought into focus the idea of life adjustment education, the concept of the whole child, and the child centeredness approach. First of all, it was a rebellion against the formalism of traditional education, its strict discipline, uninteresting and dull drill methodology, and passive type of learning. In its place were substituted such ideas as the child-interest approach, problem-solving, co-operation as opposed to competition, education is life rather than for life, shared experiences through democratic processes, and recognition of individual differences (10–96). Progressivism believed the test of knowledge was whether it could be used. It believed in the child experimenting and gaining experience through democratic processes.

Progressivism has been criticized because of its approach which placed the emphasis on the child instead of the subject matter. It believes in the child-interest approach and its student self-direction concept has been attacked as too permissive. There has been a shift away from this point of view the last decade where the demand for more emphasis on subject matter and more discipline has led to the decline of progressivism as a position. The shift in emphasis was largely due to the launching of the Russian Sputnik followed by the attack on education by such critics as Rickover (3) and Conant (4) (5). However, progressivism introduced many new and worthwhile innovations and changes in American schools and its

eclipse is probably a temporary thing. It will probably rise again in some of its many forms. Its basic structure is predicated on the concept of change to meet change and any such philosophy has something of significance to contribute in today's world of rapid change and turbulence.

Perennialism

Where progressivism was basically pragmatic, *perennialism* is essentially realism, but some of its practices are supported by idealism. It is not difficult to see why the idealist prefers the perennialistic approach over progressivism. The basic belief on which perennialism rests is the unchanging and constant nature of the guiding principles of education.

They are perennial from whence came the name of the philosophy. Perennialism, too, was a rebellion against contemporary schools which no doubt had adopted many of the educational practices of progressivism. While progressivism emphasis was based on the presence of change in all important matters, the perennialist emphasized the permanency and absolute nature of the basic principles. While culture and social organization do change, he contends that human nature does not. Education is not life itself but a preparation for life as it concentrates on developing the rational powers of man (10–110). It refutes life adjustment education in favor of the adjustment to truth which, like human nature, is universal and constant and does not change. There is a place for drill and repetition in acquiring knowledge—the very essence of education. There is no place for a student to waste time in discovering for himself what can be taught in a much shorter time. Since man is a rational being, he must be taught both freedom and restraint and permissiveness is frowned upon in such schools.

The Dewey philosophy emphasizes achievement of a self-actualizing person through the student's own initiative with some guided assistance from the teacher, while perennialism emphasizes self-realization through self-discipline with the teacher in the driver's seat. The self-discipline would be nurtured through external discipline. The emphasis is on subject matter, which is constant and universal and found in the great literature, history and philosophy books of the past. There is no place for vocational training. Everyone gets the same well-rounded educational program. The leader of the movement is Robert M. Hutchins who frequently quotes from Aristotle.

Naturally, this approach to education is narrow and fosters a situation where there is a sort of cult of the intellect. It is criticized because it appears to be reactionary and even undemocratic. Its aim is to challenge the gifted few. In so doing, it failed to recognize the importance of the many or to meet the needs of the average and the exceptional. Therefore, other theories arose to meet the problems and to refute the perennial approach.

Essentialism

While progressivism appealed to pragmatism and perennialism to classical realism, *essentialism* is more eclectic in its approach to education. Essentialism does not oppose progressivism to the same extent as perennialism does. In fact it accepts some positions expounded by the progressivist. However, its main position is that there is a core of knowledge, skills, and values which are essential for all students to learn. Since it is a position or movement rather than a philosophy in itself, essentialists do not agree on all their theories. This is easily understood, however, since it takes an eclectic approach and its proponents may come from idealism or realism. However, as a position, it is relatively conservative although democratic.

Essentialism differs from progressivism because it puts the emphasis back on the teacher and subject matter. It also uses traditional methodology and recognizes the importance of discipline. The "learning-by-doing" approach would not be employed except when the learning process dictated it. It expects the student to apply himself in hard work and demands discipline. This position contends that self-discipline is not self-taught but is a product of authority, and that effort overrides interest. While essentialism repudiates much of progressivism, it also differs from perennialism. It is not so much concerned with eternal and absolute truths and it does not place as much emphasis on the cult of the intellect. It is concerned with the adjustment of the student to his social and cultural environment while it places more emphasis on the physical sciences. Essentialism's recognized leader is William Brickman, editor of *School and Society*.

A criticism of essentialism is that it is not dynamic and changeable enough to meet the needs of a rapidly changing culture. Also, its critics say it places too much emphasis on the physical sciences at the expense of the social sciences. Opponents claim, too, that the student does not learn to think for himself since the emphasis is on acquiring subject matter. The methods of teaching, emphasis on subject matter, and dominant role of the teacher are deterrents to independent thinking and the democratic process.

Reconstructionism

Reconstructionism is an extension of pragmatic progressivism. Its basic position contends that culture must be reconditioned or redesigned along lines of the democratic ideals. Zeigler states it is farther to the left on the educational spectrum than progressivism or what he calls experimentalism (15–252). It maintains most of the beliefs of progressivism, recognizing the vastly changing social and cultural environment, maintains that the primary purpose of education is to do something about society so that it can adjust to the cultural crisis. Unlike the progressivists who do not believe a curriculum can be planned in great detail too far in advance, the reconstructionists would have a clear-cut well-constructed program with both social and political implications. The democratic process must be the central design in reconstruction and action must take place now in setting up a new social order since time may be running out in the light of man's potential for self-extermination. Education takes place now and the reconstructionist teacher leans toward the existentialist position in his approach to the new order, since he provides the knowledge for choices and consequences but leaves the decisions up to the student. Education is education for the future and preparation for life in the society and culture that will finally emerge after the process of redesigning. Education must change both as a means and an end to meet the demands of the present cultural crisis and the current findings of the behavioral sciences (10–124).

Critics of reconstructionist philosophy believe the position is too utopian and will not work in a pluralistic democratic society where one set of social values is unlikely. Also, its basis for education is knowledge from the behavioral sciences which are known for their disagreement where values are concerned.

IMPLICATION OF PHILOSOPHY FOR PHYSICAL EDUCATION

While it would be misleading to say that philosophy has become a fad in all fields of learning, it can be said that philosophy has become a component part of life in general for the educated man and for all disciplines and fields of endeavor. Since philosophy is a system of values, it behooves all of education and especially physical education to establish a better value system based on principles from science and philosophy as a process. Since philosophy is a study of values, the philosophical process enables the professional to study the meaning, nature, importance and source of existing values and in the process to establish new ones and to re-direct existing ones.

There seems to be a greater need now than ever before for an adequate system of values. Technology and scientific inquiry are providing us with more "know-how" than man has ever experienced in history. Knowledge has expanded greatly in all areas and all disciplines. With all the advancement in "know-how," however, the "know-why" has not kept apace. Old values are threatened because they do not provide enough meaning and relevance to the individual in his profession or his personal life. No longer does the educated man accept beliefs on which to base his actions and behavior without question. There are many such "beliefs" in education and physical education today which come within the province of this statement. They may even have become cliches, such as "the worth and dignity of each individual," and then planning a program where five percent of the students get ninety percent of the budget. When some beliefs are held up to the light of study and reason, they become vulnerable in the light of new evidence and study. Through study, research, and reflective thinking current basic assumptions, hypotheses and purposes can be examined, analyzed and evaluated. In the light of new knowledge and further reflective thinking, interpretations and generalizations can be made. When this is done, there are sure to be some changes in the course of the profession and the behavior of the professional. As assumptions and hypotheses are clarified through philosophic functions such as criticism, analysis, synthesis and reflection, new data will lead to further generalizations and perhaps to new principles.

Certainly there is a need in physical education at the present time for both the individual and the profession as a whole to work toward verification of data and the formulation of principles. Until recently the physical educators involved themselves little, if at all, in the philosophical areas. As a result, they knew little about the foundations on which philosophy rests and could not apply its processes. All that is changing even though there is much "catching up" still to be done. Most professionals are more knowledgeable now and a few are approaching the expert level of competence. The next step will lead to the establishment of a sounder system of values for both the individual and the profession. In turn the sounder system of values will lead to more clearly defined aims, objectives, and standards. The more clearly defined goals and directions will lead to a more uniform approach and should improve practices, procedures and techniques.

The philosophic process starts with an understanding of the general philosophies and these lead to a sounder philosophy of life. When this sounder philosophy of life is applied to the problems in education, this should lead to a more modern approach to education and a systematic philosophy of education. It is difficult to separate one from the other. One's philosophy of life will shine through and be revealed in one's philosophy of both education and physical education.

However, developing one's philosophy of life is not simple; neither is the development of one's philosophy of education. Where does the professional student start? How does he make sense out of all the philosophical discussion and controversies? Which ones are right and which are wrong? These controversial questions run the gamut from methods of instruction, types of administration, curriculum content and professionalism to student-teacher relationships and evaluation and grading. There are many approaches to all of these.

Kneller suggests several points in the building of one's philosophy (10). First, the professional must either select one of the basic philosophies as a starting point or he may take an eclectic approach where he chooses from several. The important thing if he selects the eclectic point of view is to be consistent in his philosophy and select elements which are compatible. He should not select objectives for his program which are inconsistent with his process. Zeigler has suggested that the individual examine himself and find his place on an "Educational Philosophy Spectrum" (15), which runs the gamut from reconstructionism on the extreme left to scholastic realism on the right. (See Fig. 2–1.) When one's position on the continuum has been found, the following questions should be asked of oneself. "What is my purpose in life?" "What are the values which I prize most highly?" and "What are the knowledges and skills that are the most worthwhile?" This is a process of self-examination and self-analysis into the elements which make up a philosophy. When these questions are answered along with others into the nature of educational problems, the professional may find his place on the spectrum and be in a better situation to defend his positions on educational questions and give better direction to his practices in education and in life.

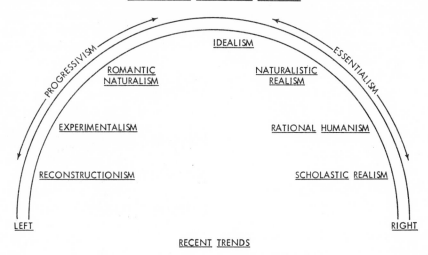

FIGURE 2–1.   Educational Philosophy Spectrum*

REFERENCES

1. Bookwalter, Karl W.: This Matter of Promotion. Procedures, National Association for Men. Published by American Association for Health, Physical Education and Recreation, 67th, January, 1964, pp. 1–5.

2. Broudy, Harry S.: *Building a Philosophy of Education.* New York, Prentice-Hall, Inc., 1954.

3. Bucher, Charles A.: *Foundations of Physical Education.* St. Louis, C. V. Mosby Company, 1968.

4. Conant, James B.: *The American High School Today.* New York, McGraw-Hill Book Company, 1959.

5. Conant, James B.: *The Education of American Teachers.* New York, McGraw-Hill Book Company, 1963.

6. Cowell, Charles C., and Wellman L. France: *Philosophy and Principles of Physical Education.* Englewood Cliffs, N. J., Prentice-Hall, Inc., 1963.

7. Cowell, Charles C.: Philosophical Foundations of Physical Education, Gymnasium, ICHPER Review, Vol. IV, Issue 1, 1967.

8. Dewey, John: *Democracy and Education.* New York, Macmillan, 1916.

9. Davis, Elwood C., and Donna Mae Miller: *The Philosophic Process of Physical Education.* Philadelphia, Lea & Febiger, 1967.

10. Kneller, George F.: *Introduction to the Philosophy of Education.* New York, John Wiley & Sons, Inc., 1964.

11. Slusher, Howard S.: *Existentialism and Physical Education.* Physical Educator, Vol. 20, December, 1963, p. 4.

12. Van Dalen, D. B.: Philosophical Profiles for Physical Educators. Physical Educator, Vol. 21, October, 1964, p. 3.

13. Van Dalen, D. B.: Philosophical Profiles for Physical Educators. Journal of the Arizona Association for Health, Physical Education & Recreation, Vol. 9, No. 1, October, 1965, pp. 4–6.

14. Webster, Randolph W.: *Philosophy of Physical Education.* Dubuque, Iowa, Wm. C. Brown Company, 1965.

15. Zeigler, Earle F.: *Philosophical Foundations for Physical, Health and Recreation Education.* Englewood Cliffs, N. J., Prentice-Hall, Inc., 1964.

16. Zeigler, Earle F.: *Problems in the History and Philosophy of Physical Education and Sports.* Englewood Cliffs, N.J., Prentice-Hall, Inc., 1968.

* Zeigler, Earl F.: *Problems in the History and Philosophy of Physical Education and Sports, 1967.* Reprinted by permission of Prentice-Hall, Inc., Englewood Cliffs, N. J.

Chapter 3

Physical Education—
Its Aims and
Objectives

INTRODUCTION

Education has been defined as a change, a modification, or an adjustment on the part of the student as a result of educational experience. These modifications lead to some end and when these ends are sought they become goals. There must be guidelines to give direction to these changes or modifications. Thus, guidelines are points of reference and as used in this text are goals. In turn, goals may be divided into levels or areas dependent upon the amount of distance or remoteness from the individual or group in question, or the degree of specificity with which they indicate direction. While these goals are not really discrete areas, for the sake of better understanding, three levels of goals shall be discussed: namely, *aims*, *objectives* and *outcomes*. The source of such goals is found in ascertaining the needs, interests, and abilities of the individual and the needs of society in general. Educators and physical educators under pressure from other individuals and groups face the problem of establishing goals which are relevant with these needs, interests and abilities.

There is no common agreement on the use of these terms by authorities in the field. They have been used along with other terms such as purposes, goals, and ends as synonyms on occasion, and at other times to mean different levels of direction but not always in the same way by all authorities. In order for there to be a clear-cut understanding on the part of the student who reads this textbook, the levels of direction or goals shall be construed to have the following meanings. They are all goals and are necessary as points of reference.

WHAT IS AN AIM?

First, the most remote goal is referred to as an *aim*. In the area of education the starting point of one's basic beliefs probably begins with the establishment of a value or a series of values which form around a central purpose known as a liberally educated person or perhaps just an educated person. In the case of physical education, these values make up a physically educated person. This ideal is arrived at through conceptualizing the type of individual which is needed by society and this is a function of philosophy. The achievement of this concept or ideal is the central purpose of education. An aim, then, would be an ultimate goal, it would indicate direction and would be quite remote and general in nature. While ideally all goals should be within the probability of achievement, in practice there are some that are so remote and general in nature that achievement is difficult or impossible. Such goals are never-ending ones and in actuality are never really achieved. If the original goal is reached, however, it long since has ceased to be an ultimate goal and has been superseded by an even more remote goal. Thus, an aim revolves around a center of purpose, it is abstract, never fully realized, and represents an ideal. Generally in talking about goals, there should be but one aim for education or a field of study. However, the aim for a field of study might well be one of several objectives of education.

Another point about an aim concerns its durability. Is it tentative and dynamic, or is it an absolute and static? Since an aim evolves from philosophy, since philosophy emerges from theories and principles, and since theories and principles are based on data and their interpretation, an aim will not change as long as the interpretation of the data remains constant. However, when new data are discovered and new theories and principles are formulated, aims will change according to the changes that are assessed. However, since an aim is remote and general in scope, it will in all probability change only over long periods of time.

WHAT ARE OBJECTIVES?

If guidelines are more immediate, they are referred to as *objectives*. By immediate is meant they are more specific, more concrete, and capable of attainment. They are not as abstract as an aim, but they still may be stated in somewhat general terms. They should be inexorably related to the aim of which they are a part, and they should indicate certain steps or levels along the line of direction pointed out by the aim. There are usually a number of these steps or levels, and they may be stated in somewhat broad terms. They are usually measurable if not by quantitative methods then by more qualitative techniques. It is these more remote objectives which give direction in terms of the values sought—values embodied in the aim. While the objectives are capable of being attained by superior persons, it is probably true that most persons fail to achieve all the objectives or achieve them only in part. However, this does not preclude the importance of objectives in the educational processes because as indicators of direction they make it possible to bring about desirable modifications and adjustments which are compatible with the values sought, even if the ultimate is never achieved. The fact that some individuals progress at a faster rate than others along the line of direction is incidental in assessing the importance of objectives. The student who understands the principles of individual differences will know that individuals progress at different rates along the line of direction, but that they are all pointed in the same direction by the objectives.

WHAT ARE THE OUTCOMES?

Guidelines may be further broken down into specific goals called *outcomes*. An outcome is a highly specific objective that is entirely capable of being achieved; it can be measured during progression or after its attainment. There are numerous outcomes for the individual to achieve. They may be stated in terms of the behavior of the individual as specific attitudes, appreciations, skills, physical changes, and knowledges and insights, and revealed as the ability to serve properly in tennis, to display good sportsmanship, or to practice good health habits. There are numerous outcomes under each of the major objectives. These outcomes are more immediate than objectives are, hence more likely to be achieved by the student.

Succinctly stated, a remote goal is referred to as an aim, the more immediate goals as objectives, and highly specific ones as outcomes. Admittedly there are other possible frameworks for these levels of direction, but this approach seems logical and can be explained and interpreted. If the education of the individual is thought of as a change or modification, there must be an ultimate direction toward which education is pointed. Since this ultimate is quite remote and general, there need to be some points of reference nearer at hand. It is at this juncture that objectives are used to indicate steps along the way toward the realization of an aim. Since the objectives are still stated in somewhat general terms and cover large areas of direction, outcomes which are highly specific, concrete and attainable are used to denote the short-term goals. Thus, through aims, objectives and outcomes, it is possible to give direction to educational processes and to the learning of the individual, thereby bringing about modifications and adjustments in terms of the values selected.

GOALS OF EDUCATION

In Chapter 1 the thesis was expounded that physical education is an integral part of education and has the same goals. Further there should be no conflict between their purposes. The values sought in physical education should and must be in harmony with those of education. Programs of physical education must be related to the aims and objectives of education in general. It has already been stated that the aim of physical education might well be listed as one of the objectives of education. In fact, the aim for any subject area might be considered an objective of education. The individual to be educated is made up of many unified and interrelated parts. Educators are presented with the problem of articulating the aims of specific subject matter areas with the goals of education in general. In order for the needs of each of these to be met in education, there must be a number of remote objectives involved to guarantee emphasis on each. While these are interrelated, each is perhaps more indigenous to a particular facet of the total individual. The aim of physical education, while it may emphasize the physical, does not separate man into disparate entities. It is in harmony with the holistic concept and must have relevancy to general education.

Who formulates educational goals? While it has already been established that basically goal formulation is a function of philosophy, frequently philosophy may be used to criticize and evaluate goals that might already exist. In any event educational goals in a democracy are generally the result of a combination of the philosophical and empirical methods where teachers, administrators, pupils, parents, the general public, and frontier thinkers all share.

One of the most difficult tasks of the educator is establishing criteria by which goals can be evaluated. If the goals themselves do not always come from philosophy, certainly the criteria and standards in those criteria for judging them do. However, such criteria would not be developed from just one of the philosophies mentioned in the previous chapter but would come more from the eclectic approach.

Aim of Education

The Educational Policies Commission in its bulletin "The Central Purpose of American Education" (6) contends that the central purpose of education is *the development of the rational powers of man*. These powers are the essence of the ability to think. On the surface this aim or remote purpose appears somewhat rigid and restricts education to an intellectual process thus propagating or continuing the dichotomy of the individual. However, this purpose is to be interpreted in its broadest sense. It is the hub of the wheel around which all other purposes of education revolve. This development of the ability to reason is central and unique because it is through such rational power that man achieves the ability to realize all the goals of society as well as his personal goals.

This central purpose does not negate the importance of all other educational objectives such as the Seven Cardinal Principles (4) or the four groups presented by the Educational Policies Commission (5), both of which are discussed in the next few paragraphs. Instead, through man's powers he is able to achieve not only these traditional objectives which have been formulated in the past but also new ones which may be necessary to serve new needs brought on by a rapidly and relentlessly changing world. It serves as the thread that can bring all valid purposes of education into an integrated whole. Thus, the central purpose becomes a means as well as an end. This might well be the aim of education while the goals set forth in the Seven Cardinal Principles are the objectives.

Objectives of Education

American education since 1928 has been influenced by the Seven Cardinal Principles of Education (4). Some authorities believe these so-called prin-ciples have become outmoded and have lost their validity in modern education. Traditionally, they have had great impact on educational change and modification. While they are called "principles," they are used in the same sense that the term "objectives" is used in this text. These seven objectives of (1) *health*, (2) *worthy use of leisure*, (3) *ethical character*, (4) *citizenship*, (5) *command of fundamental processes*, (6) *worthy home membership*, and (7) *vocation* are still fundamental in setting standards. They are as valid today as they were over four decades ago when they were first formulated, in spite of all the change that has occurred in our modern society and in educational processes.

These objectives are embodied in the values for a liberally educated person. They have not changed although the means for attaining them have changed, along with the need for attaining them. Physical education can contribute directly to the objectives of *worthy use of leisure, ethical character* and *health* and indirectly to the remaining four. Thus, the objectives of the physical educator are compatible and in harmony with the objectives of education.

A second study of the Educational Policies Commission in 1938 presented the objectives of education in four groups as follows (5): (1) The objective of self-realization, (2) The objective of human relationship, (3) The objective of economic efficiency and (4) The objective of civic responsibility.

In a sense these restate the same primary purposes of education as expressed by the Seven Cardinal Principles. Physical education can contribute its share toward the realization of these broad goals. For example, physical education can contribute to self-realization by teaching a philosophy of life which includes play as part of the good life and an enhanced appreciation of one's own body. It can contribute to economic efficiency by teaching that one's effectiveness in a vocation or profession is dependent to a large extent on health and fitness. It can contribute to civic responsibility by teaching leadership, citizenship and responsibility. These are only a few of the many examples which could be given to show the relationship between education and physical education in matters of direction and goals.

GOALS OF PHYSICAL EDUCATION

The Aim of Physical Education

In formulating an aim of physical education it is necessary to revert to the first part of this chapter concerning philosophy. It was succinctly stated that all goals are determined by philosophy. Philosophy deals with ultimates and in any particular field of learning, it is unequivocally the source of the aim for that field. Naturally philosophy does not operate in a vacuum. It is dependent on knowledge and inquiry— on scholarship and the scientific process. With the student's knowledge based on scholarship, the scientific process and philosophy, he should be able to formulate for himself an aim for physical education.

There are several characteristics of an aim that should be kept in mind in the process of formulation. First, it must be general enough to be inclusive of everything in the field. However, it must have enough specificity to delimit within that specific field. It must be relatively permanent and not be subject to the whims and fancies of the times. If it changes at all, it would change only over a long period of time, perhaps a century. It must not be readily attainable. In fact to be most operable, it must present, like Excelsior, a neverending challenge. It must have the power to inspire toward greater effort. It must be in harmony with educational outcomes thereby establishing educational validity.

The aim of physical education must be inexorably related to the qualities of a physically educated person. Thus, it is not only an essential ingredient of biological life, but also man's mental, social, emotional, and spiritual life. Many authorities have made statements concerning the aim of physical education. In general they all take a similar tack. Probably one of the most concise and at the same time all-inclusive is by the Bookwalters (3–3):

> The aim of physical education is the optimum development of the physically, socially, and mentally integrated and adjusted individual through guided instruction and participation in selected total-body sports, rhythmic, and gymnastic activities conducted according to social and hygienic standards.

This statement emphasizes the holistic concept discussed in Chapter 1 by mentioning the integrated and adjusted individual. It delimits the sphere of influence for development—through instruction and taking part in activities involving the "big muscles" and the immemorial racial movements of man. It further qualifies this sphere by placing limitations on the motivation behind those activities—they must be sports, dance, and gymnastics commonly thought of as play type activities. It implies that the activities shall be carried on under good leadership and under conditions that are healthful and hygienic. A key word in this aim is "optimum" which is in contrast to "maximum." Optimum implies that which is best for the purpose or the most favorable amount or degree. Thus, this aim would embody the qualities of a physically educated person and would be inseparably a part of the aim of education.

Objectives of Physical Education

Since an objective is a more specific statement of purposes than an aim, it is neither so remote nor so abstract. Objectives are really short-term aims, and they are a part of a whole. It has been previously pointed out that for a field of learning there will be a number of major objectives, perhaps from four to seven. Each of these must fit into the mosaic of the whole by being inseparably related to the values expressed in the aim, and at the same time uniquely related to each other in keeping with the organismic theory. In the four objectives to be presented in the succeeding paragraphs, the reader may identify the interrelatedness.

Authorities in the field of physical education have not been in complete agreement on its objectives. This diversity of opinion probably stems most from two points of view. Some practitioners lay claim to too much for the field while other more thoughtful and scientific professionals take a conservative approach. The latter group want to base objectives on evidence obtained from the scientific process and the best held opinions of the experts.

All leaders now recognize that many of the objectives formulated in the past do not have equal weight or importance, or perhaps from the standpoint of priority, physical education does not share equally in the achievement of these objectives. As the reader continues this unit of study, it may be noted that all objectives listed in this chapter are subject to this type of discrimination. Some of the objectives are unique to physical education, and no other fields in the educational family make much contribution to them. These must be of *primary* concern to physical educators because if they do not do their job well here, no one else will. On the other hand, some of the objectives are plainly *shared* objectives with other areas. These objectives must not be considered as secondary in importance. However, since they are shared, they may tend to be weighted somewhat less importantly than the primary objectives from the standpoint of the implementation of program, time allotment, grading, and the like.

The following is a hierarchy of objectives which have been agreed upon by many outstanding authorities in the field. Probably the basis for these major goals was first established by Hetherington (7) in the early part of the century and later elaborated upon by Nash (9), Williams (12), and others (8), (10).

1. ORGANIC DEVELOPMENT INCLUDING FITNESS. The organic aspect of development generally is concerned with health and vigor along with the development of stamina through vigorous activity. More specifically it is physical fitness or the more restricted term of motor fitness. The former in its broadest aspect takes into account such facets as nutrition, posture, health habits, physique, rational exercise, and other aspects including the removal or reduction of the strains and drains of life on the human mechanism. When these are removed and the training process is practiced, the individual gains physical power which enables him to perform with endurance, power, speed, agility, strength, and the like. These add up to fitness and this objective is one mentioned as being unique to physical education (see Chapter 10).

2. PSYCHOMOTOR DOMAIN INCLUDING SPORTS SKILLS. This objective, too, is one of the unique goals of physical education. It has a more general and more specific application. Generally, it means the development of body control and coordination so that the individual may perform with grace, ease, and efficiency. More specifically it concerns the various skills of sports, dance, and gymnastics. These are the specific skills for each activity, and they are distinctive to that particular event. Sport skills are highly specialized and unique

in this respect. However, they form the heart and core of the physical education program since they form the medium through which all objectives can be more nearly attained (see Chapters 11 and 16).

3. COGNITIVE DOMAIN INCLUDING KNOWLEDGES AND UNDERSTANDINGS ASSOCIATED WITH SPORTS, EXERCISE, AND DANCE. This is the intellectual aspect of development and is closely related to what the Educational Policies Commission calls the central purpose of the school—the use of the rational powers of man (6). If this be the paramount goal of education and if physical education is to be an educational experience, it, too, must make a contribution in this area. However, it is clear that this is a goal shared by all fields in the educational spectrum. It deals with the accumulation of knowledges and understandings and with insights. These knowledges, understandings, and insights provide the substance for intellectual power. From these come the ability to interpret, to evaluate, to make judgments, and to think. The educated man is a thinking man, and this might well be said, too, for the physically educated man. In fact, science has now come to look upon thinking not so much as a mental process as a process of the entire body. This relationship between the body and the mind was brought out in some detail in Chapter 1 (also see Chapters 15 and 16).

This intellectual development objective of physical education involves several facets or areas. First, it involves motor skills, and this requires thinking on the part of the individual in order to coordinate the mind with the muscles. The learning of a skill is not an automatic process but requires mental awareness, alertness and effort.

Second, not only does thinking take place with respect to the skill movement itself but there are myriads of associated learnings which accompany skill learning. These associated learnings take the form of rules, techniques, strategies, and terminology which make up sports, dance, and gymnastics. These are necessary knowledges in performing the whole activity well and in appreciating its importance.

Third, an understanding of the principles of health, good body movements, and exercise as a way of life is most important. There must be an awareness of the value of good health and fitness and knowledge of how they may be developed and maintained. Such knowledges and insights gained in physical education help the individual to understand, to make value judgments, to discriminate where choices are presented, and to interpret situations where logic is needed. It is this knowledge and awareness that make possible the achievment of other major objectives of organic, neuromuscular and emotional development.

This facet of physical education has been given a lot of lip service in the past. The whole area of knowledges and understandings, in practice, has generally reverted to information concerning rules, techniques, strategy, terminology, history, and benefits of sports and games along with some health concepts and principles of applied physiology. Until recently the field claimed to have a body of knowledge but such a conceptual approach was totally unorganized and vague as to content. It was a myth as far as any widespread effort was made to teach it. However, professionals still emphasized the importance of these knowledges and understandings as a part of becoming physically educated. In most cases, however, the physical educator has been activity-oriented and his program has emphasized the skills and fitness objectives almost to the exclusion of the mental and social objectives. Some professionals even classify their objectives into primary and secondary with the social and information objectives falling into the latter category. Thus, there has not been a great demand for this body of knowledge on the part of the general practitioner.

There is another side of the picture. Being physically educated means, among other things, that one possesses those knowledges, understandings and insights which will enable him to understand and appreciate the area of games, sports and dance and to know the physiological principles that guide his movements and the bases on which his health and fitness rest. Some years ago as an extension of the Youth Fitness Project of the AAHPER, another AAHPER committee was delegated the task of designing a test over knowledges in physical education. In a sense this test was to measure achievement and status in the knowledge area in much the same way that fitness and skill tests were to measure status in their respective areas. However, when the time came to develop the tests, the committee could find no formal body of knowledge on which to base tests. They therefore changed their attack and developed "Knowledge and Understanding in Physical Education" (1), a publication of the NEA. This publication marks a milestone in teaching physical education. For the first time there is now a formal body of knowledge to be used by classroom and specialist teachers at the primary, intermediate, and high school levels. An achievement test has been prepared by the Educational Testing Service to measure the knowledges and understandings in this book. It will now be possible to measure the achievement levels in physical education knowledge in the same manner that they are being measured in other academic areas.

4. AFFECTIVE DOMAIN INCLUDING EMOTIONAL AND SOCIAL DEVELOPMENT. The emotional and social aspects are re-lated because it is only when the emotional aspect has been properly developed that the individual can make the most contribution socially. Thus, this objective is concerned with helping the student make proper adjustments first as an individual and second as one of a group. Once again, it is obvious that this is a shared objective. It is shared first to the extent that the home, church and community in general each makes a contribution as well as the school, and then within the school it should be shared by all subject matter fields. Under good leadership, sports, dance, and gymnastics present a wonderful media for proper social and emotional adjustment. In fact the nature of these activities is such that the physical educator has a better chance and more opportunities than teachers from any other area (see Chapter 14 on Values).

This is the area of concomitant learnings where attitudes, appreciations, and values play a leading role. They are the bedrock elements in the emotional and social picture because they provide the ways in which the student makes his adjustments to himself and to his group. Every physical education activity is a social experience and most of them involve the emotions. In participating in such activities, the student finds outlets for his emotions—his aggressions, his competitive drives, his desire to belong and to be accepted, and his sense of service. Physical education provides a multitude of situations for the student to manifest an attitude, an appreciation or an ideal, and these can be expressed only through behavior.

These learnings are less precise and less definite than skill, fitness, and knowledge and are more difficult to measure. However, they do have specificity, because attitudes, appreciations and values are not general, but specific as they are revealed in a highly specific way through behavior. They are inevitable concomitants of skill learning and are always present, even if the teacher and the coach is unaware of their existence. Not only is the learning of a movement affected by attitudes, but the learning of attitudes is equally affected by skill learning. One of the great challenges in the field of teaching and coaching is to project learning in the area of movement in order to carry students further than mere skill and fitness. The implication here is that social and emotional learnings must be planned for in the educational process if they are to occur in the right way. They must be taught by both precept and example and practiced in the social environment over an extended period of time before they can emerge as character and personality traits (see Chapter 14).

These four objectives serve as guides to the aim stated in this chapter. When they have been achieved, they embody the values which have been previously established for a physically educated person. They are helpful as points of reference in revealing the progress the individual is making toward that value. They emphasize the whole individual concept and are supportive of the idea that a physically educated person is more than one gifted in sports and fitness. In addition to these he has acquired knowledges, understandings, and insights about sports, fitness and himself as well as such attitudes, appreciations and ideals which will make him a more intelligent, discriminating, skillful, and socially accepted performer. While each of these objectives is unique and separate from the others, they are inexorably related to the others. It is this interrelatedness which is consistent with the holistic concept.

Outcomes of Physical Education

It can be seen that the four intermediate objectives discussed above are pretty general and it would be difficult to evaluate attainment in them with any great degree of objectiveness. Also, while they do indicate direction in rather broad areas, they fail to help the physical educator pinpoint his aim at close range in his day-to-day endeavors. Under each of these four intermediate objectives, there are sub-goals or sub-groups or sub-objectives, and under each of these are highly specific goals generally listed in terms of behavior. For example, under the objective of neuromuscular skills, a sub-objective would be the development of the ability to play tennis. Under this short-term objective would include such behavioral outcomes as learning how to serve properly, learning how to use the forehand, learning how to use the backhand, and learning the types of shots such as drop, chop, lob and drive.

Since the four intermediate objectives are related, there would be outcomes associated with playing tennis under the other objectives such as courtesy and fair play on the courts under the emotional and social development and knowledge of rules, strategy, and pacing one's self under the interpretative development objective.

These outcomes are short-term goals and they enable the physical educator to be more specific in his planning and at the same time enable him to better evaluate the degree to which they have been met. It is currently true that standards for these outcomes according to age and sex have not been established universally and many existing ones are imprecise. Much more research and study needs to be done in this area. Critical learning period levels need to be established. However, it is these outcomes which are detailed, concrete, and specific and when they are achieved by the student, they give the most vivid picture of the physically educated person. It is these outcomes which are revealed through the behavior of the person. If

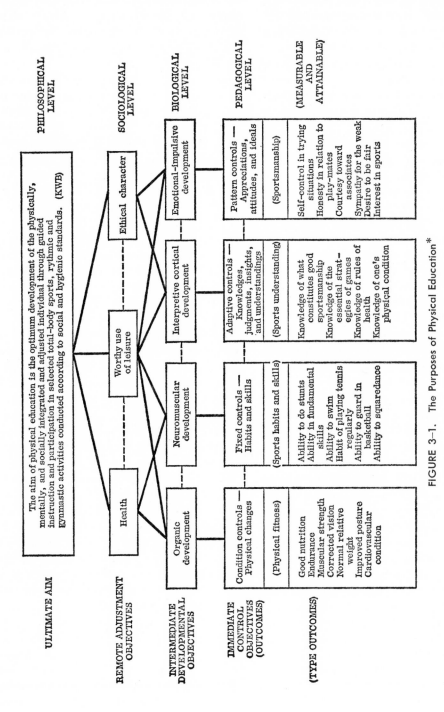

FIGURE 3–1.   The Purposes of Physical Education*

* Bookwalter, Karl W.: *Physical Education in the Secondary Schools, 1962.* Reprinted by permission of The Center for Applied Research in Education, Inc., New York.

he is a physically educated person or is becoming one, he will reveal desired outcomes through his behavior. He is well skilled as shown by his performance in a wide number of sports and activities. He is a fit individual and is able to show the stamina, endurance, and other qualities of physical fitness such as normal weight, good posture and the like. He is a knowledgeable person in the area of sports, dance, and exercise and in the area of self-knowledge concerning his own fitness and health. Also, because he is fit, healthy and participates, he uses his mental faculties with more alertness and awareness. He is emotionally and socially adjusted because he does show self-control under pressure, he is courteous to both teammates and opponents, he is honest and plays fair, he does not alibi in defeat nor does he boast in victory. In short, through his behavior he reveals his attainment in the myriad of outcomes of physical education.

Perhaps the most graphic illustration of the hierarchy of goals—aims, objectives and outcomes—in physical education is the one shown in Figure 3-1 (2–13). This arrangement is typical of the work of Karl W. Bookwalter who is a master at fusing the thinking of leaders into an integrative and meaningful whole. This chart of goals shows the relationship of physical education to education through the Seven Cardinal Principles of Education. It relates the work of Hetherington (7), Williams (12), Nash (9), Staley (10), and Bookwalter (3) into a structure which shows the vertical and horizontal relationships of each level as well as the interrelationships within and between levels.

REFERENCES

1. AAHPER: *Knowledge and Understanding in Physical Education.* Washington, D.C., NEA, 1969.
2. Bookwalter, Karl W.: *Physical Education in the Secondary Schools.* Washington, D.C., The Center for Applied Research in Education, Inc., 1964.
3. Bookwalter, Karl W., and Carolyn W. Bookwalter: *Purposes and Results in Physical Education.* Bulletin of the School of Education (Indiana University), Vol. 38, September, 1962, pp. 1–6.
4. Commission on the Reorganization of Education: *Cardinal Principles of Secondary Education.* Department of Interior, Bureau of Education, Bulletin No. 35, 1918, Washington, D.C., United States Printing Office, 1928.
5. Educational Policies Commission: *The Purposes of Education in American Democracies.* Washington, D.C., National Education Association, 1938.
6. Educational Policies Commission: *The Central Purpose of American Education.* Washington, D.C., National Education Association, 1966.
7. Hetherington, Clark W.: *The School Program in Physical Education.* Yonkers, World Book Company, 1922.
8. LaPorte, William R.: *The Physical Education Curriculum.* Los Angeles, College Book Store, 1968 (Edited by John M. Cooper).
9. Nash, Jay B.: *Physical Education: Interpretation and Objectives.* New York, A. S. Barnes & Company, 1948.
10. Staley, Seward C.: *The Curriculum in Sports.* Philadelphia, W. B. Saunders Company, 1935.
11. Webster, R. W.: *Philosophy of Physical Education.* Dubuque, Iowa, W. L. Brown Company, 1965.
12. Williams, J. F.: *The Principles of Physical Education,* 7th Ed. Philadelphia, W. B. Saunders Company, 1959.

Chapter 4

Historical Foundations of Physical Education

INTRODUCTION

History is a systematic account of man's past. It provides a means of evaluating and interpreting the course of human affairs and past events, placing things in their proper perspective. Through knowledge of this past and how it has shaped and molded the present, this present is more adequately revealed, evaluated and understood and it can be more effectively interpreted and explained. Because of this better understanding of the past and the evaluation and interpretation of the present, man is not only able to live more effectively in the present but he is also better prepared to meet the future and to predict it, and thereby to help shape it. Thus, history is a product of what has been and is currently going on, and the future will be a product of both as influenced by impinging factors and conditions of both.

IMPORTANCE OF HISTORY

The professional student in physical education should be interested in the background and history of physical education for several reasons. First, history enables him to understand the present status of physical education when he becomes aware of the influences which have shaped it and which have led to its establishment and the purposes for which it was promoted in various societies. History shows that physical education since time immemorial has been a tool of society to further its own purposes and goals. Second, he can use this knowledge to help verify and clarify principles from the behavioral and social sciences. This competency in turn enables him to help control his future behavior and to shape his environment by revealing trends and by showing causes and relationships. It should be evident, too, that the history of physical education cannot be separated and divorced from history in general. The influences which have been responsible for modern physical education are like threads running through the fabric of all history dating back into preliterate times. One cannot fully understand or appreciate the history of physical education when it is taken out of this context. The influences leading to physical education are related to almost all aspects of society—political, economic, religious, social, educational, and military. Physical education has been touched in some way by all of these and in turn has touched and had impact on them. Modern physical education has been shaped by a multiplicity of influences and will continue to be molded and directed in the future by the same factors. Physical education has evolved from the influences of history, but at the same time it has also been influential in making history. Through history, it has been twisted and shaped to serve the needs and purposes of the place and times. It reflects the social order that uses it, and has been employed to serve high and noble goals as well as for exploitation.

PHYSICAL EDUCATION AMONG PRIMITIVE PEOPLE

It is obvious that physical activity has been a part of the lives of all people. Man's evolution started with movement, and his very development into modern man is largely dependent on action of the muscles. It must be conjectured that primitive man's physical activity was related first to survival activity— the incessant search for food, clothing, shelter and protection from a hostile environment, and the propagation of his species. Prehistoric man's activities are revealed in two ways. First, through studies of archaeologists and anthropologists, interpretations have been made concerning primitive societies. Second, through a study of modern primitive man now found in certain areas of Africa and Australia, inferences and conclusions can be drawn based on their current mode of living. The present Aborigines are still in the stone age and provide a fertile field for study of modern primitive man. However, care must be taken in drawing inferences and making generalizations from modern primitive man because he may not represent the typical. He may have been detoured into a blind maze and out of

the mainstream of evolution and therefore the very thing that is generalized into a fact may be the reason the people have remained primitive and ineffective as a culture. However, through these studies it is known that primitive man participated in both games and dance. Perhaps more than people in any other time, primitive man placed great emphasis on the dance. Among other things, dance was a mode of communication. For people whose language was less than adequate, dance was a means of expression. It has been said that even in certain tribal societies today when strangers meet, the greeting is not "What do you say!", but "What do you dance!" There was a dance for the expression of all human emotions and for the portrayal of all aspects of his limited social order. Play and games, too, were an important part of living for these primitive people. Their games served several purposes. First, play was that part of their total activity which was motivated by fun and spontaneity as opposed to satisfaction of some basic necessity of life or struggle for survival. Second, it became a means of preparing youth for adult life, as games were taken from life's activities. Third, games and play became a recognized way to improve one's strength, speed and skill, qualities necessary for survival.

Fitness in primitive times was necessary for survival and generally always took care of itself. As man evolved socially and his environment changed as he learned ways to control it, his physical activity also evolved. As civilization advanced and man emerged from a savage state and evolved up through the various levels of Eolithic, Paleolithic and Neolithic man, his games and sports no doubt reflected this change. However, there was no need for organized physical activity in a primitive society. It was only when man learned to control his environment through his culture and ceased his nomadic existence, that leisure entered the picture. As civilization became more complex, so did man's play. As society had to become more structured to keep pace with the complexity of civilization, organization of man's physical activities in play and military training became inevitable.

PHYSICAL EDUCATION AMONG ANCIENT NATIONS

Two of the most ancient civilizations —China and India—have nothing to offer in the way of influences on modern physical education. They were similar in many respects. Both civilizations were reactionary, and individuality and self-expression were suppressed for the masses. There was participation in games and physical activities and sometimes these were related to life in their groups. Yet physical activity was neither an instrument of education nor of nationalism. These nations were characterized by religion, intellectual pursuits and a static social order. Once they had achieved a level of social order which suited their limited goals, they reverted to a status quo type of culture and resisted change. In China, particularly, the topographical isolation which prevailed was a deterrent to aggression from without and to progressiveness from within.

In the Near East a somewhat different picture prevailed. Sumer and Egypt are generally recognized as the cradles of civilization with records extending back to 5000 B.C. Sumer and Egypt were followed by Assyria, Babylonia, and the Hebrews. These nations were not hampered by the ancestor worship, the mystic philosophies and the rigid social order of the far east. They were dynamic and forward looking and believed in living a full life. Motivated partly by military goals and partly by the spirit of advancement, the people in these nations participated in a wide variety of physical activity ranging from horsemanship and archery to ball games and the dance. These activities were a part of the total living of the people. Perhaps the Hebrews have had greater influence on world history and physical education than any of the others. This is true because they nurtured the Judeo-Christianity and the idea of brotherhood of mankind. Out of Christianity grew many forces both antagonistic and conducive to physical education.

Perhaps physical training as such reached its highest level, until this point in history, in ancient Persia. Persia was a nation of conquerors and its main goal was military aggression. A program of training was structured by the state and was aimed at the physical and moral education of youth. The boy's training was started at the age of 6 years and was rigorous. It consisted of horsemanship, archery, hunting and active games for training of the physical and a commitment toward the truth in moral education. Because of this emphasis on health and fitness with a military motive, Persia became the greatest military power of its time. It continued to flourish until vice and corruption weakened the nation internally by corrupting both the moral and physical fiber of the people. This failure to remain virile and physically and morally strong led to the downfall of the empire and the Persian army was defeated by the emerging Greek states.

PHYSICAL EDUCATION IN GREECE

For all practical purposes it is unnecessary to go back in history beyond the time of the Greeks to identify those influences shaping modern physical education. No nation before or after the Greeks has placed as much emphasis not only on the intellect but also on physical perfection and achievement. While Sumer was the birthplace of civilization, it grew to maturity in Greece. The Greeks reached the highest pinnacle of civilization known to man in such aspects as government, literature, art, architecture, philosophy, and gymnastics. One can only conjecture at the combination of circumstances which occurred in this small mountainous peninsula to kindle its rise to such prominence. No one knows for sure how it occurred. Perhaps it was a combination of its heritage from other civilizations brought to fruition along with its geographical location in a mild climate, beautiful mountains and seas, and political expediency. In any case whatever the combination of events and causes, the Golden Age of Greece was launched. In the span of its greatness the pursuit of excellence became a Greek ideal leading to such heights of intellectual and artistic achievements that modern historians are still amazed. There is no parallel in the past where so many of the world's top thinkers, artists, philosophers, and scholars have come from so small an area as Athens which of course was the epitome of Greek greatness in these matters.

In any discussion of the Greeks, one has to keep in mind these two facts. First, Greece was not a separate nation with a fervor for nationalism, but a group of city states which varied in their philosophy and cultural patterns. These city states were incessantly at war among themselves or with outsiders, and while this military motive may have had something to do with the rise to such a high cultural level, in general it must have been a deterrent especially in the case of Sparta. Also, Greece— particularly Athens—was a stratified society with only a relatively small percentage of its people possessing citizenship. The remainder of the population were slaves who did the work. Where technology now serves man, in Greece the wonders produced in the construction of their public buildings as well as the mundane work of ordinary life were products of slave labor. However, the cultivation of the physical became a way of life for the citizen. While the motive may have varied for this with the city state, the goal of military strength was no doubt present. Yet, in Athens, which embodied the nearest thing to our modern concept of a democratic society and which developed a way of life as civilized as any the world has ever seen, the cultivation of the physical was much more than for purposes of the military.

Athens believed in the development of the total individual and the interrelationship of all life's aspects, and looked upon gymnastics as a means of educating the individual mentally, morally, and socially as well as physically. Like so many concepts which govern modern thinking, the Greeks conceived the idea of the unity of man and put it into practice. The ideals of beauty, symmetry, and perfection of the body in a harmonious relationship guided them in this quest and no doubt were reflections first of their innate sense of the artistic and second their high regard for health and fitness. While no society has ever approached the Greek ideals and accomplishments in either education or physical education, it is possible that as the future unfolds and technology advances along with education in leisure becoming more effectively used, modern man might again rise to the heights of the Greeks in his striving to live at the highest possible level of achievement. Just as the slaves freed the Greek citizen for cultural and intellectual pursuits, so may modern technology do the same for man in the future.

All city states did not have equal heritage in culture. Sparta was somewhat like the Persians and placed great emphasis on military power. Citizenship was a means and not an end. Life was rigorous and the word "spartan" has become synonymous with severity, courage, bravery and discipline as well as laconic since the Spartan was taught to talk little. Bachelorhood and obesity alike were crimes against the nation and were punishable. The training of the male was taken over by the state at the early age of six years. From that point on he became a chattel to the state and lived his life apart from close family ties. Women assumed a prominent role in Spartan life and were required to develop themselves physically so they might become strong mothers capable of bearing strong and sturdy soldiers. This emphasis on the military and physical development provided Sparta with the strongest army in the known world but was costly to them in loss of individual freedom and a lower level of cultural advancement.

On the other hand, while Athens emphasized the military to some extent and like all Greeks always gave a good account of themselves in battle when it was necessary, they did keep the military in proper perspective. The citizen enjoyed individual freedom in a democratic society. His early training was much different from the Spartan youth. He studied not only gymnastics, but also music and grammar. He met his military obligations when he became of age, but if no wars were in progress, he was released from the military service after two years and entered into a profession or an occupation. However, regardless of his occupation, he became a gymnast for life. The Greek gymnasium became not only a place for citizens to further their interests in gymnastics but also a center of political, social, and intellectual life.

The Greek festivals assumed a place of great importance. There were a number of these each honoring some Greek deity. The most famous was the Olympian festival honoring the god Zeus. Historians have placed the beginning of these games around 776 B.C., although there is evidence that they may have begun much earlier. They were held every four years thereafter until 394 A.D. (some historians place the date as 392 and others as 393) when they were abolished by the Roman Emperor Theodosius because of their pagan influence. The importance attached to these games by the Greeks was attested to by the fact that during times of war, truces were declared so the games could go on as usual. This is to be contrasted with the modern day Olympics when, since their inception in 1896, the games have been cancelled three times—1916, 1940 and 1944—because of world wars. To the Greeks, the Olympics were more than a sports festival—they were a way of life. The striving for excellence in athletics carried over to the struggle for recognition in all walks of life. Their fierce desire to excel in the intellectual and artistic realms as well as the physical placed the Greeks in a class by themselves. In the earlier centuries the festivals were guided by the lofty ideals of the Greeks. Only free citizens were permitted to take part. All contestants took the Olympic oath and conducted themselves accordingly. The emphasis in these games was on all-around development and sportsmanship. The Greeks believed in development to the fullest without engaging in anything to excess. However, as the lofty ideals and noble objectives of the Greeks began to give way to the more Roman influences, the tenor of the games changed accordingly. Professionalism, evil practices, emphasis on brutality as opposed to skill, and "spectatoritis" took over. The games declined in significance until their abolishment near the end of the fourth century.

However, the Greeks have left their imprint on our modern culture in almost every phase of life. Many of our modern concepts which have governed thinking and practice originated with Plato, Aristotle, Socrates, and the myriad of other Greek scholars. The ideals of universality were nurtured. The foundations were laid for most modern sciences. The very essence of democracy was cradled in both thinking and practical application. In fact, the use of man's rational powers to think were expounded for the first time in history. Art took on the classical principles of proportion and harmony and reached a degree of perfection still unequalled. Doctors are still administered the Hippocratic oath. No people before or after them have ever so emphasized the development of the physical within the context of the complete individual.

PHYSICAL EDUCATION IN ROME

The Roman Empire has left an indelible imprint on civilization as probably no other ancient culture has in terms of many aspects but especially efficient government, massive conquest, precise laws, and organization on an immense scale. It is somewhat difficult to generalize concerning the Romans because their civilization spanning its rise, flourishment, and decline lasted for some 1300 years and each era brought some dramatic changes in spite of the Roman desire to remain traditional. The early Romans were a practical and steady people who recognized their limitations. These characteristics may have been partly responsible for their failure to achieve the heights scaled by the classical Greeks in literature, art and philosophy, as well as gymnastics. While the Roman looked to the Greeks for classical culture, he never accepted the Greek's belief in all-around development and participation for the good of the total individual.

For the Roman, physical development was a practical matter and, on an organized basis, was chiefly due to a military motive. As the empire grew in opulence with Rome, the Eternal City, as the center of Roman grandeur, taste and influence, the Roman citizen became more passive in his physical participation as his quest for knowledge and his emphasis on material things increased. As he became more of a spectator, he became more callous and vulgar in his amusements. He demanded more and more violence. The Roman was at his best as a soldier, an engineer, or a ruler; he was at his worst in the pomp, the callousness, and the debauchery of his leisure pursuits in the later centuries. The Roman never was famous as an athlete, but he recognized good performance in others and promoted it on a professional basis. Professionalism in sports was accepted and emphasis was placed on those activities like chariot racing and gladiator combats where no holds were barred and the life and limb of the contestants were at stake. These contests were marked by violence, cruelty and brutality rather than fair play and skilled performance so revered by the Greeks. The populace bet on the outcome and the charioteers and gladiators became idols. If they survived long enough, they grew wealthy and occupied a place of high status in society. However, the fallen gladiator was not only at the mercy of his adversary, but also of the mob. If the mob turned thumbs down, the fallen died. The stadia held great throngs who came to be entertained.

The most famous stadium was the Circus Maximus in Rome, a huge arena which seated 200,000 spectators. Chariot races were the main event here. The gladiator combats were held in the Colosseum, an arena 150 feet high seating 50,000 people. However, Roman cities had sprung up throughout the empire and each had its own stadium and colosseum. The carnage and brutality found in the stadia and colosseums were unequalled in public displays of depravity. They still appall modern thinking and surely reflect the depth to which the Roman Empire was sinking in its declining decades. The leaders yielded to the cry of the masses— bread and games—and the games had to become more exciting and bloody to satisfy lowered tastes.

Another facet of Roman life which relates to physical education was the *therma*—the public bath. In a sense what the gymnasium was to the Greeks, the public baths were to the Romans. In Rome alone there were hundreds of these and some type was open to all people. In modern times there is nothing comparable to these. They were a Roman institution providing for much more than bathing and cleanliness. They became a center for exercise, recreation, socializing, and in some cases for art and learning. There is an old saying that Rome was not built in a day. With all its splendor and grandeur in public buildings, however, and riches, excess and extravagances of almost unbelievable nature by the nobility and upper classes, the slums of the cities were some of the worst the world has ever experienced. While modern man depends on technology for much of his work and the erection of his elaborate buildings, the Romans, like the Greeks, had slave labor for these purposes.

The Roman Empire declined and finally fell before the onslaught of the barbarians from the northern part of Europe. Its decline and fall was due to many reasons but basically because of the moral and physical decay of the people which had been in progress long before the official date of the fall in 476 A.D. So, as Rome was not built in a day, neither did its fall come about in a quick coup. Rome's strength turned out to be its weakness. Success in war and the development of a vast empire changed the Roman way of life. Through contact with outsiders, incessant wars, excesses in luxury and pleasures, economic ruin, military failure, misgovernment and breakdown in central government, corruption in both public and private life, the empire gradually disintegrated from within. The biologic stock of the people had become impoverished due to the loss of manpower in wars, gladiator combats, sensual excesses, and low birth rate. Along with the lowered biologic stock came an accompanying weakening of the moral fiber and the cities and provinces one by one fell to the invading barbarians.

However, the Romans over the long centuries had fulfilled their destiny and while the empire fell, the Roman heritage lived on. Parallel with the decline and fall of Rome was the rise of Christianity and the Church with influences more powerful than all the Roman legions. The Church became a great repository for both Greek and Roman culture and during the Dark and Middle Ages when the barbarians were slowly rising to a cultural level to appreciate and use Greek and Roman culture, it preserved the great heritage of these ancient civilizations. While the Romans have shared with the world a heritage which still has great impact in most areas of human endeavor, it is somewhat strange that this legacy falls short where physical education is concerned. The lessons to be learned from ancient Rome in physical education are generally of a negative nature. If history is to fulfill its role in helping to understand and interpret the present and thereby directing the course of a better future, the heritage from Rome lies chiefly in what not to do. In more ways than in its philosophy of physical education and sports are there similarities between decadent Rome and modern America. Such parallels which do exist should serve as danger signals if history is to fulfill its role of helping to direct the course of the future by interpreting the past.

PHYSICAL EDUCATION DURING THE DARK AGES

The disintegration and final collapse of the Roman Empire in 476 A.D., although it had been in the making for over a century, brought on the Dark Ages. Civilization lapsed into a period where almost all learning ceased on an organized basis, central government was destroyed, and economic progress no longer existed. Chaotic conditions prevailed throughout the empire. The barbarians from northern Europe overwhelmed all of Rome and except for the Church which was largely responsible for keeping the candle of civilization dimly lighted, the glory that was Greece and the grandeur that was Rome went into a period of dormancy. However, all was not lost entirely. These same barbarians whose conquests caused the lapse furnished the basis for nations who would spend the next ten centuries in rebuilding western civilization out of the elements of Greek and Roman civilizations under the guiding hand of the Church, and would someday surpass even the feats of both Greece and Rome.

At the fall of Rome its people were weak both physically and morally. The biologic stock of the nation was depleted and in need of replenishment. The barbaric Teutonic invaders set civilization back for more than a thousand years, because that is how long it took them to become assimilated and to slowly rise again to the cultural level comparable to the people they conquered. However, the barbaric invasion had its positive effects, too. These people brought with them to all parts of the disintegrated Roman Empire their strong, virile bodies and their sturdy traits of moral character to offset the physical deterioration and moral degeneracy of the Romans.

PHYSICAL EDUCATION IN THE MIDDLE AGES

Asceticism

Two forces evolved out of the Middle Ages which had an impact on the progress of civilization and which influenced physical education in a negative manner. The first of these grew out of Christianity. In the declining years of the Roman Empire the Church had assumed a position of greater prominence. Early Christian philosophy placed emphasis on the spiritual aspects of man and not the body. Therefore, neither the ideals of the Greeks which epitomized the body, nor the materialism of the Romans which led to sensual excesses appealed to the Christians. Thus, in a sense the Greek and Roman influence indirectly brought on the philosophy of *asceticism*. In the beginning it was no doubt a sort of revolt against the social evils existing in sensual Rome, but as time passed it cast society in its mold and became not only a philosophical approach to life but also a way of life for the masses. Asceticism subordinated the flesh and sublimated the spirit. The soul was glorified at the expense of the body. It was a philosophy that placed emphasis on life hereafter and in its harshest form resulted in extreme subjugation of the body through mistreatment and self-inflicted punishment. The ascetic had no time for self-improvement in the sense of the Greek ideal nor in self-expression. Since the ultimate objective was to prepare himself for life after death, he lived to that end. Often asceticism took the form of punishment of the body in all sorts of ways.

Asceticism no doubt was inimical to progress in the Dark and Middle Ages since its very existence would rule out individuality and initiative. Physical education activities played no part in the culture of this time. While the philosophy of asceticism no longer exists as a recognized philosophy today, there are still fragments of its beliefs which have been carried over from early time to the present. These are seen in certain attitudes which not only held back progress for centuries but which still plague education, especially physical education. Perhaps the best example of these attitudes in America concern the Puritan traditions where joy, happiness, and self-expression were considered sins. Play was evil because it was fun and involved self-expression.

Scholasticism

A second influence which came out of the Middle Ages concerned the belief that knowledge was the most essential matter. This attitude was called *scholasticism* and it, too, arose out of the Church, particularly the monasteries which served not only as repositories of learning but also centers of education. The medieval universities evolved from these and nurtured scholasticism. Thus, scholasticism evolved and functioned in a theological setting. While it served the purpose of stimulating intellectual pursuits after centuries of dormancy, it did shackle progress because of its dogmatism and restrictive nature. Where the ascetic placed emphasis on the soul as opposed to the body, the scholastic placed emphasis on the mind, glorified the intellectual and degraded the body. The deification of the mind still persists in some circles. It was this philosophy which brought about the separate mind and body concept and which has perpetuated the dichotomy until the present. The whole theory of formal discipline was based on this belief. While it has been stated in Chapter 1 that both science and philosophy have accepted the concept of the unity of the individual, the dualism of the mind and body still holds sway in many places. It is not so much that scholasticism is still believed in as a philosophical approach to education but rather it has become a hold-over attitude that still influences educational practice.

Medieval Sports

Perhaps another significant development in the Middle Ages which has been especially important to physical education was the evolution of sports. While this movement was no doubt held back by not only the ascetic temper of the Church but also the political repression of autocratic and aristocratic governments, it still continued to grow and most of the sports which exist now were carried on in some simpler form in the Middle Ages. This heritage is a significant one to America today for the very basis of modern physical education programs is one of games and sports and these originated and evolved during the medieval times. American heritage in games and sports perhaps comes chiefly from the English but not entirely since sport in the Middle Ages was not limited to England. Records show that sports were played by all groups in some form or other.

Feudalism and Chivalry

Other than sports evolution, the Middle Ages contributed to physical education in another way. Feudalism existed as a way of life, having evolved out of the chaos following the fall of Rome. All political, economic and social life was centered in feudalism. Only two opportunities for a vocation were open to the upper-class young man. He could become a clergyman or a knight. Both fields were characteristic of the feudal system which had arisen out of the Dark Ages to counteract or compensate for the fall of central governments. The Church required a religious and intellectual education for its clergy. Since before the fall of the Roman Empire, the Church had been growing in both influence and affluence, and through the Dark and Middle Ages became a force of great import. Men of the cloak occupied places of prominence in all societies and the Church itself became a bulwark of strength in the chaos of the times. However, this Christian influence suppressed physical education and especially took a strong stand against sports.

The other field of endeavor was chivalry which required a special kind of physical and military training needed for self-preservation in the warlike feudalistic society. Chivalry no doubt made a contribution to the uplifting of civilization from the depth of the Dark Ages by bringing more refinement to living and life. However, the skills of the knight were highly utilitarian and were not motivated by the idealism of the Greeks. They were used in fighting real battles in wars between the nobility or the crusades of the Church, or in the mock battles of the tournaments and jousts. Tournaments and jousts were both individual and group combat and were to medieval society what the Olympic games were to the Greeks and the spectacles of the stadia and colosseums to the Romans.

The training of the knight was not guided by the high ideals of the Greeks, nor was it characterized by either the nationalism or patriotism of the Roman. The training of the knight encompassed stages, and as he progressed from one level to another in his approach to the age of knighthood, he not only received his physical and military training but also a type of social education designed to equip him for the courtly life in the castle. His military training included horsemanship and the skills of the sword, lance, shield, and mace. To toughen and strengthen his body he wrestled, boxed, fenced, and swam. He participated in distance running for endurance. The making of a knight took

years of training but it was entirely physical and social without any emphasis on the intellectual. Physical education played an important role in the molding of a knight during an age when the only vocation the nobility had was fighting and their chief avocation was the imitation of warfare in a setting of feudal pageantry.

PHYSICAL EDUCATION DURING THE RENAISSANCE

The Middle Ages were brought to an end by a period in history known as the Renaissance which took place in general between the 14th and 17th centuries. This period has great significance for physical education because it marks the beginning of a new era where emphasis of the physical as a part of man's totality became an important part of his belief and in a more limited sense his education. In essence the Renaissance was that period in history when people in a blending of the decadence of Rome with the barbarism of the Teutons, finally climbed out of the abyss of the Dark and Middle Ages and achieved a level of civilization where they could once again assimilate and understand the cultures of ancient Greece and Rome. The word Renaissance itself means rebirth and when applied to this period of history means a revival or rebirth of the learning of classical Greece and Rome in a setting molded by the Middle Ages. However, it was more than a revival of the old; it marked the beginning of philosophies, theories, and practices that were to change the course of history and chart the path for modern times. No doubt many of the causes of this revival were rooted in the gradually accelerated progress that was made through the Middle Ages. The religious Crusades triggered many changes indirectly and directly. Directly they led to vastly increased trade and commerce. The pilgrimages to the Holy Land started a chain reaction that affected all of Europe intellectually, spiritually, socially, and economically and these in turn brought on great changes. Asceticism with its emphasis on preparation for the hereafter lost its hold on the people, scholasticism with its dogmas gave way to intellectual inquiry and exploration, authoritarianism began to be replaced by individual freedom, and emphasis shifted to the more human side of life. A new class of people rose to a place of prominence along with the clergy and nobility. These were the middle class led by the merchants. All of this led to invention, exploration, trade, and new ideas in literature, art, medicine, theology, philosophy, and education. Mercantile activity spelled the doom of feudalism and undermined the foundation of scholasticism.

Humanism

The classical learning of the Greeks and Romans was rediscovered. The first part of the period was dominated by the philosophy of humanism because it recognized the human aspects as opposed to the more spiritual approach to life. It reemphasized the classical idealism of the Greeks along with the art and literature of both Greece and Rome. The Greek scholars were thought to have a greater understanding of values and life than did medieval scholars. This movement was originally initiated in Italy for a number of reasons but later spread to all parts of Europe. In early humanism, education of the physical had a place.

Realism

However, as time passed, the humanistic movement along with the movement of moralism characterized by the Protestant Reformation became rigid and dogmatic. Moralism, which at first was marked by a revolt against the Church, culminating in the separation of the church and state, led to Puritanism. Puritanism, a philosophy which was to have great impact in the American colonies much later, promoted the idea of glorification of work, frugality in living, and condemnation of play and idleness. There was little room for emphasis on physical education in this setting. As a revolt against this newer formalism and dogmatism, the philosophy of realism arose again. Realists originated the idea of an education that was much broader in scope than any before and one that would emphasize the real things in life. While even the realists evolved from one stage to another, they in general developed a type of education that emphasized a preparation for life and one for which there was a place for man's body in the scheme of things.

Thus, the dualism of man—physical vs. mental or physical vs. spiritual—while still evident in the attitudes and customs of the people as a carry-over from medieval asceticism, scholasticism as well as Renaissance Puritanism, came to an end at least in the beliefs of the frontier thinkers like Locke, Bacon, and Montaigne. However, in only select schools were these new beliefs put into practice. Education was chiefly for the sons of nobility and only in some of the most advanced schools did physical education have a place in the curriculum. Perhaps this concept is best exemplified in the early era of humanism by the school directed by Vittorino da Feltra (1378–1446) in Italy where, incidentally, the whole humanist movement was initiated. Da Feltra combined the classical Greek learning in a medieval setting of chivalry. Physical training became an important facet of the total program of education. Perhaps it might be said that the modern philosophy of physical education began with this impetus and can be traced to the present from that modest beginning. Not since the Greeks had anyone stressed the unity of man in practice. Da Feltra's school, while reviving the Greek ideal of mind-body concept, served as a model for later practices.

EUROPEAN BACKGROUND FOR MODERN PHYSICAL EDUCATION

As the Renaissance grew to a close coinciding somewhat with the occurrence of the Protestant Reformation which had broken up the Church Universal, civilization in Europe moved into a period of nationalism. Nationalism marked the emergence of modern society. Strong national states began to take shape under the control of monarchies. This movement toward a stronger political universal had been a long time in the making. The Dark Ages had brought an end to all centralized government; feudalism and the Church rose to meet the needs of the time and continued to do so for centuries. The highly complex cultural patterns emerging from the Renaissance—political, social, economic, educational, and religious — forced changes. Feudalism had served its purpose and its restrictive organizational structure could not adjust to new conditions. It disintegrated and gave way to monarchy. Newer methods of warfare including the use of gunpowder made obsolete the skills of knighthood. The religious upheavals curtailed and finally brought an end to the civil powers of the Church. Since the emerging new middle class made up largely of merchants were leaders in both the revolt against the Church and support of central government, capitalism and nationalism began to join hands.

Nationalism

The nationalistic movement carried with it the principle of universal education. If nationalism was to achieve some measurement of success, citizens must develop a loyalty to the state and some of the qualities necessary to work toward its improvement. Thus, a scheme of education was developed toward that end. In this period physical education achieved a prominence it had not enjoyed since the time of the Greeks. Systems of physical education involving sports, games and gymnastics became an integral part of formal programs of education. If national groups were to become united or if nations were to maintain their autonomy and resist pressure from outside, their people must be vigorous and strong. Therefore, it seemed there must be some organized programs of physical training to bring this about.

The period of nationalism came to fruition in the eighteenth century and marked the beginning of the era of modern educational principles. Perhaps the movement is best traced in France and revealed in the works of Rousseau (1712–1778), who expounded his educational theories in many ways as he attacked both the Church and state. His views on political matters predated those of Thomas Jefferson and his ideas on education were revealed in his treatise *Emile*, which not only became a model for years to come in education but also physical education. He revived again the Greek ideal of the indivisibility of the mind and body and recognized the educational value of physical education including sports.

While Rousseau laid the theoretical foundation for modern physical education, the practice was left up to others. This practice is in sharpest focus perhaps in Germany and began with the work of Johann Basedow (1723–1770), who was influenced not only by the work of Rousseau but also by da Feltra. Basedow got his start as a teacher in Denmark and was no doubt influenced by ideas indigenous to that country. However, he returned to his native land of Germany and originated an experimental school known as Philanthropinum. This school featured many innovations including the admittance of students from all classes of society and the inclusion of physical training as a part of the total school curriculum. The teaching of Rousseau came to life in this school, and it served as a model for many other institutions which were developed later.

Another person who had great impact on education and physical education in this era was a Swiss educator, Johann Pestalozzi (1746–1827). He was acquainted with the works of both Rousseau and Guts Muths but he went beyond them both in his theories. He promoted the ideas of special teachers for games and gymnastics, progression in the teaching of activities, and recognition of the principle of individual differences. He placed emphasis on physical education as an education through the physical as opposed to an education of the physical.

Germany

Perhaps the best known of these schools was organized by Salzmann (18). He employed a young man, Guts Muths (1759–1839), as teacher of physical training. Guts Muths stayed on at the Schnepfenthal Educational Institute for fifty years and became known as the founder of modern physical education in Germany. He is considered the "Grandfather of German Gymnastics" because of his ideas and practices which are recorded in his several publications including "Gymnastics for Youth" and "Games." These were the first such books ever published by a specialist in physical education and they still stand as a testimonial to his greatness as a pioneer in a field where little had been done previously to serve as models. Guts Muths was a follower of Rousseau's teaching as he placed gymnastics on a

scientific basis and brought games and swimming into his program (15).

It was at this time that three other men came on the scene in Europe and made tremendous contributions to the cause of physical education both in Europe and in America. Since these men were approximately the same age, each made his contribution in his respective country at about the same time. Each man had a similar background of culture and refinement and each was imbued with the spirit of nationalism and a patriotic zeal for his country. This triology was composed of Jahn from Germany, Ling from Sweden and Nachtegall of Denmark (14). Perhaps the one who subsequently had more influence on physical education in the United States was Friedrich Jahn (1778–1852) of Germany. If Guts Muths was the grandfather of gymnastics in Germany, then Jahn has certainly earned the title of "father" of German gymnastics. Imbued with the great desire for independence and nationalism, Jahn saw the necessity for a strong and vigorous youth. His system of gymnastics known as the Turner movement was devised for this purpose. German gymnastics spread throughout Germany and later the entire world. His legacy to the German people was the Turnverein, a club where individuals not only exercised in German gymnastics to build strength and vigor but also used it as sort of a social institution. Such modern gymnastic apparatus as the vaulting bucks, parallel bars, and horizontal bars were introduced by Jahn.

Jahn's Turner system of gymnastics was carried on chiefly in the many Turnvereins which had sprung up all over Germany. However, these gymnastic societies catered chiefly to older youths and adult men. It was left up to Adolph Spiess (1810–1858) to introduce gymnastics into the schools in Germany. Spiess, using Jahn's system as a base, formalized it almost completely. He advocated and put into practice a special type of program for girls and made modifications and adaptations for younger children. His chief objectives were the complete development of the body along with the development of discipline and moral and social values through his methodology and program content. His school gymnastics were directed at education whereas Jahn's system was more political in its direction.

Sweden

Per Henrick Ling (1776–1839), after experiences in education in other countries, returned to Sweden and founded a system of gymnastics which has since become known as Swedish gymnastics. Like Jahn and Nachtegall, he was no doubt influenced by Pestalozzi and Guts Muths but made his own unique contribution in several ways. He was a pioneer in professional preparation as he established the Royal Central Institute of Gymnastics where students were trained in one of three phases of his program—educational gymnastics, military gymnastics, and medical gymnastics. While Ling was educated in theology, he had some training in medicine and it was natural that he began to place emphasis on the scientific aspects of physical education as revealed by anatomy and physiology. His contributions to the area of gymnastics were many but one that has had great impact was in the realm of apparatus. The stall bars, booms, rings, swinging ladders and climbing ropes were introduced as a part of Swedish gymnastics. Ling's system was finally accepted in the schools of Sweden and much later was introduced to the United States and interpreted first by Baron Posse in 1891.

Denmark

In Denmark, which experienced a similar political fate to that of Sweden,

the need for a program of physical education was met by Franz Nachtegall (1777–1847). Due to his influence, physical education became a requirement in both the elementary and secondary public schools. This increased the demand for trained teachers and this need in turn led to the development of a teacher-training program. Also, Nachtegall took the lead in developing courses of study for the guidance of this trained leadership in their work. Because of these accomplishments Denmark moved ahead of other nations and became the leader among European countries in progressive physical education.

England

While Denmark, Germany and Sweden in their efforts toward nationalism were developing systems of gymnastics, the British were engaging in games and sports. In fact, the legacy in matters of physical education which they have passed on to English-speaking people everywhere is in the form of sports. There were reasons why the surge toward nationalism never became as important to the British. They were blessed with a type of geographic isolationism in the English Channel which was a natural barrier to conquest. Therefore the English people were never motivated as strongly by the military as they were by their heritage of play and sports. This heritage reaches back to the Middle Ages where it became a feature of English life. Over the centuries the various sports evolved. Sports and sportsmanship are an important characteristic of the Britisher and have been used in the school programs to develop those positive qualities of the individual which are synonymous with the sturdy British traditional character. It has been said that the Battle of Waterloo was won on the playing fields of Eton. In any event such sports and games as golf, tennis, cricket, bowling, archery, rowing, boxing, wrestling, hockey, football, track and field and many others became a way of life and as the British Empire spread around the world, so did its sports.

However, England did not escape having a "system" of gymnastics. Archibald Maclaren (1820–1884), a Scot by birth, combined his knowledge of medicine, sports, and gymnastics to develop a system of gymnastics for the British army and navy. The program was used to supplement sports and games already in use. Maclaren, drawing heavily from already existing systems of the Germans and Swedes, really contributed nothing new, but he did try to bring about a measure of professionalization through his writing. He attempted to place gymnastics on a sounder scientific basis. However, his system later gave way to the Swedish system. The British were never completely sold on "systems" and, although some thought that more formal programs were needed for developing health and fitness and should be used to supplement sports and games, basically they remained true to their long heritage and used sports not only as forms of recreation but also as a means of education.

AMERICAN HERITAGE

Colonial Period

Physical education in America is a mixture of European tradition and New World expediency. Its early history might be divided into the colonial period up until the Revolutionary War and the period of nationalism up to the Civil War. The first period was characterized by pioneer life and while the second period was more advanced especially near the eastern coast, it too always had its frontier not too unlike the pioneer era. During this colonial era there was no organized physical educa-

tion as such. The lack of a system or the presence of one is always a product of the times as well as the place.

Much of the country was still wilderness and the people were too busy carving a civilization out of this wilderness to have either leisure or a need for additional physical exercise. Wresting a living from the soil was a back-breaking job in colonial times. Added to this expediency angle were religious overtones such as those of Puritanism which considered both play and idleness as sins. However, as the country grew in size and population and cities began to assume more prominent roles in the economic and social life of the nation, the picture was changed. At least for some people the times did not provide the needed exercise and the seeds were sown for some practical substitute.

It would be a mistake however to assume that the colonials did not play and have their games (13). The English brought with them their heritage of sports and games. The Dutch, too, brought with them their Old World sports and participated in them in the New World. The only part of the country that did not have games was New England, and this section was still pretty much under the control of the Puritan influences. Also, among the pioneers and later on the frontier where life was difficult and rigorous, games and play became an integral part of man's work as he labored to overcome his demanding environment. Log rolling, husking bees, barn raising and other cooperative activities were engaged in both as work and play. Both competition and cooperation were present in these pursuits.

Nationalism—1776–1820

Following the War for Independence there was a period when the spirit of nationalism and patriotism grew weak after being present to a great extent during the war. These qualities developed very slowly in the early decades of the young nation in the face of its political, social, and economic problems brought on by the times. During this era there was little change in the status of physical education. Following the War of 1812, the states did catch the spirit of nationalism that had been lacking earlier but, unlike their European antecedents, nationalistic fervor was not accompanied by an upsurge of interest in physical education. Nationalism and fitness have not been principal objectives for physical education in America. At no time prior to the 1850's did colleges or public schools officially assume any responsibility for physical education programs. The doctrine of formal discipline prevailed and schools were considered only as agencies for the education of the mind. The three R's were the only subject matter. Moral and character education were relegated to the home and the church while physical education was left to chance. However, during this era of growing nationalism, interest in physical education did exist both unofficially in the schools and among out-of-school groups.

The Beginning of the Systems—1820–1860

The period of the 1820's marked a significant time for the evolution of American physical education. It was in this decade that Jahn's German gymnastics were introduced into this country. Three German political refugees who were "Turners" and proficient in German gymnastics were responsible. All three were intellectuals and protégés of Jahn. They were forced to flee from Germany under the intolerance of Metternich. The first of these was Charles Beck who was employed at the Round Hill School and who started the first gymnasium in America. This was in 1825 and the following year his friend and fellow countryman, Charles Follen, began a similar program both for Harvard and the city of Boston. Follen was succeeded by Francis Leiber who continued these programs for a few years. For a time German gymnastics became popular and thrived as it spread to other institutions and parts of the country. Several facts stand out concerning gymnastics during this era. First, the persons who initiated and conducted the programs earned their livelihood by some other means. For example, Beck, Follen and Leiber were academicians and teachers by profession. Beck and Follen were classical scholars and Leiber was a historian and later initiated the Encyclopedia Americana. Second, colleges and public schools assumed no responsibility for gymnastics as a part of the formal curriculum. However, some private schools and female seminaries did. In fact a number of academies, where education was directed toward a preparation for life, encouraged games and exercises as an after-school activity in the late afternoons. Third, the interest in German gymnastics waned as the novelty wore off and by 1830 no vestiges remained. People more American in origin could see no parallel between their own needs and purposes and the spirit and purposes of Jahn. The native American was by now a product of his own democratic environment which had molded him into an individual with zeal for personal independence and freedom of choice. While this first effort to introduce German gymnastics into America failed, it did pave the way for its revival in the late forties and fifties. Many Germans had come to America following political upheavals and had settled throughout the country but particularly in the Middle West. When the Turner system was introduced in these predominantly German communities, it was well received and flourished.

During this period there was, however, a recognized need for exercise, and many educational institutions attempted to meet the need through manual labor. This combining of intellectual training with manual labor thrived for a time but finally proved to be impractical. Also, during this era the names of two people stand out among those who made contributions to the development of modern physical education. One of these was Dr. J. C. Warren who taught at the Harvard Medical School and promoted physical education in his spare time. He recognized the need for exercise and recommended various types of activity including both gymnastics and sports. He helped establish the Harvard and Boston gymnasiums and advocated suitable exercises for women. He was among the first to use the term *physical education* and he also used the word *calisthenics* derived from the Greek words meaning "beautiful strength." Another name was that of Catherine Beecher who ran a girls' seminary at Hartford, Connecticut. She included physical education in her curriculum but modified her program to more nearly meet the needs of young women. She really contributed nothing new but her system was a combination of exercises borrowed from Old World sources and adapted to the New World experiences. Her ideas on physical education were later published in two books. Miss Beecher should probably be recognized as the originator of the first system of physical education by an American. However, it must be noted that she was ahead of her time since her ideas and practices failed to be accepted because they were in conflict with American customs and ideas on femininity and the role of the female in society.

The 1860's marked a new era in the evolution of American physical education. The nationalist period between 1776 and 1860 for physical education was characterized by meager founda-

tions having been laid for future growth and progress. The development which occurred between 1825 and 1850 in gymnastics, sports, and exercise led to an increased tempo for the fifties and this period was marked by continued growth both in the schools and out until interrupted by the Civil War. The German gymnastic movement was revived in 1848. The influx of thousands of immigrants from Germany, driven away by the Revolution of 1848, created in America many communities dominated by people of German ancestry. They brought with them their customs and ways from the old country including their gymnastic system. The first Turnverein was organized in Cincinnati in 1848 and the movement spread rapidly to other cities. Where German gymnastics had failed earlier under Beck, Follen, and Leiber, it now flourished chiefly because it was carried on by German people who were already somewhat knowledgeable and whose political and social background was more in keeping with the aims and purposes of gymnastics.

Also, in the years just before and during the Civil War a new champion for the cause of physical education appeared on the scene. The "New Gymnastics" of Dioclesian Lewis became popular and was even accepted into some public schools for a time. Dioclesian Lewis was neither scientific nor original in his work but his system comprising a constellation of exercises gleaned from many sources brought him into the limelights. He was undoubtedly a gifted salesman and his system succeeded temporarily chiefly due to the force of his dynamic personality, along with the fact that times were ripe for the appearance of a system of American origin. Little if any of this system remains today but Lewis did leave his mark on the growth and development scale of physical education in several ways. First, he recognized the need to have trained teachers of gymnastics and he organized the first successful school in America designed to prepare special teachers in gymnastics. This was the Boston Normal Institute for Physical Education, founded in 1861. He also published the first American journal devoted to physical education. Then, the acceptance of his system into selected public schools, while in itself was not widespread, did lay the foundation for future requirements and paved the way for expansion into educational programs following the war.

Period of Growth and Expansion— 1860–1900

The Civil War brought a temporary halt to the modest expansion which had been initiated in the fifties. However, with the end of the war in 1865, some significant events occurred which began to shape and mold the modern era of physical education. While education itself was at a low ebb, the progress of gymnastics along with sports was rapid. The foundations laid by Beck, Follen, Leiber, Warren, Beecher, and Lewis along with some significant developments growing out of the war were beginning to bear fruit. Both gymnastics and sports were becoming a part of school programs and interest in sports by the general public was growing rapidly. However, it might be pointed out at this time that while sports were being played in colleges and public schools, they were still not considered a part of the gymnastic programs, and the schools accepted no responsibility for their organization and administration.

The gymnastic "systems" which carried over from pre-war years were German gymnastics, Lewis' "New Gymnastics," and revised forms of the Beecher system. To these were added the Swedish gymnastics and the Delsarte system along with several systems more

American in origin. These systems along with sports and military drill competed for supremacy in what Weston has called the "Battle of the Systems" (24–24). Most of these systems recognized the necessity for trained leadership, and this period is marked by the establishment of a number of new institutions for the training of this leadership. The Boston Normal Institute by Dio Lewis has already been mentioned. The Turners had originally started a training school for their leaders in 1861 but it failed to function because of the war. However, the idea was revived again and in 1866 the Normal College of the American Turnerbund was established and has been in operation ever since. It is now located in Indianapolis and is a part of the School of Health, Physical Education and Recreation of Indiana University and is still known as the Normal College of the American Gymnastics Union. German gymnastics no doubt dominated the seventies and eighties and many of its outstanding leaders campaigned for the inclusion of physical education into the public schools.

However, men of more American origin began to assert themselves and be heard. One of the first of these was Dr. Edward Hitchcock, a physician, who became the first college director of physical education with faculty status when he became head of the Department of Hygiene and Physical Culture at Amherst College in 1861. Dr. Hitchcock was truly a pioneer as he developed a system of physical education centered around gymnastics, calisthenics, and sports (22). He was also a pioneer in anthropometric measurements and emphasized health as an aspect of his program. He was joined in his almost lonely position a few years later by Dr. Dudley Allen Sargent and Dr. William G. Anderson. These three formed a triology of eminence equal to that of Jahn, Ling, and Nachtegall in laying the foundation for modern American physical education. Dr. Sargent was director of the Hemenway Gymnasium at Harvard and his many contributions to the field place him at the top of the list among early American physical educators. His work ran the gamut from teacher training, through the organization, administration, and instruction of his own unique system, to scientific research and writing. His system was unique because it was eclectic as he drew from all the existing systems and then added his own special principles and techniques. His was the most comprehensive and the most scientific system yet devised. His work in teacher training resulted in two different schools. The Sargent School of Physical Education was organized in 1881 and later became the Sargent School of Boston University. The Harvard Summer School which was organized for the benefit of teachers wanting in-service training during summer vacation was organized in 1887 and prospered for a time.

Dr. William G. Anderson became interested in physical education through his early work with the YMCA. He later became the director of physical education at Adelphia Academy at Brooklyn before moving on to Yale as professor of physical education. He was an intelligent and gifted teacher and leader who is best remembered perhaps because of his efforts in behalf of the development of unity and organization in the field. It was he who called the now famous meeting in 1885 out of which the present AAHPER ultimately evolved. At this meeting the organization was ordered and called the Association for the Advancement of Physical Education. It later became the American Physical Education Association, and finally health and recreation took their rightful place along with physical education and the modern title of American Association for Health, Physical Education and Recreation came into usage in 1938. Dr. Anderson saw the need for trained professional leadership and he established the Brooklyn Normal School for Physical Education in 1886. Chronologically this school ranks fourth among such normal colleges. He is also credited with initiating the School of Physical Education as a part of the Chautauqua Assembly at Chautauqua, New York in 1886.

Out of the confusion of ideas and conditions of the eighteen seventies and eighties came several other movements and events that have had their impact on the development of modern physical education. One was the growth of the YMCA and YWCA movements (6). Along with the social and educational objectives as a part of these organizations' religious goals, leaders now began to see the importance of the physical. Therefore, gymnasiums became an important facet of "Y" programs and full-time directors were in demand. This led to the establishment of the International Training School of the YMCA at Springfield, Mass., and in 1887 a department of physical education was added and has been one of the many wellsprings for development of leadership ever since. Robert Roberts took the lead in this movement. Another development during this era was the introduction into this country of Swedish gymnastics. The Swedish Movement Cure based on Ling's medical gymnastics first made its appearance in America just prior to the Civil War. It later reached a period of common acceptance under the leadership of Hartvig Nissen. Nissen was also instrumental in introducing Ling's educational gymnastics. However, this phase of Swedish gymnastics was made popular in America due to the efforts of three other people—Mary Hemenway, Amy Morris Homans and Baron Nils Posse. Mrs. Hemenway, a woman of great wealth and humanitarian interests, and Amy Homans, a gifted teacher, were instrumental in introducing Swedish gymnastics into the public schools in Boston. Baron Posse, a Swedish immigrant, took over the leadership of this system and Swedish gymnastics enjoyed great popularity in the eastern part of the United States. To supply the trained leadership needed to teach this system the Boston Normal School of Gymnastics was organized in 1888 and later became the Department of Hygiene and Physical Education of Wellesley College. Both Posse and Homans were employed as teachers in the early years of this institution. Swedish gymnastics became so popular that it now rivaled the more entrenched German gymnastics for a place in the sun. Shortly after the introduction of Swedish gymnastics came still another system called the Delsarte System of Physical Culture, an import from France. This system was initially designed to develop dramatic and singing abilities through physical exercises. However, the system seemed to have benefits other than in the arts as its exercises emphasized graceful and dramatic movements and soon became one of the fads of the time.

During the era before 1900 there was a widespread interest manifested in sports (11). Sports had begun to play a minor role in colleges prior to the Civil War but afterward the interest increased and by the eighties had assumed an important place in campus life. The colleges took the lead in setting sports trends but all athletics were student-sponsored and student-controlled; students organized and administered their own programs. At first the educational authorities attempted to legislate against athletics and then tried ignoring them. However, in the eighties when it became apparent that interschool competition could not be eliminated, school authorities started to exercise some controls.

Intercollegiate competition had gotten under way with a boat race between Harvard and Yale in 1852. The first baseball games were played between Amherst and Williams in 1859 and the first intercollegiate football game was the Princeton-Rutgers game in 1869. Interest in football grew until by the eighties it was the most popular sport at the college level, and in a sense has maintained that position ever since. Both tennis and golf became popular, along with bowling. National organizations to regulate them came into being. Basketball was invented by Dr. James A. Naismith in 1891 at the YMCA Training School at Springfield, Mass., and became popular immediately in school programs as well as in recreation agencies. Volleyball, too, was invented four years later by William Morgan at Holyoke YMCA and for the same purpose as basketball, which was to provide a winter indoor sport. Track and field events became popular, and with the revival of the Olympic Games in 1896 under the leadership of Baron DeCoubertin interest continued to increase.

However, sports and athletics were not confined to colleges and schools. They were becoming popular everywhere as leisure activities and community sponsored projects (11). Professional sports made their beginning shortly after the Civil War with the first professional baseball team—the Cincinnati Red Stockings in 1869. Under the leadership of A. G. Spalding, the National Baseball League was organized in 1876 and the American League, now called the junior circuit, did not come along until 1900. Track, cycling, handball, wrestling, boxing were among the sports where professionalism thrived. In fact, professional athletics and the spirit of professionalism grew to such an extent that an organization was founded in 1879 to combat the evils of professional athletics and to promote athletics on an amateur basis. This organization was the AAU (Amateur Athletic Union) in 1888. The AAU, then as now, exercised jurisdiction over many sports and activities and attempted to promote participation in them in the frame of reference of amateurism. However, the college sports did not come under this jurisdiction directly and it was not until 1905 that college representatives formed their ruling organization which has now come to be the NCAA (National Collegiate Athletic Association) (12). It might be pointed out that these two powerful organizations—AAU and NCAA—have come to the point of confrontation in regard to which shall have control of amateur athletics, especially where the Olympic Games are concerned. Individual institutions had, however, in the eighties attempted to exercise some control over their own athletic programs to reduce the evils which had crept in and in order to make them more educational in nature. Individual institutional control was followed by the formation of conferences, notably the Big Ten, and conferences in turn led to controls more national in nature. High schools patterning themselves after the colleges also developed athletic programs. The same problems on a somewhat lesser scale became prevalent. These school authorities went through the same process of gaining control and establishing standards. Control was begun on the local level first and then moved to conference and state control. The first state high school athletic association was organized in Wisconsin in 1896.

Two rather significant things should be pointed out at this time. First, athletics and gymnastics were completely separated in the schools. While some schools did sponsor sports and games along with gymnastics, for example Dr. Sargent at Harvard, in general teachers of physical education and gymnastics did not serve as coaches of interschool teams. At the same time, however, many institutions were beginning to exercise some control of formerly student-controlled athletics but they had not yet assigned them to physical education for administration and coaching. The second point has to do with the leadership of physical education programs. The colleges were turning to physicians to head up those programs considered educational in scope. This was done for two reasons. First, if heads of departments were to be given faculty status along with academicians, the philosophy of the times required comparable levels of training. No specialized school of physical education or gymnastics could provide this amount. Secondly, physical education was connected with health and it seemed logical to involve physicians where matters of health were concerned.

Probably one of the most significant things to come from the last two decades of the nineteenth century was the laying of the groundwork for professionalization of the field. The conference out of which the AAHPER developed has already been mentioned. Perhaps an even more significant conference was one held in 1889—the Boston Conference. Representatives from practically all groups or systems of physical education attended this meeting, except leaders in sports and games. Why the latter were left out is easy to understand, since athletics existed entirely outside organized physical education. The main accomplishments of this meeting were the sharing of ideas and the recognition that each of the systems had strengths and weaknesses, and that no one system could possibly fill the growing needs and interests brought on by the times. In 1897 the Society of College Gymnasium Directors was founded with membership open to men who held administrative positions in colleges. This organization is now the National College Physical Education Association for Men and its membership is open to all college personnel in physical education. A similar organization was organized for women in 1924 and it is now called the National Association of Physical Education for College Women. An organization of eminent professional leaders was founded in 1904 by Dr. Luther Gulick called the Academy of Physical Education and its membership is open only by election of the body. Many organizations and groups began publications of professional literature. The most significant of these was the forerunner of the Journal of Health, Physical Education and Recreation which was begun in 1896.

PHYSICAL EDUCATION IN THE TWENTIETH CENTURY

The first two decades of the twentieth century marked an end of one war and the entry into another. The Spanish American War and the First World War were followed by similar patterns in physical education. Historically during times of war, nations have always leaned toward a fitness-type program and seem to become more cognizant of their physical shortcomings, thus becoming more health conscious. Between these two wars the battle of the systems continued unabated with the main struggle between the German and Swedish gymnastic programs on the formal side and systems more American in origin on the informal side. In general, during this era the formal programs held the upper hand. However, this period for physical education was more than a struggle between the systems. It was a transition period because of a new concept which was to change the whole course of both education and physical education. Chiefly due to the vision and efforts of three men—Wood, Gulick and Hetherington—this new philosophy took hold in physical education and began to gain momentum.

A new concept expounded by John Dewey, the renowned philosopher of education, culminated in an educational philosophy known as *progressivism* where life-adjustment education became the focal point. In this new philosophy Dewey placed emphasis on social education and learning by doing in creative experience (see Chapter 2). He expounded the idea that the learning of a physical act was more than just physical, but also mental and social, and that play had a part in the development of the total individual including his personality. For the first time physical activities were looked upon as contributors directly to the educational processes. Sports and games under the best conditions could supplement the entire educational spectrum. In physical education this new concept began to take shape and exert force. While it was no doubt influenced by Dewey's philosophy, the idea had also been nurtured in the minds of these three men even before Dewey had become spokesman for education. In any event, due to this new emerging belief that physical activity could make important contributions to educational processes in its own right, physical education became an integral part of the school curriculum in the first quarter of the twentieth century.

A Trilogy of Great Leaders

The new idea resulted in the new concept in physical education sometimes called the "Natural Program" which was based on games, sports, outdoor activities, and selected gymnastics from the older systems. The concept was new but the parts of the program were as old as the customs of the peoples which made up America at this time. In this new approach which was not too unlike the program envisaged by Rousseau and Guts Muths long ago, stereotyped procedures and the nonfunctioning parts of the traditional systems were eliminated and activities based on the immemorial racial activities of man were substituted.

Thomas Denison Wood (1865–1951), a product of Oberlin College as was Gulick, got his early professional experience at Stanford where he worked with Hetherington for a time. He later moved to Teachers College, Columbia University. He was a man of wisdom and insight and gave leadership of the highest type to the evolving "New Physical Education." He brought sports, games and tumbling into his program. Since development of the physical became a means rather than an end in this new philosophy, Wood also became a leader in the fast growing movement of school health. His ideas and practice encompass a great deal of current programs.

Luther H. Gulick (1865–1918) has already been mentioned for his contribution to the YMCA Training School at Springfield College. Sharing a similar philosophy, Gulick, too, emphasized the natural activities and was chiefly responsible for arousing interest in camping and outdoor activities. He assisted in the organization of the Camp Fire Girls' movement, and made many other contributions to physical education. He is best known for including sports and games in his program and emphasizing the social values which might accrue from participation including sportsmanship. He originated the idea of awards in athletics and promoted state-wide competition.

Clark W. Hetherington (1870–1942), known as the modern philosopher of physical education, came to New York University by way of the University of Missouri and Wisconsin (2). However, he had known Wood earlier at Stanford and was no doubt influenced in his thinking and practices by Wood's con-

cept of the "New Physical Education." The basis for his theory that play could influence behavioral patterns was nurtured in these years and culminated in his belief and practice that sports and games were prime factors in character development. At the University of Missouri he had made popular, as a part of planned programs, such natural activities as the "hunting" type of games or "chasing-and-fleeing" games which still make up a significant part of the primary and elementary programs. Hetherington was a dedicated teacher and became a lecturer of note; many of his lectures were published in various media.

Hetherington's only book was *School Program in Physical Education* which he reluctantly permitted to be published (5). It is still a classic even in modern times and embodies much of present day philosophy concerning aims, objectives and purposes. While his work and philosophy paralleled that of Dewey's, historians (16) seem to think that he arrived at his theories independently of Dewey's influence. It is probable that both men were perceptive enough, even though working in different cultural milieu, to see this new philosophy emerging from the social and cultural changes which were taking place in the early twentieth century. It is certain, however, that Hetherington was impressed by both Wood and Gulick and their views of the natural idea of play and thus indirectly Dewey might have been somewhat influential since both Wood and Gulick knew of Dewey's work and no doubt their thinking had some impact on Hetherington. Thus, once again another trilogy of leaders arose to give direction and vision to the cause of physical education where it came to be looked upon as education through the physical rather than of the physical.

Later on after World War I, the new physical education of Wood, Hetherington, and Gulick found worthy disciples in Jesse Feiring Williams and Jay B. Nash. Williams became Wood's successor at Teachers College and Nash was brought from Oakland, California, by Hetherington to later become his successor at NYU. Williams, a graduate of Oberlin, became the standard-bearer for the natural program and physical education through the physical. His philosophy, emphasized in his teaching, lecturing, and writing, was consistent in its direction and brilliancy as it clearly marked the way for physical education in the twenties and thirties. In fact it still dominates the field perhaps more than the work of any other single professional. Nash was of equal stature and together with Williams and Charles McCloy among others kept the profession moving during the depression years and World War II. McCloy epitomized the new scientific era which forged progress in research and tests and measurements.

New Developments in Teacher Education, Health, Recreation and Dance

The first quarter of the twentieth century brought phenomenal growth in many facets of physical education. In teacher education there was a shift in direction marked by the private non-collegiate teacher training institution affiliating with colleges and universities. This was made necessary for financial reasons partly and partly to enhance the status of these institutions. An example of this was Arnold College which became an affiliate of the University of Bridgeport. Also, departments of physical education began to establish teacher education programs in many colleges and universities including Illinois in 1905 and Oregon in 1907. Four years of college became the accepted minimum for undergraduate training and a bit later graduate work was recommended. These graduate programs did not come

along until the mid twenties when both NYU. and Columbia University as well as the YMCA. Graduate School of Nashville, Tenn. (23) began graduate work.

Health education grew in interest and scope. Educational developmentalism led to an increasing interest and emphasis on both health service and health instruction. Health took on new meaning in 1918 when it was placed at the top of the list in the Seven Cardinal Principles of Education (3). The playground movement along with athletics represent similar movements and both movements sponsored activities that were later adopted by physical education. Out of the playground movement grew the recreation movement and it, too, expanded rapidly. The first important dateline after the Boston Sand Gardens in 1885 was the founding of the Playground Association of America (later to become the National Recreation Association) in 1906. Dr. Gulick was a leader in this movement and became the association's first president. However, the real philosopher of the playground movement and the one who gave it its educational direction was Joseph Lee. To the recreation movement was added camping also contributed to by Dr. Gulick. The basis was laid in these years for both private and school camps and interest grew to such an extent that the Camp Directors' Association (later the American Camping Association) was founded in 1910. The YMCA movement, which had gotten its start in the 1920's, expanded rapidly in the first part of the new century. Once again it was Luther Gulick who left his imprint on these programs from the time of the training school in 1888.

Perhaps one of the most dramatic steps forward was made in the area of the dance which by now had become an integral part of physical education. The two types of dances which became most popular were the folk dance and natural dance. Isadora Duncan was the creative genius who was more influential in stimulating interest in the interpretive dance. Gertrude Colby also worked in the natural dance but introduced folk dance into education. The natural dance was the harbinger of modern dance which made its appearance in the 1930's and formed a link between modern dance and the aesthetic dance of the late nineteenth century.

Professional Literature and Scientific Research

This period was also a time of expanding horizons in professional literature and scientific research. Many of the agencies promoting some aspect of health, physical education, and recreation started or continued professional journals. Many of the professional leaders presented their philosophies and specialities in their writing and many books and articles appeared in print. Much of the research of the era led to the development of tests and measurements. The measurement programs of Sargent and Hitchcock were expanded and the emphasis shifted first from anthropometry to strength and then later to achievement including physical efficiency and athletic achievement testing. New statistical techniques enabled scientific methods and procedures to be employed.

Sports in the Curriculum

In the meantime, the sports and games which had always been indigenous to American people through their heritage principally from the British continued the phenomenal growth which started in the last quarter of the nineteenth century. Through the efforts of Wood, Gulick, Hetherington and others the games and sports had grown to a place of such prominence in the school program that they had begun to challenge the supremacy of the formal program of gymnastics. Track and field and combative activities were the first such sports but later basketball and volleyball as well as individual and dual sports were added. At the same time, outside of physical education but still within the school, a transition was taking place in the sports and games for students. While athletics grew in great popularity, their control was passing from the student to the faculty and administration. The colleges led in the expanding sports and games movement, and the high schools were quick to follow in their footsteps. College athletics were so popular and created so much interest among alumni and area spectators that they became big business. Football became the symbol for college athletics and created such legendary sports figures as Alonzo Stagg, Walter Camp and Knute Rockne. In the early years of the century, the game had become so brutal and overemphasized that something had to be done to save it. In fact some schools did abolish it. Leaders gathered to study the matter, however, and in 1905 the Intercollegiate Athletic Association of the United States (the forerunner of the NCAA) was organized. The organization was not the power structure it has now become but it did make recommendations and set standards which helped in the conduct of athletics on a more favorable basis (12).

In general the American people were becoming more sports-minded as they not only became participants but millions became spectators. The rise in interest was due to several things including more leisure, more wealth, better transportation, and increased publicity. In high school, the state high school athletic associations movement which had started in 1896 with Wisconsin grew steadily during the early part of the twentieth century until every state in the union had some type of association. In 1920 the National Federation of State High School Athletic Associations was formed to protect and regulate the interstate school athletics.

World War I had an important impact on physical education in several ways. First, the draft statistics revealed the rather deplorable physical condition of the American male. Second, there was a return to the more formal type program during the war but afterwards the sports and games interest boomed more widely than ever. Third, the interest in physical education plus the revelation of the draft statistics promoted state level efforts for more physical education. Many states enacted legislation requiring physical education in the schools. These compulsory laws created many job opportunities and immediately placed the onus on teacher-training institutions to train more and better leadership. Also in the period of prosperity of the early twenties, great progress was made in the construction of new gymnasiums and outdoor facilities.

The immediate result of World War I was a return to the more formal program. However, during the twenties the informal natural program advocated by Wood and Hetherington and emphasized by Williams and Nash as well as a host of others took over so that both school and college programs consisted of the sports program augmented by some gymnastics and calisthenics and dance. For the next two decades the pendulum continued to swing toward sports and the battle of the systems was over. The prosperous years of the 1920's found many changes in both education and physical education. The most significant one in physical education was the fall of the systems in favor of the natural program accompanied by a need for more facilities, better leadership, and an increased time allotment.

The draft statistics of World War I together with the emphasis on physical prowess in time of war were perhaps instrumental in many states enacting laws for physical education requirements.

A Time of Crises and Professionalism

The first half of the twentieth century left its mark on physical education in many ways as it did on all aspects of man. There was one crisis after another — World War I followed by an unprecedented but false period of prosperity, then the crash and the great depression of the thirties which really did not come to an end until the beginning of World War II. Of course after this has come the cold war with communism along with two undeclared wars in Korea and Vietnam. The professional association which had gained in scope before World War I declined during the war due to the drain of leadership and resources toward the war effort. However, following the war there was a decade of great growth and development under the able leadership of many fine professionals. The depression years marked a period of crisis for the association as well as the profession itself. However, in spite of the economic cutbacks and the struggle to exist, some significant events happened in the 1930's. The old American Physical Education Association became the American Association of Health, Physical Education and Recreation in 1938, and perhaps a more important event occurred just prior to that time in 1937 when the association merged with the National Education Association where it became a department. The official seal of the association, a sculptured profile of the typical American college boy and girl, was designed by Robert Tait McKenzie, noted sculptor, anatomist, educator, teacher, and writer. Another major milestone in the progress of the professional association was the authorization in 1938 of a full-time executive secretary-treasurer and thus the beginning of the modern headquarters staff which now numbers two dozen full-time consultants and project directors. Up to the present time only three persons have held the important job of executive secretary—Neils Neilson, Ben Miller, and Carl Troester. In 1941 the association was structured along lines similar to its present organizational plan with the Board of Directors and Representative Assembly and divisions for areas of interest. The state and district affiliates, too, have grown in size, influence and structure.

The association has two awards for outstanding service to the profession. The Gulick Medal established in 1923 is awarded for distinguished service to the profession by the association to one of its members. It is the highest honor the profession can bestow. The Anderson Award established in 1948 is made outside the membership to persons who have made significant contribution to the field of health, physical education and recreation. The association has become a major force and has extended its influence into many facets of education. However, several of these have taken priority. Following World War II the association took the lead in helping to plan for much needed sports and recreation facilities and professional preparation of teachers. The latter need was met by two conferences held in the late 1940's where desirable standards were established for both the undergraduate and graduate curricula. The undergraduate conference was held at Jackson's Mill, West Virginia in 1948 and at Père Marquette State Park in Illinois in 1950 for the graduate. The association has continued to increase its membership and services with special emphasis on conferences, consultant services, and publications. Numerous publications on many facets of health, physical education, recreation, athletics,

dance and safety have been added to the Journal and Research Quarterly. Also, the association has been aggressive in promoting fitness and international relations.

Since 1950 the professional efforts have exploded into many facets as the field of physical education, health, recreation, athletics, dance and safety have become more and more proliferated. Those facets which seem to have encompassed the most scope and many still continue to be high in priority were: emphasis on fitness, professional preparation and accreditation, advancement in the scientific area, international relations, ballooning interest in sports, and a close working relationship with the American Medical Association among others.

A Time for Fitness

Probably more time and attention have been given to fitness during this period than to any other facet (see Chapter 10). Fitness historically has always assumed a place of importance during times of war and political crises. This was apparent during the Civil War, the Spanish American War and both World War I and II. As generally happens following a war, there is a return to normalcy where fitness is concerned. This means that in general fitness no longer becomes a concern as far as survival and supremacy are concerned. This happened after World War II. Then the Kraus-Hirschland study, that expounded the differences between the American and European youth on the Kraus-Weber Test, was made public (9). The test results were widely publicized and caused a great deal of concern over the apparent softness of American youth. President Eisenhower took the initiative in calling the first Conference on Physical Fitness of American Youth in 1956. This was followed by the establishment of the President's Council on Youth

Fitness with Shane MacCarthy as the first executive-director. In the fall of the same year the AAHPER sponsored its first Conference on Youth Fitness. Several states held Governor's Conferences on Fitness and established state fitness committees or councils. The AAHPER started the Youth Fitness Project which resulted in the AAHPER Youth Fitness Test and a country-wide Operation Fitness USA program designed to make fitness a national concern. President Kennedy gave able support to the cause even before he took office when his article entitled "The Soft American" appeared in *Sports Illustrated* (8). Another article under his byline appeared a few months later (7). In both articles he emphasized the vital need for fitness both from a national as well as an individual viewpoint. He, too, called a conference on fitness and appointed "Bud" Wilkinson, former football coach at the University of Oklahoma, as his special consultant on fitness. Kennedy's aggressive support of the cause lent both prestige and momentum to the efforts of the AAHPER and professional workers.

Professional Preparation

Professional preparation and accreditation have been a source of much study and work at both the graduate and undergraduate levels. The work of NCATE and the many state-operated accrediting agencies have been a means of upgrading professional training programs in many institutions. NCATE has become the closest thing to a national official accrediting agency. The profession itself has been active in developing criteria for self-evaluation and study. Professional preparation councils, panels, committees and associations exist at the state, district and national levels. While much has been accomplished, there are still many weak programs and many aspects of programs in

general which cannot be agreed upon by the authorities in the field.

Research and Professional Acceptance

The scientific area has in many ways been the means of developing physical education to its present high level of acceptance by other disciplines and professions. As more researchers have been trained in the field and more research has been done, physical education has grown in prestige and status, as well as in know-how and know-why. This has had its impact on other disciplines and since much of that research has implication in physiology, psychology and sociology, it has been the means of drawing these fields closer to us. To the names of McCloy, Brace, and Cozens who spearheaded the scientific movement in the 1920's and 1930's were now added such stalwarts as Steinhaus, Cureton, Henry, Karpovich, and Jokl and still a host of others.

International Relations

With the advent of the jet age and increased interaction between people from all over the world, it was only natural that physical education extend its sphere of influence and efforts in behalf of world understanding and peace. Many professionals have actively promoted international relations through world conferences and international organizations. The Peace Corps, the Olympic Games, student exchange programs, research and study grants, and many other forms of international sports competition have all been instrumental in their own way in promoting international goodwill and understanding. Direct services are made through a number of sources including agencies and international federations for sports, for teachers, and even for professional organizations.

The Athletics and Sports Boom

Athletics and sports have continued their booming growth in all aspects. At both the college and high school levels there is a continued growth both in the number of sports included in the program and also in the number of participants involved in each sport. There is a trend toward tighter controls; regulations have eliminated or minimized many of the evils which formerly existed in both high school and college athletic programs. However, this does not cover up the fact that many evils still exist. The emphasis on winning forges a vicious cycle that frequently takes both intercollegiate and interscholastic athletics out of the realm of the educational spectrum. There is a trend toward more competition for children, if not in the schools directly, it is organized and sponsored by well-meaning but sometimes ill-informed outside groups. Competitive athletics for girls and women are beginning to be stressed more, and the play days and sports days no longer seem to meet either the needs of the girls or the objectives of professional leaders. Intramural sports for both men and women have developed since the earlier days of Elmer Mitchell. It is the competitive sports program for all the students and probably best symbolizes how well physical education instructional programs are functioning. While amateur athletics grew to new heights in both variety and participation, the greatest expansion has come about in professional athletics. Professional athletics now provides a career for the gifted in sports and one of the great media of entertainment for the public. Radio and television coverage has brought professional sports into the home and helped make them an important part of the cultural milieu.

REFERENCES

1. Ballou, Ralph: Early Christian Society and Its Relationship to Sports. Proceedings National College Physical Education Association for Men, 71st, January, 1968.
2. Bronson, Alice Oakes: *Clark W. Hetherington: Scientist and Philosopher.* Salt Lake City, Utah, University of Utah Press, 1958.
3. Commission on the Reorganization of Education: *Cardinal Principles of Secondary Education.* Department of Interior, Bureau of Education, Bulletin No. 35, 1918, Washington, D.C., United States Printing Office, 1928.
4. Cozens, F. W., and F. S. Stumpf: *Sports in American Life.* Chicago, University of Chicago Press, 1953.
5. Hetherington, Clark W.: *School Program in Physical Education.* New York, World Book Company, 1922.
6. Johnson, Elmer L.: A History of Physical Education in the YMCA. Proceedings National College Physical Education Association for Men, 70th, December, 1966.
7. Kennedy, J. F.: The Vigor We Need. Sports Illustrated, Vol. 17, No. 3, July, 1962, 12–15 pp.
8. Kennedy, J. F.: The Soft American. Sports Illustrated, Vol. 13, No. 26, December, 1960, 15–17 pp.
9. Kraus, H., and R. Hirschland: Minimum Muscular Fitness Tests in School Children. Research Quarterly, Vol. 25, No. 2, May, 1954, 178 p.
10. Leonard, F. E., and G. B. Affleck: *A Guide to History of Physical Education.* Philadelphia, Lea & Febiger, 1947.
11. Lewis, Guy M.: 1879: The Beginning of an Era in American Sports. Proceedings National College Physical Education Association for Men, 72nd, January, 1969.
12. Lewis, Guy: Theodore Roosevelt and the Founding of the National Collegiate Athletic Association. Proceedings National College Physical Education Association for Men, 69th, December, 1965.
13. Manchester, Herbert: *Four Centuries of Sports in America.* New York, Benjamin Blom, 1968.
14. Matthews, David O.: A Historical Study of the Aims, Contents, and Methods of Swedish, Danish, and German Gymnastics. Proceedings National College Physical Education Association for Men, 72nd, January, 1969.
15. Moolenijzer, Nicolaas J.: Johann C. F. Guts Muths' Contributions to Athletics. Proceedings National College Physical Education Association for Men, 70th, December, 1966.

16. Moreland, Richard B.: The Pragmatism of Clark Hetherington. Proceedings National College Physical Education Association for Men, 72nd, January, 1969.

17. Rice, E. A., J. L. Hutchinson, and Mabel Lee: *A Brief History of Physical Education.* New York, The Ronald Press Company, 1969.

18. Salzmann, C. G.: *Gymnastics for Youth or a Practical Guide to Healthful and Amusing Exercise.* Philadelphia, William Duane, 1802.

19. Schwendener, Norma: *A History of Physical Education in the United States.* New York, A. S. Barnes & Company, 1942.

20. Van Dalen, D. B., E. D. Mitchell, and B. L. Bennett: *A World History of Physical Education.* New York, Prentice-Hall, Inc., 1953.

21. Vanderzwaag, Harold J.: Nationalism in American Physical Education (1880–1920). Proceedings National College Physical Education Association for Men, 69th, December, 1965.

22. Welch, J. Edmund: *Edward Hitchcock, M.D.: Founder of Physical Education in the College Curriculum.* Greenville, N.C., East Carolina College, 1962.

23. Welch, J. Edmund: *The YMCA Graduate School of Nashville.* Unpublished paper presented to the Research Section of the National Convention, AAHPER, March, 1968.

24. Western, Arthur: *The Making of American Physical Education.* New York, Appleton-Century-Crofts, 1962.

PART II

The Profession

Chapter 5

Leadership and Promotion of the Profession

LEADERSHIP AND MAN'S HERITAGE

Since time immemorial, man has assumed positions of leadership and played these roles in numerous ways. Leadership appears to be a fundamental human trait. Since there can be no leaders without followers, followership is also a part of man's heritage. Hence, leadership and followership become social dimensions of great import in all social groups. Leadership no doubt evolved as a part of social man. His initial efforts to organize into small groups for protection against a hostile environment must have been lessons in leadership development, and this evolved along with his culture. The leadership of these primitive groups was either bestowed by the group or seized through force by the would-be leader. Through some type of democratic process or through his own ability to assert himself in an autocratic or even militant manner, this individual took over the role of leadership. He no doubt possessed certain dominant characteristics. These may have been his skill, size or strength or his intelligence, or the

weapons at his disposal, the sheer force of his will or the magnetism of his personality. In all probability, it was a combination of these with emphasis on physical prowess, since this complex of qualities has always been a prime factor in the emergence of leadership.

HOW LEADERS ARE SELECTED

The qualities needed by the leader depend in a sense on the functions to be performed by the group, the skills needed, and the level of acceptance by group members. These qualities also may have some relationship to how the leader came by his status in the first place. Leaders emerge in the following ways: (1) through appointment by some authority, (2) through election by the group, and (3) through usurping the leader's position. In all three cases the person qualifies for his leadership role in the same manner. In the case of appointment and election, he probably demonstrated to the authority or the elective group powers or qualities needed to fulfill functions needed by the group. In the case of usurping the leadership role, he demonstrated these same qualities of dominance. In either event the leader evidently possesses qualities which command the respect of the group or which the group believes can accomplish its avowed purposes. On rare occasions a leader emerges because he possesses such unusual qualities that his followers regard him as having a type of charismatic quality that is worthy of great dedication and loyalty on their part.

QUALITIES OF LEADERS

The leader has two main objectives. First, he must obtain and then attempt to keep the position of leadership to which he aspires. Second, he must possess a concern for the welfare of his followers and the cause or causes they pursue. In a sense, the two are germane. The leader is accorded the position of leadership by the group because they feel he has the necessary qualifications and commitment to look out for their welfare in serving their cause and solving their problems. This encompasses not only the cause of the group but also the needs of individual members of the group. Together the leader and the group should interact for a common goal and for each other.

The important elements in leadership are the competencies possessed by the leader — those which are best suited for getting the job done that is required by the group. The requirements vary for the situation and leadership appears to be specific to the task. One might venture that the situation makes the leader. Although the components of leadership have been studied on numerous occasions, no universal traits of leadership have been established. However, skills that are specific to particular situations have been isolated and it has been shown that these can be learned and improved through participation.

Time is replete with examples of persons who have forged names for themselves as leaders as they changed the course of history and events. In fact, history in the making may have been the situation which catapulted some to the heights of leadership. In history much of this leadership has been associated with politics, social change, economic conditions, the military and the like. Much of it was concerned with actions of the government and their many ramifications. Commerce and industry have provided classic examples as well as religion and the professions. The importance of this single type leadership cannot be denied, however, because it is the most important component of a collective group quality called professional leadership which will be discussed later. Good or bad, this individual type leadership is always the catalyst which initiates and gives momentum toward goals. The techniques and methods of leadership will vary depending on the degree of democracy present in the leadership process. Leadership is at its best perhaps when there is a smooth interchange of ideas and an interaction between the leader and the group as they pursue together the avenues leading to decision-making. This togetherness process is known as the democratic-cooperative type of leadership. While the leader may be symbolic of the group and the ideas and decisions it projects, and while traditionally the role of the leader has been decision-making, the goals for any particular group are more readily attainable when democratic processes are followed. The specific skills and qualities of leadership needed for the teacher are discussed in the next chapter.

The above concept of the democratic process does not in any way detract from the importance of strong individual type leadership which has just been mentioned. The most democratic and skillful leader may arrive at many important decisions in a democratic manner through interpersonal relationships. He may be sensitive to the needs of the group and not impose his own will on it although he can and should communicate his ideas. Then, through democratic, dynamic interaction of the leader with his group, plans may be formulated, goals determined, and decisions made. Once decisions are made, however, the leader becomes the generating force which directs and stimulates the group toward realization of the ultimate goal and bringing to fruition the purposes expressed in the decision-making. In the democratic concept of leadership there is frequently a sharing of the leadership role where one of a group is a follower part of the time as well as a leader. The group functions more effectively when leadership is shared.

In another context, some leadership is not democratic at all. In fact, some individuals are unable to accomplish the purposes for the group and work toward its causes through the democratic process. For them, the more autocratic methods seem to work best. In a democratic society even when leadership is somewhat authoritarian and decisions are made by the one in charge, there must always exist the right to disagree and to express opinions by the group. However, inevitably something is lost in total commitment when group participation in decision-making and planning is stifled or lacking entirely. Group members are denied the growth and development which are products of accepting responsibility and initiative. Leadership, like other aspects of the social being, is a learned characteristic and is a result of the "doing" process. Autocratic leadership leads either to rebellion or mediocrity because only limited learning can take place under its yoke. For learning in leadership to take place, groups must plan, make decisions and mistakes, and then benefit from such action.

In still another context, the most democratic leader must at some time make decisions on his own. He may even have to make decisions contrary to the will of the group, because this is his prerogative if he believes his knowledge and experience are such that he feels his decision is best for the cause of the group. In some leadership capacities the leader has a commitment to his superiors for the success of his group and the work they pursue and he alone is held accountable to them. In the case of the administrator, for example, he not only has the authority but a demanding responsibility to make what he considers the right decision. It is probably good in this instance when there is a delineation into areas — some which lend themselves more readily to group discussion and decisions and some which remain the prerogative of the leader.

TYPES OF LEADERSHIP

Leadership runs the spectrum from democratic-cooperative to authoritarian. In turn, authoritarianism runs the gamut from benevolent despotism where the leader is the patriarch who does all things for the group in the spirit of loving kindness to the dictator who cracks the whip, demands that his followers fall in line, and exercises maximum control. The democratic type, too, runs the spectrum from the permissive laissez-faire administrator who delegates all powers, asks no questions and volunteers no answers, to the other end of the continuum where the leader always keeps his hands on the pulse of things but lets the group share with him in all solutions and decisions involving its sphere of interest and involvement.

Leadership per se can neither be labeled as good or bad. There are classic examples of leaders who are both good and bad. Every gang has its leaders as well as a code of conduct for its followers. Some of gangland's most wanted criminals have been brilliant leaders in some respects. The test of leadership as a social function is inherent in the purposes or causes promoting it. Whenever there is leadership, there must be this cause to be served — good or bad. In a sense, each member of the group from the lowest to the highest status makes a contribution to that cause. Socially speaking, leadership runs the gamut from good to bad depending on the worth of the cause. Whether or not a leader's role is acceptable to society is chiefly inherent in this cause. If the cause is worthy and if the ends sought are acceptable to society and come within the norms of that culture, the leadership fostered by the situation will in all probability be accepted as good although ways, means and procedures may be, and frequently are questioned. However, there is a particular kind of snobbery connected with how leadership is viewed. The higher the status for the role of leadership, the more esteem is accorded the leader although such esteem may not always be related to the worthiness of the cause as much as the status. For example, the coach of an athletic team is frequently accorded more esteem by the public than the classroom teacher chiefly because the status of coaching usually rates higher in the public's eye. Such high esteem has nothing at all to do with the cause served. The cause served by the teacher in his place of leadership in many cases may make a far greater contribution to the objectives of education and the purposes of society than those of the coach. Also, the success in role playing by the teacher may be relatively greater than the success of the coach and still not rate the esteem due to a lower status for role playing.

PROFESSIONAL LEADERSHIP

Society is predicated on responsible and dedicated leadership. Democratic leadership is predicated on such concepts as the worth and dignity of the human personality as well as other ideas and ideals inherent in the democratic process. Individual leadership gave way to the group type leadership. As theology, medicine, law, and education began to shape up and take on the distinguishing characteristics now recognized as the criteria of a profession, the role of leadership began to assume a different connotation. It was no longer relegated to the force of a single individual but to the work of a great number of people working first as individuals but second as a group welded together by the common bonds of service, responsibility, and speciality. It is this collective type group quality of leadership which will be dealt with next.

In the sense of a profession, the need for good leadership is evident. Progress in a profession is indispensable and progress is closely related to its leaders.

Basic to this leadership need are several components. Among them perhaps the most pertinent are *scholarship*, *philosophy* and *inquiry*. These three make up the fundamental parts to a professional cycle (2). The term cycle implies that this trio of values moves in a circular pattern. If it moves, there must be some force which starts it in motion and then keeps it moving. Bookwalter says at this point that professional leadership assumes great import since it is the dynamic force which starts and continues to turn the wheels of professional growth and progress (2). The key to this cycle is the dedicated work of many individuals who make up the profession and who are professionally trained. They make up the professional leadership as they promote themselves and the profession. Together they can accomplish much which could not be done as individuals.

When one is promoting his profession, he is literally promoting himself both directly and indirectly. Directly he is gaining stature and status as he earns a name for himself in proportion to his ability and to the amount of contribution he makes to his profession. Indirectly he shares in the gains of his profession as a result of his work. A man and his profession are inexorably bound. When status and image of the profession are enhanced as its standards, practices, and work are upgraded, the professional person gains in stature. By the same token, when the image of the individual professional takes on luster because of his contributions through his work and his professionalism, it rubs off on the profession as it, too, gains in influence and prestige. Also, there is still another facet. Leadership is not some quality that is bestowed on one by chance; it is partly a learned ingredient made up of many qualities. Since all learning is a result of doing and since leadership is partly a learned attribute, there must be practice in leading. When one gains practice in making contributions and displaying leadership, that experience is important in raising the level of one's worth or stature. This is an important concept for the student to accept. He should not wait until after his formal training is finished to start this process of professionalization. He should share, participate, and gain experience in professional leadership activities — major clubs, fraternities, committees, and the like—while he is still a student.

Knowledge, philosophy, attitude and skills are the prerequisites to positions of leadership in physical education. When these components are followed by acceptance of responsibility, the keys to professional growth and development are assured. All members of a profession have an obligation to help in carrying a share of the professional load. Each qualified person occupies the status of a professional. Whether he accepts the responsibility for playing that role comparable to that status is something else. The true professional has a moral obligation not only to himself but also to his profession to assume his share of the professional responsibility and to play his role.

There are levels of excellence and participation in professional leadership. Probably the most professional expressions of leadership have as their focus these three aspects. The first has to do with "being" — with the possession of the necessary competency — being the right type of person, knowing one's field, having the technical know-how and possessing the specialized expertise. The second has to do with "doing" — with doing the job at hand either as a student in professional training or later as a professional worker in service. In this regard it is possible for one to "be" but never "do." This may be the most important aspect of the three. Third, after one's obligation to one's self and one's job, there is "helping." Often complementary to the other two factors, helping has to do with levels of leadership expressed in the profession itself and its professional association — membership, officer, committee member, and worker at whatever task that needs to be done.

Professional leadership takes many forms. There is the leadership of the department head or dean of a school over his staff in an administrative capacity. There is the leadership of the instructor over his class as a teacher and counselor, or of the coach over his team. Then, there is the leadership of the student officer in a local professional club as students gain practice and training outside the formal curriculum. Also, leadership is displayed by the professional person in his professional society or organization as he sets about enhancing and promoting himself, his profession, and his work. Then there is the scholar who through his research and

4

writing has great influence on the professional and the profession. These and many others may all appear different. Yet, they have many commonalities.

However, one does not become a leader in his profession by accident. The mantle of leadership falls on one because his background of experience and training, together with his possession of vital personal characteristics, qualifies him. These all add up to professional competence. However, before the matter of professional competence is considered, it might be well to consider the nature of the profession itself.

WHAT IS A PROFESSION?

What is a profession? How does an area of work or an occupation evolve to the point where it can be considered a profession?

It is apparent that the long-established professions are a result of evolution, and they have developed to their present place of prestige over a long period of time. In the progressive swing upward, these fields must have employed some common procedures or followed similar patterns of approach. The achieving of professional status in any field has not been an easy accomplishment, and did not come about through chance. Traditions, taboos, superstitions, ignorance, and still other obstacles were barriers to the emergence of full-fledged professions. As these barriers gave way to principles and laws based on facts and valid judgments, to the concerted efforts of specialists, and to the pressure of existing social demands, true professions were born.

In physical education today there is a sincere desire on the part of its practitioners for public recognition and acceptance. They want their field to be accepted as an academic discipline and they wish to achieve professional status. If this aspiration is to become a reality, then it will be necessary for physical educators to follow procedures similar to those followed in the other recognized professions as these slowly emerged to professional stature. As these classic professions gained in expertise for their specialities, they also gained in respect and acceptance. This is not an easy course to pursue, however. There are some roadblocks ahead for the teaching profession and particularly for the physical educator. In the past, far too many physical educators have not conducted themselves as professionals. In the beginning they operated first as exhibitionists and later as technicians and craftsmen. Even now there are far too many who are governed by apathy and lack of motivation and involvement.

One of the best ways to define a profession is to distinguish it from a trade. A trade is carried on by tradesmen or technicians. These individuals know rules, methods, and techniques, and can get the job done by means of their knowledges and skills. In most cases these methods and techniques can be obtained without a great deal of formal schooling. Much of it can be gotten while the practitioner is on the job or as in the case of the apprentice, an in-service type of training. There is no guarantee that this practitioner has developed a sense of responsibility to the public for his knowledge and skill. For example, as a group they may withhold their services from the public for long periods of time in order to enhance personal gain or for self-aggrandizement. It seems that teaching in general is getting farther away from the usual concept of a profession. As teacher groups become more like labor unions and as they become more militant in their demands for personal gain, they slow down the progress toward professional acceptance. At this juncture the speculation may be made that the same thing could happen to teachers in a labor union that has happened to other workers. They could grow more apathetic and submissive under the structure of trade unions than they are now.

It is further apparent that while principles and theories and a large scope of academic matter may underlie these trades, there is no requirement that the tradesmen understand the rationale of his practice. He can do an adequate job at his trade without knowing this large body of knowledge which is basic to his work. The electrician can effectively wire a house for lights and appliances without any deep understanding of the principles of electronics. In general, occupations and trades are concerned with things as contrasted to people. Too often people in physical education still conduct themselves as tradesmen. The football coach too often considers his work as a technique rather than an art – as coaching football rather than coaching young men. As technicians some people in the field have not been aware of the scientific and philosophical bases on which their practices rest. A true profession is based on scientific and philosophical facts obtained through scholarly endeavor. It differs from a trade in several respects. Individuals who wish to enter a profession do so for a combination of reasons but generally for prestige, material gain, and social consciousness. There are some commonly accepted standards for professions which distinguish them from all other work or vocations and make them unique in man's work. The following are criteria which may be used for judging professional status (2), (3), (8).

CRITERIA OF A PROFESSION

The statement has already been made that professions evolved into their present status. If this is true, it would seem to imply that some areas of work are currently professions and some are emerging professions not quite evolved to the point where they are accepted by other professions and by the general public. Some areas meet certain of the characteristics listed below and perhaps are striving diligently to meet others. It is possible they fall short entirely in others. Some have a sort of semi-professional status. Bucher suggests that physical education is an emerging profession and has not yet gained full status (3). Shivers states that recreation, too, has only quasi-professional status in its attempt to approximate the qualifications of the recognized professions (8–209). Some of these semi-professions or quasi-professions generally fall short in the area of humanitarianism and in the criteria of examination and certification or registration along with powers to police their own ranks. In the area of humanitarianism Shivers suggests that their specialities may be predictable and concern things rather than people (8–197). However, all of the recognized professions now meet all or practically all of the criteria listed in this chapter.

Scientific Basis

Perhaps the first criterion of a profession is that it must render a unique social service with a scientific basis. If it has a science-oriented basis, it must be dependent on research. The principles and practices of physical education come from a wide area of learning. In fact, they are interdisciplinary in scope since they are derived from the natural and physical sciences as well as the behavioral and social sciences. Like the doctor of medicine, it is necessary for the physical educator to have a strong scientific background. The fundamental principles of physical education come from biology, physiology, anatomy, kinesiology, psychology, sociology and anthropology. From these sciences the physical educator obtains his principles which in turn determine his technology and methodology. However, these principles should not be obtained at the expense of the humanities. All principles must take into consideration the needs of society and must reflect social purposes. If man is to survive in the years ahead, he will need to know most of all, perhaps, how to adjust socially and how to get along with others. This aspect of behavior is best obtained from the humanities. Thus, physical education is eclectic since it is both an art and a science but it is the science which makes it a profession in the frame of reference of the non-predictability of the humanities. However, physical education has been weak in the identification of its unique social service. It now means too many things to too many people.

Extended Period of Preparation

The professional does not become a professional overnight. He must undergo a prolonged period of preparation in which he studies and is trained in the necessary aspects of his field. He must acquire the specialized knowledge and skill required to make him more than average in adequacy. This is his expertise and it is not come by lightly. He must be competent to make his speciality available to the public. There was a time when one could be a gym teacher with a three-months course in gymnastics. All recognized professions now require years of advanced preparation and a specific kind of training providing knowledge and skill unique to the field. Four years of higher education and a baccalaureate degree will only give one the impetus toward professional status and academic acceptance. The five-year program or a graduate degree should become the minimum. With the rise in professional excellence along with the explosion of knowledge coupled with the demanding needs of a more intellectual society, the professional must know more now than ever before. To attain a place of acceptance in his profession and

in society, he must not only be a highly trained and knowledgeable specialist, but also a cultured person in a liberal arts sense (see Chapter 6, Professional Training). Professional programs in physical education must rise above the mediocrity now found in many institutions. This can be done only through self-regulatory autonomy in such matters as accreditation of the professional training institution, certification of candidates, and enforcement of codes of ethics.

Specialized Skills

A third quality of a profession is that it is distinguished by specialized skills. These may be both intellectual and technical. The specialized skills, knowledges, and techniques are unique to a particular profession and they are obtained through the extended period of preparation. Because this expertise is denied the average person or the non-professional, it gives the practitioner a very special competence and produces in him a superior type of status. The professional understands the guiding principles and the basic concepts of his field and has the ability to modify and innovate when emergencies arise and traditional rules and methods have failed. These specialized skills are developed in the extended period of preparation mentioned in the number two criterion above and are the result of professional preparation. These professional competencies which distinguish physical education will be discussed in the next chapter.

A producing person in physical education is not only a knowledgeable person in an academic sense, but he is also one who possesses a high degree of specialized skills. These skills and knowledges in physical education are unique and separate and form the very core of its order. Basically, everything taught in physical education and every experience valued is dependent upon specialized human movement—either a sport skill, a dance technique, a gymnastic stunt, or an exercise. While physical education may be an academic discipline, it becomes so only in the frame of reference of human movement. Most professions have subdivisions and physical education is no exception. Once past the baccalaureate level, the physical educator can specialize in many areas and can spend a lifetime in attaining success and proficiency in any one of them.

Service Motive

Another quality of a profession is that there must be a service motive. Basically, this indicates a deep realization of a social function to perform and a moral obligation owed to mankind. All persons in a profession presumably are committed to two things—the improvement of the society in which they live and the improvement of the profession. Each profession must ultimately justify itself on the basis of this public service it renders. Public service and humanitarianism are among the chief commitments of the professional. He assumes a sense of responsibility to the public for the specialized service he has to offer. This sense of responsibility and commitment may be the most distinguishing characteristic of a profession.

Ideally the professional is motivated intrinsically by a sense of fulfillment at making his speciality available for the welfare of others.

This does not negate the practitioner's own betterment through the profession. It is to be expected that when one spends an extended period of time in preparation and invests heavily in both time and money for his education, there will come a certain amount of personal gain, monetary reward, and perhaps prestige. However, these economic and social rewards should be secondary to the service motive. The public loses

confidence in a profession and respect for the professional when economic gain takes precedence over the service motive. In some areas of education today, teachers are moving farther away from professional status when they take on the characteristics of a labor union. In general, the teacher today is faced with a choice. In order to improve his working conditions and salary schedules, he may either resort to his professional society or he may band together with others in a labor union. Some think that if he chooses the latter, he forfeits his status as a professional. It is probably safe to state that those who do not have a sense of service and a feeling of humanitarianism should not go into physical education and its related areas because they will never be adequately paid in money for their time and commitment.

Body of Literature and Scholarly Achievements

A fifth quality of a profession is concerned with research and scholarly achievements. For any profession there are a great many books, journals, monographs, theses, abstracts, and articles written by members of the profession and used to educate individuals in the profession, or to communicate with the public in general. The amount and kind of professional literature indicates in a meaningful way the stature not only of the professional worker himself, but also the profession. The quality of its literature and scholarly achievements is far more important than the quantity. The promotion and dissemination of research is a major professional responsibility.

Physical education is reaching a point where some literary contributions are rich in meaning and achieve a high level of scholarly accomplishment. Most experts agree that the literature in physical education must maintain a balance between theory and practice—a balance between intellectualizing its work and making it more scholarly on the one hand, and being practical on the other, as it makes its approach to the unique contribution through movement. Movement education can be an intellectual experience and if physical education is to educate for life, it must invest the student's learning with an intellectual challenge. The physical has meaning only in a setting where the unity concept is the rule rather than dualism. Movement education challenges the whole man intellectually, socially, and spiritually as well as physically, and the literature should reflect this concept.

Code of Ethics

Next, a code of ethics should provide a definite behavior by which the professional is guided. All recognized professions have these specific standards of conduct for the moral behavior and ethical practice of their members. Medicine has its Hippocratic Oath and a code of conduct for its members. So does law. It is important that ethical relations and idealism exist between the professional worker, his peers, his profession, and the people whom he serves. Most codes of ethics are formulated from within by the professional practitioners themselves. They are generally self-imposed and self-regulated and are accepted in good faith by the members of a profession. There should be some means of insuring compliance with the code. This is best done by the profession itself in the same manner as it handles other matters through its self-regulating powers. A true profession should have the right to eliminate the incompetent and unfit as well as those who fail to abide by the ethical and moral standards of the group.

When such a code does exist, it becomes one of the most distinguishing characteristics differentiating a profession from a trade. Probably no profession can excel in its speciality unless it has this code and the determination along with the judiciary powers to police its ranks. Such a system of intrinsic discipline can raise standards of performance to high levels if applied in moderation. However, if the code of ethics is truly functional, the internal disciplinary powers must never be used to keep out the worthy and competent.

While education is sometimes called the mother of all professions, evidence shows that teachers in general and physical education teachers particularly, may be at the bottom of the totem pole among recognized professions. Perhaps among other things, a code of ethics is needed to lift the standards higher, or perhaps what is needed most is to give more than lip service to already established codes. Just as there seems to be a need to strengthen the moral fiber of the individual in America today, there needs to be a strengthening of the moral fiber of the profession. If the public is to take the physical educator seriously in the modern process of education, he must demonstrate his fitness to educate in the same manner that other professions have demonstrated their fitness to provide their specialities. Like the doctor, he must possess an expert technical competence but equally important is his attitude of dedication, perseverance, and integrity of purpose which places the interest and welfare of his people first. A strong code of ethics is needed to challenge the professional to more nearly achieve his potential. The teaching profession is weak in both its desire and the machinery to police its own ranks when standards of ethics have been breached. Indirectly, the profession seeks to do this by exercising pressure on the professional training institution through accreditation first and later by means of selection, retention, and certification policies. However, there is no machinery to enforce sanctions on the practitioner already turned loose on the profession and society.

Professional Associations

An important characteristic of a profession is that it has an organization or society to promote its own interests and to professionalize its members. Professional associations place emphasis on those aspects on which the profession is founded. For example, the specialized techniques are the bonds of commonality which draw the practitioners together. Ideally the profession has one master association which examines for professional competence, provides for registration or certification of members, establishes a code of ethics, and possesses judiciary procedures for the enforcement of the code of ethics. The medical doctors have the American Medical Association. In physical education there is not one organization working in this area of promoting and professionalizing, but there are several representing various specialities and interests. Perhaps the most important from the standpoint of size, accomplishments, and influence on the greatest number is the American Association for Health, Physical Education, and Recreation. It has its sub-organizations at the local, state, district, and national levels and some affiliates which are international in scope. There are several others which should be mentioned here including the National College Physical Education Association for Men, the National Association for Physical Education of College Women, Phi Epsilon Kappa, National Recreation Association and the American School Health Association. They all have the same purpose—continued growth of their members and an opportunity to share in experiences through conventions, conferences, workshops, projects, committee work and various ongoing work. However, it is obvious these societies are weak in autonomy and self-regulatory powers.

The AAHPER, while it has been a department of the NEA since 1937, still retains a large degree of autonomy. It is democratically organized and operated at not only the national level but also the district, state, and local levels. Many services are provided at all these levels and there is even an extension into the international level. Each state has its organizational structure and in turn the states are grouped geographically into six districts each with a governing structure somewhat similar to the national structure. These districts are: Central, Eastern, Midwest, Northwest, Southern and Southwest. Both the states and districts are involved in convention type programs and a limited amount of ongoing projects. The Southern District has changed its structure to place more emphasis on ongoing professional work.

At the national level there is a Board of Directors which serves as the executive branch of the association and which conducts most of the business of the organization. This board is made up of elective officers including a president and the vice presidents representing the divisions and the district representatives representing the six districts. A much larger Representative Assembly, democratically organized from the board of directors, divisions, sections, districts and states carries on association business including election of officers, changing constitution and by-laws, and approving action of the board. While originally the association was convention-oriented, it currently has a great amount of ongoing work which is carried on through numerous committees, councils, panels, and task forces. Much of the ongoing business as well as the convention planning is initiated and carried on by division executive councils and committees.

Almost a score of related national organizations are affiliates of the

AAHPER and they work with the association on problems of mutual interest and concern. In addition to its affiliates, the AAHPER works cooperatively with many other agencies and groups. The headquarters staff headed by the executive secretary is made up of full-time professionals and specialists who serve in administrative or consultative positions.

There is no doubt that while there are a number of organizations promoting professionalism in the fields of health, physical education and recreation, the AAHPER can speak for more people who are engaged in some facet of its program. It cuts across areas horizontally such as physical education, health, recreation, dance, athletics, and safety and at the same time it combines the leadership of vertical areas such as elementary, secondary and college levels. It also cuts across types of schools at all levels. Perhaps the best idea of the scope of association work can be gotten from this listing:

> The Association is currently involved in a program of action which includes annual conventions, national conferences, and workshops, consultants services, representation in other national and international groups, publications, informational and public relations programs, and specific services to state associations and individual members. It is concerned with raising professional standards, improving programs of instruction, promoting more nationwide activity in our specialized areas of education, creating and sustaining professional interest, informing the public of the contributions of our areas, and building better understanding of the significant role played in our society by health education, physical education, athletics, outdoor education, recreation, and safety education (5).

The professional must participate above the level of just belonging to his professional societies. He must be dedicated to his profession through his professional society and be aware of the fact that his destiny is in his own hands.

He must accept responsibility for his professional behavior. The acceptance of responsibility is a basis of all growth and development in a profession. Physical education will be judged by other academic disciplines and professions partly by the strength and prestige of its professional association. In the same context, the physical educator will be judged by his own colleagues also on the basis of his contribution to his professional organization and his acceptance of the responsibilities that accompany professional autonomy.

There are three levels of excellence and participation in professional leadership for these associations. The first two levels which will be mentioned are not exactly negative but neither are they highly positive. The lowest level of leadership displayed in a profession is merely paying one's dues and belonging to a professional association. The second level might include some passive participation by merely showing up for meetings and conferences without assuming any other responsibility. The third and highest level of participation is to take part in an active manner. Paying dues and attending meetings are the bases out of which the true professional can make many contributions in an active manner as he becomes a leader in his profession. Belonging to a professional society is not a one-way street. It is a two-way process with lines of communication open both ways. There are both professional obligations and privileges. Some practitioners in physical education are like parasites. They don't belong or pay dues. They take many of the privileges without assuming any of the responsibilities. If there is strength in unity, they sap the strength without making any significant contribution to the unity. There are many privileges as a result of the accomplishments of professional societies as leaders work together in achieving them. The nonmember may share in many of these benefits and advantages without sharing the work, effort and cost of gaining them. If all practitioners would belong and pool their resources, there would be more benefit for all.

Accreditation

Another quality of a profession is accreditation. Accreditation is the practice of an association or an agency approving an institution or a program of study in that institution for an area of specialization when that institution or program has met standards in certain preconceived criteria. Historically, such professions as law and medicine have risen to their present place of prestige chiefly because of accreditation on a national scale. Inevitably this process led to the improvement in the standards of the professional training institution and subsequently to the practices in the profession. It also led to the elimination of the sub-standard institution or program. Since this beginning, other professional groups have adopted the practice of accreditation on the national level.

A profession is characterized by a sense of service and responsibility to society. If it is to meet this responsibility, it must assume some measure of control for the competence of its practitioners. It must protect society from those whose training has not provided them with the necessary competence and expertise. To do this it must use its authority first to encourage and influence higher standards in those facets of professional education designed to provide that competence, and second, to evaluate and approve the program when it measures up and conforms. Such accreditation does not always guarantee a competent and qualified practitioner because there are other facets which contribute to competence other than formal professional training. However, this professional training—in a recognized professional school or program—is rated by authorities as the most important contributing factor to successful professional experience. No one is better qualified to determine what is acceptable practice in the profession and thus what competencies should be emphasized in professional training than the profession itself. Thus, accreditation should be in the hands of the profession and professionals should either directly or indirectly set the standards.

Accreditation in teacher education is done in several ways. The only national agency which provides for accreditation is NCATE—National Council for Accreditation of Teacher Education (see Chapter 6). The standards and guidelines adhered to by this body have been established by educators and represent the composite thinking of many groups. Many of the teacher education programs in the nation have been evaluated by this agency. In most cases the institutions have been approved, rejected, or placed on probation. Where NCATE is not called in for purposes of accreditation, states have set up their own machinery for this purpose. Most of them have standards and guidelines patterned after NCATE.

A weakness of the teaching profession in general and physical education in particular is the fact that NCATE has not become the lone accreditation agency. Some institutions are unwilling to be approved by NCATE even though their standards might easily qualify. Other institutions are unable to meet acceptable standards and still continue, in some states, to prepare teachers. Since preparation in a recognized professional preparation institution should be the only grounds for entrance into the profession, the implementation of accreditation on a national scale should become a mandatory procedure. It should be pointed out that the processes of accreditation are such that any institution can maintain its autonomy and uniqueness within the frame of reference of accreditation standards and guidelines.

Certification or License

Another quality of the true profession is that there must be some form of license or certification to support high standards. The idea behind this criterion is again one of discrimination – discrimination in the sense that the incompetent is kept out of the profession. The mere fact alone that one has passed through an approved and accredited professional preparation program should be no guarantee of admittance to the teaching profession. A doctor must have a license to practice. A lawyer must pass the bar examination. A public school teacher must be properly certified in the appropriate speciality to teach. In the case of the first two, the profession has autonomy and possesses self-regulatory powers. The profession itself administers the procedures of admittance to the profession, and it also controls the procedures of exclusion and suspension. This is done through licensing by the medical profession according to standards which the profession has set up and by examinations prepared by the profession in law. There are good arguments for this self-regulatory approach. In the case of certification of teachers, this procedure is done by the respective state departments of education. However, in some states the state approves the institution and the institution does the certification. It might be pointed out that in most cases the standards for certification and admittance to the profession have been developed by the state departments of education in collaboration with professional personnel in the institutions of professional preparation. Of course certification applies only to those who wish to be employed in the public schools.

One does not have to be certified for admittance to some avenues in the profession. For the teacher at the college level there is no certification, and only the degree requirements which are in force for all instructional personnel protect against incompetence. Most institutions of higher education establish their own standards, but many of them are lenient where physical education is concerned (3). It must be emphasized, however, that promotion of a profession is far more than certification or licensing. Such procedures merely set minimum standards. A profession should be motivated to achieve higher levels.

Certification in many states has become an abused area. The most common abuse is the emergency certificate. Even though good procedures for certification are established for those who pass through the front door to the profession, the emergency certificate opens the back door for the untrained and the incompetent. It is paradoxical that a modern society is willing to trust the education of its youth to the mediocrity brought on by emergency certification but not its medical or legal care to the same policy. One does not want to be defended in a court of law by a lawyer who came into the profession with an emergency license, or to be operated on in a hospital by a doctor with emergency certification. In this light it could not be done at all because there is no emergency certification in law or medicine. In some states the only qualifications for the emergency certificate in education is that the individual be eighteen years of age.

PROFESSIONALIZATION

There are many ways to become professionalized. The extended period of preparation should provide one with the necessary training in scholarship and techniques. This can be done both within and outside the formal curriculum. Somewhere in the professional training the concept of professionalization must be emphasized. There must be ample opportunity provided outside the classroom work for the major student to gain experience in professionalizing activities. Such activities as student professional organizations, building of professional libraries, participation in community projects, working in intramural and recreation programs, assisting in activity classes, committee assignments, and hearing outstanding professional speakers are excellent means of development of the budding professional.

Professional education and professionalization is really a career-long process. Once the practitioner has entered the profession, he should recognize the four-year undergraduate preparation as but a basis for future growth and development. He must continue his study and inquiry, and improve his other professional competencies through some type of in-service training. In addition to getting his job done with efficiency and dispatch, he must become a worker in the profession and make his contribution to his professional societies.

Too much cannot be said about one's responsibility to the profession and the contribution of time and effort to the professional association. The assuming of this responsibility contributes to professional growth. However, in some cases, the contribution of time and effort may reach a point of diminishing return. For example, some practitioners, either for gratification of their own personal prestige or out of a deep sense of service, devote more time to the profession than their job can afford. The practitioner must strike a balance.

Perhaps when all is said and done about the profession and the professional, it is not more specialized training in skills and knowledges, nor a strong professional organization, nor contributions to this organization, nor research, nor sounder philosophy, nor certification which counts the most in becoming professional. All of these are highly important and singularly essential as has been pointed out. However, the greatest contribution that one can make as an individual to his profession, and the one which alone can make one a true professional in a valid sense, is excellence on the job for which his speciality qualifies him. This may be teaching, administering programs, research and counseling, or combinations. If one is sincerely concerned with professional status and being accepted by other academic disciplines and the public, this excellence on the job is a first order.

The true professional is one who makes use of his scholarship, his philosophy, and the research and literature in the field to more adequately get his job done in service. He uses his extended period of preparation and his professional societies for growth and development in not only his speciality but also his relations with others. This combination of specialization and humanitarianism is the very key to success in his field. It furnishes the foundation out of which he becomes more challenging, creative, imaginative, and dynamic. The practitioner who is professionalized is adaptive because he is able to meet and to recognize new problems. He then is able to make changes and adjustments in his work in order to keep in touch with the main issues of his time. For the true professional there can be no crystallization into complacency. All too often there are too many practitioners who lack the motivation to take a stand. They shy away from involvement and are content with the status quo. Involvement always means commitment, and commitment means more work. In the future, the bona fide professional will become more involved. Unlike the wage worker, he will find his services more in demand, his working hours longer, and he will be forced to spend a lifetime devoted to the cause of acquiring new knowledge in his speciality and how to make use of it.

Professionalizing oneself in physical education means many things, not the least of which is acceptance by other academic disciplines. If this is to occur, the practitioner must not only know his stuff and do his stuff in his own field of physical education, health, recreation, dance, or safety but he must be able to meet people from other disciplines on either their own or neutral grounds. Too often physical educators have not been able to communicate with anyone but other physical educators. The word scholarship has been mentioned again and again as a mark of a profession. Scholarship implies the effective use of the English language and this effective use of language is the hallmark of culture and the trademark of a professional. The physical educator must develop an "at homeness" in an academic setting. If he wants his field to be accepted by professionals in other disciplines, he must first be accepted as an individual. When he is thus accepted as a peer, his program and his profession will also be accepted.

REFERENCES

1. AAHPER: *Developing Democratic Human Relations.* Washington, D.C., AAHPER, 1951, 101–115 pp.
2. Bookwalter, K. W.: This Matter of Promotion. Proceedings of Annual Meeting (January 8–11, 1964), National College Physical Education Association for Men, 1–5 pp.
3. Bucher, Charles A.: Physical Education: An Emerging Profession. Journal of Health, Physical Education and Recreation, Vol. 39, No. 7, October 1968, pp. 42–47.
4. Cratty, Bryant J.: *Social Dimensions of Physical Education.* Englewood Cliffs, N.J., Prentice-Hall, Inc., 1967.
5. Esslinger, Arthur A., and Carl A. Troester, Jr.: Our Association Today. Journal of Health, Physical Education and Recreation, Vol. 31, No. 4, April 1960, p. 24.
6. Knapp, M. L., and F. Todd: *Democratic Leadership in Physical Education.* Palo Alto, The National Press, 1952.
7. Pape, L. A., and L. E. Means: *A Professional Career in Physical Education.* Englewood Cliffs, N.J., Prentice-Hall, Inc., 1962.
8. Shivers, Jay S.: *Principles and Practices of Recreational Services.* New York, The Macmillan Company, 1967.
9. Tead, Ordway: *The Art of Leadership.* New York, Whittlesey House, 1935.
10. Ulrich, Celeste: *The Social Matrix of Physical Education.* Englewood Cliffs, N.J. Prentice-Hall, Inc., 1968.

Chapter 6

Promotion of Professional Competence

INTRODUCTION

Professional preparation of teachers for the 1970's and 1980's must be relevant. It must be geared to meet the needs of teachers who will grapple with the problems presented by this approaching era. This approach will be a mixture of the traditional with the new. The traditional—not because it is traditional—but because many of the same concepts expressed about teacher preparation at the Jackson's Mill Conference (9) in 1948 and the National Conference on Professional Preparation (2) by the AAHPER in 1962 are still valid today. The new—not just because of innovation and change for the sake of innovation and change—but because the complexities of our time have made education infinitely more complex and thus the role of the teacher more complex and demanding, and because leaders have the sensitivity to perceive the need for change. Thus, it will be necessary to break with tradition in many aspects, and creativity, innovation and imagination must furnish new ideas and concepts to be interwoven into the fabric of the best of the old. Yesterday's and today's solutions may not work in tomorrow's world. Education must strive for relevance.

Technology and the explosion of knowledge along with exploding population have brought sharply into focus some new concepts and new terms like auxiliary personnel, flexible and modular scheduling, differentiation of staff, interdisciplinary, computer programming, team teaching, individualized learning, personalized instruction, the teaching machine, and feedback. These are all new approaches to teaching and in some degree must become a part of the professional training program for teachers.

The sweeping social changes which have occurred and will continue to occur unabated in the immediate future have placed an added burden on teachers. Perhaps it will not be possible in the future to train teachers who can go into the field and make their adjustments to any and all situations. However, some things are known. A teacher's chances of making adjustments to new situations brought on by social upheaval and change are in proportion to the direct experiences provided for the teacher in professional training programs. Professional training programs in the future must reflect these complexities in the competencies planned for in the program experience.

In the program of teacher education there must be greater understanding of learning, of teaching, and of learning to teach. It has been said that one literally learns his way through life (7–5). If this be true, one has to learn how to learn. Institutions must place greater emphasis on good models since it is known that students tend to teach as they were taught. All teachers engaged in professional preparation must become more aware of their influence on the student's competency to teach. While academic freedom will still prevail, the college teacher's classroom will become less his ivory tower as faculties will be evaluated for their own competency in personal and professional effectiveness. It is probable in the future that promotion, salary, and tenure will no longer depend upon the sacred white cow of years of training and experience, but on the results of effective evaluation in the competencies needed to make an educational program function. Most promotions at the college and university levels now are dependent on contributions in research and scholarly activities and status in learned societies and professional associations. These are highly important aspects of the higher educational process, but to these must be added good teaching.

Professional preparation programs in physical education must keep pace with the times as has already been pointed out. There is frequently a cultural lag between the needs of society and the fulfilling of these needs by social institutions and agencies. This lag will be evident in accreditation of professional preparation institutions and in the certi-

fication of the professionals themselves. However, in the current holocaust of change brought on by the many factors of our culture, the professionals and the professional institutions themselves must take the lead. They must identify the urgent needs facing education today and then set about trying to gear their programs to meet these needs. Eventually some of the concepts and innovations may find their way back into certification and accreditation. However, the profession itself, as well as the training institution, can generally work within the framework of current certification and accreditation to achieve some of its worthwhile goals.

In a time when there is community unrest, militancy and deviant behavior in the cities, professionals must be prepared to teach and work in the inner city. This new breed of teachers on whose shoulders rests the success of educational processes in a militant environment must have more training in the social and behavioral sciences. More professional laboratory experiences must be provided for these teachers who expect to face the problems of the inner city schools. Either through internships or some similar program, the student must gain experience in the environment before he can be expected to become a full-time teacher. Along with the training of new teachers, it will also be the job of the professional training institution to develop programs for the administrators where city and county directors and chairmen of departments can be trained for the role they must play. Special attention must be given to professional standards regarding ethics, union and negotiations. Since it will be one of the many jobs of administrators to develop in-service training programs, this facet should not be neglected in their training.

A definite program for training auxiliary personnel should be made. The concept of auxiliary personnel or teacher aides offers a whole new approach to educational processes. The dramatic changes in sociocultural environment demand a different and more varied approach to means. Such differentiation in education might be better served by the differentiated teaching staff. A differentiated staff might include such personnel in addition to the fully qualified teacher as subject matter specialists, special service personnel, administrators, subprofessionals, nonprofessionals such as teacher aides, student teachers and interns. Since there is a hierarchy or levels of involvement, job analysis must be developed for each level. However, this program cannot be developed and implemented by the teacher training institution alone. There must be a program of interrelationships where there is involvement in teacher preparation by the community as a whole as well as the training institution.

The professional training institutions must develop stronger programs in the field of elementary education. It is conceded that more males should be drawn into elementary education and that in the future more emphasis will be placed on the teaching of physical education in the kindergarten through the sixth grade. In a publication, "Professional Preparation of the Elementary School Physical Education Teacher" (4), the AAHPER has set up guidelines and standards for the preparation of the physical education teacher in elementary schools. There are standards for student personnel, faculty, program, and suggestions for implementation.

Attention has already been called to the National Conference on Professional Preparation by the AAHPER in 1962. This conference resulted in the report "Professional Preparation in Health Education, Physical Education, and Recreation Education" (2). This report has served in the last decade to guide institutions in establishing and implementing programs of teacher education in health, physical education or recreation. A similar conference is planned for 1972 and the entire area of professional preparation will be reviewed and new guidelines established to meet the needs of education in the 1970's and 1980's.

While the content of the last two mentioned AAHPER publications is focused on undergraduate preparation, each underscored the importance of both the masters and the fifth year programs as well as the doctoral program. In 1967 the AAHPER sponsored a conference on graduate education. Guidelines and standards were established at both the master's and doctoral levels in health education, physical education, recreation education, safety education and dance. This report, "Graduate Education in Health Education, Physical Education, Recreation Education, Safety Education and Dance" (3), is now available to institutions desiring to develop new programs of graduate education or to upgrade present ones. This report considered such overall factors of concern as faculty, graduate students, methodology and administration and the like as common to all areas, but presented different programs for each of the five different areas.

All three of these sets of standards are aimed at an average level of performance. They challenge the weaker institutions but are below the level of the stronger ones.

PRODUCT AND PROCESS

In Chapter 5 the statement was made that professional competence was basic to a profession and to the professional growth and development of its leaders. If leadership in a profession is to achieve its potential, it must be related to the "extended period of preparation" criterion mentioned in the criteria of a profession. In this extended period of higher education which includes professional preparation, there are two main facets involved. One facet is concerned with the *product* of education — the student major who is an emerging professional. The other facet is concerned with the *process* — all aspects of the extended period of preparation including professional preparation which serve as a means of educating the product. It should be made clear at this point that professional preparation is more than a specialized training in a speciality. While training for a profession is specialty-oriented and the farther up the ladder of higher education one scales, the more highly specialized his training becomes, still professional training — particularly at the base — is broad in scope and aims at culture and refinement as well as specialization.

This "extended period of preparation" process includes all aspects of the institution's approach to higher education and should provide for the student an academic climate and a professional guidance that will enable him to develop his latent capacities to the fullest. The objectives for the student are based on the abilities, knowledges, skills and values which are deemed essential for professional excellence. These qualities are numerous and cover a wide area of both tangible and intangible factors. These qualities are of two types — those which are influenced greatly in the formal curriculum of the professional training institution and those which are learned, perhaps to a greater extent, outside the formal curriculum. Just as the academic and professional climate of the institution must be one that helps to instill the tangible factors, it must also help to nurture the more qualitative and intangible ones. It would be difficult to list all the necessary requisites for professional excellence, but some of the more

commonly recognized ones are discussed below.

COMPETENCIES

Leadership which was the chief topic of discussion in the last chapter is without doubt one of the major concerns, if not the major concern, in physical education. Since the recruitment, selection, training and certification of this leadership is primarily the responsibility of the professional education program of the institution of higher learning, leadership is directly related to professional preparation. If professional preparation is to achieve ultimate results in this process, it must have some definite goals or objectives to work toward. What are the goals of the profession for its leaders with respect to its work? These goals must inevitably be related to the duties and responsibilities of professional workers. At the onset it must be recognized that the duties performed by members of the profession are multiple and vary all the way from those by the instructor in the basic program at any educational level to those of the research scientist who pioneers in the areas of the unknown. Yet there are certain qualifications which might not only serve as a core of commonalities for all professionals, but also which are particularly pertinent for those in the formative years of professionalization who aspire to a career in teaching. Most professional preparation programs are teacher-oriented. Many authorities have expressed themselves in this matter and while they may have used different approaches, in general, they are pretty much in agreement on the major abilities.

What are the abilities that are needed for success in the field of physical education? They are most commonly referred to as competencies. The word competence itself might be defined as qualifications or abilities needed to achieve success in a particular field.

They may be divided into *professional* competencies and *personal* competencies.

Professional Competencies

In the case of professional competence, this means the ability to successfully carry on one's special field of endeavor or the possession of the necessary requisites for success in the speciality of that profession. The institution engaged in professional preparation of physical education professionals should prepare its students to assume the duties of a physical educator after graduation. The professional competencies listed below are needed by leaders in order to assume their many duties. This list of competencies is the result of composite thinking of many professional leaders when they met in a conference on undergraduate professional preparation in physical education, health education, and recreation (9–7).

Appreciation of the place and contribution of our schools in society, including the school in relation to the community

Knowledge of the development and organization of our communities and schools

An understanding of child nature and development

An understanding of the learning process and how to expedite it

Skill in the adjustment of learning experiences to the nature and needs of people

Knowledge and skill in the use of resource materials and of teaching and leadership aids

Skill in the use of the appropriate teaching and leadership techniques

Proficiency in evaluating the outcomes of learning experiences

Skill in making school and community life an experience in democratic living

Mastery of basic and related materials involved in the area of leadership responsibility

Knowledge and skill necessary to share in meeting common needs of people without reference to the nature of the teaching or leadership assignment; for example, health education, physical education and recreation needs, and guidance and counseling needs

Skill in relating learning materials to the total learning experience of the individual

Effectiveness in working with others, including pupils, colleagues, parents, and community

A point of view in education and recreation which requires that practices be adjusted to all people and their welfare

Personal Competencies

In addition to the professional competencies mentioned above, which incidentally are the responsibility of the professional education institution, a great deal of emphasis should be placed on personal qualities which the professional should possess. These are qualities which are more or less common to success in all teaching. Needless to say, some of these qualities will be present when the student seeks admittance to the professional institution and are a result of the innate and the acquired. Many of these are the intangibles mentioned previously and they are most important in determining the effectiveness of the professional worker. As has been mentioned before, these qualities should be emphasized in the formal curriculum but perhaps to a greater extent outside where the academic climate of the total institution must accept an area of concern. The personal qualifications listed below are a result of the same composite thinking as were the professional competencies (9–7):

Faith in the worth of teaching and leadership

Personal concern for the welfare of others

Respect for personality

Understanding children, youth, and adults and appreciating their worth as citizens

Social understanding and behavior

Community-mindedness

Interest in and aptitude for teaching and leading

Above average mental ability and common sense

Above average health status

Voice of good quality and power, intelligently used

Effective use of language

A sense of humor

Energy and enthusiasm sufficient to the requirements of effective leadership

THE PROFESSIONAL INSTITUTION—ITS SELF-STUDY, EVALUATION AND ACCREDITATION

At the onset the statement might be made that the product in education is inexorably related to the process. Thus, the physical education professional major is no better than the institution which trained him and a superior process should always be reflected by a superior product. However, at the present time, there is no scientific verification of its existence. Through logic it is assumed to be true that this relationship does exist. If this relationship does exist, the product and the process complement each other. By improving the process of the physical education professional institution, the product is upgraded. By the same token, if the candidate for the product is more effectively recruited, selected and trained, the process is upgraded. Good students demand and stimulate a better process. A good process keeps out the incompetent, commands respect, and attracts a better product.

What is this process of professional preparation in physical education and how can it be established, evaluated and upgraded? In its initial stages it differs little from the process of teacher education in general. All subject matter specialities share a common approach. Under the constitution each state has been charged with the responsibility of education. In the final analysis a society can guarantee quality teachers only by assuming some measure of control over the institutions which prepare them. The state must assume responsibility for the training of its teachers and it does this through a process of evaluating and accrediting institutions and their programs of teacher education. This form of accreditation is the same as referred to in the criteria of a profession. It is related to certification. It is different from certification, however, because it involves approving institutions rather than individuals, but it is similar because it involves many of the same criteria which are involved in certifying the individual. Accreditation is a process of recognizing the performance and integrity of educational institutions so they may merit the confidence of the public and each other. The aim of institutional accreditation is to promote the continued improvement of the professional leader in education and this could well be the aim of certification.

General Accreditation

There are several approaches to institutional accreditation for teacher education. The first step is *general accreditation*. General accreditation of institutions is implemented by means of six regional associations of colleges and schools geographically distributed throughout the United States. These six regional associations granting general accreditation are as follows: (1) Middle States Association of Colleges and Secondary Schools, (2) New England Association of Colleges and Secondary Schools, (3) North Central Association of Colleges and Secondary Schools, (4) Northwest Association of Secondary and Higher Schools, (5) Southern Association of Colleges and Schools and (6) Western Association of Schools and Colleges. There is a Federation of Regional Accrediting Commissions of Higher Education which represents and speaks for these six agencies (6). These are nongovernmental voluntary agencies which have assumed a role of accreditation. They establish criteria for evaluation, provide (upon request) a visitation team, and an evaluation and subsequent approval of institutions which meet the criteria.

All states require general accreditation for their teacher training institutions. The procedure is something like this. All institutions engaged in the training of teachers undergo a self-study, followed by a visitation, evaluation, and accreditation by their respective nationally recognized regional accrediting agency. This self-study is important because it requires each institution to examine or re-examine its concepts, goals, and operations. The regional accrediting agency first visits the institution and then evaluates the educational aspects as a whole and approves it for its effectiveness as educational processes. It then reports back to the institution. While the agency may be interested in specialized programs and schools, it does not provide specialized accreditation. However, the National Commission on Accreditation recommends that the graduate programs in colleges and universities be a part of general accreditation (6). Thus, general accreditation is the first step in specialized accreditation and is a paramount one. Institutional accreditation by such regional agencies, while it may differ in some minor aspects, presumably will guarantee general overall acceptance in such facets of educational process as financial stability, effective administration, adequate facilities, adequate student personnel program, a strong faculty, quality instruction, and appropriate curriculum (1). These aspects are really criteria and there are minimum standards in each of them which must be met. A point of reference here should be made, however. General accreditation by a regional association does not imply that institutions must be alike with respect to goals, process, and product. Each institution may maintain its uniqueness within the frame of reference of the standards which have been devised to assist all institutions to achieve maximum educational effectiveness. In a sense, such accreditation establishes the academic integrity of the institutions.

Specialized Accreditation

It may be apparent to some, however, that even when these standards established by a regional agency are met by an institution, there is still no assurance that good teachers will come as byproducts and that a good program of teacher preparation is present. Regional accreditation does not accredit specialized or professional programs. Some quality institutions make teacher preparation just an appendage or some make physical education an adjunct for the athletic department. There has to be another vital step in the approach to excellence just as there is in other professional schools. This second approach involves *specialized accreditation*. In this second approach the state must once again take the lead and require that each institution be accredited for professional preparation of teachers. Similar procedures to general accreditation are followed as the institution undergoes another self-study and visitation followed by evaluation and accreditation for its competence specifically in the program of teacher education – the whole institution as well as each subject matter area separately. Unfortunately there is no single agency which does this as is the case with approximately 30 other fields including law, medicine, architecture, engineering, and physical therapy. However, there is one agency which is responsible either directly or indirectly for most of it. Most states accredit their institutions through NCATE – National Council for Accreditation of Teacher Education. This is the recognized accrediting agency on the national level and its standards and guidelines are already established. NCATE is recognized along with 30 other professional agencies by the National Commission on Accrediting. One criterion for recognition is the requirement that an agency serve a definite social need. In some states the state education department has established its own approved program approach to teacher education (12). In most instances these states have patterned their standards and guidelines after those of NCATE. Both standards and guidelines are requirements which must be attained by institutions which seek approval from the state to train teachers. In general, the specialized accreditation procedure is one means of protecting the public welfare—by guarding against incompetence (1). Its criteria serve to give guidance and direction to professional programs in meeting the needs of society and the profession itself. Regardless of how valid institutional general accreditation is, it does not meet this specific need. Most specialized accreditation agencies require general accreditation first, however (1).

Whether specialized accreditation is done by NCATE or by the state, there are standards, guidelines, and evaluative criteria involved in the process. In general, these standards recognize that teacher education is an institution-wide approach. They presumably guarantee that the institution has met minimum levels of general excellence in all aspects of the institution which could conceivably be connected with professional preparation, and that teacher education is not an appendage. In North Carolina, for example, there are standards which refer to conditions which must be met by the institution preparing teachers (12). These standards concern overall policies, student personnel programs and services, faculty, curricula, professional laboratory experiences and facilities, equipment, and materials for both the graduate and undergraduate programs. In a sense these are similar criteria as those used in general accreditation but the emphasis is shifted to include preparation of teachers. In addition to the standards described above, there are guidelines for the curriculum in the three areas of (1) general education, (2) professional education and (3) subject matter specialization. These guidelines give flexibility to the program. At the same time they guarantee that the student will have adequate experience in the liberal arts and professional education as well as his subject matter speciality. They further describe the nature, scope, sequence, and amount of emphasis in the courses for subject matter specialization. Eventually, it would seem that all states must follow this pattern of evaluation and accreditation. It is the only sound approach — one which will either strengthen or weed out the weak institutions and the weak candidates.

In the "Standards and Guidelines for the Approval of Institutions and Programs for Teacher Education" by the State Department of Public Instruction of North Carolina, the following guidelines have been established for the three areas of general education, subject matter specialization, and professional education (12):

GENERAL EDUCATION (12–18)

1. The program should assure that all teachers are able to read, write, and speak the English language clearly and effectively.
2. The program should develop a critical understanding of and a sensitiveness to the aesthetic, philosophical, ethical, and imaginative values expressed in literature, art, music, religion, and philosophy.
3. The program should develop an understanding of the development of world civilization, an understanding of the basic concepts of the social studies, and an understanding of democracy as a way of life.
4. The program should develop an appreciation and understanding of the structure of science, of scientific inquiry, and of the main scientific principles.
5. The program should develop an appreciation of the structure and applications of mathematics.
6. The program should develop the knowledge, habits, and attitudes necessary to achieve and maintain sound physical and mental health.

SUBJECT MATTER SPECIALIZATION IN PHYSICAL
EDUCATION AND HEALTH (12–34)

1. The program should lead to the development of principles compatible with current educational philosophy.
2. The program should provide basic knowledge in the sciences.
3. The program should provide for knowledges and competencies in regard to organizing, planning, administering, and evaluating the various aspects of the total program of physical education.
4. The program should provide knowledge of and skill in a wide variety of activities; ability to analyze motor skills, and knowledge of methods and materials in teaching and coaching.
5. The program should develop knowledge and understandings in the various aspects of healthful living.
6. The program should develop competencies that will enable the teacher to plan or assist in planning and conducting programs of health service, healthful living, and health instruction.
7. The program should include sufficient preparation for later pursuit of graduate study in the area of physical education and health.

PROFESSIONAL EDUCATION (12–52)

1. The professional education program should provide an understanding of the normal sequence of human growth and development, with special emphasis on the pupils of the school age to be taught.
2. The professional education program should provide an understanding of the nature of learning, the learning process, and the psychology of learning.
3. The professional education program should provide an understanding of methods, special techniques, and materials appropriate to the specific levels or areas of the prospective teacher's subject-matter concentration, and skill in applying them in the classroom situation.
4. The professional education program should provide an understanding of the purpose, organization, and administration of school systems, with special emphasis on the role of the school teacher in the total education program.
5. The professional education program should provide a broad historical, philosophical, and sociological orientation to schools in our society and to the profession of teaching.
6. The professional education program should provide an extended period of continuous full-time student teaching experience in the grade levels or subjects to be taught.

Beyond Accreditation

It is at this point that even a third approach must be taken in the professional preparation of teachers of physical education. Once the academic integrity of the institution has been established by regional accreditation and its general competence revealed for professional education by NCATE or its state equivalent, the institution must go beyond minimum standards. The standards developed for accreditation are directed at the average. In one sense they represent a minimum. This may be good but good is not good enough in dealing with the preparation of professionals. The better institutions go beyond the average. The crux of the problem is to get the mediocre institution up to or above the average and the good institution to do better.

If physical educators are motivated by the desire to produce high level teachers and professionals who can meet their responsibility with respect to their speciality and expertise, the physical education process must undergo constant self-study, self-evaluation, and improvement (see Chapters 17 and 18). This procedure may have nothing to do with accreditation because it is at a level above and beyond average standards. It should, however, give leaders in the profession at the institution level an opportunity to diagnose strengths and weaknesses of their respective programs —weaknesses which may not be revealed in the first two approaches mentioned above. However, this ongoing evaluation could be directly related to both general and specialized accreditation. Most accrediting agencies review status of institutions periodically—some every five years, some every ten years. This review of status periodically does encourage continual self-study and evaluation. The factors which are most influential in teacher preparation and which come under scrutiny in the above approaches to accreditation are discussed in the next unit on the *product* of professional education.

THE PRODUCT AND THE TEACHER EDUCATION PROGRAM

In the preceding paragraph the three approaches for improving the professional education process were discussed. In the final analysis, the emphasis must shift back to the product. The good process is a good process only if it meets its responsibility in the matter of the product — his recruitment and selection into the program, his retention in the program, and finally his certification. Perhaps the follow-up should be added to this list since the ultimate test of competence comes much later in the form of the degree of success on the job. This responsibility starts with selection, however, but desirable follow-up methods must be developed.

Selection and Recruitment

Only those students who show genuine promise should be selected for training. A great deal has been said about recruitment and selection of the major student. Many institutions have set up criteria by which majors are admitted to the professional program. Presumably if institutions are forced by regional and state accreditation agencies to set up high standards in the criteria listed under the professional institution, these standards will include criteria for admission not only to the institution but also to the teacher education program. However, experience has shown that this is not enough. Additional criteria must be established for admission to the major program in physical education by

the department, division, or school of physical education itself.

Acceptable standards must be used for admission to the major program, and authorities in the field have from time to time used all or some of the following criteria for screening candidates who apply: health, personality, motor ability, sport skill, fitness, scholarship, native intelligence, attitude, interest in teaching, social and emotional qualities, weight control, and oral and written English. These are generally the personal type competency, since the student will have had no orientation into the professional competencies. When students meet reasonably high standards in these selective criteria for admission to candidacy as physical education majors and have been admitted, then what?

Retention

The very fact that these students have been admitted to the institution as students and then to candidacy as physical education majors in an institution whose academic integrity has been validated in both education and physical education by both regional and state accrediting agencies, still does not guarantee professional excellence. It merely indicates capacity to be educated. The burden is still on the institution to take this neophyte — this diamond in the rough — and provide him with a full measure of opportunity to achieve the competencies which authorities think are desirable in the field of physical education and for which he seems to have the potential.

A great deal has been said in recent years about retention policies. It is recommended by leaders in professional preparation that the student be eliminated from the teacher education program when he fails to measure up. It is comparatively easy to set up standards in criteria for retention. They are similar in nature to those criteria for both admission and certification. The criteria are those competencies deemed essential for professional excellence. Broadly speaking, they may be categorized into scholarship in general education, scholarship in the field of physical education, skills, fitness, mental and emotional health, character, personality, dependability, and professional attitude. The competencies centering around scholarship, skills, and fitness can be learned in the formal curriculum and can be rather accurately evaluated with scientific techniques.

However, the real test of the quality of the student lies in the area of the intangibles – such qualities as character, personality, dependability, and professional attitude. These are the human values on which the welfare and good of a society are predicated. These are competencies which are influenced to some degree in the formal curriculum but they are learned to a greater extent outside the curriculum. The professional climate of the institution must be one that helps to nurture these intangibles. Such qualities are far more difficult to instill than the more measurable skills and knowledges. Like many of life's finest qualities, they cannot be measured by objective techniques and their presence cannot be expressed in quantitative terms. However, many of these qualitative factors may be far more important in becoming a competent teacher and a good professional than are the more tangible and objectively measured traits.

Few students come to their professional preparation institution as mature men and women. Most come with a fair background in physical activities and a potential for scholarship if the institution has maintained its integrity in admission standards. Also, if the teacher education program along with the department or school of physical education has done a good job in screening for ad-

mittance to the profession, they have good potential as teachers. However, almost all students come to their professional preparation program completely naive in the many areas of professional pride and attitude, and the basic philosophy of the role of teacher and coach in today's society. If this be true, professional students in physical education must change their values, their attitudes, and their behavior. The actual test of this change during the retention period is not found by evaluating the verbalized responses of candidates but by observing their behavioral patterns. Students do not always behave as they say they would behave.

Present thinking among some of the authorities in teaching would seem to indicate that perhaps the number one professional competency of the good teacher is his ability to use the group process. Historically, in physical education while we have talked about democracy and group dynamics, our programs have not borne this out in practice and neither have its methods. There is a need for the teacher of physical education to possess a problem-solving tolerance and in this context to become aware of Mosston's (8) idea of teaching for inclusion rather than exclusion. Through the problem-solving approach, movement exploration, awareness of self, and dynamics of small groups, the teacher can individualize his instruction for mass groups and organize group management on the basis of individual needs.

The basis for individual needs are diagnostic services which are now available in most schools. When these needs are found, they are the basis for the learning process. It is at this point that the group process must become a part of the teacher's approach to his problem of self-direction and discovery. However, the crux is to internalize this attitude in the budding professional teacher. This is one of the many challenges of teacher preparation institutions.

What happens if those who are admitted to the professional education program fail to meet the standards in the criteria which have been established for retention? The answer is simple. They should be eliminated. If the criteria have been properly established and if proper evaluation techniques have been used to measure competency in them, and if the student fails to measure up, the institution should be committed to dropping him from the program at any point along the training period.

If the profession is to fulfill its responsibility to itself and its obligation to society for policing its own ranks, the place to start is in the professional training institution.

Standards have been too low in this area of teaching and coaching. They have been low not only in the selection of good candidates for training, but also in the training program and teaching personnel themselves. In order to offset this problem and to refute much of the criticism now directed toward the discipline of physical education, special effort has to be made by leaders in the profession and by accreditation and certification agencies. The aim of teacher education programs in physical education should not just encompass placing the emphasis on the selection of the good candidate to train. It should reach out and encompass much more. The Greeks talked about the pursuit of excellence and physical educators have more or less given a lot of lip service to this ideal. In professional education if the pursuit of excellence is to mean anything, the emphasis must be placed on "excellence" and not just "good." When standards are being raised, *good* could result in a form of mediocrity.

Certification

The final step, an important one, in professional preparation is certification. It is tantamount to admission to the profession as a practitioner with all the rights and privileges thereof. In many states at the present time, the state approves the institution for professional preparation either through NCATE or through its own approved program approach. When this is done the institution does the certifying. In still other states the institution makes application to the state department for certification of its students and the state does the certifying. Before the institution does the certifying or recommending for certification and puts its stamp of approval on the student, it has a commitment to see that the student has measured up and has met standards of adequacy in the competencies which are recognized as minimum requirements.

Naturally he must meet minimum standards of scholarship in not only his area of (1) subject matter specialization, but also in the areas of (2) general education and (3) professional education. These will vary from one institution to another. One common denominator might be a minimum standard on the National Teachers Examination. Some authorities are opposed to such practice, and have a good point since it does not always seem justice to eliminate an individual on the basis of one single exam score. However, there are two sides to this coin. Such a requirement is a way of raising extremely low standards and eliminating the weak candidate scholastically. Actually the NTE is made up of three parts: (1) professional education, (2) general education and (3) teaching area examination. The first two of these are combined into the Weighted Common Examination. It should be understood this exam does not reflect the personal competencies mentioned earlier in this chapter, but at the same time it does provide much information regarding the professional competencies. It should give evidence of one's knowledge in the three areas listed, especially the teaching area. It also reflects one's verbal skills. Since teaching and coaching are highly verbal activities (11), this portion of the test could reveal a teaching weakness that should be corrected before certification. Sommerfield points out that education exists for the benefit of the student and ultimately society and not for the teacher. It is unfair to both children and society to permit persons to come into the profession without the necessary academic aptitude and competence (11). Therefore, if education is to achieve excellence, its teachers must show evidence of at least minimum levels of academic preparation. Perhaps the concept of differentiated staff, when implemented, may find a place for those whose verbal skills do not meet minimum requirements. It is difficult to see how anyone can oppose a practice which tends to raise the standards in a discipline which is commonly regarded as being near the bottom of the totem pole of academic disciplines.

In addition to the minimum level of scholarship, the candidate should meet minimum levels of skill, be physically and mentally fit and healthy, and have demonstrated his competency to teach in his practice teaching situation. However, at some point just before the stamp of approval is placed on him as a teacher in the profession, all of these competencies along with the more intangible ones should be wrapped into one big whole and a general overall evaluation should be made of each candidate. This evaluation should be a departmental affair and be made by all the staff members who are acquainted with the student. It is here that a rating scale can be used to rate the student not only on his scholarship, skills, fitness, and health, but also the more important intangibles of character, personality, human values,

interest, professional attitude, and others (see Fig. 6–1).

Admittance to the professional program and completion of the course requirements for the physical education major should not guarantee certification and admittance to the profession as a teacher. Other than selection procedures, this is probably the only way the profession can exercise discriminatory powers to keep out those who are incompetent. However, when desirable standards are met in all the competencies needed for success in teaching, the constituted authority representing the institution or state can put its stamp of approval on the student and recommend him as a candidate eligible for certification. The professional institution has no commitment to graduate all candidates any more than they have to admit all who apply for entrance in the program. It is the responsibility of the professional institution to exercise care in the recruitment and selection of its candidates, to see that candidates are not retained in the program during their training period if they are failing to measure up, and as a last resort not to place the stamp of approval on the candidate who in the last analysis fails to achieve his potential. Some students are selected in the program because of their potential and are still retained in the hopes they may begin to achieve according to their capabilities. However, in some cases after they are continued in the program for four years on the basis of their potential, they eventually run out of it and they become poor bets for certification. Such candidates should never receive the stamp of professional approval solely on the basis of original potential.

There is still one facet over which the institution has no control. This involves the matter of the emergency certificate. Most states provide for some means of obtaining the necessary teaching person-

Name of Student_____

Home Address _____

Professional and Personal Traits	Excellent	Good	Average	Below Average	Inferior	No Opportunity to Observe
PERSONALITY (How one affects others)						
PROFESSIONAL ATTITUDE 1. Membership and participation in Professional organization						
2. Desire to achieve success in a requirement						
3. Willingness to serve beyond a requirement						
ABILITY TO EXPRESS ONE'S THOUGHTS 1. Use of oral English						
2. Use of written English						
MOTOR ABILITY (Fundamental skills)						
ACTIVITY SKILLS 1. Team sports						
2. Individual sports						
3. Gymnastics						
4. Aquatics						
5. Dance						
SCHOLARSHIP (Knowledge of subject and academic areas)						
TEACHING POTENTIAL (Ability to apply knowledge, skill and understanding)						
PERSONAL APPEARANCE (Neat, clean, and well dressed)						
DEPENDABILITY (Highly reliable and punctual in meeting responsibility)						
SELF-CONTROL (Emotional stability)						
SOCIAL QUALITIES (Poise, dignity, and tact)						
COOPERATION (Ability to work with others)						
LEADERSHIP (Initiative, Resourcefulness, Magnetism)						

GENERAL COMMENT _____

Date of Graduation_____

Date_____STAFF, DEPARTMENT OF PHYSICAL EDUCATION
WAKE FOREST UNIVERSITY

Signed_____
          Chairman

FIGURE 6–1   Rating Scale for Physical Education Major Student (Courtesy Department of Physical Education, Wake Forest University)

nel at the local level. If properly certified persons are available, this privilege is rarely abused by the good administrator. However, when the demand exceeds the supply, or when some administrator seeks a coach for his athletic prestige but one who is not properly certified, this privilege is abused and teachers are permitted to come into the profession by the back door.

Follow-Up

The ultimate proof of the adequacy of the process and the worth of the product is found on the job much later in the professional student's career. What counts most is the job the teacher does in service. If an institution is really interested in the ultimate in evaluation of its process and its students, it must plan and implement a follow-up program. This program must be constantly sensitive to the needs of the schools, and the follow-up appraisal processes must be a two-way process where there is communication between the schools and the teacher training institutions.

REFERENCES

1. AACTE: *Standards and Evaluative Criteria for the Accreditation of Teacher Education.* Washington, D.C., AACTE, 1967.
2. AAHPER: *Professional Preparation in Health Education, Physical Education, and Recreation Education.* Washington, D.C., AAHPER, 1962.
3. AAHPER: *Graduate Education in Health Education, Physical Education, Recreation Education, Safety Education, and Dance.* Washington, D.C., AAHPER, 1967.
4. AAHPER: *Professional Preparation of the Elementary School Physical Education Teacher.* Washington, D.C., AAHPER, 1969.
5. AAHPER: *Self-Evaluation Check List for Graduate Programs in Health Education, Physical Education, Recreation Education, Safety Education, and Dance.* Washington, D.C., AAHPER, 1969.
6. Hegener, Karen C. (Editor): 1970—*The Annual Guides to Graduate Study, Book VI. Education.* Princeton, N.J., Peterson's Guides, Inc., 1970.
7. Klopf, Gordon J., Garda W. Bowman, and Adena Joy: *A Learning Team: Teacher and Auxiliary.* Washington, D.C., U.S. Office of Education, U.S. Government Printing Office, 1969.
8. Mosston, Muska: *Teaching Physical Education.* Columbus, Ohio, Charles E. Merrill Books Company, 1966.
9. National Conference on Undergraduate Professional Preparation in Health, Physical Education, and Recreation: Jackson's Mill, West Virginia, May 16–27, 1948: Report, Chicago, 1948, The Athletic Institute.
10. Snyder, R. A., and H. A. Scott: *Professional Preparation in Health, Physical Education and Recreation.* New York, McGraw-Hill Book Company, 1954.
11. Sommerfield, Roy E.: Just How Bad Is The NTE? North Carolina Education, Vol. 36, No. 6, February, 1970, p. 10.
12. State of North Carolina: *Standards and Guidelines for the Approval of Institutions and Programs for Teacher Education.* Raleigh, N.C., State Department of Public Instruction, 1962.

Chapter 7

Opportunities for One Who Is Trained in His Profession

INTRODUCTION

It is one thing for the professional student to know about his profession and how one becomes professionalized, and still another for him to understand many ramifications of his extended period of preparation—the teacher training institution and its program. It is still another, however, for the budding professional to know the opportunities that are available to him in the field of service as a result of his training and how these fit in with his own personal qualifications.

Physical education is a broad field and offers many opportunities to those who have the necessary training including the important professional and personal competencies mentioned in Chapter 6. Probably in most professional training institutions, the emphasis is placed on the preparation of the professional physical education teacher rather than the recreationist, the therapist, or health educator. Thus professional preparation is decidedly teacher-oriented. This is only logical, since there are so many places open in the teaching profession,

and more people go into this field than any other.

Teaching as a part of the school and college program is merely one aspect of the broad range of opportunities open for not only the beginner, but also the person who is already in service and is looking for advancement. The person who is surveying the field with an eye toward specialization needs to know what might be in store for him in the way of getting a position and advancing in his speciality, after a tour of duty in that speciality. Career days in high schools could provide students with much of this knowledge. Orientation programs during the early part of college years would also help. The person who has committed himself to a career and his professional training is already under way also needs to be made aware of the many other avenues for service in his chosen field. While the undergraduate degree is essentially a generalized education, it does permit some specialization. For example, it is possible in some institutions to major in either health, physical education, or recreation. Also, one may be certified either at the elementary or the secondary levels.

However, it is never too early for the physical education major student to be planning his professional life for the future. He needs to do this with certain things in view. For example, he may have options in his professional training. Today there are many good teacher preparation institutions which, in addition to meeting certification requirements, permit some leeway in training for specialization. Thus, the young trainee will let his professional preparation play a role in the selection of the kind of service he wishes to render, or by the same token plan his program according to the career he wishes to pursue. In this case he may plan on the basis of his aptitude and abilities as well as his interests, or he may take the expedient course and choose on the basis of his best chance of getting a job. If he is perceptive and inquiring, he will want to know the opportunities for continuous employment and advancement in his contemplated field and something about salary, retirement, and tenure. If he is even more discriminative, he will be concerned about the opportunity for creativity and self-expression in his work and the status that his position will occupy in society or the role he will play in that status. Also, since it is important that all people obtain a certain amount of happiness and satisfaction from their work, he will want to evaluate himself in the light of the setting for his work. He should be able to evaluate himself in this regard in many ways—his interests, abilities and attributes which could lead to success or failure. Another important consideration, and perhaps closer to home, is the requirements for his professional preparation. The trainee should be familiar with them from the outset and know what is involved for certification or pre-requisites to additional training or other specialized jobs.

In any event, once the student knows the opportunities in the broader field, the more likely he will be able to enter an area of endeavor which is to his liking and which is compatible with his abilities. Also, he is more likely to appreciate the importance of doing those things which will insure him the best chance of professional advancement. This process has been discussed at length in Chapter 6, but the trainee should be schooled in the ways of advancing himself in whatever setting he chooses. While the setting may vary and there may be differences in the requirements for preparation, the criteria for advancement are essentially the same for all types of positions. Perhaps the best way is for the worker to do the best job he can while he is on the job. However, while success on the job is a necessary attribute to advancement, there is something more. There must be a willingness to develop in one's self the kind of leadership that is referred to in Chapter 5. The requirements for leadership will vary for the various types of positions and settings but in general most of them are similar to the requisites for advancement in education. In teaching, the worker must be willing to professionalize himself, he must be willing to go the second mile in such things as continuing education in graduate school, working to improve himself in service, supporting and promoting his professional organizations, and seeking self-improvement through independent study and research. At the higher levels particularly, the production of scholarly material for publication and undertaking quality research are the stepping-stones to advancement. These same criteria would apply to the worker even if he went into recreation, health, or therapy. In any of these areas of work in the future, success, status, and expertise will require a great deal more of the specialist's time and effort. However, more and more jobs will become available. In addition to the new jobs which are created by a burgeoning increase in the services required to meet the population explosion and the constantly increasing demands of an affluent society, for smaller classes, enriched curricula, special programs for the exceptional, and federal funding, there are many positions already in existence which become vacant each year because of resignations, marriage of women who leave the field, retirements, deaths, and the constant mobility of people who move into other fields.

The person with a background in physical education has many possibilities for job opportunities. In order to simplify the long list of agencies and institutions where physical education activities and services are needed, they will be categorized into the following areas: schools and colleges, health agencies, recreation, service agencies and clubs, therapy, and governmental agencies.

SCHOOLS AND COLLEGES

Physical education has always been an important part of the school program from grade one through college. With the current emphasis on movement education and its relation to neurological organization for the child, both the kindergarten and nursery school can now be added to the list. In recent years there have been fewer persons available in the field of education than there are jobs. This is due to several reasons including the absorbing of men into the national defense efforts either directly as a member of the armed forces or as a worker in some form of industry supporting the war effort, draining of eligible college graduates into more lucrative positions in business and industry, and early marriages taking

many trained women out of the profession at least temporarily. Thus, there is a demand for qualified persons to fill the vacant positions that occur each year. There is a particular need for more men especially at the elementary level. Overall needs in the elementary and secondary schools as revealed by statistics released by the Research Division of the NEA show an increase of 200,000 from 1967 to 1977 (9). During the same period the need for instructional staff in colleges will rise by 130,000. These projected needs are in line with the increase of 2,000,000 elementary and secondary pupils and almost 3,500,000 more students in institutions of higher learning. During this same period the cost of operating elementary and secondary schools will rise by over ten billion dollars and higher education by almost twelve billion. Much of this rise in cost will go into not only more job opportunities, but higher salaries and better working conditions (2).

Normally jobs are available in each of the following levels: elementary, junior high school, senior high school, two-year colleges, and four-year colleges and universities. Physical education is generally a requirement at each of these levels; in most instances it is taught by a specialist except in the elementary school where the self-contained classroom teacher still is responsible in the majority of cases. However, there is now a trend toward changing to specialists even in the elementary grades because leaders believe that good physical education programs properly taught and conducted here are perhaps more important than at any other level. At the present time this possibility is limited by two things. First, many schools do not have the necessary finances to hire enough full-time physical education teachers, and second, there is not enough motivation yet to attract a sufficient number of specialists into this field. It is probably true that some persons are reluctant to enter the profession at this level since the financial remuneration is not as high in the lower levels as at the college level. There is a tendency to look toward college teaching and involvement as an advancement in both status in the profession and personal benefits to the individual. This is not entirely without basis, for research reports published in 1969 showed the following salary averages: elementary — $7,676, secondary — $8,160, public junior colleges — $9,165, and colleges $10,235 (9). Perhaps as physical education gains more momentum at the lower level, it will be possible for more status as well as opportunities for advancement to those people who chose this area for a career. In the past and even now the salaries are generally higher at the college level chiefly because more advanced training and experience are the criteria for qualifying. There is a demanding need, however, for better qualified teachers and supervisors at the elementary levels and these positions should offer the same opportunity for advancement in salary, rank, and status as well as self-satisfaction as the college positions.

The junior and senior high school positions are similar since they are both usually involved with intramurals and interschool athletic coaching and teaching of health in addition to teaching similar physical education activities. A physical education specialist for both girls and boys is generally employed. In some states a double major is possible whereby the physical education teacher may have some classroom teaching in a subject matter area in addition to his physical education. This dual major enhances the worker's chances of obtaining a job at the beginner's level particularly. This is a plan which is used more often at the junior high school level and there is some advantage even in extend-

ing it downward to grades five and six to include the middle years of school in terms of the ages of students. Since the teaching of health in public schools is a requirement by law in most states, there is some demand for the health specialist. However, most health instruction is still taught by the specialist in physical education, who also is required to have some health training as a part of his major. Some states now have a certification plan called 4 through 9 which makes it possible for the student to have two areas of concentration with one of them being physical education. Obviously this plan opens up further job opportunities at the upper elementary level for one who holds such certification. It is one method to get more individuals qualified at the middle grade level. The private schools in many cases have better programs than the public schools. However, these differences are generally in degree rather than kind.

At the college and university level there are a number of things which have led to the demand for more trained professionals in physical education. Of course the greatly increased enrollment figures are partly the key to the increased demands. However, there is a trend toward more services and a burgeoning growth in professional preparation programs in order to supply the need for trained men and women for all of the groups needing services of physical education, health, safety, recreation, research, and therapy. Another source of many new jobs is the phenomenal growth of the junior colleges. Added to the many old-line junior colleges are the new two-year community colleges which have sprung up in the last decade. Many states are just beginning to build their community college complexes so this movement should be a continuing source of job opportunities. Physical education should play an important role in these schools since for many students they provide a terminal education and a last chance to become physically educated.

Colleges and universities offer more opportunity for diversity in specialization. In general, college positions can be divided into: (1) work in the required program; (2) intramural administration; (3) professional preparation in physical education; (4) coaching athletic teams; (5) graduate program; (6) health and safety; (7) research, and (8) administration. These various aspects speak for themselves in most cases. Perhaps the greatest demand in terms of number is the required program which serves more individuals than any of the others. It is also true that a single professional worker is rarely assigned to just one of these areas. He may have areas of responsibility in two or even more. For example, he may teach some classes in the required program, and others at the professional preparation level and also have coaching responsibilities. Frequently the same person teaches at the undergraduate professional level and in the graduate program and may also be involved in research. It is true of course that not all colleges and universities are concerned with all of these specialized areas, but most four-year colleges are involved with the majority of them.

While teaching at the college level has been deemed to be the highest level of achievement for a professional worker, it also has the most demanding requirement as prerequisites in qualifying for a position. The master's degree is a common requirement for all positions and in the case of those who teach in the graduate and the undergraduate professional preparation programs, the doctorate is frequently mandatory. Advancement in salary, rank and status is similar to that in other academic disciplines. It is based on achievement as a teacher, scholarly works including either research

or writing, and involvement in one's professional societies. While in many institutions advancement in rank is still based on degrees and the number of years in service, there is a trend toward the superior performer being recognized for his excellence in one or more of these three areas. Teacher evaluation for merit, although unpopular in the past, may become a necessity in the future.

Administration is one facet of work at the college level that requires a complex of diversified qualities. The administrator is generally one who has had a great deal of experience in the field and some advanced specialization, and who has demonstrated the qualities of leadership that are necessary for the conduct of the overall program. Coaching, too, is a highly specialized area and offers many opportunities for either part-time work in combination with other phases or perhaps even full-time as has become so prevalent now, especially in football and basketball. However, while it is still helpful for the graduate to be hired for a position on the basis of his athletic reputation, the time has come when he must demonstrate his competency to teach and carry the load in other facets of the program if he is to advance in his profession. Another highly specialized area today is research. This is not to imply that all research related to physical education is carried on in the colleges and universities; the major portion of it is. Many graduate programs especially at the doctoral level demand research in fulfilling the requirements for the degree. Some master degree programs, too, have such a requirement. In addition to this vast source of creative work, many positions now have release time for independent research on the part of the professional worker. In fact, it is now almost a requirement in many institutions for professional advancement in some specialities. It is now possible for the undergraduate to begin directing his training and experience toward a career in research. Just as more opportunities will become available at the college and university level, it is equally true that outside foundations, government, and even industry are sources for job opportunities for those trained in research techniques and know-how.

Another rich source of career potential in the public schools particularly are the supervisory positions. These positions vary all the way from those at the state level in the state department of education to those at the local level in the elementary schools. As more and more emphasis is placed on education through the physical, there will be increased pressure for well-organized and well-conducted programs. As school units grow in size and complexity, there is the need for better direction and the answer to this problem is good supervision.

These positions will become more common at the city and county unit levels. Like the position of the administrator, supervisory positions will require special kinds of competencies and should be filled by persons who have had a number of years of experience as teachers and advanced special training in the techniques of leadership and supervision.

Another career open to people in the field is health education and safety in the schools. The schools offer a broad area of opportunity for those who have a background in health and physical education. Health is a relatively new teaching field as a speciality but has been taught for a long time in combination with the program of physical education by physical educators. Most colleges now offer courses in health as electives and many of them have health instruction as a part of the general requirements. Some colleges are instituting a professional preparation program for training teachers in health and safety.

In addition to teaching health as a subject, some of these positions require the health education specialist to coordinate health services and health instruction as a part of the overall health education program. It is probably true, however, that much of the teaching of health as a subject in the public schools will continue to be taught by the physical education teacher, since most schools do not yet have the finances to hire a full-time specialist. Some schools are hiring directors of safety who direct the school safety program including driver education.

In general there has been a significant improvement in the lot of the professional worker in education over the last few years. In spite of great enrollment growth and added pressure due to the explosion of knowledge, the teacher's working conditions are better, salary, tenure, and retirement plans have improved, and the work has made some progress toward achieving professional status.

In the field of education a great deal of lip service has been given in the past to the principle of individual differences. Perhaps at no time in the history of education has so much been done in the way of administering to the needs of the exceptional or atypical child. The exceptional child ranges all the way from the gifted on one end of the continuum to the mentally retarded and the physically handicapped on the other. The needs of some can be met in regular schools by classification and adaptation. The physical educator must help meet these needs in individual physical education in the regular school.

In many states and communities it is the philosophy that the needs of all students should be met in the schools. Thus, special education programs, and in many cases special schools, have been provided for the deaf, blind and visually handicapped, mentally retarded, socially

and emotionally maladjusted and crippled. In order to care for those who do
not seem to have the capacity to obtain
an education through normal channels,
technical, vocational and trade schools
are growing rapidly. Since programs
must be adapted to the individual needs
of the pupil, special training is needed in
order to adequately administer to these
needs and physical education becomes a
part of the specialized program of each
group.

HEALTH AGENCIES

In addition to the needs of the schools
and colleges for specialists in health,
there are numerous possibilities for employment in other areas. The health
specialist is needed in both private and
public agencies in greater number each
year. The federal and state governments have many positions open in their
departments of public health and local
needs in county and city health departments are many. There is further demand by both the federal and state
rehabilitation programs and programs
for the physically handicapped. There
is need for the health specialist in private
organizations and foundations who are
promoting health, as well as business and
industrial firms. For example, the state
and national heart associations, the
American Cancer Society and the National Foundation (formerly the National Foundation for Infantile Paraly-
sis). Health specialization even takes
on an international flavor with jobs now
available throughout the world by the
World Health Organization (WHO).

An increasing number of institutions
are now providing a professional preparation program for the health specialist. While the public schools do absorb
some of these specialists in their program, the majority still go into college
health teaching and to national, state,
and local agencies and foundations
whose primary responsibilities are the
promotion of health. The undergraduate
professional preparation in health offers
a sound basis for specialization in public
health at the graduate level. Many
physical educators, as they grow older
and have less desire and capability to
continue teaching physical activities,
move into the health field on a full-time
basis, where teaching is generally relegated to the classroom. As previously
pointed out, the opportunities for full-
time teaching of health in the public
schools are not so numerous. However,
it is expected that these positions will
grow in demand as more funds become
available for public education and as
more administrators and boards of education recognize the importance of
health as a major objective of education.

RECREATION

Recreation in its broadest sense ranks
right along with education as one of the
basic needs of society as well as one of
the fundamental needs of the individual.
There are many settings in which recreation occurs and a special type of training is required for each. In general over
the years the majority of recreation
workers have come from the ranks of the
physical education major. There is a
trend now, however, for the recreation
field to require its own standards of
personal and professional competence.
More and more the recreation worker is
trained in a professional training program for recreation and there is a very
definite body of knowledge now being
formulated with recreation as its focus.

There are also definite specialities
within the special field of recreation such
as hospital, industrial, rural and municipal recreation in addition to the many
federal and state programs involved with
state and federal parks, forests, and
other projects. Jobs in recreation range
all the way from the worker on the playground in a public or community program to the camp director in camping or

the nature specialist in a national park. In addition to recreation personnel employed in the schools, there are many positions open in public recreation such as city director, playground director, special activities director, supervisor of centers and pools, and many others. Similar jobs are open in industrial recreation where employee programs either supplement or take the place of community programs.

The armed forces furnish the setting for a great deal of supervised recreation and jobs are open to civilian personnel. There are numerous industrial recreation programs which require leadership and some business firms offer similar opportunities. Organized camping is now operated on a large scale and furnishes one of the most important educational as well as recreational developments in America. There are literally thousands of camps operated by many agencies and voluntary organizations on a nonprofit basis as well as private camps which are run for profit. There are job opportunities for camp directors, camp specialists, and nature specialists.

THERAPEUTICS

There are many opportunities in the area of therapeutics for the qualified specialist. The physical education major offers an excellent foundation for work in the various areas of therapy and many such programs offer the necessary prerequisite for special schools. However, in general, therapeutics require a high degree of specialization beyond the undergraduate major in physical education. There are four major areas of specialization as follows: physical therapy, occupational therapy, recreational therapy, and exercise therapy.

Perhaps the area that attracts more physical educators than any of the others is physical therapy. Around the country there is a dearth of well-trained therapists and jobs are plentiful in general, service, and veterans' hospitals, in both public and private clinics, and clinics for crippled children, and agencies providing rehabilitation services. This speciality is definitely medically orientated since the physical therapist usually works under the prescription of a medical doctor and since most physical therapy schools are under the guidance of medical schools. At the present time there is need for more men to enter this profession.

Occupational therapy also is medically orientated since its services, like physical therapy, are prescribed by the medical profession. The occupational therapist works toward restoring and rehabilitating both physical and mental faculties and is usually employed in some type of hospital. These settings vary from mental hospitals to orthopedic and children's hospitals, and from work in veterans' hospitals to centers for vocational rehabilitation. The occupational therapist's field of work is as varied as the vocational opportunities provided by man's culture. However, the arts and crafts area, home economics and shop work are among the most important areas. The rewards of personal satisfaction and fulfillment in one's work are great, although the evaluation of immediate as well as long-range objectives for the patient may be difficult.

Recreational therapy has similar objectives to those of occupational therapy. Work is here again with the mentally and physically handicapped. However, the ends sought are achieved through different means. All types of sports, games, and recreational activities are employed to treat the problems of both adults and children. The recreational therapist, too, works under the direction of the medical doctor and his work may be conducted in conjunction with the occupational and physical therapists. The setting for such work is in hospitals and clinics.

The latest area of therapy is the exercise therapist. This speciality received impetus during World War II when all divisions of the armed forces carried on rehabilitation exercise programs in VA hospitals. The idea was to shorten the time that servicemen would spend in hospitals. Like the other therapists, the exercise therapist works with the doctor, and through special exercise programs works directly with patients in order to develop their strength and fitness as well as to help restore body functions and correct remedial defects. This work is chiefly carried on in veterans' hospitals.

SERVICE AGENCIES, ORGANIZATIONS, AND CLUBS

There are many positions open in public, private and semi-public organizations which are designed to serve the needs of both youth and adults. Professional opportunities are usually open to young men and women who have a background of undergraduate preparation in physical education. The list of such agencies would be long but the following are examples of the ones most commonly thought of which serve youth: YMCA, YWCA, Boy Scouts, Girl Scouts, Camp Fire Girls, Young Men's Hebrew Association, Young Women's Hebrew Association, 4-H Clubs, Boys' Club, American Red Cross, American Youth Hostels, Inc., Settlement Houses, United Service Organizations, and Future Farmers of America.

The service agencies mentioned in the preceding paragraph all have much in common. Much of their leadership comes from persons with undergraduate professional preparation in physical education or recreation. In general, their programs are voluntary and attempt to supplement the programs found in the schools and home and other community agencies such as recreation departments and churches. Most of them have programs which are wider in scope than just sports and games but these do occupy an important place in the order of the services they render. Opportunities for advancement of the professional worker are similar to those in other related areas and the techniques of advancement are also similar. Some of the agencies do offer opportunities for work in foreign countries.

However, most of these agencies do require some specialization which must be obtained outside the usual physical education major. This is generally attained through graduate study, short courses in special schools, or in some cases, an in-service program. However, in general the activities of physical education are the core of that part of the program which would require the service of trained physical educators. Many of the youth agencies are under religious auspices such as the Catholic youth organizations, the Young Men's Hebrew Association, and others which were originally established for religious training. The church itself now finds it important to administer to the physical side of man's unity and many churches and synagogues have facilities and provide leadership.

GOVERNMENT AGENCIES

Aside from the schools, health services, municipal recreation, and armed forces which are governmental in nature if not in function, and which have already been briefly discussed in previous sections, there are a reasonable number of job opportunities in other governmental services. Many of these stem from the government's entry into the area of social welfare and its funding of extensive programs in these areas. This is particularly true of the federal government. However, there are also opportunities at both the state and local levels although in many cases these opportunities are in programs which are sponsored by state and local governments but are funded by the federal government.

The National Park Services provide opportunities for park directors as well as camp directors along with nature specialists. The same is true for state parks and forests. There are still a few positions open in the Office of Indian Affairs. However, perhaps the programs which have assumed the largest role in supplying jobs in government for people trained in physical education are the Peace Corps and those associated with the Office of Economic Opportunity. Hundreds of physical education majors have gone into the Peace Corps in recent years and have given service in more than fifty nations around the globe. The work is challenging and the satisfactions that come to the worker from contributing to the rise of disadvantaged people in needy countries are great and somewhat offset the limited pay.

The Office of Economic Opportunity sponsors several programs where persons trained in physical education might qualify for positions. Perhaps the most inclusive one is the Job Corps, a training program with setting usually in a camp or outdoor situation where the culturally deprived and the disadvantaged youth might be assisted toward becoming better citizens. This program is similar to the Civilian Conservation Corps of the 1930's, but is combating the school drop-out problem and cultural deprivation rather than economic depression. Head Start is another program, part of the Economic Opportunity Act. The idea behind this service is to provide for the disadvantaged child a pre-school experience either before first grade or kindergarten in order to narrow the gap in experiences between the culturally deprived and those who are not. The program has worked so well that it is now extended throughout the year instead of the pre-school experience.

Other possibilities for job opportunities include work in penal institutions and correction institutions for juvenile delinquents. The philosophy toward the social deviate who comes into conflict with the law has changed greatly the last few decades. The emphasis is now on correction and rehabilitation especially for the youths who have not yet become hardened criminals. In any such re-education socially, the services of physical educators will play an important role. With the current social problems of society, there will be even more demand for the services of the recreation director and physical educator in such settings as state and federal prisons, reformatories, detention homes, prison farms, and workhouses.

REFERENCES

1. Bucher, Charles A.: *Foundations of Physical Education*, 5th Ed. St. Louis, C. V. Mosby Company, 1968.
2. Department of Health, Education, and Welfare: Projections of Educational Statistics to 1977–78. Washington, D.C., U. S. Government Printing Office, 1969.
3. Johnson, G. B., W. R. Johnson, and J. H. Humphrey: *Your Career in Physical Education*. New York, Harper and Brothers, 1957.
4. Knapp, Clyde, and Ann E. Jewett: *Physical Education: Student and Beginning Teacher*. New York, McGraw-Hill Book Company, 1957.
5. NAPECW and NCPEAM: The Physical Educator as Professor. Quest, Vol. 7, December, 1966.
6. Nixon, John E., and Ann E. Jewett: *An Introduction to Physical Education*. Philadelphia, W. B. Saunders Company, 1969.
7. Palmer, Chester L.: Physical Education as Your Career. Journal of Health, Physical Education and Recreation, Vol. 24, No. 3, March, 1953, pp. 17–19.
8. Pape, L. A., and L. E. Means: *A Professional Career in Physical Education*. Englewood Cliffs, N. J., Prentice-Hall, Inc., 1962.
9. Research Division: National Education Association: Economic Status of the Teaching Profession, 1968–69. Washington, D.C., National Education Association, 1969.

PART III

Scientific Bases and Principles

SECTION A
Principles

Chapter 8

Principles—Their Meaning and Source

INTRODUCTION

The statement already has been made that a profession or discipline is based on scientific facts. These facts are the foundations on which a field of study rests. Such facts lead to basic beliefs. Basic beliefs serve as guides to the professional; they are the very capstones of his status as a practitioner. Naturally the good professional in service as well as the professional student is curious and at the same time concerned about the bases upon which his work and profession are predicated. He should be concerned for several reasons, but chiefly because he knows that his actions and practices will be dictated to a large extent by his basic beliefs. If he is truly a professional, he will want to know that his actions and practices will be outgrowths of valid facts from experience and scientific inquiry. As a professional he must know that this is expected of him by the public as a part of his responsibility to them, and that it is a part of his code of ethics.

Basic beliefs which have been verified are necessary for any discipline or profession. The practitioner of a trade, as was pointed out in Chapter 5, does not need to know the fundamental concepts on which his trade rests. He is concerned only with rules, methods and techniques. Conversely, the practitioner of a profession, by the very essence of his being a professional, performs a different function and has a different relationship to his chosen work. By the very nature of this work, the professional is called upon in a multitude of situations to take action, make judgments, come to decisions, and in general act in a responsible manner to carry out his speciality in a humanitarian way.

Since the keystone of a profession is responsibility, the professional must make all possible effort to take action, make his decisions, and govern his conduct according to some underlying basic beliefs arrived at in the best manner possible. Basic beliefs must be as valid as science, philosophy, and experience can make them. The perceptive professional will develop an acute awareness of the fundamental concepts and causes, and an attitude to know the "why" as well as the "how."

WHAT ARE PRINCIPLES?

Basic beliefs are principles. The word principle is derived from the Latin word *principium* with the connotation of origin, primary, or source. It further carries with it the idea of fundamental or ultimate. *Principles* may be defined as truths or general concepts based on facts and used as guides for taking action and making choices. These facts are arrived at in a valid manner through both scientific and philosophical methods.

One of the characteristics of principles is their permanence — their universal nature with respect to origin and ultimate truth. However, theoretically even scientists are suspicious of the idea of universals if by universality is meant absolutes. In science there is a respect for tentativeness and a certain amount of flexibility where the door is always open for old hypotheses to be revised or even discarded completely (4). Whenever a belief once accepted as truth ceases to function or explain in an effective manner, or when new discoveries through scientific research or philosophical method add new light and/or discrepancies, hypotheses and beliefs are subject to modification. However, while theoretically again, truth may not be absolute, its data from many sources are readily generalized into principles. In turn these principles are used to direct behavior and give guidance. The principles of an area of work give it professional status. They actually indicate the quality of the professional himself.

The acid test of a principle concerns its verification and ultimately, of course, its application. However, just because a belief exerts an influence and controls actions is not just cause alone to indicate its validity. While it must be capable of application and it should control action, it must also be based on the best held scientific and/or philosophical evidence at the time. An unverified controlling belief may be applied and may dictate action as it is held to rigidly by the practitioner. However, it may be a generalization which has been based on unsupported evidence, on prejudice, on false reasoning, on faulty interpretation of data, or for that matter on taboos and superstition. Verification must rest on supported evidence of either a scientific or philosophical nature (9–7).

HOW DO PRINCIPLES FUNCTION?

Once principles have been established, they serve as guides toward purposeful action as they may govern practices and behavior. They serve to give direction and identify purposes. They are means for clarifying misconceptions, misunderstandings, and criticisms. They enable one to make discriminating judgments when decisions have to be made on controversial subjects for they furnish facts for alternatives and at the same time consequences of action. They enable one to take an issue out of the realm of the personal and place it on the higher level of the professional good.

The difference between a trade and a profession once again shows the function of principles. Since the professional is guided by principles and has a knowledge of them and the tradesman does not, the professional is in a better position to act in new situations and take a more creative approach to his work. He is more resourceful when his actions are dictated by principles rather than by rules and methods. He further is able to work in a more cooperative manner with other professionals if they share a realm of commonality in the fundamentals of their discipline. Principles provide a better guarantee that practice will arise out of the theory and not just experience alone. Oberteuffer suggests that practice without principle is a headless horseman (7–440).

All true professions operate from principles which are based on scientific facts and no area of work can improve and grow to professional status without these valid and reliable statements of basic beliefs. These beliefs are the guidelines by which the profession is conducted and through which professional practice and behavior are controlled. When data from many sources are generalized and principles formulated as these tend to cluster around an area of concern or a field of endeavor, it marks the emergence of a profession. Those professions which are now moving ahead the most rapidly are doing so because of research and inquiry. Those areas of work which seek professional status must engage in more scientific investigation and philosophical inquiry if their practices are to rest on primary causes and corroborated facts. However, it must be pointed out that the solution to all problems and answers to all questions in education and physical education cannot be found in the scientific process strictly speaking. There are many gaps for which science in its present form cannot be applied. These gaps become the province of philosophy. In its broadest sense, however, even philosophy may be considered a science since it has been defined as the science which investigates the facts and principles of reality. The philosophical process uses the scientific method to reason, reflect, examine, analyze, synthesize, and finally to generalize.

VARIABILITY OF PRINCIPLES

Do principles change? The idealist might insist that truth is truth and it does not change while the realist and pragmatist would insist that truth is relative and will change if the situation or circumstances change. However, as a general rule the statement can be made that principles can change and some do but in general they have a certain amount of permanency (10–150).

Principles based on scientific facts as a result of accumulated data are more universal and thus more readily acceptable as absolutes than principles based on philosophical facts since they are looked upon as more fixed and unchanging. In some instances the particular sciences are so well established that scientific facts derived from them seem immutable and principles based on them will not change unless the facts have originally been erroneously interpreted. However, even in the case of principles based on scientific fact, it is difficult to declare them universal and absolute. This is true because with the new techniques and methodology in science, new truths are formulated based on the discovery of new scientific data. As these truths become validated and are applied, principles may have to change to be consistent with the new evidence.

Principles based on philosophic reasoning as a result of understanding, experience, and insight gained from the social environment are more tentative and are subject to alteration and modification. The data used in their verification are generally of an abstract or subjective nature and are more difficult to validate. Such principles based on experience and insight are less likely to have stability than principles based on scientific facts. The principles based on philosophy are concerned not only with the social heritage of man but also how this heritage relates to economics and politics. Since evolutionary processes are still operable in these areas and since social structures differ from nationality to nationality, less assurance can be placed in the validity of accumulated data from them. Time, place, and new experience in a complex and changing social order nurture an atmosphere where stability is unlikely.

While the nature of man, biologically speaking, is relatively universal and varies little throughout the world, his social and political structures are as unique as nationalities. By the same token, principles emerging from the facts of man's biological nature are relatively permanent for all people everywhere but principles emerging from the facts of political and social structure will differ in proportion to the customs, traditions, and mores of people. Facts from a particular social and political structure are subjected to philosophical inquiry and generalizations are made and emerge as principles. These principles tend to be as unique as the culture and social structures of the nationality that produced them. While customs and tradition along with other aspects of social heritage within a nation change rather slowly, they do change. When they do, principles derived from them will also change and be modified in accordance with the new concepts.

Since political, economic and social concepts are subject to change and to different interpretation, there are no absolutes for principles in this area. However, over long periods of time some concepts have shown themselves to hold up under the demands of both time, place, and social order and are viewed as time-tested, having all the force of principles based on scientific facts. It must be kept in mind, however, that in a rapidly changing world, even these time-honored concepts could become outmoded. Succinctly stated, in spite of the scientist's fear of the absolute and his aversion to immutable facts, and the rapidly changing nature of the social environment, principles should vary but very little over a period of time if they were truly principles in the first place. However, by the same token, man's present world is characterized by an era of accelerating change.

SOURCES OF PRINCIPLES

Physical education is eclectic inasmuch as it draws its principles from many sources (6–129). Its facts and truths come from three main sources: first the basic sciences but principally biology, anatomy, physiology and kinesiology, second from the humanities including history, political science and philosophy and third from man's social heritage including psychology, sociology and anthropology. The first source is founded in man's nature while the second source is from his nurture. The third source cuts across the boundaries of both nature and nurture. Data are collected from all of these sources, scientific method and inquiry and philosophical thinking are applied and facts revealed. These facts involving primary causes and fundamental premises are generalized to form the systematic concepts necessary for shaping conduct and guiding behavior in a profession. After generalizations are drawn from the available data and facts revealed by the data, they are applied. If they prove workable, then principles can be formulated.

These three sources mentioned in the preceding paragraph are not separate and disparate. They are inexorably related and they are classified into the above three areas chiefly for convenience and for better understanding. Man cannot be separated from his environment, and his behavior and actions as an individual always take place in a social setting. Thus, out of an interaction and interrelationship of nature and nurture —psychological and physiological man with the sociological — scientific and philosophical facts are revealed, fundamental premises are made and principles emerge. Barriers between disciplines have been gradually disintegrating. Just as man is no longer looked upon as a dichotomy of mental versus physical and that there is an interrelationship of all his parts, so too is this true with respect to disciplines and the professions with specialities in those disciplines. Evidence of the holistic concept is once again attested to by the fusion of the biological, sociological and psychological thought into principles, carrying with them the idea of the unity of man.

Data from these three general sources are combined to generalize into principles. For any particular question or problem there would need to be a great deal of data available for purposes of tabulation, understanding and then generalization. For most subjects where data are available, they are generally not available in sufficient amounts to the individual professional for him to devise his own principles. Therefore the job of establishing or formulating principles becomes the responsibility of authorities in the field (8–201). These authorities or experts are the theorists and possess the necessary experience, training, and background which qualify them to analyze data, interpret data, synthesize results and draw conclusions from all of these to make universal generalizations. If these individuals are truly authorities, once they have formulated these principles, such generalizations become the basic beliefs in a discipline and an integral part of the professional's domain. All professionals have an obligation and a demanding responsibility to place these principles in operation as a part of their practices as well as their beliefs.

THE APPLICATION OF PRINCIPLES

What should be the relationship between principles of a profession and the professional himself? What is the obligation of the professional with respect to principles which have been formulated for his profession out of scientific and philosophical processes? In other words, should principles of a profession always be applied and adhered to by the professional? In general, these questions can be answered in this manner and there may be two different answers depending on circumstances. When a professional accepts a body of knowledge as being relevant and out of this body of knowledge or facts principles have been formulated, and these principles have been made a part of the fundamental bases on which that profession rests, the professional has a responsibility to observe these fundamental concepts and be guided in his actions by them (11–22). The highly professional person's practices will always coincide with his principles. He does not accept one set of values in theory and suggest that they won't work in practice. The true professional, once having accepted a principle, will be motivated by the challenge of trying to apply it.

Reference in the above paragraph was made to a second answer to the questions presented. Are there times in the career of the professional when he might be tempted to discard a principle when it might appear expedient to take other action? Every professional will face crises in his career when his dedication to his principles and devotion to his profession will be challenged. To compromise his principles may seem to be the only solution to a sticky problem. Are there times when the exigencies of the situation justify the abandonment of principles?

Perhaps there are no absolutes in the answer to this question. However, the true professional will use a principle to guide him in his answer to his own question "Shall I compromise my principles for expediency?" Since these matters are always highly personal, the professional must be very objective in his approach to his answer. He must be aware of the dangers which are inherent in compromising his principles. Such actions may lead to a loss in a personal sense of integrity and a permanent compromising of values. Also, the professional must be cognizant that when he makes a decision to act on expediency rather than principles and justifies his reasons in a manner that seems logical, that he might be rationalizing his actions and that he could be acting from purely personal or selfish motives. Only he can be sure what his real motives are, and he can only be sure if he is fully aware of the pitfalls and dangers of acting on expediency.

When does one desert a principle for expediency? The true professional will always make such decisions on a professional basis rather than a personal one (11–24). If abandoning a principle will ultimately bring an advantage to the profession and society in general, it might be worth the risk. If such abandonment merely results in an advantage for the professional and there is no accompanying advantage for the profession, the compromise is a poor risk. Williams suggests that the professional might compromise a minor principle in order to gain a major one or he might give way on even a major principle now if such compromise might be the means of gaining a greater good for a legitimate cause (11–24). In this case the means would be justified by the ultimate end which might be the greater good of the greater number. Sometimes one accepts a present defeat on application of a principle in the hopes that such action may lead to a later victory.

REFERENCES

1. Bookwalter, Karl W., and Harold J. Vander-Zwaag: *Foundations and Principles of Physical Education.* Philadelphia, W. B. Saunders Company, 1969.
2. Cowell, C. C., and L. F. Wellman: *Philosophy and Principles of Physical Education.* Englewood Cliffs, N.J., Prentice-Hall, Inc., 1963.
3. Davis, E. C., and D. M. Miller: *The Philosophic Process in Physical Education.* Philadelphia, Lea & Febiger, 1967.
4. Educational Policies Commission: *Education and the Spirit of Science.* Washington, D.C., National Education Association, 1966.
5. Nash, Jay B.: *Physical Education: Interpretation and Objectives.* New York, A. S. Barnes & Company, 1948.
6. Nixon, John E., and Ann E. Jewett: *An Introduction to Physical Education.* Philadelphia, W. B. Saunders Company, 1969.
7. Oberteuffer, Delbert, and Celeste Ulrich: *Physical Education.* New York, Harper and Row, 1962.
8. Shephard, N. C.: *Foundations and Principles of Physical Education.* New York, Ronald Press Company, 1960.
9. Shivers, Jay S.: *Principles and Practices of Recreational Services.* New York, The Macmillan Company, 1967.
10. Webster, R. W.: *Philosophy of Physical Education.* Dubuque, Iowa, Wm. C. Brown Company, Publishers, 1965.
11. Williams, J. F.: *The Principles of Physical Education,* 8th Ed. Philadelphia, W. B. Saunders Company, 1965.

PART III

Scientific Bases and Principles

SECTION B
Bases and Principles Related to
Physical Objectives

Chapter 9

Biological and Physiological Bases

INTRODUCTION

In Chapter 3 the objectives of physical education were discussed. The most important concern facing the teacher and coach is the realization of these objectives. If they are to be achieved, they must be understood in their depth and breadth. Each of the listed objectives is surrounded by a body of knowledge and is concerned with a set of principles. Each is a focus around which clusters the concepts, knowledges, and understandings which make that area unique, at the same time expressing unity and relationship with all the other objective areas. Before the physical educator can continue the education cycle effectively —developing the educational process through selecting appropriate activities, methodology, and evaluation techniques —he must understand this body of knowledge and know the principles germane to it. The purpose of the next eight chapters is centered on this problem.

Perhaps the most basic one of these objectives concerns the biological nature of man and more specifically his organic development. While the concept of unity is always paramount in our think-ing and all the objectives are important because of their interrelationships as well as their particular uniqueness, this organic development objective is more concerned with life and with the giving and sustaining of life. This area deals with man's physiology, his health, his fitness and life itself. Knowledge of organic development is founded in the biological sciences—zoology, physiology, anatomy, kinesiology and genetics. Man is first of all a biological organism, and only secondarily a mental and social being. In the order of his origin, the biological was there first and is ever present throughout evolution and is still perhaps more of a key factor in the present than educated and socialized man is generally willing to admit or accept.

It is the intent of this chapter to provide the student with a basic orientation in this area so that he may have an adequate background for other professional courses with the science concept and furthermore to provide him with a better understanding of some features of his biological self.

BIOLOGICAL BASIS OF LIFE

In the process of evolution mentioned in the last section, as one stage or level followed another, in the beginning it was the muscular system that triggered the process in a chain reaction that spanned millions of years. As evolution proceeded from the one-celled organism which first came into being in the Archaeozoic era two billion years ago to multicellular animals with the necessity of moving about in the environment, muscular tissue evolved. The evolutionary scale began its more complex climb with the appearance of the rudimentary muscular elements of the single cell. It was at the point when locomotion became necessary that the process of specialization appeared. As a muscular system became more efficient in locomotion, it became less efficient in its other processes. In response to the needs of the muscular system as it became more specialized, other systems arose to take over special functions of food and oxygen supply and removal of wastes. The nervous system along with the digestive, respiratory, circulatory, and excretory systems were eventually developed.

Thus biologically speaking, man's organic system today is highly related to the muscular system because the muscles came first in the order of things and the other systems came into being in response to the needs of the muscular system. Organically speaking, man can only develop in strength, power and stamina through the action of the muscles. None of these systems are directly under the voluntary control of the mind. While they may be affected by emotions and psychological stresses, the only way they have of developing and being strengthened and maintained outside of nutrition and proper living habits is through the exercise of the voluntary skeletal muscles and particularly the "big muscles" or "fundamental muscles" of the trunk and upper legs and arms.

Thus, exercise is a basic need of life. This need is deeply imbedded in man's biologic nature as well as his attitudes and psychologic urges by the countless ages during which the evolutionary processes operated to make him an active moving being. These needs have existed for millions of years and over the last several thousand there has been relatively little change in the kind and amount needed for growth, development and maintenance. By the same token, it is reasonable to expect no appreciable change for the next few thousand years. Biological evolution took millions of years before primitive man arose and since his arrival, the span in time up to the present represents only a short period. Also, the last century, when man's environment had changed so dramatically from one of hardship and labor to one of automation and ease, represents only a minute part of man's life since primeval times. While man is the most adaptive creature on earth, it seems unlikely, in view of the ages it has taken for biological nature to vary through genetic change, that biological needs will change over such a short period. Thus, man is stuck with his heritage both from the standpoint of his heredity and his environment. He can change neither—only his mode of living in that environment.

The biological basis of life is particularly true with the nervous system. There is this inextricable relationship between the mind and the muscles (see Chapter 16). Movement does not just occur in a vacuum but must be initiated by a stimulus of some sort or by the thought processes. Through action of the muscles, the nerve centers are developed and strengthened. This point will be more fully developed in Chapter 15, but the muscles originally were responsible for bringing the organism into a more varied and richer environment and for furnishing myriads of stimuli which ultimately led to a mind and to the process of perception. Also, it must be pointed out that the fundamental muscle groups mentioned above are phylogenetically older and tougher than are the smaller muscles controlling the hands and the feet. Thus, that part of the nervous system controlling them is older and less complex. It seems to be a law of nature that proper functioning of the fundamental muscles along with the nerve centers which control them is necessary for the later efficient functioning of the accessory muscles and the cortex of the mind.

The mind's development in the earlier years of a child is tied largely to the movements initiated by the muscular system. Phylogenetic development shows that the cortex started to develop in complexity as the finer coordinations of the hands came into use. This fact emphasizes the importance of erect posture and the biped position which left the hands free for manipulation. This later development appeared first in the primates and later on the scale, actions of the hands are thought to be the integrating agent which eventually led to the active and creative mind and eventually the thinking mind (9). Thus, it is as President Kennedy once said, "The relationship between the soundness of the body and the activities of the mind is subtle and complex. Much is not understood. But we do know what the Greeks knew: that intelligence and skill can only function at the peak of their capacity when the body is healthy and strong" (4).

It is now known that this biologic need for exercise is permanent, and while contemporary environments no longer seem to demand exercise for survival, man's nature does. It is becoming increasingly apparent that man's ability to survive and to live at a high level of efficiency and happiness in existing and future environments is dependent upon his ability to fulfill the needs of his biologic heritage. Since his en-

vironment no longer forces him into activity, his sense of values should. He must discipline himself to choose — either to gain this end through his work and his play, or to run the risk of lowered biologic efficiency through inactivity. Man has knowledge of his own evolution and its implication (see Chapter 13). His destiny in life's aspects related to it then is in his own hands. Since he has the knowledge, it now becomes a matter of values as he can choose accordingly.

DISINTEGRATING FACTORS

Many forces are currently at play in our modern society which compound man's difficulty in meeting the needs of his biological heritage. These forces generally constitute in part at least what is known as civilization. Contemporary society in modern civilization is now highly dominated by science, technology and innovations. This is particularly true in the United States where men's lives are directed and dictated by the vast technological changes which have occurred in the last century and especially the last decade. Many of these changes in themselves are not necessarily bad and on the contrary have advanced civilization significantly. They have been largely responsible for a much higher standard of living — in fact the highest standard of living ever known to man — and they hold the promise of still even higher levels probably even beyond man's fondest dreams. However, inherent in these changes are some alarming aspects which have significant implications for man and his biological integrity.

In the future, society must demonstrate not only its desire but also its ability to overcome or adapt to certain disintegrating forces and factors associated with them, if man is to live at that promised level. These forces have in them the potential for destruction. Just as important as the atomic threat which may some day be responsible for man's destruction are some elements within himself which could lead to self-destruction. Some of the disintegrating forces which characterize modern society and which could act adversely on man's biologic nature are discussed below.

Emphasis on Cortical Activity

The social inheritance of man the last few decades has been slanted more and more toward the use of the mental faculties and less and less toward physical activity. It is obvious that social order is predicated more on the use of the mind now in making a living and getting along in the automated and computerized world than on hard physical labor. Society now generally places a higher price tag on mental things. Success criteria are now equated with intellectual pursuits. Because of the explosion of knowledge and the requirements of the space age, both formal education and the public are demanding more time and money for education of the mind. Intellectual achievement now has the highest priority. No one deplores this greater use of the mental faculties, but in the process of using the mind to meet the challenge of an increasingly complex world, man must not ignore his biological heritage. It must never be forgotten that in the processes of evolution the biological preceded the psychological by millions of years. This priority will not change. His need for fitness through movement is just as demanding now as it always has been. It would seem that even these same mental processes which are demanded by an automated and enlightened society are based on biological fitness and if they are to function at the peak of their capacity, they must be based in a fit body. President Kennedy stated, "If we fail to encourage physical development and prowess, we will undermine our capacity for thought . . ." (4).

Sedentarianism

Modern life is characterized by sedentarianism. Since more emphasis is now on the mental aspects and since modern technological know-how has removed the need for much of the physical work, and as the automobile and other modes of travel have revolutionized transportation, unless man chooses to do so, he no longer has to lead an active life. Automation has created a new class of workers who sit at their work for hours each day. The toil and drudgery are gone from much of work, and the golf cart has replaced walking on the links. Much of the action has been taken out of recreation, and many adults as well as youths gain the joys of exercise vicariously through passive recreation and on the TV screen. Sedentarianism is not only prevalent in work but also in living in the home and at school. It could be that unless our ideas regarding the importance of these matters change, irreparable damage will be done. No one would advocate returning to the horse and buggy days even if it were possible, but the problems of sedentarianism must be met from the other end of the line. The forces of the environment will not change except perhaps to be accentuated even more toward sedentarianism. Therefore, the problem must be met from the other end of the continuum. Thus it is incumbent on society to change its attitudes, its sense of values, and its behavior where exercise is concerned.

Mechanization and Automation of Work, Play and Industry

There was a time in history when man could get from his work much of the needed physical exercise that was required for adequate levels of fitness. Since the time of primitive man when he first became a tool user and later a tool maker, much of his waking hours have been spent in overcoming the obstacles of a hostile environment—obstacles to living a safe and comfortable existence. Due to the great changes elicited by the Industrial Revolution in the last century and the advent of the atomic-jet-space-age in the last decade, man has now moved into an era where his work is characterized by a push-button type of existence. He has won the struggle and achieved a soft comfortable existence. Mechanization has replaced his muscles and automation is now rapidly supplementing both his muscles and mental process. The computer reduces thousands of hours of mental work to a few minutes. For the youth under 16 there is no real work any more and even for the adult, hard physical labor is almost a thing of the past. These marvelous changes have brought man into an era which has endless possibilities for living at a level that exceeds all previous expectations.

However, there are some dangers involved that cannot be denied. Technological advances have led to a softer and easier life. In fact, it would sometimes seem the chief purpose of these advances is to create a world of ease where physical work will soon disappear. Moreover, with this softer life has come the temptation to forego the vigorous physical activity so necessary for a healthy body. It is possible for such a society to become one which places such limited requirements on man biologically that in times of freedom from stress and emergencies, those with low physiological capacity can still exist. It may be only during times of challenge and great stress that the individual and nation can recognize this weakness. Then, it could be too late.

Modern Society Places Undue Stress on the Nervous System

Our modern world is characterized by speed, hurry-up-and-wait, noise, along with numerous other tension-producing factors. The twentieth century is truly an age of tensions. The stress placed on the nervous system by the demands of our economic system and devotion to intellectualism can be tremendous. Modern life is characterized by the development of these stresses without providing or requiring the necessary outlets. City and urban life have become so complex that it is the cause of many of these tensions. The situation will grow worse. It has been suggested that this growth in complexity of man's affairs amounts to three percent per year. Both the business man as well as the professional worker is involved in a stepped-up kind of existence where the complexities of his work and interrelationships are severe stresses, placing great strain on both the mental and emotional processes. In the future the professional will have greater demands on his expertise; also this speciality will require a lifetime of education and re-education. However, the large majority of the world's people will not belong to the professions. Modern man lives in an age of competition. His world is a competitive one, but unlike the competitive world of the professional athlete, the physical is not primarily involved.

Biologically speaking, man evolved to live in an environment much more physically oriented than the one he now finds himself in. It is a paradox that in America we have reached the highest level of physical comfort known by man, and thus, should be a nation comparatively free from anxieties, apprehension and feelings of insecurity. However, in spite of being a nation rich in the material blessings, American people are searching for escape in many ways and display a disturbingly high percentage of emotional problems and mental disorders (14–1).

Leisure in Abundance

There was a time when the average man was so busily engaged in earning a living and digging a civilization out of the wilderness that he had very little free time on his hands. Work historically has always been the central requirement of life for the great majority of people. That situation is now changing for a great many people as they experience a degree of leisure heretofore unknown to any culture. Automation is related to leisure since it is through technology that large amounts of time are now available to the average person. The long working day and week have gradually been reduced for most people and the trend is for further reduction. Holidays and vacations are more numerous and of longer duration. The atomic age may bring such freedom as man never before imagined where leisure for most people might well become the core of living rather than the periphery. However, as was pointed out in the previous paragraph, the professional in all too many cases will not share in this abundance of leisure. He will continue to have more and more demands made on his speciality, and if he is true to his service motives, he serves.

Leisure has been defined as time free from work. In this light there are many people who even now have large amounts of free time. They can spend that time either in a constructive way or to the detriment of both themselves and society. Thus, leisure may cause more problems than it solves in the future. Once again it is incumbent on society to make leisure an asset rather than a liability. If some of this leisure could be spent in socially accepted physical activity, the time would be valuably spent both from the standpoint of the individual and the nation, because physical vigor and fitness is one of the most important resources of a nation. Paradoxically once again, our nation seems to have both the leisure and the material wealth to achieve high levels of fitness, but too many people still live on the fringes.

Joy and Self-Expression Have Been Taken from Most Work

The assembly line, a product of automation, is now characteristic of man's work. No longer is there any self-expression and joy of creativity in the finished product when one man's share is a small task repeated over and over many times each day in an air of monotony.

This specialization of work not only is degrading for morale and for interpersonal relationships, but also it fails to provide man with an environment rich in stimuli. Also, the same assembly line takes away the hard labor as well as satisfying skills of work. Perhaps a competence in leisure activity could help to restore both of these. The skills of sports and fitness seem best suited to this purpose. Even the office worker who is destined to sit at his desk all day loses his identity and becomes anonymous in a sea of faces.

Environment No Longer Conducive to Working off the Stress Influences

The pace and frustration of modern living causes an increase in the flow of secretions from glands, especially the adrenals. The adrenal glands are small button-like glands which lie over the kidneys. In emergencies sudden emotions of fear, anger or excitement stimulate them to instant action. As epinephrine is secreted into the blood stream, it triggers the body for action of the extra effort type. Blood pressure drops, the heart beats faster and respiration increases markedly. Historically this increased flow of chemicals in the blood caused by great emotional stress served a useful purpose. It prepared prehistoric man to fight for his life or run to save it. The process increases the capacity of the muscles to perform with more speed, force and endurance. Another physiological reaction to such stress is the increased flow of sugar into the blood stream for extra energy. These phenomena are no doubt associated with survival activities as a part of the evolutionary cycle. In prehistoric man there was always the need for such responses to emergencies as he battled the hostile and demanding environment for survival. In this confrontation his life often depended on these reactions. Either he had to stand and fight for his life or food, or he had to flee. In either event he needed these compounds triggering his extra effort. Under the stress of great emotional reactions of fear or even anger, it is possible that our prehistoric ancestors might have set astounding records in running, jumping and climbing.

Nature discards such behavior very slowly, if at all, even when there no longer appears such frequent use for it. Man's nature is replete with rudimentary remains of useless organs and behavior which infect, dysfunction, and interfere with modern life (2–17). Our social order is such that man's glands are stimulated to dump these potent secretions into the blood stream under great emotional stresses and tensions brought on by the many conflicts in our modern era. However, that same social order does not, in most instances, provide either the opportunity, the motivation, or the social approval for the vigorous actions needed to neutralize the chemicals. Thus, man smothers his day-to-day stresses and is left literally to simmer in the stew he has created for himself. It is nature's way to take care of such products in the blood stream through vigorous exercise of the big-muscle type, or the residue may manifest itself in organic or mental disorders. The principle of fight or flight must be balanced out in modern living with a design of exercise to use up these energy materials and epinephrine. While man's environment has changed, his problems creating pressures and stresses

have not. Modern automotive society has made obsolete the fight or flight philosophy, but it cannot influence the autonomic nervous system's response to stress as part of man's biological legacy. Ulcers, degenerative heart and circulatory disorders, and spastic colons seem to have become a way of life.

High Standards of Living

Never before in the history of any nation has the standard of living for the average person been at the level it is at the present time in this country. With some exception the United States citizen is the best fed, best clothed, and owns more of the luxuries of life than any other people. Modern technology with great mass production has kept pace with the increase in income and a high mass demand. Commodities in vast quantities are now available for the almost insatiable needs and wants of all. Most of these are designed to make life easier, more luxurious, more comfortable, and less vigorous. Thus, modern man lives in an age of materialism where material goods are paramount and standards of living grow each year. This standard of living can create for all men a type of life beyond all imagination. It can be a godsend if used wisely. However, inherent in its very strength lies the potential for weakness and degeneration biologically. Such a standard of living is related to knowledge and mental prowess. Is it unusual then for the processes of education to give first priority to the development of intellectual excellence? To understand modern technology and space problems requires mental prowess. It is not hard to see that a high standard of living tends to make a second-class citizen out of the physical.

BIOLOGICAL WEAKNESSES

As a result of man's heritage, by nature he is equipped to live in one type of environment demanding physical prowess, but finds himself in another which is characterized by the disintegrating forces mentioned in the last unit. There are certain weaknesses which now show up in man and which may in some way reflect these forces. Such biological weaknesses are in no way permanent since they do reflect forces outside of man and presumably he still has the power as well as the know-how to direct his own destiny. Whether he has the will and the desire and the sense of values is left to be seen.

Perhaps there are many facets to his problem of overcoming these disintegrating forces. However, the most significant one is no doubt education. Some weaknesses that are showing up in man now as a result of the disintegrating forces are either caused by these forces or reflect them to certain degrees. These weaknesses are either of a biological nature or have in them the potential to affect biological well-being.

Lack of Physical Fitness and Particularly Motor Fitness

A great deal has been said in recent years about the relative physical unfitness of the nation. There is substantial scientific evidence now to reveal that fitness levels are lower than that considered normal and desirable. Fitness tests administered in the armed forces during World War II showed an alarming lack of strength and fitness among inductees (3) (7). Since these were selected from the most fit group—the 4F classification was not included—the overall picture was perhaps slightly worse.

The first studies on children were made in the fifties and showed a marked inferiority of American children compared with European children (5). More recent research shows some improvement in youth fitness but low levels of fitness are still widespread. The high rate of rejection of draftees, the poor physical condition of those who were accepted together with the lack of fitness in school children and youth reflect man's way of life in America—a way of life that grows "softer" with each new convenience and innovation (see Chapter 10).

Low Skill Levels

The level of sport skill, particularly among youth, while showing some improvement, is disturbingly low. While low skill is not in itself a biological weakness, it is related to it because sports offer one of the best means for obtaining optimum levels of fitness. It goes without saying that if skills are low, it will follow that fitness will be somewhat related.

Again, World War II statistics showed how limited the skill training had been among inductees (7). Until recently more than half of the boys and girls had no physical education program in the high schools (1). With the increase in facilities and improved leadership, this percentage has no doubt risen but the population explosion has placed great strain on both leadership and facilities and many children still have either no programs or poor programs.

Skill level is interrelated with such other aspects as fatigue and safety. The skilled performer is more efficient and gets more rest. Also, he is better able to control the force of his activity and movement and is less subject to injury.

Prevalence of Hypokinetic Diseases

In spite of the fact that medical skill and knowledge along with medical care and the wonder drugs have given a new dimension to life and longevity, the rate of incidence of hypokinetic diseases has increased abruptly. The horizons are being pushed back constantly in revealing new information about these diseases; at times it appears that man is on the threshold of discovering measures of their control. However, there is still much that is shrouded in darkness. Some facts revealed by science stand out clearly by now. The presence of these diseases is frequently related to the kind of life one leads. Heart disease is associated with high levels of cholesterol, while it has been shown that cholesterol may be controlled through proper diet and regular vigorous exercise.

Lack of adequate exercise can lead to debilitating stresses which, in turn, can have both physical and emotional effects. For example, emotional effects of day-to-day living in a pressure environment (technological, innovative and computerized) can best be offset by action of the voluntary muscles. Since these muscles are either directly or indirectly related to such aspects of living as circulation-respiration, metabolism, endocrine imbalance, posture, body mechanics, bone structure, and emotions, lack of sufficient exercise may affect each of these adversely and thus lead to any one of the disabilities known as hypokinetic diseases.

Prevalence of Mental Disorders

All statistics point to the increase in incident of mental and emotional disorders. Such disorders can partly be attributed to the mode of life man is currently leading. While the problem is no doubt many-faceted, at least part of the difficulty might be alleviated by more emphasis on physical activity, along with a wiser use of leisure to offset the strains and stresses of modern living. Vigorous physical activity is needed in youth to strengthen the basal centers of the nervous system. A continuous exercise program is needed throughout adulthood to afford release from tension and stress placed on the emotions and nervous system. The fundamental muscles, when sufficiently exercised, act as a safety valve as they react and respond to stimuli and stresses placed on the emotions and nervous system.

Thus, it would seem that mental and emotional disintegration is concomitant to physical disintegration, and that both are outgrowths of the current trend toward soft living and inactivity.

Malnutrition

In spite of the fact that youth today in America is taller, heavier and healthier than any generation before, there is a certain amount of malnutrition prevalent. Some undernourishment is associated with the poverty growing out of racial discrimination and from technology. Aside from the undernourishment associated with poverty, there is the malnutrition caused by eating the wrong kinds of food even among the affluent. Man by nature is adapted to rough, coarse foods, but now finds himself eating more to please the taste than to meet the needs of this biological heritage. A recent survey shows that the more affluent the stratified level of society, the less likely the diet is balanced. Malnutrition is not always limited to the poverty stricken. As automation and innovation have taken over and characterized our society the last few decades, there has been an accompanying tendency for a more permissive society. Parents particularly have shown this inclination with children. The child and youth does not always eat what is best for him in the light of his heritage. Also, the culture of today is changing the behavior patterns in the home. Fewer home prepared meals are now being served in proportion to those being served outside the home. The franchise quick-order food establishments are rapidly changing the eating habits of people as well as the quality of the food. There is another facet to this problem. Due to overpopulation in some areas of the world and lag in agricultural science, millions of people today go hungry. This problem concerns America as a "have" nation who must share its affluence with the "have nots." However, it has been estimated that unless immediate and drastic action is taken in population control, the population of the world will double in the next 30 years. At that time the world may have to face up to a large-scale famine. When this happens, for the American, the Citadel approach is not possible in our economic system, any more than it now applies to our political and military systems.

Poor Posture and Body Mechanics

First, it might be well to point out at this juncture that man's biological heritage has left him somewhat vulnerable in the area of posture and body mechanics. As man scaled higher and higher on the evolutionary ladder and assumed the biped position, several adverse effects resulted to skeletal and muscular systems, and it was necessary for them to undergo adaptations. Added stress was placed on both the digestive and the circulatory systems as well as the skeletal and some adjustments were made in the evolutionary processes to offset these ill effects. However, incomplete evolutionary adaptations to the biped position have left man with problems which have been accentuated by his mode of life. However, the physical educator must understand that the tendency toward weakness is still there and only through maintaining good posture and the cultivation of proper body mechanics can these effects be minimized. It is obvious that a strong musculature is needed as a framework for good posture and body mechanics. The part played by muscles in maintaining good body position, posture and bone structure cannot be underestimated. The viscera are held in place by good musculature. Good posture not only has a relationship with health, but it also has psychological implications. It is even related to economics. Since good posture has esthetic appeal, one makes a better impression and can thereby impress more people in business and professional life.

GROWTH AND DEVELOPMENT

An important aspect of the organic area has to do with growth and development. Although growth and development in general follow a pattern, there are wide variations and differences within this pattern. While growth is generally viewed as increase in height, weight or size, development has to do more with the functioning of that body mass. Growth, then, represents an increase in mass while development indicates an organization of that mass with respect to its functional abilities. These may go on simultaneously but may also proceed independently of each other.

There are many factors which influence growth. Basically heredity furnishes the frame of reference for lines along which growth and development take place. More will be said concerning this matter in a subsequent unit on genetics. Some characteristics of structure and physical makeup as well as levels of intelligence are results of combinations of genes from the parents. These combinations make up heredity and place limits upon the individual. Important as heredity is in the growth and development of the individual, there are wide limits within which environmental factors may become influential. Perhaps heredity does set the boundaries, but environment and impact of nature dictate how one falls within these limits. Environmental factors which can significantly influence growth and development are: nutrition, climate, outdoor living, fresh air, sunshine, exercise, and rest.

Both heredity and environment provide for great variation in growth. These variations complicate the job of the educator but especially the physical educator. It is obvious that within the variation of heredity, growth and development proceed along many lines. In fact, even within one family there are many physiques and structural differences.

GENETICS

It is important for the physical educator and the professional student to know some genetics. There are some things that are inherent in the life of the individual and cannot be changed significantly. He perhaps needs to know that heredity sets the limits and that he cannot change factors beyond those limits.

Genetics is the branch of the biological sciences which deals with heredity. It teaches that some traits and characteristics, both mental and physical, are passed to the child from the parents. Genetics even tells us the mechanics of this transmission process. In the process of reproduction, the female ovum is fertilized by the male sperm and this fusion produces a *zygote*. Within both the female and male germ cells are myraids of genes which are the clues to the traits and characteristics in heredity. They are the most powerful of all living forces because they control patterns of growth from generation to generation. They are the building stones of life and they provide the variety within the limits of stability needed to preserve the species.

In the process of fertilization of the ovum, there are thousands of male sperm available and the principle of random selection is operative as to which one is finally brought into combination with the ovum. Thus, from thousands of sperm only one is selected through chance. Each of the cells, male and female, carry one-half of the whole of a particular characteristic. In the process of combining, the characteristics emerge as heredity. Every human body is composed of trillions of cells and is a product of repeated cell division from the original zygote as it continues to multiply. Within each cell as it divides are chromosomes and these contain genes. Chromosomes are chainlike structures within the cell and get their name from the absorption of dyes—stains—used to study them. Genes in turn are made of the famous DNA (deoxyribonucleic acid), the determiner of specific traits. Each cell has twenty-three pairs of chromosomes and in cell division the process of *mitosis* produces a replica of each in the two new daughter cells except the terminal sex cells. Sex cells or gametocytes go through a process called *meiosis* in which the gamete contains only one of the chromosomes from a pair. This self-reproduction process of meiosis thus leads to variability in the offspring of any mating pair. Mitosis leads to hereditary stability since its cells reproduce exact replicas of themselves and meiosis leads to variability since it is a matter of chance which traits are passed on to the offspring. It is conceded, however, that science may be on the eve of a new era when "programmed evolution" can take place through gene manipulation. Through selected variables it may become possible in the future to control the sex, physical patterns, and even the intellectual qualities of the embryo during fetal development. In fact, it is not only conceivable but highly probable that manipulation can be carried on outside the human body.

However, while it is true that certain characteristics like the color of the eyes and hair cannot be permanently altered within the limits set by heredity, there are great variations even within the individual. Thus, each individual has the opportunity to develop within the range of his potential, and environmental influences are very powerful even in the physical and mental areas and are the deciding factors in personal and interpersonal relationships. The physical educator must be cognizant of this genetic factor and make alterations in his program in accordance. This would seem to indicate that each teacher must become much more cognizant of the principle of individual differences and be more aware of the diagnostic services which are available now in most schools to individualize his program to a greater extent.

BODY TYPES

The combination of genes even within one family is almost limitless. This great variation in heredity is one of the bases for the principle of individual differences. In the population as a whole the law of chance operates and people in general tend to fall along a curve of normal distribution on all traits. Thus, variation in heredity is followed by variations in body types, and body types follow a continuous distribution. They do not readily quantify themselves into dichotomous or trichotomous schemes for classification.

In general the young follow a rather definite pattern of growth and development. As they pass from one stage to another, no definite prediction can be made about the age level at which the growth processes will occur. In general the first six years of life are characterized by a rapid growth. This period is followed by a slowing down process in the rate of growth during which time, of course, some growth does occur, but the emphasis seems to be on development. This period is followed by another stage of rapid growth sometimes called the "adolescent growth spurt." There is great variation in the chronological age at which this growth spurt starts. It possibly could occur as early as 10 and as late as 15 and it is not unusual for fairly large groups of the same age level to show three-year differential in the time of this growth spurt. Girls are generally about two years ahead of boys in development during this rapid growth age. Following this period there is a tapering-off process until the plateau of maturity is reached. The reaching of this plateau is also variable. Some girls reach this at a very early age. Some boys mature early and reach their maximum weight and height while still in high school whereas some of their classmate peers continue to grow well along into college. See Chapter 17 for growth and developmental characteristics of the various age levels.

The physical educator has always been interested in body physique and body types. One's body type is no doubt influenced primarily by his heredity. However, his physique as we have commonly come to look on it is a result of his way of life and comes as a by-product of exercise, diet and care. One's occupation as well as climate are factors in long-term modification of body type. Both psychologists and physical educators have been concerned with the classification of individuals into types of body builds. The psychologist was perhaps primarily interested in the relationship between body types and personality traits and secondarily in physiological aspects. Sheldon, an anthropologist, sought answers to the question can temperament be predicted by measurement of the body (12). To date, there is no definite relationship found between personality and body build (12–19). Sheldon and others, however, found a persistent low positive correlation between physical structure and both mental and social traits—not high enough to have predictive value but high enough to seem likely that such relationship does exist and might be scientifically determined if other important variables could be controlled (12–19). Sheldon's chief contribution to this area is his photographic technique which permits an individual to be typed with ease.

The physical educator is more concerned with body type because of the necessity to adapt his program to the different needs which might be present because of different body types. Objective evidence has been established to show that body build is related to success in physical activities (8–105). There are several methods of classification for body types. Probably the best known method to the physical educator is the one proposed by Sheldon (11). Patterned somewhat after a method presented by Kretschmer (6), a German psychiatrist, where body builds were classified into the three categories of pyknic (short, thick and rounded figure), athletic (muscular, well-developed and strong), and asthenic (tall, slender and shallow-chested), Sheldon also divided people into three types as follows: endomorph rated as 7–1–1, mesomorph rated as 1–7–1, and ectomorph as 1–1–7 (11). The numbers represent the amount of each component present with 1 the least amount and 7 the most possible. Sheldon found that pure types seldom existed but that people in general did exhibit a body build with predominant features of one specific type. (Sheldon suggests that while somatotypes probably are directly a result of heredity or indirectly because of the influence of heredity on the chemistry and physiology of the body, environmental influences may play a role as well as endocrine function). The three types are listed below with dominant characteristics.

Mesomorph (1–7–1). Mesodermal embryonic layer. Square, hard, and rugged with excellent musculatures, prominent bones, and heavy underlying tissues.

Endomorph (7–1–1). Endodermal embryonic layer. Dominant viscera with roundness and softness.

Ectomorph (1–1–7). Ectodermal embryonic layer. Linear, fragile, and delicate body with slender bones and thin muscles and greater surface area in proportion to mass.

In practice, no one person conforms to any of these three categories. There are 88 somatotypes which have been isolated and recognized for men. There is some evidence to indicate similar types for women. Thus, there are not dichotomies or trichotomies in body types, but rather a sort of continuum where the concept of variation is scaled along a dimensional axis. Also, an aspect of body type known as *dysplasia* is indicative of the disharmony between the several regions of the body proposed by Sheldon (12–7). This simply means that any given individual might have predominately ectomorphic characteristics in one section but perhaps endomorphic or mesomorphic in others.

However, somatotyping has been used very little with men and still less with women. Perhaps it is only in extremes that any great use can be made of this classification procedure in physical education. There is a tendency for people with certain body types to choose particular activities and avoid others. This no doubt stems partly from the fact that some body types are better adapted for success in some activities, and the individual chooses to do those things where his chance for success is greater. For example, the endomorph type would avoid running events in track and field but might choose the weight activities. The ectomorph type would choose the distance runs over the weight events. However, it must be pointed out that the classification into body types is not highly reliable because such factors as chronological age, physiological age, skill, strength and fitness as well as motivation and levels of aspiration can many times offset the disadvantages of body type or physique. The experienced physical educator and coach will know that you can't always select athletes from a group on the basis of the way they look—their body types.

Probably one of the most important jobs of the physical educator is to help students understand the nature of body types and to accept their particular or peculiar heredity for what it is. Like the giraffe and the pig, it is sometimes better to be tall and sometimes short. It is imperative that each individual learn to understand his body type, to accept it as a part of his inheritance, and to gain a measure of happiness with it. It is true, however, that our modern culture looks on the ideal male physique as more the mesomorph type where the shoulders are broad, the hips somewhat narrow and the musculature prominent, strong, and skilled. On the contrary the ideal female in that same culture is somewhat reversed with broad pelvis, narrower shoulders and little evidence of muscles. However, the student must understand once again that there are wide deviations from this norm. Members of each sex exhibit some of the secondary characteristics of the opposite—some a great deal more than others. This bi-sexuality of physique is referred to as *gynandromorphy* and may be independent of somatotype (12–7). The male physical educator will see many evidences of the feminine type among students in his male classes and the female teacher will also see some of her girls with more masculine characteristics in physique. Unfortunately this latter type girl has become identified with athletics, particularly highly competitive athletics and the Olympics. This has been somewhat of a deterrent for the image of girls who are feminine and who do wish to be associated with sports and athletics. Under careful guidance by the trained physical educator the point can be made that the

test of masculinity or femininity is not type of body or physique, or in the case of girls, competence in sports. Hereditary variations in physique may be greater within one sex than are the differences between the sexes (10–82).

A more recent method of classifying body types is the Wetzel Grid (16). This technique divides both boys and girls into nine different body types or physiques. Since this technique is based solely on age, weight and height and provides in addition to physique a number of other important variables, it offers one of the best means of evaluating growth and development.

POSTURE AND BODY MECHANICS

Upright posture and the biped position was an achievement in man's ancestry that cannot be overrated in the process of evolution. The biped position with the subsequent freeing of the front paws to be used in prehensile activities was a preliminary condition to the development of the brain and its mental processes. However, the upright position required great adaptation in both skeletal and muscular structures. Posture underwent modification in three distinct areas in the process of evolving man. The first occurred in the forearm-shoulder and chest areas as modifications became necessary when the hominoids adapted to brachiation (swinging and hanging by the arms). The next change occurred as later hominoids became ground creatures and the pelvis and legs underwent great changes in order to adapt to the standing and walking positions. Perhaps this adaptation was the key that lifted man to his erect two-legged upright position. The pelvic area changed greatly in order to adapt to the vertical position, to form a support for the vertical spine and to provide a foundation for the internal organs. However, the pelvis itself changed its shape and size but little from that of the quadruped. The last significant change occurred in the skull with marked modification in the face, jaw, and the size and shape of the cranium. Also, there had to be a shift in the set of the skull on the spinal column. The evolution of man's skeleton below the head was completed a half million years ago. All changes that have occurred since with some minor exceptions have been in the head area.

Upright posture not only brought about adaptations in man's skeleton but also made necessary some major adjustments in the circulatory, digestive and nervous systems. The vertical position for standing and bipedal locomotion is man's and man's alone. However, for this uniqueness he pays a price. Vertical terrestrial biped position has not only made man more vulnerable to the forces of gravity in the maintaining of balance but also to other possible weaknesses such as poor circulation leading eventually to heart failure, varicose veins, hernia, defective feet, back pains, sinus trouble, excessive curvature of the spine and digestive disorders.

As was pointed out earlier in this chapter, man has made incomplete evolutionary adaptation to the biped position. This has left him vulnerable where good posture is concerned. Cratty has suggested that man may be several thousand years away from accommodating to the upright stance (2–17). While his skeleton has undergone a process of resculpturing, it still leaves him imperfectly balanced. Instead of the line of gravity being at the spine with the organs and remainder of the body distributed around it, the center of gravity is in front of the spine, and this design toward weakness can only be overcome by the muscles and ligaments. Man can overcome his inherent weakness in body mechanics only by developing those muscles that are used in maintaining good body posture — sitting,

standing, walking, running and exercising. Perhaps the keys to this challenge are twofold: the development of strong muscles in the trunk and abdominal areas and an attitude of good posture to insure proper body balance. This attitude is a matter of education and transfer.

Posture and body mechanics are related to physique and body type because the more modern approach to posture emphasizes that there is no one best posture but that there are many postures. Posture becomes an individual matter chiefly because of body types. The guiding factors as to what constitutes good posture are many and varied but all of them are related to body type. Each person must develop a good body posture within the framework of his body build. Good posture is characterized by the best mechanical efficiency, the least interference with organic function, and the greatest freedom from strain (15–4). When these criteria are applied to the framework of specific body type, good posture will be characterized by good balance and proper alignment of the various body segments. However, since there is so much variation in body types, no two people will be identical, and the pattern of posture will always vary slightly in accordance with physique and body type. Thus, posture development comes within the province of the physical educator.

HEALTH

Certainly the organic aspect in its biological setting is highly related to health. Health is discussed at this point in this chapter because it is related to what has been discussed—growth and development and especially body type— and what is to follow in Chapter 10, fitness and how it can be attained and maintained.

Health is defined in the dictionary as freedom from disease. A more searching look into this subject would show that health is more than this. While it is true that freedom from disease, sickness, deformity and malfunction is a part of health, there must be considerably more. Dr. J. F. Williams defines health as "that quality of life which enables one to live most and serve best." (17–13) This definition, though somewhat nebulous and needing explanation, implies that health is more than "wellness" and freedom from disease and malfunction. The implication is that health may be a continuum along a linear scale from near death at one end to optimum health at the other. There is more involved in achieving levels of health than just the physical. The mental, social and spiritual are a part of the unity mosaic as the unitary concept once again enters our thinking. The term optimum health has been used instead of maximum for maximum health is too far beyond the limits of normal expectancy in a demanding and complex society. However, even optimum health is an ideal which is perhaps achieved by only the few. Optimum health or fitness would be that level which would enable the individual to live life to the fullest. It would mean that one could meet the requirements of his vocation with enough energy and strength, and then have enough vitality to meet any avocational interests with zest or any special demands placed on him by emergencies.

As a nation perhaps the United States would rate very high in health status if compared with most other nations. No doubt this high rank is due to many factors—a high standard of living, better medical service, better education for the masses and the like. However, as was pointed out earlier in this chapter, there are some alarming danger signals and to back them up some revealing statistics as supportive evidence to show that levels of health are not as high as the

potential might promise. It is increasingly apparent that a great need exists for more to be done in the way of providing for adequate medical care along with better education for the masses. One of the serious weaknesses in the armor of this goal toward optimum health for all is that people don't do and practice the things they know or should know in an educated affluent society. It is no longer infectious diseases and epidemics that cause the majority of illness, other health problems, and death now as much as it is disorders which are related to the way of life brought on by modern living. It is a paradox that in modern society success seems to be achieved through these factors which are proving so detrimental to biologic and psychological health—affluence in a society already with a high standard of living, industrialization, automation, urbanization, sedentarianism with the rise of professions and demand for white-collar workers, and a life where physical ease and comfort is a primary goal.

The evidence points to the fact that there must be some escape from the dilemma of a modern technological culture and these social forces mentioned above. Perhaps the answer lies somewhere in the study of etiology (science of the causes of diseases) which inevitably reverts to human ecology; since human ecology concerns itself with the relation of man to his environment and to each other. Man is only now becoming acutely aware of his needs ecologically and as polluted land, air and water become more prevalent, this may well become one of his major challenges of the future. Health is a result of both heredity and environment. Someone has said that one's chance for living to be a ripe old age is to choose the right ancestors. There is apparently much truth in this adage. As has been pointed out, health is related to body type and body type is primarily an inherited character-istic. Also a study of genetics reveals that weaknesses of the parents are some-times passed on to the offspring and even compounded in some instances. These weaknesses are either like nervous and mental disorders and abnormalities, or they are weaknesses which tend to make one more susceptible to disease and thus are indirectly causative to health problems. No doubt much will be discovered in the future concerning the etiology of familial diseases and per-haps some control may be established to a certain degree over heredity where health is concerned. However, it is es-sential that efforts be centered now on environmental influences and recogni-tion given to the fact that the etiology is a multi-faceted problem where both heredity and environment play a role. Some dramatic work has been done in the control of hereditary factors in lower forms of life by geneticists. The frontier is now open for genetic engineering in animals. It is only a matter of time until someone tinkers with the birth of man. However, this is a frontier of the future, and while it is an exciting possibility and offers an intriguing po-tential, at the same time it has its grimmer side. It could presage both a moral as well as a social confrontation in addition to having great political impli-cations. It might be possible at some point in the future for some nation, through manipulating the genetic code, to produce a super race and take control of the world and space beyond. Society must decide this issue of human manipu-lation in genetics. If man is already the greatest of the world's wonders, is there not danger in upsetting the throw of the genetic dice in his heritage?

6

REFERENCES

1. AAHPER: President's Conference on Fit-ness of American Youth. Journal of Health, Physical Education and Recrea-tion, Vol. 27, No. 6, Sept., 1956, p. 9.
2. Cratty, Bryant, Jr.: *Movement Behavior and Motor Learning*, 2nd Ed., Philadelphia, Lea & Febiger, 1969.
3. Karpovich, P. V., and R. A. Weiss: Physical Fitness of Men Entering the Army Air Force. Research Quarterly, Vol. 17, No. 3, Oct., 1946, p. 186.
4. Kennedy, J. F.: The Soft American. Sports Illustrated, Vol. 13, No. 126, Dec., 1960, pp. 15–23.
5. Kraus, H., and R. Hirschland: Minimum Muscular Fitness Tests in School Chil-dren. Research Quarterly, Vol. 25, No. 2, May, 1954, p. 178.
6. Kretschmer, E.: *Korperbau and Character*. Berlin, Springer, 1921.
7. Larson, L. A.: Some Findings Resulting from the Army Air Force Physical Training Program. Vol. 17, No. 2, May, 1946, pp. 144–146.
8. Larson, L. A., and R. D. Yocom: *Measure-ment and Evaluation in Physical, Health, and Recreation Education*. St. Louis, C. V. Mosby Company, 1951.
9. Nash, J. B.: Those Hands. Quest, II. Monograph no. 2, April, 1964, pp. 53–59.
10. Oberteuffer, D., and C. Ulrich: *Physical Education*. New York, Harper and Row, 1962, p. 82.
11. Sheldon, W. H.: *Atlas of Men*. New York, Harper and Bros., 1954.
12. Sheldon, W. H.: *The Varieties of Human Physiques*. New York, Hafner Publish-ing Company, 1963.
13. Ulrich, C.: *The Social Matrix of Physical Education*. Englewood Cliffs, Prentice-Hall, Inc., 1968.
14. Ward, Judson C.: Where Does "The Phys-ical" Fit into Education. *Educational Comment*. Toledo, College of Education, University of Toledo, 1961.
15. Wells, K. F.: *Posture Exercise Handbook*. New York, Ronald Press Company, 1963.
16. Wetzel, N. C.: Grid for Evaluating Fitness. Cleveland, NEA Services, 1948.
17. Williams, J. F.: *Personal Hygiene Applied*, 9th Ed. Philadelphia, W. B. Saunders Company, 1950.

Chapter 10

Principles Concerning Fitness

INTRODUCTION

Fundamental to success in education or any facet of living for that matter is good health, and this cannot be achieved in youth unless growth and development take place in an acceptable manner. Under any hypothesis, a sound fit body is necessary for the school child to achieve his full educational potential. Unless he has the capacity to develop his physique in strength and fitness within the limits set by heredity, few, if any, of the objectives of education as well as physical education can be attained. While fitness is not synonymous with health, it certainly plays an essential role in all aspects of health. Health and fitness are inexorably related. Good health provides a solid foundation on which fitness rests and at the same time fitness provides one of the most important keys to health and living one's life to the fullest. Freedom from disease, organic development, efficient movement, alertness of mind, and emotional adjustment provide the framework of fitness. It has been said that fitness not only adds years to one's life, but life to one's years. Thus, fitness is not a state for the young; it is for all ages.

Fitness is a product of exercise, and exercise and training have been shown through research to possess important implications in the general health of people. However, fitness is more than a product of exercise. While exercise is necessary to obtain and maintain fitness, there is more involved than mere physical activity. Proper nutrition, adequate rest, relaxation, health appraisal, and good health habits are all facets of implementation. Also, just as in the case of good health, heredity probably sets the upper limits which one can achieve through his health practices and exercise habits.

Because of this bridge between health and fitness, there has been a renewed interest in fitness and a resurgence of effort toward attaining and maintaining it. Too often, however, when fitness is thought of at all, it is viewed within its narrower context of the physical—a sort of cult of muscle. More knowledgeable people, physical educators and medical people particularly, now talk about total fitness. Total fitness is a third dimension of fitness viewed as the capacity to function in every way at one's best. A new concept of well-being is included that involves the mental and social as well as the physical. Perhaps this idea of total fitness makes sense for several reasons. Most importantly, of course, one is reminded as always of the unity concept of man where he exists and functions as a whole. Physical fitness is but one aspect of total fitness with the other parts of the whole forming a cluster of many interrelated qualities. Thus, when total fitness is used in its modern context, it includes the emotional, social and mental as well as the physical components. While these will differ in importance depending on the situation and the circumstances, all components play a significant role in living a full life throughout life.

Fitness is no doubt a relative matter depending on the individual. Yet there are commonalities applicable to all. Certainly no simple set of standards could apply to all people. The continuity of life's processes is constantly changing as well as the demands of an ever-changing environment interacting with those on-going life processes. Thus, there is probably an optimum level of fitness for each individual dependent upon his age, sex, body type, vocation, and avocation. As one grows older or changes vocations there is a shift in the needs and emphasis for fitness. The 20-year-old needs a different type of fitness than the 40-year-old and the longshoreman has needs different from the white-collar worker. The football player needs a different degree of fitness than the cross-country runner, and the Sunday golfer has needs which are different from either of them. Women and men of the same age may have different requirements because of sex differences just as the ectomorph and the endomorph. Thus, fitness is somewhat hard to pin down and becomes a bit on the elusive side when one thinks in terms of "fitness for what?" However, when purposes are spelled out and other facets are taken into consideration, fitness becomes a bit easier to define.

DEFINITION OF FITNESS

The American Association for Health, Physical Education and Recreation defines total fitness as:

> . . . that state which characterizes the degree to which the person is able to function. Fitness is an individual matter. It implies the ability of each person to live most effectively with his potential. Ability to function depends upon the physical, mental, emotional, social, and spiritual components of fitness, all of which are related to each other and are mutually interdependent (1).

COMPONENTS OF FITNESS

The American Association for Health, Physical Education and Recreation also presented the following list of interdependent attributes or components of total fitness (1).

1. Optimum organic health consistent with heredity and the application of present health knowledge.
2. Sufficient coordination, strength, and vitality to meet emergencies, as well as the requirements of daily living.
3. Emotional stability to meet stresses and strains of modern life.
4. Special consciousness and adaptability with respect to the requirements of all of life.
5. Sufficient knowledge and insight to make suitable decisions and arrive at feasible solutions to problems.
6. Attitudes, values, and skills which stimulate satisfactory participation in full range of daily activities.
7. Spiritual and moral qualities which contribute to the fullest measure of living in a democratic society.

TYPES OF FITNESS

Total Fitness

In the definition and the components presented above, reference is being made to "total fitness" and concerns not only the individual's ability to survive in his environment but also his capacity to do this in an effective manner. Total fitness would imply that in addition to demonstrating acceptable degrees of performance in physical attributes, that the individual must also demonstrate social adaptability, emotional stability, mental efficiency and perhaps even positive moral and spiritual qualities as well as cultural.

Physical Fitness

When the idea of a constellation of aspects into a unity mosaic is analyzed, physical fitness becomes a limited phase of the totality. However, under any hypothesis, it becomes an important aspect; but from the standpoint of the physical educator, it no doubt assumes a dominant role. It is not that the modern mature physical educator is a follower of the cult of muscles necessarily, but rather that the contribution he can make to the cluster of qualities is largely done through the physical aspects of motor performance. Let it never be forgotten that the physical is his special field to plow and that he is uniquely alone in this quest while many other areas share the other aspects of the fitness cluster. Thus, physical fitness is a means to an end and is not an end in itself. The end sought through physical fitness is the good of the total individual.

Cureton has divided physical fitness into three aspects: (1) physique, (2) organic efficiency and (3) motor efficiency (9–19). The points concerning physiques have been covered somewhat in Chapter 9 in the unit on body types. However, for clarity the characteristics of the *physique* aspect as listed by Cureton are shown below (9–19):

1. Health and robust appearance.
2. Muscular development strongly in evidence.
3. Good posture with appearance of ease, alertness, and poise.
4. Good proportions of bone, muscle, fat quotas.

5. Normal bones, joints and muscles.
6. Good size for age and sex.

The second aspect, *organic condition*, has the following characteristics listed (9–19):

1. Normal sense organs—sight, hearing, smell, taste, feeling.
2. Fit heart and circulatory system with marked resistance to cardiovascular fatigue.
3. Fit glands of internal secretion and blood.
4. Fit digestive system and good teeth.
5. Fit muscular system in development and tone.
6. Fit nervous system for rhythmic alternation of abundant energy and relaxation.
7. Normal sexual vigor and vitality.
8. Normal excretory and evacuation systems.

The third aspect of fitness is *motor fitness* and Cureton lists four specific points (9–20):

1. At least average capacity in a wide variety of fundamental motor activities—balance, flexibility, agility, strength, power, and endurance activities.
2. Sufficient swimming ability to save a life.
3. At least average skill in basic skills of running, jumping, climbing, crawling, throwing.
4. Some specialized skills for adult social recreation: golf, tennis, swimming, archery, ping pong, bowling, shooting, riding, cycling, skating, skiing, etc.

Motor Fitness

The physical educator understands the term *motor fitness* a bit more clearly because it is more limited in scope and loses some of the elusiveness of physical or total fitness. *Motor Fitness* has been defined as "a readiness or preparedness for performance with special regard for big muscle activity without undue fatigue" (5–125). It includes the capacity of the individual to move efficiently and with strength and force over a reasonable length of time. While motor fitness is only a limited phase of physical fitness and does not include in its meaning many of the factors listed by Cureton in part two above, nevertheless it does reflect them to a high degree. It is highly related to total fitness in the same manner. This view is consistent with the idea that each individual is an integer and cannot be separated into divisible parts for development.

Motor fitness is generally judged by performance, and this performance is based on a composite of many factors. It is these factors which most fitness tests attempt to measure, and therefore such tests are actually motor fitness tests. The following list of factors has generally been conceded as being the most commonly mentioned components of motor fitness: strength, endurance, power, speed, agility, balance, flexibility, and stamina. These factors are discussed and defined in some detail in Chapter 11.

HISTORY OF FITNESS

Fitness, in essence if not in name, has always been a concern of man. Physical prowess from prehistoric times down through history has been equated with survival and power. Primitive man was fit or he perished. This quality was present in Sparta and Athens during the golden era of Greek history and again in the early centuries of the Roman Empire. Down through the centuries—the Middle Ages, the Renaissance, the Reformation and later—it has been emphasized in such historic activities and philosophies as chivalry, humanism, naturalism, nationalism, Nazism and the like. Few formalized programs were devised until the late eighteenth century. From this point on there has been a constant interest in physical efficiency, and the threads of contribution from many individuals and nations have led to a world-wide concern and interest in the concept. In America the emphasis has always shifted toward this physical ability during times of war and great national emergencies. However, once peace was restored, interest waned. World War II created a demanding need for fitness in the military as shown by studies listed in the last chapter (Chapter 9). The Army's position in general was that schools and colleges should place more emphasis on this aspect in their programs. In turn, the armed forces themselves were forced to develop their own crash fitness programs including measurement. However, after the war was over and peace declared, the emphasis on fitness that had been created during the war once again dropped from sight.

While physical education programs and accomplishments were not at a standstill during these postwar years, apparently the fitness aspects of the programs were being somewhat neglected. The first public awareness of this fact came about through the Kraus-Hirschland study. This report entitled "Minimum Muscular Fitness Tests in School Children" was published in 1953. While it did not immediately flame the fires of public interest, it was the catalyst that eventually led to national concern (13). In brief, the report concerned a study made with the Kraus-Weber tests, a six-item battery designed to measure strength and flexibility of the trunk and leg muscles. The subjects were several thousand American boys and girls age 6 to 19 and a comparable number of European children from Austria, Italy and Switzerland. The results revealed that almost 58 percent of the American children failed one or more of these test items, whereas only 9 percent of their European counterparts failed. Somewhat later this report reached the desk of Dwight D. Eisenhower, President of the United States. The results of this study and their implications were made known to the President by Senator John B. Kelley, Sr., who was a staunch supporter of physical vigor. Eisenhower was alarmed and immediately showed his concern for this apparent weakness in American citizens. From this point on the fitness crusade began to gather momentum. It continued during the latter half of the 1950's and reached a peak of interest and involvement in the early 1960's. The federal government has continued to help focus national attention on the need for individual and national fitness and programs for implementation.

The Kraus-Weber test itself is a somewhat controversial testing instrument, and the conclusions drawn based on the percentages of American and European children who failed test items have been interpreted in many ways. In general, physical educators tended to look with skepticism on the validity of these conclusions and interpretations. Whether all of this negativism was academic and a result of scientific interest or an over-sensitivity to the inferences being drawn about failures of physical education programs to achieve success in their unique bailiwick—the physical and its well-being—is not quite clear. Be that as it may the fitness movement was under way and whether the Kraus-Weber test is an inadequate measure of fitness or not does not alter the fact that it was the catalyst that started it. There has been nothing in the field of physical education to compare with the promotion and publicity through the various communication media that has been received other than sports on the sports pages. In radio, television, newspapers, magazines and various other public relations media the fitness crusade received wide support for over a decade.

Many individuals, groups and agencies have shared in the vast amount of promotion, planning, and implementation of fitness. However, there are three agencies which have been largely respon-

sible for the consistent work over a period of time. These are the American Association for Health, Physical Education, and Recreation, the President's Council on Physical Fitness, and the American Medical Association. The AMA has given the movement prestige and an adequate medical and scientific basis; the President's Council on Physical Fitness has lent outstanding service in prestige and promotion, and the AAHPER has borne the brunt of the work in planning, implementing, and creating programs and attitudes in youth as well as doing its share in promotion.

Perhaps the one individual who did most to further the interest and public concern in fitness was President John F. Kennedy. Even before his inauguration in January 1961 Kennedy had written an article for publication in *Sports Illustrated* entitled "The Soft American" (11). In another article, again written under his byline in a 1962 issue of *Sports Illustrated* (12), the President reiterated the need of physical fitness for national strength and gave a progress report on the involvement of the federal government in promoting fitness. Kennedy continued to support the cause through speeches, spot announcements and many other ways.

The AAHPER has been concerned about fitness since the inception of its predecessor, The American Association for the Advancement of Physical Education in 1885. Early leaders who were prominent in the promotion of physical ability and efficiency were Drs. Sargent, Hitchcock and Anderson (see Chapter 4 on History). However, due chiefly to the philosophy of Hetherington, Williams and Nash (see Chapter 4), the pendulum swung away from this aspect of the program and slanted more toward the natural program based on sports, games and related activities. While many of these games can, under suitable conditions, develop certain levels of fitness, many of them are just not that vigorous, and besides too many school programs which emphasized sports were too poorly organized and taught for the overcrowded sports classes to be active enough in developing fitness.

Thus, it was the Kraus-Weber tests and the subsequent Kraus-Hirschland research report with its implications regarding the physical fitness status of American and European youth that resulted in a chain reaction of events leading to the fitness movement. A National Conference on Physical Fitness, called by President Dwight D. Eisenhower and directed by Vice-President Richard Nixon, was held at the United States Naval Academy in July 1956. Out of this conference evolved the President's Council on Youth Fitness and a President's Citizens Advisory Committee. Shane McCarthy became the first executive director of the President's Council and gave effective support to the promotional aspects of fitness throughout the country. Individual states got into the act by calling governors' conferences on fitness and appointing fitness committees, councils, or commissions. Organizations such as the National Collegiate Athletic Association and the National Association of Intercollegiate Athletics became active in support of the cause. During this particular era a great deal of attention was given to the concept of total fitness which not only emphasized the physical aspect but also the mental, social and spiritual. It is probable that the totalitarian concept resulted in a somewhat nebulous approach to the implementation of specific programs in these early years. Also, while President Eisenhower was the instigator of the nationwide approach, he did not express the personal involvement and concern that was needed to create wide national interest and support.

However, when John F. Kennedy became president in 1961, his unflagging interest and zeal for the national welfare made fitness a popular topic. Kennedy not only had a burning personal interest in fitness but he was cognizant of the importance of fitness to the welfare of all citizens. Charles "Bud" Wilkinson, highly successful football coach at the University of Oklahoma, was appointed as special consultant to the president with the charge to formulate a youth fitness program at the national level. Wilkinson reorganized the President's Council on Youth Fitness, and the Council working in cooperation with many agencies and governmental units and especially the American Association for Health, Physical Education and Recreation accomplished some notable achievements. In February, almost immediately after his inauguration, President Kennedy called a National Conference of Physical Fitness of Youth. The conference was structured to find answers to these two questions: first, how could the federal government best support programs of youth fitness? Second, how should the federal government work in cooperation with state and local governments in the promotion of fitness?

Under the direction of Wilkinson and later Stan Musial and James Lovell, the President's Council has evolved into an agency with a broader base. It became the President's Council on Physical Fitness in 1964 in order to meet the needs of fitness for all ages, and in 1968 it became the President's Council on Physical Fitness and Sports. The addition of sports no doubt reflects the interest and concern of the sports people and particularly the Lifetime Sports Foundation. The Council has carried on a vigorous program of promotion and interpretation of fitness through all communication media. It has sponsored clinics, encouraged and participated in research, promoted legislation, provided large quantities of films and educational aids and in general has been an effective promoter of fitness and has made an outstanding contribution to the fitness programs in America. Since all of its early involvement and much of its later work has been done for the fitness of youth, the Council has worked within the framework of the schools and has collaborated with the AAHPER. Several of its publications have been used extensively in the school and recreation programs. These include "Youth Physical Fitness—Suggested Elements of a School Centered Program" (15), "Physical Fitness Elements in Recreation—Suggestions for Community Programs" (17) and "Adult Physical Fitness" (16).

In the Council's "Youth Physical Fitness—Suggested Elements of a School Centered Program" the following recommendations were made:

1. Identify the physically undeveloped pupil and work with him to improve his capacity.

2. Provide a minimum of fifteen minutes of vigorous activity every day for all pupils.

3. Use valid tests to determine pupils' physical abilities and evaluate their progress.

Perhaps it was a matter of semantics in the recommendation but number two above led to some misunderstanding on the part of administrators who interpreted the "minimum of fifteen minutes" to be a recommended length of the physical education period. The idea behind the recommendation of course was to insure that each student receives at least fifteen minutes of vigorous activity as a part of the total period. This recommendation was aimed at the programs where most of the students stood around for most of the period.

The American Association for Health, Physical Education and Recreation has given outstanding leadership not only to the promotion of fitness but also in helping to plan and to implement programs. In September 1956, the AAHPER

Fitness Conference was held in Washington, D.C. Statements of philosophy and position were prepared and foundations laid for future implementation. In 1958 the AAHPER Fitness Testing Project under the direction of Paul Hunsicker developed the AAHPER Youth Fitness Test (3). These seven test items have been administered to literally millions of students not only in America but also in foreign countries. In 1958 when these tests were administered to several thousand British boys and girls, these children scored significantly superior to their American counterparts in practically all test items. The results of these comparisons seem to bear out in part at least the findings of the Kraus-Hirschland Study.

In 1965 Hunsicker and Reiff (10) conducted a restudy using similar techniques to the first study and established new norms for the test items along with some minor revisions of the test battery. Results of this study showed that both boys and girls in America had made significant gains in fitness levels since 1958. As a part of the testing project the AAHPER has developed an elaborate award system which has been adopted by many schools and which serves as a motivator of students to greater efforts.

The AAHPER Test Project became a part of OPERATION FITNESS—USA, a symbol and a medium for fitness created by the AAHPER and the NEA. OPERATION FITNESS served in many ways other than measurement and program materials. It became a catalyst of ideas and a service center for projects and suggestions for fitness programs. Many of the projects initiated by OPERATION FITNESS—USA were implemented and completed during the 1960's. However, some are just reaching the fruition stage. The Sports Skill Test Project under a team of test makers headed by Frank Sills now has presented skill tests for a number of sports for both boys and girls including basketball, football, softball, volleyball, and archery. A Sports Knowledge Test Project, coordinated by Dorothy Mohr, took a different turn and finally led to one of the most significant developments in the field. The Mohr Committee concluded that no knowledge test could be valid until there existed a recognized body of knowledge commonly accepted by members of the profession. The committee changed its tack and developed "Knowledge and Understanding in Physical Education" which now serves as the basis for the body of knowledge (2). A knowledge test has been developed over these materials under the direction of the Educational Testing Service (ETS). These are only a few of the many highlights of OPERATION FITNESS—USA. Others involved tennis, track and field, K–4 project, and numerous publications, brochures, films, and clinics, meetings and conferences of many types.

Perhaps one of the most significant contributions to the cause of fitness has come from the AMA. This prestigious professional association has given active support to the fitness movement in numerous ways. The most important are statements for the public benefit promoting fitness and several joint publications with the AAHPER and other agencies including "Exercise and Fitness" (4). Many individual members of the AMA have given avid support to the cause. Perhaps the best known is the famous heart specialist Paul Dudley White, who has been unflagging in his promotion of the part fitness can play in personal health.

In 1960 the House of Delegates of the AMA passed the following resolution and reaffirmed it again in 1969:

School and College Physical Education

WHEREAS, The medical profession has helped to pioneer physical education in our schools and colleges and thereafter has encouraged and supported sound programs in this field; and

WHEREAS, There is increasing evidence that proper exercise is a significant factor in the maintenance of health and the prevention of degenerative diseases; and

WHEREAS, Advancing automation has reduced the amount of physical activity in daily living, although the need for exercise to foster proper development of our young people remains constant; and

WHEREAS, There is a growing need for the development of physical skills that can be applied throughout life in the constructive and wholesome use of leisure time; and

WHEREAS, In an age of mounting tensions, enjoyable physical activity can be helpful in the relief of stress and strain, and consequently in preserving mental health; there be it

Resolved, That the American Medical Association through its various divisions and departments and its constituent and component medical societies do everything feasible to encourage effective instruction in physical education for all students in our schools and colleges.

Other groups that have made major contributions in fitness are: The American College of Sports Medicine, the Lifetime Sports Foundation and the Athletic Institute. Of these three groups perhaps the American College of Sports Medicine has contributed most to the cause of fitness. It is an affiliate of AAHPER. Among its purposes is involvement in research into the scientific aspects of sports and related activities and their relationship with fitness. The Lifetime Sports Foundation, which incidentally is a private foundation, funded a special project of AAHPER—the Lifetime Sports Education Project. Fitness has been promoted through this project by promoting participation in sports of the carry-over type like golf, tennis, bowling, and archery. The Athletic Institute contributes to fitness indirectly by emphasizing sports and recreational activities through many approaches including films.

Fitness has not only become a national

concern of this country but has become of worldwide interest. Fitness is a universal need just as biological heritage is universal in nature. Many countries around the world are interested in fitness on their own initiative while others seem to have been motivated by the fitness movement in America. There are many international organizations and groups which either influence fitness directly or indirectly. These groups include sports, recreation, health, physical education, sports medicine, and research and in one way or another have made contributions to the cause of fitness.

If nations will but look to history, they can find some of the answers concerning both individual and national fitness. One of the great lessons from the past is that historians have been able to trace the rise and fall of nations by what people have done about fitness in their leisure. The English historian Toynbee wrote that of the 21 great civilizations of the past, 19 of them fell because of the physical and moral decay from within. Therefore, it is hoped that the promotion of fitness becomes a basic and continuing policy of the United States government. President John F. Kennedy stated this issue clearly in his belief that "the physical fitness of our citizens is a vital prerequisite to America's realization of its full potential as a nation and to the opportunity of each individual citizen to make full and fruitful use of his capacities." (11)

America is a land of paradoxes where fitness is concerned. It presents the picture of a nation which has enough leisure and the material wealth to use it wisely. Yet it is a nation which finds itself physically unfit. Too many people confuse issues. The fact that our youth are taller and heavier than any other generation is not a reflection of their fitness status. In a nation that has the best medical facilities and know-how, there is the highest rate of deaths from heart attacks and related causes. Another paradox equally alarming concerns its culture. As a nation it has scaled the highest peak of physical comfort known to man, yet it is a nation with the highest percentage of mental diseases and emotional disturbances in the world (19).

Historically, then, fitness has assumed an important role in the scale of events. Scientists have expounded the necessity for exercise. Historians have written about the lack of it in those nations which fell. Educators request more time be given to fitness activities in the school programs. Politicians have demanded it as a measure for national survival. Ministers have even preached about it from the pulpits. Poets have written about the want of it. Many years ago before the age of automation had taken its toll, Rudyard Kipling wrote these words which so aptly express the issue of national fitness:

> Nations have passed away and left no traces
> And history gives the naked cause of it—
> One single, simple reason in all cases,
> They fell because their people were not fit.
>
> Nothing on earth—no Arts, no Gifts, nor Graces—
> No Fame, no Wealth—outweighs the want of it.
> This is the Law which every law embraces—
> Be fit—be fit! In mind and body be fit!
>
> This is the lesson at all Times and Places—
> One changeless Truth on all things changing writ
> For boys and girls, men, women, nations, races,
> Be fit—be fit! And once again—Be fit!
>
> —Rudyard Kipling

BENEFITS OF EXERCISE AND TRAINING

The student should by now understand that fitness is not conferred on one by immunization or heredity, or through some process of sorcery. Physiological fitness can be attained only through exercise.

Until recently there were only two times when the average person seemed interested in fitness. These were in athletic competition where winning is important and during times of war when survival is at stake. In general women are somewhat more concerned about some aspects of fitness since most of them are style-conscious and are interested in a streamlined figure. In spite of this feeling, however, few of them are engaging in an all-out war on obesity and flabbiness. However, there is another group who is becoming interested in fitness. This is the fast growing numbers who have become aware of the needs and benefits that can accrue from training. Many of them are literally running or training for their lives on doctors' orders. These are the people who know the "Why's" and "How's" of training and fitness. These knowledges and understandings include the benefits of exercise and training to the individual.

Man is essentially a lazy animal more prone to do what he wants to do today which gives him pleasure while ignoring the vigorous activity which holds promise of rewards to him tomorrow. He may have good intentions but puts off until "tomorrow" the exercise program he should be doing today. He may start his program of activity only to become discouraged because he does not seem to be making any short-term progress. It is true that in becoming fit a person who begins with a low level of fitness will require hard work over a long period of time before he can show any clear-cut superiority over those who have procrastinated and have never exercised. Also, young people tend to ignore the call for higher fitness levels because they have difficulty compromising with middle and old age. In fact, when one is young, he thinks he will live forever.

The individual who aspires for higher fitness levels must work hard physically and apply the overload principle. He must work hard and perhaps sweat some and do this regularly for a long period of time. Once he has acquired a state of optimum fitness, he must continue to exercise if he is to maintain that level. Fitness cannot be stored. Failure to continue exercise will lead to deterioration and a reversal of all the benefits that accrued as a result of that exercise. This will be discussed in the succeeding paragraphs.

Endurance is lost more rapidly than strength, and strength and endurance are lost more rapidly than the skill which also comes as one of the by-products of participation.

The changes brought on by exercise training are of two types. Some of them are considered *immediate* effects and occur in most all strenuous exercise for either the trained or untrained individual. The other set of effects occur gradually and over a long period of time and are called *chronic* effects. However, it is true that in the trained individual the immediate effects eventually terminate into chronic effects since with regular exercise the short-term effects become more efficient thereby making them chronic in nature. Perhaps these benefits can be categorized by body systems to facilitate understanding. However, the student must keep in mind again that these benefits are related to the unity concept, and that they imply interrelationships as opposed to dichotomies.

In discussing the "benefits" of exercise in the next few paragraphs, exercise is assumed to mean regular, vigorous activity which places demands on the heart and circulatory systems. Also, it must be clearly understood that there is no claim that exercise can provide immunity from communicable and infectious diseases, nor can it alone entirely offset the effects of other disintegrating forces of the environment.

Benefits of Exercise to the Heart and Circulatory System

The key to physiological fitness is the heart and circulatory systems, sometimes referred to as the cardiovascular system. This combined system is the sustainer of movement by the muscles. The key to this system's well-being is exercise. The cardiovascular system is the body's vital transport system. It transports the necessary food materials and oxygen to the cells and serves as the garbage collector removing waste products from the cells and transporting them to the elimination centers. The blood serves as a carrier through which materials are moved through the network of arteries, veins and capillaries. The force which keeps the system running is the heart. The heart is a pump vital to the efficient performance of all other systems in the body. It is a muscle not too unlike other muscles of the body except it is the strongest and most efficient. It has great powers of endurance and operates under a wide margin of safety. The healthy heart cannot be injured through exercise, and it is highly resistant to strain.

Just as the heart is the key to the well-being of other systems, the muscular system is the key to the well-being of the heart. Since the heart is a muscle, and muscles are meant to be used, the heart too must be used. Like any muscle, it is subject to the laws of use and disuse. The more it is used, the more efficient it becomes. The less it is used, in a sense, the more stress is placed on it. It must be taxed beyond the ordinary needs of day-to-day living in a modern society. However, the heart cannot be exercised directly; the only way it can be challenged beyond normal limits is through the voluntary muscles—particularly the skeletal muscles. Thus, through exercise of the muscles, the demands on the heart and circulatory system are increased as they meet their responsibility of pumping and carrying blood to all areas of the body involved in the stepped-up process, and if this exercise is carried on over a reasonably prolonged period of time, positive adaptive changes will take place. The increased demand on the heart and circulatory system triggers the whole process of physiological fitness. The process acts cataclysmically to start a chain reaction in all body systems. When these positive changes are combined, Cooper calls them "training effects" as they lead one closer to the physiological capacity of one's body to function efficiently as an integrated whole (8).

Thus, in keeping with the law of use and disuse, the heart and circulatory systems themselves become stronger and more efficient after a prolonged period of regular vigorous exercise. The normal heart through this training has an increased volume per stroke. It contracts more forcefully and relaxes more completely thereby pumping more blood per stroke. The systolic pressure increases more rapidly and goes higher in order to force the blood through the circulatory system at a faster rate to meet the stepped-up needs of the cells. The conditioned heart can do more work in fewer beats. Also, the heart rate goes up less during strenuous work than the untrained heart and returns to normal more quickly. The resting rate of the trained heart is lower. All of these add up to a more efficient heart and a great saving in energy at rest and in work along with providing more blood to the body tissues. The average well-trained distance or cross-country runner generally has a heart rate between 50 and 60 beats per minute whereas the average untrained person will generally have 70 to 90. A heart that beats only 60 times per minute gets 18 days more rest per year than one that beats 80 times per minute. An "athlete's heart" was once thought to be a weakened heart which was injured through too strenuous exercise. There is no scientific basis for this belief since the normal heart cannot be injured through exercise. Thus, an "athlete's heart" is a strong and efficient heart.

Another benefit to the circulatory system is an improved venous circulation particularly in the extremities. The muscular contractions brought on by strenuous exercise force the blood back into the heart by increasing the venous pressure and the higher the venous pressure, the better the circulation. The capillary circulation in the muscle tissues is increased by almost half because latent capillaries are opened and new ones formed. More efficiency is obtained in temperature regulation through more effective dilation of the peripheral blood vessels. With training there is a lower blood lactate concentration for the performance of a given amount of work and an ability to achieve a higher blood lactate concentration before exhaustion sets in. There is also an increased storage of glycogen in the muscle fibers and a greater utilization of anaerobic energy reserves. Also, the amount of hemoglobin per unit volume of blood is increased since strenuous prolonged exercise can increase the number of red corpuscles by as much as 100 percent. Thus, the amount of blood and its payload of oxygen made available to the cells is conditioned by a stronger and more efficient heart with its increase stroke volume, arteries that can adapt readily to the increased needs of the cells by adjustment in size to speed the flow of blood, increase in the number of functioning capillaries, enrichment in the composition of the blood, and improved venous circulation and ventilation in the lungs for removing waste products.

Exercise of a strenuous nature has been positively related to the resisting of progressive cardiovascular diseases. Such diseases have become the nation's number one health problem. More than half the deaths in this country which occur annually are a result of heart trouble and related diseases. The great challenge to medicine and public health is not only to learn more about these diseases, but to educate the public in the knowledge which is already available concerning care and prevention. Currently there are still many unanswered questions concerning cause and prevention, and certainly there is no single cause but a multiplicity of causes. Research has related the following conditions among others to cardiovascular diseases: high blood pressure, high cholesterol count, high fat level in the blood, tension, stresses, overweight, and sedentarianism. These are related to exercise. A program of regular exercise of a strenuous nature can provide the fitness level which has been recommended by heart specialists as a protection against those conditions which seem to lead to heart attacks. Thus, this becomes the ultimate benefit of exercise to the individual since it may not only be a means of living a fuller life, it may mean life itself to him.

Exercise graded according to age and level of fitness is one of the important means now being recommended not only to prevent heart attacks and accompanying degenerative diseases, but also to lessen their severity once they occur, and to hasten the time required for recovery. Most of the cardiovascular diseases seem to be related to the fatty deposits which collect inside the arteries. As the inner walls collect more and more of these deposits, the inside diameter of the vessels is reduced in size and the flow of blood is impeded. Not only does this clog the arteries but it reduces the elasticity of the walls and may produce a hardening of the walls and other degenerative changes. There is a relationship between a cholesterol-rich diet and the fatty deposits. Also, there is the danger of portions of these fatty deposits tearing loose and lodging in arteries in the heart to produce a coronary attack or in the brain to produce a stroke. Regular vigorous exercise has been shown to be effective in offsetting these degenerative conditions. Another danger to the untrained heart is what happens when some physical, mental or emotional stress or strain suddenly throws the heart into a state of ventricular fibrillation. Unless quick action is taken by someone who is trained to act in such instances, this condition results in cardiac arrest and death. The trained heart is protected from this state by its built-in governing system.

Benefits of Exercise to the Respiratory System

Paralleling the more efficient heart and circulatory system through training and exercise there is a corresponding increase in the efficiency of the respiratory functions in order to obtain the vital oxygen so necessary for body processes. This relationship is to be expected since the respiratory system is an important link in the cycle of getting oxygen into the blood stream. Dr. Kenneth Cooper believes that oxygen is the key to the efficient functioning of not only the heart and brain but all other systems of the body including the muscular system (8). Since the body cannot store a supply of oxygen, as it can food materials, it must depend on a constant source of oxygen supply even when at rest. When the body is placed under anaerobic exercise stress (oxygen debt), the demands by the cells are increased many fold. Oxygen must be pumped through the body systems effectively. Oxygen is the key to life's processes since it must be present in the tissues for oxidation of the food materials to produce the energy needed for movement

and heat. Thus, without oxygen the heart and brain cease to function in a matter of moments. The more demands made on the body, the more oxygen is needed. The true test of an individual's cardiovascular fitness is the efficiency with which his system can process and consume oxygen during maximum effort. Therefore, the respiratory system is the first important link in getting the vital oxygen into the transportation system and on its way to the working tissues. The efficiency of this first necessary step can be maximized by training.

Due to training there is a slight decline in the rate and depth of respiration during rest. This is accompanied, however, by a slower, more even, and deeper respiration during exercise and a return to normal more quickly following it. There is an actual increase in the pulmonary ventilation as the lungs can take in more air with each inspiration. There is an increased efficiency in *external respiration* where oxygen and carbon dioxide are interchanged more effectively between the lungs and the capillaries within the alveoli. There is an increased efficiency in absorption of oxygen per liter of ventilation during exhausting work along with the more efficient elimination of carbon dioxide. This is accompanied by an increased ability to attain a greater minute volume of ventilation partly due to the increase in the surface of alveoli, thereby increasing the area from which oxygen can be absorbed (5).

A greater mechanical efficiency of the system is effected due to the increased flexibility of the chest and a strengthening of the respiratory muscles. The lungs do their work as a result of the action of the diaphragm. Like other muscles, the more they are exercised, the stronger and more efficient they become. At the same time the volume of the blood is reduced by as much as one-fourth with some of the fluid being forced out of the blood vessels into spaces in the tissues. This process provides for a higher concentration of blood and enhances its oxygen-carrying capacity. There is also an increase in the efficiency of *internal respiration*. The amount of oxygen and carbon dioxide per unit of blood exchanged between the blood in the capillary system and the muscle cells is enhanced through more efficiency in the process of osmosis.

Benefits of Exercise to the Muscular System

The muscles themselves develop in strength, power and endurance and thereby result in improved muscular performance. First, there is an increase in the size of the muscle known as hypertrophy. This increase is due to the smaller and unused fibers becoming functional. The elastic walls of the muscle fibers, called sarcolemma, grow thicker and correspondingly tougher. The connective tissues within the muscle itself also increase in amounts. These changes not only enable the muscle to become stronger but also better able to withstand the strain of hard work and emergencies. Along with the increase in the size of the muscle, there is also an increase in the strength of the muscle since strength is in proportion to the muscle's effective cross-section. The stronger the muscle, the more likely work will be performed by parts of the muscles acting in relays while other parts rest. This permits some muscle units to rest and recover, while other units carry the load and thus enable the individual to do more work over a longer period of time. Also, exercise enhances the quality of the muscular contraction. It functions more smoothly and contracts more forcefully with less effort thereby developing the ability to sustain effort. With the increase in size and strength of a muscle

there is a gain in endurance which is out of all proportion to its gain in size (5).

The trained muscle becomes more effective in combating fatigue through more efficient chemical reaction. Since fatigue is produced by waste products building up in the muscles and by a lack of oxygen in the cells, the more efficient cardiovascular system can prolong the time for the onset of fatigue. There is less of the main by-product of exercise (lactic acid), and also there is more efficient resynthesizing of lactic acid for reuse.

Also, through exercise the postural muscles can be kept toned and strengthened; this can lead to improved posture and reduce fatigue. In this regard an important point is that while one's body type is an inherited characteristic, his "figure" is built through exercise and diet control.

Benefits to Other Vital Organs and the Nutritive System

The benefits of exercise and training are not relegated to the cardiorespiratory and muscular systems. Exercise tends to result in benefits to other organs and functions. The digestive system along with the excretory system increases in efficiency as greater demands are placed on them through exercise. There is not only an increase in efficiency of these organs, but also an increase in size so that digestion, assimilation, absorption, and elimination are all improved.

The endocrine glands are related to the effects of exercise. The adrenal glands increase in size and efficiency. The epinephrine and norepinephrine secreted by these glands enable the individual to sustain muscular activity more efficiently over a longer period of time. Epinephrine activates the muscular functions more efficiently and the higher output of norepinephrine provides for increased energy. Exercise also helps in the output of hormones from the pituitary gland which in turn aids in the further production of epinephrine.

Muscular exercise increases the capacity of the cells to build their nutritive powers. Use of the muscles and the functioning of the power-building cycle are highly related. Through exercise the glycogen is burned. Heat and energy are released. This brings on a demand for more oxygen and food materials from the blood. There is an increased efficiency in the elimination of waste. The economy in function of the internal organs increases since they all share either directly or indirectly in this power-building cycle.

Even the nervous system, acting as a controller to the patterns of movement involved, is strengthened and receives many other benefits from protracted exercise. In childhood and youth exercise and physical activity are the main way the mental powers develop (see Chapter 16). Throughout life physical activity is perhaps the best antidote for tensions and stresses brought on by complex living behavior, and thus enhances mental health.

Other Benefits of Exercise

Health and fitness are inversely related to overweight and obesity. Obesity is a contributor to the etiology of degenerative diseases since it is a recognized fact that the obese person is subject to greater incidence of heart attacks and related conditions than the individual with normal weight. Excessive obesity subjects the heart to an overload, and the mortality rate is considerably higher for the overweight persons. The fat individual is a poorer surgical risk than his thinner counterpart.

In addition to the health hazard presented by obesity, there are psychological and emotional disadvantages. Obesity does not enhance the development of a good body image especially in adolescence. This lack of respect for one's own body image is a deterrent to the development of a proper self-image and hence becomes a social liability. In fact, it is now possible that society is partly responsible for this condition due to its condemning and critical attitude toward the obese. However, obesity is frequently related to mental depression, and it may be that in some cases mental depression leads to obesity rather than the reverse.

Both exercise and proper nutrition are important factors in the control of overweight. The best answer to creeping overweight and obesity is therefore not only a reduced caloric intake but also a regular vigorous exercise program. The abdomen and the hips are two areas of the body which collect excess fat first. These areas are easier to control through prevention than through weight-reducing techniques after the damage has been done. The streamlining effect of these areas of the body becomes a by-product of strenuous regular activity plus a strict control of diet. Neither alone will accomplish the purpose.

While the average citizen of this country does not ordinarily eat a balanced diet, he apparently eats too well since it is estimated that fully one-third of the population is overweight. Overweight and lack of exercise to tone the muscles produce a flabby citizen.

Another value of regular exercise which is related to weight control is the toning up of muscles which gives a firmness to the body as opposed to flabbiness. This naturally enhances good posture and gives a more pleasing appearance. Poor posture is related to chronic fatigue and is thought by some medical authorities to be associated with minor illnesses.

The strength and endurance increment as a result of regular exercise helps delay the onset of fatigue and tiredness of day-to-day living. This is an advantage which enables one to be more alert, to meet not only the requirements of the daily job more effectively but also to enjoy leisure time pursuits and become better company at these times. Also, it provides one with the necessary reserve to meet any emergencies which might arise in one's life above and beyond the ordinary task of one's daily life.

Since this book has constantly emphasized the unity concept and the aspect of the whole individual, it is reasonable to conclude that a vigorous regular exercise regimen has a positive influence on all components of the human organism. By the same token, lack of exercise has a negative influence. There is some evidence to indicate that participation in physical activity plays a role in postponing the aging process.

IMPLEMENTATION OF FITNESS

Since health is vital to education and living life to the fullest and since fitness is an important aspect of health, the question arises as to how fitness may be attained and how maintained once it has been gained. Perhaps these are essentially the same and differ only in a matter of degree. It has already been suggested that fitness is more than a product of exercise and that it includes such aspects as nutrition, rest, relaxation, medical care, good living habits, and moderation. However, the dominant factors of fitness are stamina, strength, endurance, and power. These are directly the result of physiological efficiency, and this efficiency is gained and maintained through some type of an exercise regimen.

Along the way of a protracted exercise type program there are some valid principles and practices which apply. First, of course, it must be emphasized that the normal body is sensitive to training and will respond in a positive manner. It will function within rather extensive limits of safety when normal and healthy. However, even with this

knowledge in mind, the basis of any fitness regimen should be a medical examination to assure the participant of his ability to function without harm. Next, since fitness is relative and will vary with the individual for many reasons, no two people will have the same starting point. The important thing is to start where one is and gradually go on from there. The word *gradually* is to be emphasized because high levels of fitness take time and do not come about either quickly or easily to the young who are forming their fitness habits for life and who have much free time to do it, or the adult who is trying to regain or maintain optimum levels and who may have a minimum of time. It is desirable for adults in a fitness training program to be supervised by a qualified person who has experience in training techniques and who knows the principles behind training. This individual must be aware of moderation in the beginning and the necessity of gradually increasing the load. In addition to a medical examination for the trainee, it would be desirable for him to have a preliminary testing program in order to provide him with a workable starting point. Pollock suggests that the program be individualized, heart rates should be checked periodically, warm-up and tapering-off procedures be observed, leg and foot problems anticipated and prevented, and variety provided for motivation (14).

When there is no qualified person to assist in the training, the individual who desires to begin a fitness program should take certain precautionary measures. In general, the exercise and training program should be selected and participated in according to one's age and physical condition. Fitness is an individual matter, therefore, the amount and kind of exercise are determined by the individual's degree of fitness. Too much exercise at any one time can be harmful.

The best guide concerning the amount of exercise needed is the ability to recuperate following activity. Recuperation should be fairly prompt. An individual has exercised too vigorously if his muscles become unduly sore for several days afterward, if his heart continues to pound rapidly several minutes after activity has stopped, if he is too restless to sleep the night following activity, if he is unduly tired the following day and if undue weakness is prevalent following a couple hours of rest. As a general rule, an individual out of training should not compete with or against the trained individual in strenuous activities. Also, there is a need for modification of activities as one grows older.

Regular activity with a prolonged training session (30 minutes to 1 hour minimum) is needed to achieve optimum levels of fitness. Also, the activity must be strenuous enough to place stress on the heart and respiratory system and to produce sweat. Exercise must be frequent — daily if possible — but under ideal conditions three times per week might be enough. The three principles of *duration, intensity* and *frequency* are basic in any fitness program. Exercise must be carried past a feeling of discomfort or perhaps even pain, a point that is frequently referred to as one's psychological limits. As tolerance for exercise is increased the individual can begin to reduce the difference between his psychological limit and his physiological limit— his ultimate limit. It is at this point in training with repetition of sessions of intensive type of activity that the trainee begins to experience the phenomenon of "second wind," a physiological adjustment of the cardiorespiratory system to the increased demands for oxygen and the elimination of the oxidation products. When second wind occurs, the participant obtains relief from the distress and discomfort of breathlessness and lethargy and is able to continue his efforts with renewed vigor and efficiency. While the physiological basis of second wind is not clearly understood, the changes in several physiological functions at onset are easily distinguished. There appear to be adaptations in not only the cardiorespiratory system but also the muscles, peripheral circulation and the brain.

Another principle involved in fitness concerns the application of the *overload*. This principle is in operation when the exercise load is increased in intensity so that the intake of oxygen no longer meets the demands of the exercising muscles and an oxygen debt is induced. Muscles gain in size and strength in only one of two ways: through maturation and through the application of the overload principle. This principle can be applied in three ways: (1) by increasing the resistance (weights, etc.), (2) by increasing the speed of repetitions and (3) by increasing the number of repetitions.

The trainee should have a knowledge of how the overload can be used in acquiring muscular strength, muscular endurance and cardiovascular endurance. The individual is working at a *normal load* when the oxygen supply is more than adequate to meet the body needs during activity. He is working at a *crest load* when the oxygen supply balances the needs of the muscles as all the physiological processes are working at full capacity. Too many people seem to be operating at a normal load and rarely get into the realm of the crest load or overload. Both the crest load and the overload limits may be increased dramatically by regular exercise. Ironically both will decrease almost as rapidly through either disease or inactivity. Recent studies have found a 23 percent decrease in circulation capacity as a result of illness and bed rest over only a short period of time. Thus, fitness is transitory. It can be lost in a short time unless kept up by regular activity.

The overload principle seems to operate more effectively in youth than it does after maturity. However, advancing age does not negate the need for exercise although it may alter the amount required. One's potential for strength, endurance and agility is highest in the mid-twenties and after that, unless kept up by some type of motivation, slowly declines. However, the need for some exercise is always there. Studies show that not only middle-age men but men between age 50 to 80 can undergo training and expect significant improvements in physical abilities. Also, it has been shown that the breathing capacity of young girls can be improved to the same extent as boys through running.

Obtaining and maintaining high levels of fitness offer many avenues of approach. Basic to any of these approaches, of course, is an adequate knowledge of what is health and fitness, why they are important, and how they may be obtained. Some prefer to stay fit through some type of sports participation. This is perhaps the best way from the standpoint of motivation since experience has shown that people will continue to do that which they enjoy doing. The weaknesses of the sports area are that many sports do not place enough stress on the cardiorespiratory systems, and that sports participation is too time-consuming done on a regular basis. If one enjoys golf, it takes a minimum of four and one-half hours to play 18 holes if one dispenses with the mobile cart and walks as he should to get the most value from his exercise. Most people cannot spare this amount of time on a regular basis. Many persons are turning to body-building exercises either as a steady diet or as a part of their cardiovascular fitness regimen. These exercises can be either of an isotonic or an isometric type. An *isotonic* exercise is one involving muscular

contraction which produces a shortening of the muscle and a range of movement involving a body lever. An *isometric* exercise is one which involves a strong muscular contraction which does not produce a change in muscle length; it is sustained for a few seconds without producing movement in a body part. A favorite isotonic exercise is weight lifting. A favorite isometric approach is to work one set of muscles against another set and hold tense for a short time. However, neither isotonic or isometric exercises provide for cardiovascular fitness.

Weight training, as an isotonic form of exercise, is a favorite in applying the overload principle. There are two other methods of conditioning which apply this principle and which have become popular in training programs: interval training and circuit training. *Interval training* is a method of fitness training involving alternate periods of strenuous activity and recovery, and the routine is followed for a specified number of times. It may be adapted to a large number of sports and activities. *Circuit training* is a method of conditioning involving exercise in a number of activities in rapid order. The activities are generally set up in stations and the participants rotate from station to station as they complete the required repetitions at each station.

There are a number of programs which have received widespread interest and promotion. The *5BX* and *XBX* programs for men and women respectively are a part of the "Royal Canadian Air Force Exercise Plans for Physical Fitness" (18). These plans have been highly recommended by physicians and can be carried on in the home. Lt. Col. Kenneth Cooper of the Air Force has captured the imagination of not only the trainee in fitness and the research specialists in fitness, but also millions who read his book and articles and participate in his program of aerobics. Colonel Cooper's book, "Aerobics" (8) contains his research and recommendation for a fitness regimen. His program of aerobics has now replaced the 5BX program for the U. S. Air Force. This program is based on the principle of *aerobics* from which his book gets its name. It simply means the individual must perform hard work up to a point just short of the onset of oxygen debt so that exercise can be carried on for a prolonged period of time thereby starting the training effect which triggers the desirable changes necessary for fitness. Running for distance is the best example of this type of exercise although cycling, swimming and some sports would fit the pattern. If the exercise were to be carried past this point of oxygen debt, the heart-circulatory-respiratory complex would be thrown into an *anaerobic* state. This means that an oxygen debt would be incurred and exercise would cease involuntarily until the debt was paid thereby not achieving any training effects. Other types of anaerobic exercises would include short bursts of activity which might be strenuous. However, by the nature of the activity, it would be terminated voluntarily on the part of the trainee and would not last long enough to produce the training effects. Examples of these kinds of exercise are wind sprints, sprints in track and field, and running up a short flight of steps.

This is an age of automation and automation has taken most, if not all, of the muscular effort out of work. Paradoxically, however, that same age of automation has provided man with different machines and gadgets on which to exercise. These vary all the way from the expensive treadmill or ergometer in the basement to the set of bar bells under the bed. Many have joined the most recent trend—the jogging club. This activity along with some distance swimming provides one of the best means for

staying fit for the masses. Bicycling could become more prominent in the fitness crusade if the factor of safety could be adequately controlled. Cooper (8) places squash, handball and basketball high on his list of activities which produce training effects.

In any event, the individual exercising must be knowledgeable regarding the principles of training. In addition to the ones already mentioned, he should know the value of the warm-up and the tapering-off. Most people are more cognizant of the necessity for the warm-up than they are for the tapering-off. However, it is necessary for the trainee to continue with some moderate form of activity following strenuous activity so that the muscles may aid in increased venous circulation in order to enhance the flow of blood out of the lower extremities and to remove the excess waste products from the cells. The trainee should be aware of the cause for muscle soreness, muscle cramps, and the "stitch" in the side and know how these physiological conditions may be avoided and treated if necessary. He should know that there is likely to be a period of retrogression when he first begins work and his performance will be poorer for a time.

In a statement of the role of exercise in fitness by a joint committee of the AMA and the American Association for Health, Physical Education, and Recreation entitled "Exercise and Fitness" the following suggestions were made concerning an exercise program (4):

1. A program of exercise should be started at an early age and be continued throughout life with certain adjustments from time to time as life advances and needs, interests, and capabilities change.

2. The amount of vigorous exercise that is desirable each day is largely an individual matter. Recommendations range from 30 minutes to an hour daily as a minimum.

3. Something of interest for every individual

can be found to make exercise satisfying and enjoyable. In addition to numerous sports, the variety of choices includes daily habits such as walking, bicycling, and gardening.

4. Hard, fast, sustained, or highly competitive games and sports should not be played by persons of any age unless these persons have attained an appropriate state of fitness through systematic training.

5. All persons should be shown by medical examination to be organically sound before training for competition or other strenuous exercise. The examination should be repeated periodically and whenever special indications appear.

6. An individual in good condition may appropriately participate in an activity that might be harmful to another person of the same age who is not in a comparable state of fitness.

7. Persons who are out of training should not attempt to keep pace in any vigorous sport with persons who are properly conditioned and accustomed to regular participation in that sport. Being in condition for one sport does not always mean that a person will be in condition for another.

8. Persons long out of training, or "soft" (who have not practiced strenuous exercise regularly) will need an extended period of conditioning to facilitate gradual return to full activity.

9. A person's ability to recover quickly after physical activity is a good indication as to whether or not the exercise is too strenuous. If breathlessness and pounding of the heart are still noticeable ten minutes after exercise, if marked weakness or fatigue persists after a two-hour period, if a broken night's sleep is attributable to exercise, or if there is a sense of definite and undue fatigue the following day, then the exercise has been too severe or too prolonged for that person in his present stage of training and physical strength.

10. Medical supervision of the amount, type, and effect of exercise during convalescence is essential.

11. Persons should not compete in body-contact sports or activities requiring great endurance with others of disproportionate size, strength, or skill. If risk of injury can be controlled, carefully supervised practice periods against such odds may occasionally be warranted as a learning device for gaining experience or improving performance.

12. Sports involving body contact or traumatic hazards necessitate the provision of protective equipment. Such protection is especially important for the head, neck, eyes, and teeth. Other activities should be substituted when adequate protection cannot be provided.

13. Careful preparation and maintenance of playing fields and other areas of sports are essential to reduction of injuries and full enjoyment of the activity. Competent supervision and proper equipment are necessary for the same reason.

If adequate levels of fitness are to be achieved for all people of all ages, there must be a concerted effort by many groups. While the schools must be the core of this effort along with the home, because they are the only two agencies which deal with all of the youth, many other agencies must make a significant contribution to this overall effort. These should include all official, voluntary, and professional agencies. A committee representing the AAHPER listed the following aspects which contribute to fitness (1):

1. Physical activities, including sports and athletics, which help to develop individual fitness.

2. Experiences which lead to appreciation of and skill in movement.

3. Skills and appreciations which will enable the individual to enjoy a variety of recreation activities.

4. Health knowledge, attitudes, and practices which are applied in daily living.

5. Protective services which promote the maintenance of individual health.

6. An environment which is conducive to safety and optimum growth and development.

7. Leadership which is capable of implementing and evaluating all aspects of this program.

Once again, fitness is broader than the school program. It is for everybody and not just for youth. This makes fitness everybody's business. It is a part of education but it is also a part of life. The big question becomes: "How does one become fit and how can this fitness be maintained throughout life?" Without apologies for oversimplification, the answer is simple. One must become "physically educated." If the student would refer back to Chapter 1, he will find the physically educated person defined in terms of skills, knowledges, attitudes, appreciations, and fitness. These elements are elaborated upon again in Chapter 17 for the high school student. None of these can stand alone, however. There is an interrelationship between them and each of them must be operable in a frame of reference which overlaps with the others. Each aspect has been discussed in some detail in Chapter 3 under objectives. While skilled activity is not the only avenue leading to fitness, it seems to be one of the most rewarding to most people. While all of the aspects are important and the interrelationships have been pointed out, there appears to be a logical sequence leading up to fitness. The "Why's" and the "How's" seem important. These knowledges and understandings in physical education and fitness must be emphasized as a facet of the sequence. They are not well known, however, either by the students or the adults. If the future generations are to know them, they must become a part of the fundamentals of education. The modern youth is intelligent, selective in his behavior, and seeks relevance in his educational pursuits. He will have to know the importance of these "Why's" and "How's" before he learns them or he won't participate. Knowledge alone is not enough, however.

Fitness requires not only knowledge but what may be more important a type of self-discipline. Thus, fitness in the final analysis becomes a matter of values. Perhaps the one overriding aspect in this quest for fitness is an attitude on the part of the individual to want to participate and to be fit. This attitude must become a part of his value system. As for the leadership of those promoting fitness, perhaps an overriding need is more motivational studies to see how man can be motivated to extra effort.

This interrelationship is evident. If the attitude is present, participation and activity will result. When the student participates, he builds a base of skilled behavior. Each of these aspects—knowledge, attitude, skills and participation—in a sequential pattern leads to fitness but the process does not end there. For example, skilled behavior reacts in reverse down the continuum and influences attitude and knowledge. However, the fitness objective, important as it may seem, must not become the entire program in the schools. It is one of the unique contributions of physical education, but it must assume its proper place among the other objectives.

REFERENCES

1. AAHPER: Fitness for Youth, Statement Prepared and Approved by the 100 Delegates to the AAHPER Fitness Conference, Washington, D.C., Sept. 1956. JOPHER, Dec. 1956, p. 8.
2. AAHPER: *Knowledge and Understanding in Physical Education.* Washington, D.C., AAHPER, 1969.
3. AAHPER: *Youth Fitness Test Manual.* Washington, D.C., AAHPER, 1961 (Revised).
4. American Medical Association: *Exercise and Fitness* (Joint Statement from AMA and AAHPER). Washington, D.C., AAHPER, 1964.
5. Barrow, H. M., Marjorie Crisp, and J. W. Long: *Physical Education Syllabus.* Minneapolis, Burgess Publishing Company, 1967.
6. Barrow, H. M., and R. McGee: *A Practical Approach to Measurement in Physical Education.* Philadelphia, Lea & Febiger, 1964.
7. Bookwalter, Karl W., and Carolyn W. Bookwalter: *Fitness for Secondary Schools.* Washington, D.C., AAHPER, 1956.

8. Cooper, Kenneth H.: *Aerobics*. New York, Bantam Book, Inc., 1968.

9. Cureton, T. K.: *Physical Fitness Appraisal and Guidance*. St. Louis, C. V. Mosby Company, 1947.

10. Hunsicker, Paul A., and Guy G. Reiff: *A Survey and Comparison of Youth Fitness 1958–1965*. Cooperative Research Project No. 2418. Ann Arbor, University of Michigan, 1965.

11. Kennedy, J. F.: The Soft American. Sports Illustrated, Vol. 13, No. 26, Dec., 1960, pp. 15–23.

12. Kennedy, J. F.: The Vigor We Need. Sports Illustrated, Vol. 17, No. 3, July 16, 1962, pp. 12–15.

13. Kraus, H., and R. Hirschland: Minimum Muscular Fitness Tests in School Children. Research Quarterly, Vol. 25, No. 2, May, 1954, p. 178.

14. Pollock, M. L., Richard Janeway, and Henry Miller: *Endurance Training for Middle-Aged Men*. Unpublished Research Report, Department of Physical Education, Winston-Salem, N. C., Wake Forest University, 1969.

15. President's Council on Youth Fitness: *Youth Physical Fitness: Suggested Elements of a School Centered Program*. Washington, D.C., U.S. Government Printing Office, 1961.

16. President's Council on Physical Fitness: *Adult Physical Fitness*. Washington, D.C., U.S. Government Printing Office, 1963.

17. President's Council on Youth Fitness: *Physical Fitness Elements in Recreation*. Washington, D.C., U.S. Government Printing Office, 1962.

18. Royal Candian Air Force: *5BX Plan for Physical Fitness*. Ottawa, Canada, Queen's Printers and Controller of Stationery, 1959.

19. Ward, Judson C.: Where Does "The Physical" Fit Into Education. *Educational Comment*. Toledo, College of Education, University of Toledo, 1961.

Chapter 11

Neuromuscular System

INTRODUCTION

A word that has created a new dimension in physical education in recent years is *movement*. Movement implies motor skills and motor skill implies learning since such patterns of movement ordinarily thought of as natural processes are in effect learned. Mention has been made that everything a child knows and can do has to be learned. Excluding maturation with its unfolding of an inherent readiness, this applies to skills as well as knowledge and attitudes. In keeping with the unity concept, once again it is not possible to separate motor activity from other aspects of the whole. The performing of an organized pattern of motor skills cannot and does not exist as a physical response only, but rather as an entity which involves the psychological and sociological as well as the physiological. Performance is not just a physical or mental response alone, but is a continuum which runs the gamut from physical to cognitive, and there is always an interaction between them. The organic aspects are affected along with the personal and social facets. Much claim has been made in the areas of moral and ethical development as they relate to skills. Of course, whenever there is movement, there must be performance or learning or both. The name neuromuscular itself indicates a relationship between the physiological and the psychological. Chapters 15 and 16 are intended to cover the aspects of learning and the part played in this totality by the psychological, and this chapter—while it cannot be separated from learning and psychology — will dwell more on the aspects of skill seen in their relationship with physiology, anatomy and kinesiology. Recognition is given to the unitary concept but for the sake of convenience, the part method approach is used for our purposes.

Muscles are only robots which have certain unique characteristics, responding to certain physiological principles. The action itself can be studied and understood, but physiological bases of the learning of that movement still remain a mystery. Psychologically, movement is instigated by the brain and nervous system. It is hypothesized that the mind is analogous to the computer, and that data fed into it from the senses act as input, and when this input is processed in its highly complex integrative area, output results and movement may occur (8–2). This theory will be discussed more fully in Chapter 16.

MOVEMENT

Human movement is a concomitant of living. It is inevitable in the process of man's changing life pattern interacting with and reacting to a dynamic and changeable environment. In general, movement runs the gamut from the general type of abilities to the highly specialized patterns found in sports, exercises, dance and gymnastic techniques. Activities commonly recognized as work are certainly a part of the total movement mosaic. However, they will not be considered in this discussion except as they may relate to fundamental skills. General abilities seem to include a type of behavior that is racial in nature and while it may be learned, it encompasses activities that have historically been associated with man's incessant and inescapable search for existence—the seeking of food, shelter, clothing, and protection in the living of his daily normal life. Hence these movements have been frequently referred to as *racial* activities. On the other hand the specialized movements are highly individual and unique to certain restrictive forces. The general abilities are universal in nature, while the specific abilities are as unique as nationalities and geographical areas.

Movement is a complex phenomenon, especially willed movement. It is a mosaic with many facets. It is physical in the sense that it deals with certain mechanical principles based on the structure and function of the human body, as well as the universal laws of force, motion, and gravity. It is also physiological to the extent that muscles function in a way that is highly specific and according to principles found in the study of physiology of exercise. Further,

it is psychological to the extent that it depends on neural mechanisms for its direction. However, it is something more than any of these. Contrary to a well-known mathematical principle, the sum of the parts does not just equal the whole. Rather, when these parts are synthesized and integrated into movement, movement becomes something more than the sum of its parts.

Movement itself is like this. Simple skills are combined with other simple skills to form a more complex pattern. In turn this pattern may be integrated with other patterns to form a hierarchy. This hierarchy is something more than the sum of its individual patterns. The fusion of already existing learned patterns into a more complex hierarchy has some of the elements of transfer (8–5). Also, more complex hierarchies are difficult or impossible to develop unless the simpler patterns have been learned well (10–158).

Movement is associated with muscular contraction and the performance of either a general or a specific type of skill pattern requires muscular action in some of its myriad forms. Thus, the physiology and kinesiology of the muscular system should be understood if one is to understand movement. Muscles are the organs whose primary function is movement. The movements found in sports, exercise, dance and gymnastics, while they may be initiated by nervous impulses, have a unique function within themselves. The energy necessary for these movements is generated in the muscles themselves. In other words, the muscle has within itself the power to change potential energy into kinetic energy, work or heat. Thus, there are many levels of utilization of these forces found in muscles. By the very essence of man's own physique and nature, there are restrictions and limitations placed on his action patterns. These limitations are variable and changeable.

They change as man's experiences change. For example, the most prevalent factors of fitness are relative. They are related to man's experience and will change in relation to it. Fitness is not the same for the twenty-year-old as for the fifty-year-old. Neither is the level of fitness for the office worker the same as for the professional athlete. Furthermore, man's actions are restricted by body size, physique, and the factors of movement and conditions of learning.

The intent of this chapter is to deal with the factors and aspects which constitute movement and the elements and conditions which affect it. Since movement is a complex quality and is influenced by many forces both intrinsic and extrinsic to the individual, a better understanding might be had if some type of classification could be made. Traditionally, man's motor behavior has been divided into such categories as motor ability, motor capacity, motor educability, motor fitness, and motor skills involving sports and gymnastics.

This type of classification is perhaps an oversimplification and to a certain extent is no longer valid, but it does enable one to get a better perspective concerning movement in general. The complexity of the human body and its workings is almost beyond human understanding. The 206 bones which are moved and supported by the 696 muscles give an almost unlimited range and quality of movement. Even the simplest skills are complex involving many patterns influenced by many forces. These influences may, too, be categorized into several types. First, there are *physical performance factors* which underlie the action of all movement. These factors include speed, power, strength, agility, coordination and the like. Second, there are *structural factors* which either place limitations or restrictions on movements or which might enhance performance. Such factors include weight, height, body type, structure and posture. Third, there are certain *psychological* factors which influence behavior and ultimately influence movement to a very great degree. These factors include interest, initiative, courage, persistence, competitiveness, esprit de corps and many others. The degree to which these are present may have great influence on sports (2–114).

The physical performance factors are the ones most influential in this area. There seem to be three types. First, there are the *physical performance elements or factors* which underlie all movements, and as has been pointed out, consist of agility, speed, power, strength, endurance, balance, flexibility, and the like. Second, the factors are revealed through the *racial motor activities* which include such fundamental skills as running, jumping, climbing, throwing and hanging. These are sometimes called racial activities or universal skills because they seem to be common to all performances of all people regardless of geography or nationality. They are the framework of man's physical behavior. They provide the basis on which all patterns of motor movement are formed and seemed to be related to his evolutionary rise. They become generalized through incessant play activities in early life. When these abilities are combined into patterns for specific purposes, they lead to the third type. This third level includes the highly specialized movements resulting from much specialized training and experience, and differ from person to person. They include sports, dance, and gymnastic activities. They are obtained by the individual through much practice and specialization and are unique to each specific activity.

The relationship of these levels is rather an interesting one. The factors which are basic to all motor performance are causal in nature since they represent the first level of performance. In other words, they are the cause of the fundamental skills and ultimately the sport techniques. The fundamental skills are both cause and effect since they are the result of the basic factors and are themselves the cause or basic to sport skills. The highly specialized sport, dance and gymnastic techniques are movements which represent the result or the influence not only of the fundamental skills, but also the factors which are basic to all performances (1).

Perhaps a more sophisticated analysis of factors involved in motor skills was made by Singer (11–98). He points out that success in motor performance may depend on the following personal factors: (1) physical characteristics, (2) motor abilities, (3) sense security, (4) perceptual abilities, (5) cognition and (6) emotional effects. Another frame of reference for human movement is classification into postural, transport, and manipulative.

VALUE OF SKILL

The word skill may be thought of as either a task or an ability to perform that task. As an ability, skill involves an organized sequence of activities. The spectrum is broad ranging from the complex organization of patterns of movement to the integration of symbolic information necessary in card games and chess. In general, skills are of two types: *fine motor* and *gross motor*. Gross motor skills deal with large fundamental muscles of the body, while fine motor skills involve less active movements with a more sensitive quality and more precision. However, most fine motor skills are performed within the framework of the gross motor skills of posture and transport. At the same time most gross motor skills may have fine motor components. Thus skills are on a continuum from fine to gross motor (3–11). However, they all involve pre-

senting information from the outside— the environment—and as a corollary they require that this information be brought back to the environment in the nature of some response, usually physical.

Skill has to be the most important aspect of organized physical education. Its values to the individual and to society far exceed those of other objectives. This is true because skill is generally the vehicle through which all the other values to the individual are achieved. Without skill it is reasonable to say one could never become physically educated and thus never fully educated.

Fitness has become a most sought after objective of education. With some exceptions most people prefer to obtain their fitness through sports. It is a mistake to imply that skill and fitness are synonymous. However, fitness can only be attained through the muscles. It is difficult perhaps to achieve a high level of fitness through sports alone because some sports are just not that physically challenging. However, sports will continue to be one of the most used ways of gaining and maintaining levels of fitness.

Neuromuscular development is desirable and there is a need for every individual to become more proficient in this area. All persons need to be able to move easily, gracefully, and effectively with as little expenditure of energy as possible. This is true not only for man's play but also his work and even in his postural and locomotor activity. In carrying out one's daily normal activities the efficient use of the fundamental skills is important. One of the best means of developing these basic qualities is through sports and games.

Another objective of our time which assumes more and more importance in an increasingly complex and automated society is leisure activity. It has become more and more apparent that man's working hours per week will grow increasingly shorter and his leisure greater. This leisure can become either a burden to society or asset to both society and the individual. If man is to learn to use his leisure worthily and at the same time combine its use with other well-defined objectives, motor skills offer one of the best approaches. At the present time there seems to be a trend toward more play as a leisure activity.

It is becoming increasingly more apparent that movement in general and skill particularly are the chief media whereby many types of learning take place. Play with all its ramifications of skill patterns furnishes the pathways for development (6). The skills of play in a sense are imitations of the child's adult world which is to come. If this aspect is neglected, his adjustment to his universe will be fragmentary and partial. It is as though these formative years are the "warm-up" for his life in the adult world, and physical skills play a major role in this process. Through his play activities the developing child repeats the same movement over and over and at the same time explores new ways of behaving. It is through almost incessant play activity during his waking hours that he obtains the necessary amount of physical experience essential for learning.

Skills have become a part of our cultural heritage. Not only is this true among the boys and girls of today but it is a part of the adult world as well. For the youth of today modern culture places a high priority on skill. Perhaps there is no other factor which can affect a boy's relationship with his peers as much as skill in sports and games. Skill provides an avenue for social status (12–120).

FACTORS UNDERLYING ALL PERFORMANCE (COMPONENTS OF MOVEMENT)

Another approach to movement is through a study of its components. In order to enhance the student's understanding of the various categories of movement, it would be well first to elaborate upon these components or factors which are basic to all movement and which contribute to successful performance of skills. All of these factors are associated with muscular movement; each in its own way affects the quality of both general and specific skills. Some of these factors have been identified through empirical judgment, although in many cases components are identified through factor analysis techniques. Motor performance depends on the presence of reasonable amounts of these factors. If they are inadequate, physical performance will never be effective. If strength is not present in reasonable amounts, the tennis racket can never be handled well enough to execute good strokes. The following factors are the basis of all movement (2–115).

Strength

The basis of all movement is muscular activity and most of the factors of motor performance are dependent to some extent on strength. In varying amounts, strength is prerequisite to all fundamental skills such as running, jumping, throwing, climbing, hanging and to the underlying factors which undergird them. Strength is inexorably related then to other factors underlying movement but still remains an entity in itself, and is one of the most important facets of the whole. Strength is defined as the capacity of the individual to exert muscular force. Such force is shown through the ability of the person to push, pull, hang, lift, or squeeze. The strength in a muscle is in proportion to its effective cross-section.

Speed

Muscular action has a temporal quality as well as a force. Speed is the ability or capacity of an individual to perform successive movements of the same pattern at a fast rate or even one single movement. While speed would appear to be an innate quality, it can be improved by practice of the coordinated movements and by learning proper techniques. Speed is not unrelated to strength and an increase in strength may be accompanied by some increase in speed. The rapidity of any movement may be affected by body weight, density, muscle viscosity, and structural and nutritional features such as length of the body part or range of flexibility of the joint.

Power

Power is the capacity of the performer to apply maximum muscular contraction at the fastest rate. It is a product of the principle of force times velocity. In this case force is the strength of the muscle and velocity is the speed with which the strength is used in movement. Thus, power is an explosive action where maximum muscular force is released at maximum speed. It is one of the most basic components of movement and is a characteristic of the superior athlete. It has limitations in the same way as speed.

Endurance

Endurance may be defined as a physiologic capacity to maintain movement effort over a prolonged period of time. There are two types. One is concerned with the factor of strength and the other with the circulatory-respiratory systems. The former has to do with the ability of the muscles or muscle groups to continue to function under a heavy work load without undue fatigue over a period of time. This is called muscular endurance. It is apparent that the stronger individual can continue successive movements under work stress for a longer duration or for more repetitions than a weaker person.

In the type of endurance associated with the circulatory-respiratory system, the question of physiological fitness is involved and it is related to stress on the heart, circulatory and respiratory systems. The person exercising tends to get out of breath and if he is to continue exercise over a period of time, there has to be an adjustment in the circulatory-respiratory system to meet the stress conditions. In both cases, training can make for greater efficiency.

Agility

Agility is the ability to move the body or parts of the body in space in order to change directions quickly and accurately. In this factor the big muscles of the body are involved, and they must be coordinated rapidly and precisely. Both innate capacity and training and experience are important in the level one attains in this factor. It plays an important role in such activities as gymnastics, wrestling, high jumping, hurdling, and maneuvering in football and basketball.

Balance

Balance is the ability to sustain the body posture in a static position for an effective response or to control it adequately in a specific position while it is in motion or following motion. The first part refers to static balance and the latter to dynamic. Balance is basic to most movements and is founded in a number of elements. First, it is naturally related to what has been universally referred to as the organs of balance located in the semicircular canals of the inner ear. Second, it seems to be related also to the kinesthetic senses located throughout the body in the muscles and joints. Third, it also is related to vision since balance can be maintained much better when the eyes are open and one can see.

Static balance is observed chiefly in sitting or standing positions or in an activity like a handstand or a balance stunt on a balancing beam. Dynamic balance is revealed when the body is moved from one place to another and stability must not only be achieved during the movement but also following movement.

Flexibility

Flexibility is concerned with the range of movement in a joint. It limits the degree to which the body or some part of the body can bend, twist, or move by means of the flexion or extension of muscles. The degree of flexibility depends not only on the flexibility and extensibility of muscles, but also on the nature of the ligaments themselves which surround the joints. Flexibility seems to be a specific quality rather than a general one since there is variation in degree of flexibility from one joint to another.

Hand-eye-foot-eye Coordination

The coordination of the hands, feet and even the head with the eyes is one of the most important factors in the performance of some motor skills. These include all movements involving a ball or similar object and are concerned with a primary objective. Such skills involving catching, striking, hitting, fielding, kicking, and heading are in this category. The eye must be trained on the primary objective during the initial phase of the movement and skillfulness in this factor requires steadiness, accuracy, and control. No doubt this factor is related to other qualities such as depth perception, kinesthetic sense, agility, and relaxation.

Coordination

This is a general quality which is basic to more complex movements in motor performance. It is the ability of the individual to integrate all types of movements into specific patterns. It is undoubtedly related to many other factors but due to the uniqueness of the patterning process, it is usually considered an entity in itself. Strength and endurance are not significantly related to this factor except as coordination seems to become less efficient with the onset of fatigue. However, it is fairly obvious that there is an interrelationship with such factors as speed, balance, agility, and kinesthetic sense and hand-eye-foot-eye coordination. The integration of movement patterns into a whole for performance not only plays an important part in sports, but also in the normal activities one performs each day.

Kinesthetic Sense

Kinesthesis or proprioceptiveness is the sense which provides the individual with an awareness of the position of his body or parts of his body with respect to space. This awareness is made known to the individual through the mechanism of feedback and furnishes the information needed to control further action (see Chapter 16). These sense organs are located in the muscles, fascia of muscles, tendons, and joints. The receptors are stimulated by the stress placed on them usually by movement itself and when this information is processed, the individual is able in varying degrees of efficiency to determine the position of his body in space and to better control it. Such awareness appears to be an important factor in learning. However, much more research is needed to study the specificity and generality of kinesthesis. While it does not appear to be related to motor ability as measured by existing motor ability tests, it does seem to underlie and be a requisite for skilled performance (11–75). However, it could be that kinesthesis is a hard quality to measure accurately and when more precise techniques are found, relationship can be shown.

Accuracy

Accuracy has to do with the ability to control one's movements in relation to a specific target or object. Many physical education activities involving precision of movement for throwing, hitting, shooting, kicking and the like are dependent for success on this factor. Accuracy is no doubt interrelated with other factors such as coordination, balance, kinesthetics and visual perception, but it is sufficiently different to make it an entity in itself.

FUNDAMENTAL MOVEMENTS (RACIAL SKILLS)

The basic patterns of motor movement are embodied in the so-called fundamental skills. These are racial activities in a sense because they are common to all mankind and know no boundaries either racially or geographically. They include such fundamental movement patterns as walking, running, jumping, striking, throwing, climbing, hanging, and carrying. The quality and efficiency of these skills are dependent on the underlying factors which are basic to all motor performance, and which have just been discussed. It is obvious if an individual is to run effectively, he must have speed; if he is to jump high or far, he must possess power, and if he is to walk a fallen tree over a stream, he must have balance. These skills may be described as gross motor activities and include most postural and locomotor type activities as well as some manipulative. They are the fundamental skills which have formed the basis of man's work, play and dance since primitive times. They were the primary instigators of the evolutionary processes which raised man to higher levels as they were performed first as survival activities. Later the skills developed into more purposive forms of work extending from primitive times to the modern era of electronics. All sports, games, gymnastics and dance activities are elaborations, modifications and adaptations of these basic patterns.

This would suggest that a modern program of physical education should be based largely on these immemorial racial type skills. It is apparent that man's biological and physiological evolutions were brought about chiefly through his moving according to these patterns. Two primary reasons for physical education are for development and maintenance of the organic system. Development must in a sense recapitulate the evolution of the race, and the biological basis of life is inexorably operative. These racial activities act powerfully to fashion a sound organic and nervous system. Such activities may be engaged in directly as in running or indirectly as they are organized and integrated into patterns and forms of play, work, dance, and other activities. When fundamental skills are used properly as they are related to man's daily tasks, they provide satisfaction for the participant and make performance more efficient from the standpoint of time and energy expenditure. The implication here is that while fundamental skills are a form of natural activity, there still is a wrong and a right way for them to be performed. Thus, perhaps correct form should be taught as a part of the physical education program.

GENERAL ABILITIES

Traditionally man's motor behavior has been classified into categories chiefly for better understanding. There is some doubt cast on the traditional approach to movement as a general quality; some scientists have swung to the opposite extreme and cite that all movement is highly specific. The concept of general motor ability as opposed to specific ability has particularly been questioned. However, the traditional approach will be presented here and the arguments for and against will be presented, then the student may make his own choices. The general qualities have been divided into motor capacity, motor ability, motor educability, and motor fitness.

Motor Capacity

Motor capacity has been defined as a general overall quality which is representative of one's potential or innate performance. Dr. C. H. McCloy has developed a test of motor capacity and his test presumably predicts innate capacity or potential performance, or motor aptitude (9–114). This quality is difficult to isolate since it becomes important to identify factors which undergird it. These factors must not be educable since they are indicators of maximum potential. Pioneer work in this area was done by McCloy, and he has isolated the following four elements as indicators of capacity: size and maturity, power, motor educability, and agility and coordination (9–115).

Motor Educability

Associated with motor capacity is motor educability. This quality implies that there may be levels of learning with respect to the rate and speed with which it takes place. Implicit in this quality is the ease and thoroughness with which individuals learn skills. Some may be more educable than others when certain factors associated with educability are present to a great extent. This inherent aptitude for motor skills learning appears in a similar manner as for mental learnings. Perhaps this quality is more psychological since it is no doubt related to learning. However, the coach and teacher can readily see that there is some quality of this nature present. The student who possesses a high level of educability factors is the one who responds to teaching and coaching quickly. He is said to be a natural and usually achieves the class of championship caliber. Educability is evidently related in some sense with maturation because there seems to be a relationship between improvement and age. While motor educability is related to maturation, size, physique, and in some degree to most of the factors listed under components of movement, it seems to be influenced very little by strength and endurance.

Motor Ability

A third classification of motor behavior is motor ability (1), a term sometimes referred to as general athletic ability. Motor ability has been defined as "the present acquired and innate ability to perform motor skills of a general or fundamental nature, exclusive of highly specialized sports or gymnastic techniques" (2–122). Of course, this definition implies that motor ability is a combination of the innate and the acquired. It represents present or developed status and is subject to change in relation to the amount of practice and training. The definition further implies that motor ability is general in nature, is made up of general abilities, and does not involve highly specialized skills as revealed in such activities as sports, gymnastics and dance. Also, there is the implication in this definition that it is made up of factors which at least are relatively static and enduring in contrast to factors which may be more dynamic and changeable. This seems to imply that motor ability status would come about relatively slowly and over a period of time. Improvement would come about and be in proportion not only to one's potential but also in the amount of time and practice devoted to activity. Also, as one approaches his potential, change would come about more slowly. Once learned and practiced, these dominant abilities would be enduring and persist over a long period of time since they become a part of muscle memory. To some degree at least all the factors mentioned under components of movements in this chapter concern motor ability. Each contributes interdependently in the successful performance of skill. All these factors underlie performance and are causal to both fundamental skills and specific sport, gymnastic, and dance skills. They combine in an integration to make up total body movement. However, it must be pointed out that there has been no common agreement on the factors that constitute motor ability.

Motor Fitness

Another facet of motor performance is motor fitness. This quality has previously been discussed (see Chapter 10), but will be presented briefly here to show its relationship to neuromuscular skills. It is a limited phase of physical fitness and in many instances is similar to motor ability. However, it would seem to be more heavily weighted with the factors of strength and endurance. It is defined as "a readiness or preparedness for performance with special regard for big muscle activity without undue fatigue" (2–125). Motor fitness, like motor ability, is gauged by performance, and this performance is made up of many elements, many of which are the same as for motor ability. However because of the nature of motor fitness with its emphasis on performance without undue stress and fatigue, it would appear that some of these elements are more dominant than others. While it was said above that motor ability was undergirded by factors which were relatively static and enduring, motor fitness is made up of factors which appear more dynamic and changeable. It is heavily weighted with endurance and strength, and perhaps flexibility and power. Improvement in these factors would come about rapidly in most instances but at

the same time high level performance is lost in them unless they become a product of continuous training and conditioning. However, just as in the case of motor ability, there is no common agreement on all the factors constituting motor fitness.

SPECIFIC SKILLS (SPORTS, GYMNASTICS, AND DANCE)

The factors which are basic to all performance comprise a type of general ability which is exemplified through the fundamental skills. At a higher level are more specialized movements which are not necessarily racial in nature and are therefore not common to all individuals. These are a result of specialized training and experience. They are acquired through practice and specialization. They represent the result or influence of the factors which are basic to all performance as well as the fundamental skills. In fact, they are elaborations of these fundamental movements.

The physical educator is essentially an educator through skills such as a sport, a game, a dance, or a gymnastic technique. Perhaps the majority of that education takes place through sport skills and the major task of the teacher and coach is the development of these skills long recognized as the basic objective of their programs. These specialized skills may be defined as those physical abilities constituting each activity which are distinctive to that activity. They are unique to a specific game, dance or gymnastic stunt. Since it is obvious that games and dance and even gymnastics vary according to the custom, mores and nationality of people, these specific skills are not common to all people as the fundamental skills which come about through an interaction of maturation and practice in survival and drive activities.

A sport skill is a unit, and when combined with other units into a pattern,

7

along with certain rules, the result is a sport or athletic game. These patterns have as their basis the fundamental skills such as running, jumping, throwing, climbing, striking, and performance in them depends on the underlying basic factors to all movement such as speed, strength, agility, power, and the like. Baseball is running, throwing and striking. The quality or effectiveness of these skills is related to the fundamental factors of speed, power and coordination as well as strength and agility. Thus, sport skills are the result or effect of both the fundamental skills and the basic factors underlying them. When fundamental skills are combined into various patterns and sequences along with the functioning of the basic factors, sport skills result. These are unique and specific for each activity, as different sometimes as the mores and customs of people. Each nation has its own folk dances based on the traditions and culture of its people. Many nations have games that are different. The games themselves within a nation are as different as the rules and specialized type of skills make them.

SPECIFICITY VS. GENERALITY OF TASKS

There is the inevitable controversy between the traditional view that some abilities are general in nature and are present in amounts that can be applied to many skills and the new approach that views all abilities as highly specific. This controversy has not been resolved; much more sophisticated and careful research needs to be done in this area. However, current thinking based on recent research tends to view not only cognitive abilities but also physical abilities as highly specific to the task. This is to say that good performance in one ability would be no guarantee of excellence in others (11). Most of the research concerning general motor ability was done many years ago, when motor

ability was considered to be something general in nature. It was at this time that most of the tests involving motor ability, capacity and educability were developed. To imply that motor ability as a concept is passé and no longer exists as a quality is unfair. While it may be that research has grown in sophistication since these tests were developed, well-constructed and validated motor ability tests are currently playing a role in the success of many programs of physical education. These tests are not designed to disclose small differences in abilities nor even to predict potential in sport skills, but they are used successfully in classification schemes to screen students into the gifted physically, the average, and the low skilled. These tests have worked well for this purpose over the years and have been instrumental in facilitating teaching and learning.

However, much of the present-day research tends to point to the specificity of motor skills (5). In essence this indicates that performance from one skill to another is independent provided of course that these skill patterns are unrelated. Also, for example, research has shown that some of these factors are not a general quality but are specific to the task. The balance shown by a halfback may not be carried over to the balance that is necessary for performance on a horizontal bar. Franklin Henry and A. T. Slater-Hammel are the pioneers in this task specificity area.

Movement is a result of many variables including factors of learning. While it may be true that the psychology of learning is such that specificity of skill is indicated, there is another side to this question. Other variables connected with movement such as flexibility of joints, strength of muscle fiber, viscosity of muscle mass, the organs of balance would seem to make up qualities that could be interpreted as general in nature.

There is another point of issue. Many

of the tests used in research that have resulted in low correlations between tasks and hence to the conclusions that there is specificity of tasks have not provided reliabilities. It is a recognized fact that a test can be no more valid than it is reliable. Therefore, it could be that these tests on which conclusions are based are completely unreliable and hence not valid.

The proof of the pudding is in the eating. Motor ability tests in general have been used chiefly for classification where the program is a more or less survey type of approach. A good motor ability test which has been scientifically validated will do an adequate job of screening students into homogeneous ability levels. This is not to imply that all individuals who may have been placed in the upper 25 percent by the motor ability test will be good tennis players or gymnasts. However, it is a known fact that after a period of training and practice in these sports, they will become adequate performers and their level of skill will be higher than will those who were placed in the lower 25 percent by the original testing.

The controversy over task generality or specificity usually involves the question of whether there can be such a thing as general motor ability. At the present time this is not known because both positions still rest on theoretical reasoning and the research on either side is not overpowering. While most motor learning experts lean toward the task-specific side, there are two points of issue that must be resolved. First, in the research in motor learning, expert talks about a task, and it might be conjectured that a task and an ability are not the same thing. It is highly probable that tasks are specific. At least the research points toward this. However, an ability is broader in scope than a task and could be more general because it does include different patterns rather than just an isolated task. Second, the task-specific people base their whole case on the fact that if an individual is good in one activity, he would necessarily be good in all others if there were such a thing as general motor ability. However, this denies the fact that the traditional view of motor ability looks on it as being made up of a number of dominant underlying factors or elements which may be unrelated to each other. These have been identified as speed, strength, power, agility, hand-eye coordination, and others. Any given individual might possess some of these to a different degree than others. Also, some activities are dependent more heavily on some of these factors than others. For example, basketball is heavily weighted with agility, power and hand-eye coordination. Thus, when participating in an activity, one's success will generally be in proportion to the degree he possesses those factors which weigh most heavily in successful performance of that activity. In an activity heavily weighted with balance, strength and steadiness like performing on the horse in gymnastics and another activity heavily weighted with speed and hand-eye coordination like playing split-end in football, there might be a low correlation between any given individual's performance on the two.

Also, one other point. It is thought by those who recognize the generality of abilities that motor ability is a combination of the innate and the acquired in fundamental skills. These fundamental skills are the basic simple skills which are universal in nature and are learned and strengthened over a long period of time in childhood and early youth. When these are present in gross form, there is the possibility of rapid adaptation through transfer. Within the framework of heredity these skills become generalized so they can be used automatically under varying conditions. To say that kicking a soccer ball is highly specific and is unrelated to other kicking skills denies the fact that it is based on the simple skills of kicking which have been practiced in many forms for years during incessant play activities and have been adapted through transfer to other similar tasks.

Proponents of generality and specificity of perceptual-motor traits probably are prone to take an extremist point of view toward the issue. The "skill is specific" group is headed by such strict experimentalists as Franklin Henry who would go so far as to deny that there can be transfer between skills (11). The generality group is headed by traditionalists who continue to use unitary factors that have been arrived at over the last century through empiricism chiefly. However, there is a group of middle-of-the-roaders who would compromise and take a more in-between position. These would not deny the specific nature of most tasks. However, at the same time, they recognize the influence of more general abilities which have arisen out of past experience. They, therefore, claim that neither position is defensible. This group is headed by Bryant Cratty who has probably contributed more than any other researcher to date in the area of perceptual-motor skills. Cratty has presented a conceptual framework of motor behavior which provides for both general and specific elements (4). In fact he presents a three-factor theory of perceptual-motor behavior (see Fig. 11–1). As revealed by this figure there are three levels of supports for motor behavior. These include general supports at the base, perceptual-motor ability traits at the second level, and specific tasks at the top level. Cratty suggests that the first two levels are more important during the early years during childhood and early adolescence but as the later adolescence and adulthood years are reached, perhaps the traits at the apex of the pyramid become more influential. He concedes, however, that his theoretical framework is only partly fact and some facets of it need further verification.

PRINCIPLES OF MOVEMENT (13–344)

In the past it has empirically been recognized through observation that movement tends to follow certain principles or laws. Some of these no doubt are inherent in the neural system, while others are related to anatomy and physiology and in some instances are related to all three. The following principles apply to most motor skills when applicable.

Opposition

The principle of *opposition* is the natural tendency for a movement to make use of opposite body parts in a synchronization of action. For example, in correct form in walking or running, the left arm is synchronized with the right leg and vice versa. The shooter in basketball drives under the goal for a "crip" shot. As he shoots the ball against the backboard with his right hand, the jump or take-off is from the left foot. Some skills violate this fundamental principle and Dr. J. F. Williams points out that these have never been universally popular (13–345).

Form

Aside from the quality of a movement, it has come to be recognized that from a mechanical standpoint there is a correct *form* for all so-called fundamental skills as well as specific skills. This does not mean that form is an absolute and cannot be changed when better mechanical means are discovered. Everything else being equal, the performer who utilizes good movement form should achieve a more efficient performance than one who is thrown at a mechanical or physiological disadvantage due to poor form. While it is true that form over the years

A THREE-FACTOR THEORY OF PERCEPTUAL-MOTOR BEHAVIOR

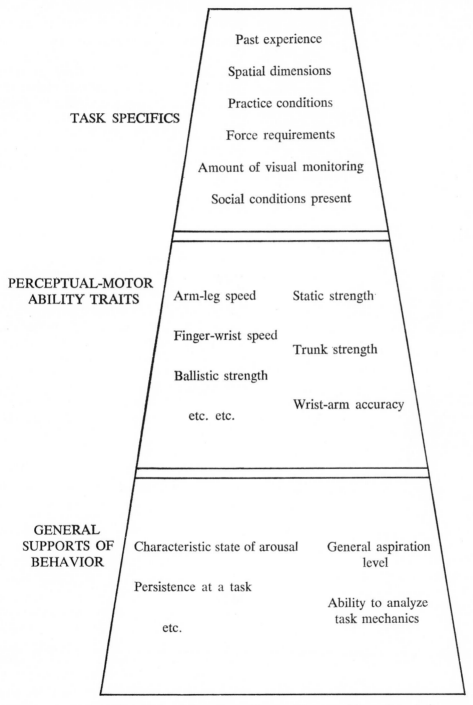

FIGURE 11–1.   A Three-Factor Theory of Perceptual-Motor Behavior*

* Cratty, Bryant J.: A Three Level Theory of Perceptual-Motor Behavior. QUEST, VI, May, 1966, pp 3–10.

has changed in some activities and coaches and physical educators are continually seeking not only better means of learning a technique but also better mechanical advantages, form still remains one of the criteria by which success is measured. It is related to the economy of movement since good form is accomplished with a minimum of energy expended. It must be pointed out that individual differences do exist due to many factors. Among these are body type, structure and psychological factors.

Quality

Aside from the form or movement pattern itself of a skill, an important factor in success is the *quality* of that skill within the framework of the pattern. In other words, it is speed, force, power or ease with which an individual performs most skills in order to become successful. Many skills, for example, must be performed with speed or within a time limit. Mechanically or form-wise, some individuals can perform quite well but either because of a lack of speed, force or power, their achievements fall short of others who have more speed or power. Since the temporal factor is a significant aspect especially in complex skills, what has been called "timing" is also a part of this principle. However, basically timing refers to ordered or sequential patterns which make up a skill hierarchy.

Primary-Secondary Objectives

Many skills involve hand-eye-foot-eye coordination. Such skills involve catching, shooting, batting, or stroking in some manner. Shooting, catching and batting usually are concerned with two or more objectives. For example, there is an order of movement involving a primary objective followed by a secondary objective. If attention is removed from the *primary* objective too soon in order to concentrate on the *secondary* objective, there will usually be an error in performance. For example, a second baseman who covers the bag on an attempted steal of second base tries to tag the runner before he catches the ball; or a flanker in football, on a hook pattern, attempts his pivot and dash down the field before he catches the ball; or the batter who moves his eyes from the ball an instant before contact and looks at the fence in left field over which he hopes to clout the ball; or the golfer who looks up for his shot down the fairway before he contacts the ball. In many instances the simple remedy is "to keep your eye on the ball" until it is hit or caught.

Principle of Follow-through

All skills involved in batting, striking, kicking, shooting, throwing are performed with a *follow-through*. This simply means that at impact or release, the movement leading up to impact or release is continued. This continuation of the movement in the line of flight provides not only for greater power, but also accuracy. Examples of the follow-through are: the golfer who hits the ball and continues the movement after impact in the line of flight, ending up with the club held high above the head, or the basketball shooter who lets his hand and arm at release continue after the ball toward the basket.

Principle of Total Movement

Most sports, gymnastics and dance skills, as well as the fundamental skills, while they may involve fine motor coordination, are basically performed out of a base of gross motor activity. Gross motor activity involves not only postural but also locomotor or transport forms of movement. Thus, most skills performed primarily by the arms or legs involve more than just that moving part. It involves the entire body in a synthesis of movement involving postural, locomotor and manipulative types of movement. Thus, the teacher as well as the performer must be cognizant of the importance of *total body movement*.

REFERENCES

1. Barrow, Harold M.: *Motor Ability Testing for College Men.* Minneapolis, Burgess Publishing Company, 1957.
2. Barrow, Harold M., and Rosemary McGee: *A Practical Approach to Measurement in Physical Education.* Philadelphia, Lea & Febiger, 1964.
3. Cratty, B. J.: *Movement Behavior and Motor Learning,* 2nd Ed., Philadelphia, Lea & Febiger, 1969.
4. Cratty, B. J.: A Three Level Theory of Perceptual-Motor Behavior. Quest, Vol. VI, May, 1966, pp. 3–10.
5. Henry, Franklin M., and Donald E. Rogers: Increased Response for Complicated Movements and a "Memory Drum" Theory of Motor Reaction. Research Quarterly, Vol. 31, 1960, pp. 448–458.
6. Kephart, N. C.: *The Slow Learner in the Classroom.* Columbus, Ohio, Charles E. Merrill Books, Inc., 1960.
7. Larson, L. A., and R. D. Yocom: *Measurement and Evaluation in Physical, Health, and Recreation Education.* St. Louis, C. V. Mosby Company, 1951.
8. Lawther, J. D.: *The Learning of Physical Skills.* Englewood Cliffs, N. J., Prentice-Hall, Inc., 1968.
9. McCloy, C. H., and Norma D. Young: *Tests and Measurements in Health and Physical Education.* New York, Appleton-Century-Crofts, Inc., 1954.
10. Oxendine, Joseph B.: *Psychology of Motor Learning.* New York, Appleton-Century-Crofts, Inc., 1968.
11. Singer, Robert N.: *Motor Learning and Human Performance.* New York, The Macmillan Company, 1968.
12. Ulrich, C.: *The Social Matrix of Physical Education.* Englewood Cliffs, N. J., Prentice-Hall, Inc., 1968.
13. Williams, J. F.: *The Principles of Physical Education,* 8th Ed. Philadelphia, W. B. Saunders Company, 1964.

PART III

Scientific Bases and
Principles

SECTION C
Social Bases and Principles

Chapter 12

Social Bases

INTRODUCTION

As a part of the entity of the individual the area of social attitudes and feelings plays an essential role. This unity concept implies that the organism reacts to any stimulus as a whole, thus the social and emotional are as much a part of the physical as psychological and biological reactions. The emphasis in physical education has been on organic aspects and on movement. Historically, the physical objectives seem to take precedence over others.

However, while man is a biological organism and in his original nature has animal characteristics, he is engulfed in an environment and immersed in a specific culture. This environment is characterized by people, ideas and things as a part of specific culture. No one or no thing can be divorced from this culture and the society concomitant to it. At birth the newborn is like an animal with all the built-in biologic drives and needs. Biologically he will grow and develop within certain limits set by the factors contained in his genes. However, that growth and development always occur in a setting characterized by other people, ideas and things. While body type and muscular potential may be genetically predestined to some extent,

personality, feelings and attitudes are not. They are a result of man interacting with his culture—culture unrelated to biological inheritance. Man's personality best exemplifies what he is and therefore how he acts because personality can only be known and revealed through his actions. Social behavior is a product of the interaction of original nature and the environment. Man is not born with an already built-in social self. Personality and for that matter the whole area of human behavior come about through a long process of socialization. While the young child is equipped with a set of forces which include inner drives to fulfill basic needs, his whole process of socialization is dependent on the social and cultural heritage of his society. Since the physical educator is concerned with the whole individual, the professional student should have some knowledge of culture and social order, and how socialization occurs. The physical educator's realm is human movement and this chapter seeks to understand social man in the context of movement.

It has been traditional in education to view man's behavior in terms of the three disciplines of biology, psychology, and sociology. If educators are to achieve their goals for educating youth, it is mandatory that they understand this behavior and the experiences which promote it. No one field alone holds the key which unlocks the doors to understanding human behavior. Rather these three traditional fields along with some others interact in special ways to provide not only understanding, but also acceptable educational experiences. However, sociology is an important dimension to this interaction since it is a study of human behavior as a part of society. The student must know and understand the basic tenets of sociology if he is to become sensitive to its implications for physical education.

Sociology is the science of social facts as they apply to human relationship with other men and with human society. It studies the origin, nature and the development of that society. Man does not live a life alone. Even Robinson Crusoe had his Friday. Man has a tendency to associate with other men because he is a social creature by nature. This becomes one of the most important assumptions on which the foundation of sociology rests. Man lives with other people and interacts with them as one of a group. This interaction leads to social organization and social control. Social organization deals with people in their culture—with personality, the social group, socialization, social change, and of course with such institutions as the family, marriage, religion, education, recreation, and politics—a network of social interaction. Social interaction occurs through action and reaction among individuals and predictable human behavior results. Ideas, attitudes, appreciation and ideals are influenced by such interaction. Basic to the process of interaction is some type of communication. Since movement is now looked upon as a mode of communication, it is as much sociological as it is biological or psychological. Since sociology is vitally concerned with human behavior, the physical educator must have an understanding of social controls. He must know the greater realm of human behavior before he can fully understand the principles of movement behavior, and he should know the part played in total human behavior by movement.

SOCIAL ORGANIZATION

Fortunately human behavior is somewhat predictable since it follows an order similar to the patterning of natural phenomena (1–5). If education is to profit most, the educator as well as the physical educator must understand these patterns of behavior. The activities which most people perform are done in a somewhat standardized way and can be predicted since they are characterized by regularity and recurrent patterns. As people act, react and interact together over a period of time, they tend to develop certain mutual expectations of one another and of the total group; these emerge as patterns of behavior. In a society these patterns of behavior become highly complex, and they are referred to as *social organization*. While these patterns of behavior become regular and predictable to a degree, they are always shifting and changing in some manner, an indication that socialization is dynamic. Social organization is not the same thing as culture. Culture refers to the standards of behavior while social organization deals with the behavior itself.

SOCIETY

Social organization is patterned human behavior carried out in a *society*. Bertrand defines society as "a collection of people with a common identification who are sufficiently organized to carry out the conditions necessary to living harmoniously together." (1–23) A society must be a large group of a relatively permanent nature existing in an atmosphere of cooperation and interaction. This interaction is the key to the social processes. It involves the behavior of members of a society as they act, stimulate, react, and respond together in some type of exchange. Such behavior is not always positive nor is it always a face-to-face relationship but it must elicit a response.

SOCIALIZATION

The process of socialization has been referred to previously in this chapter and also on other occasions. *Socialization* may be defined as a process of learning the ways of one's society and becoming a functioning member of it along with exhibiting standards of behavior in accordance with its rules, laws and customs. It has to do with the adjustment one makes to his environment. It will be shown in the next chapter on anthropology how social man evolved and how the complexities of modern society have made his problem of adjustment to his cultural milieu more difficult. What might have been a very simple type of adjustment in prehistoric man has now become a highly complex process. This total process is sometimes referred to as *enculturation* by cultural anthropologists.

The human personality is basic to the socializing process. While personality has a biological basis and is partially a product of heredity, it is more a product of one's cultural heritage. Social behavior and personality, while they may develop within the boundaries of certain hereditary dispositions, are shaped and molded by the forces of the environment —the cultural milieu in which man is immersed. No child is ever born with a personality any more than he is born a socialized being. While he is born with a biological heritage, culturally he must start from scratch. He has to learn all the behavior which will enable him to adjust to society and to become a functioning and an accepted member of it.

Many questions arise at this point. How does one become socialized? How does one become a stable functioning member of his group in a complex social world? How can one best be taught the ways of his immediate group and his broader cultural heritage—customs, traditions, folkways, mores, rules, standards, and laws? A more pertinent question might be what are the desirable attributes of personality which are essential for group living? What are the personal traits and characteristics which should become the goals of education in a democratic society for its members? The answers to these and similar questions are not always objective. The means of implementing the socialization process are never clear-cut or sharply defined. In fact, at the present time they present one of the most controversial areas in education. However, some facts seem evident, and perhaps it would help to trace some of the threads which form the fabric of social patterns.

Starting with the beginning one observes that the infant is born with complete social immaturity and is completely dependent upon others. The process of socialization is the design of life through which the child develops and is led from a state of social immaturity and dependence toward a state of social maturity and independence. Through this design, he gradually acquires the learning which enables him to live effectively in his culture. These requirements must be internalized as habits of acting and thinking and when they do become so, his behavior is somewhat predictable and he acquires a personality. Due to his interaction and close relationship with his more intimate primary groups, he never reaches the point of complete maturity and independence. The transmission of culture is a part of socialization. This transmission occurs first in the home and then in the schools as a formal process; also, it is done on a less formalized basis by other processes of transmission. Any time there is interaction between individuals, between an individual and the group, or between groups, some form of transmission and socialization takes place. Socialization is always an ongoing process because it is never complete. Secondary socialization takes over for primary socialization and continues until the end of life (3–83), (6–149). There are always adaptations to be made to changes in the cultural environment.

Since the process of socialization takes place through interaction of the individual with other individuals and with social groups there can be no socialization without interaction and every act has some effect. Both the individual and society have expectations about goals of the socialization process. The ultimate goal of socialization is culture, and the development of the personality is its product. While this process has been effective in reaching desired expectations, both the individual personality and society profit. The goals of expectation have to do with the aspiration level of the individual, and they may either limit or motivate. When aspirations are high, goals are difficult to achieve but they are worthwhile since they symbolize culture and refinement, and epitomize civilization that is revered by society. Personality of the individual is influenced through the socialization process by the development of a self-image.

Since personality emerges through the process of socialization, and socialization results in the creation of a self-image, perhaps it would be well to elaborate a little more so that the professional student might clarify his thinking regarding the self concept. Through the processes of socialization the child develops his own *self-image* by means of a feedback from others (3–10). He interprets what others think of him through the results of this feedback, and he sees himself mirrored in their expectations. At the same time he is developing his own self-image, he is also developing his concept of the *ideal-self* which, in simplest terms, is how he should behave in order to become well liked and accepted (1–59). This is an integrative process whereby he combines in his thinking the expectations of his society, his own aspirations with respect to those expectations, and perhaps information he receives from individuals from his reference group. A third level of self-development through socialization referred to by Broom and Selznick is the *ego* which involves the internalization of the ideal-self until it becomes conscience which controls behavior even when no one is watching (2–101).

However, social interaction leading to socialization depends on a number of variables. There are many factors which lead to modification of behavior. Ulrich suggests that the factors of integration lie along a horizontal continuum which runs the gamut of association (8–75). At one end are the processes of disassociation and at the other are the processes leading to the highest form of association. At the negative disassociation end are the forces of opposition including *competition, rivalry* and *conflict*, while at the positive end are the associative processes including *accommodation, cooperation* and *assimilation*. It is not to be assumed that the forces of disassociation are always bad as a part of the socializing process. As a matter of fact, all factors are related and a typical social situation might involve all of them. It can be easily observed how all of these factors would play some part in the game situations which are a prominent part of physical education. The following factors are the keys to the

[handwritten margin note: questionable in light of curr. research which assoc. aggres./competitiveness with frustration in a syndrome]

social processes as interaction leads to socialization.

Competition

First, there is *competition* which is a form of opposition on the negative side of the association continuum. It is the most pervasive and continuous type of oppositional interaction. It is a part of the original nature of man in need of modification. Competitiveness is a part of all social interaction but is a basic ingredient of sports and athletics. Competition generally is carried on under rules and standard codes of behavior. The goals, purposes or ends sought are the primary emphasis and the process is impersonal. The competitor is of secondary importance. Competition has been classified into two types: direct and indirect. Indirect competition is characterized by an attempt to achieve a standard and could be involvement without an opponent other than a set criterion, one's past record, or a conference or world record. Direct competition involves an opponent where maximizing one's own achievement leads to minimizing the opponent's. When rules are not obeyed and codes of behavior such as sportsmanship are ignored, direct competition usually degenerates into conflict.

Conflict

Second, competition can lead to *conflict*. When competition is carried to excess and over-competition results, there is conflict which is at the extreme negative end of the continuum. As a social process, conflict represents the most radical type and while in its most extreme forms could lead to disintegration of the social processes, it does have certain assets when kept within limits. In case of conflict the goal is secondary and the opposition becomes the primary consideration. Once the opposition (primary) is eliminated, the secondary goal becomes the reward for victory. Conflict is not always accompanied by physical violence but one frequently thinks of it in this nature. In modern political, economic and business worlds, conflict is characterized not by physical violence but more than likely by psychological stress. The emphasis is still on thwarting, eliminating or completely destroying the opposition rather than achieving an ultimate goal or purpose. Therefore, in the main only in athletics is conflict a socially accepted process (8). Conflict must be resolved in some manner. Either the opposition is eliminated or the conflict is solved through accommodation. Conflict is an intermittent process as such violent interaction cannot exist indefinitely.

Rivalry

Another type of opposition is *rivalry*. It is somewhere between competition and conflict since it has some of the elements of both. There is some question about which is the primary aspect— the goal which is the source of competition or the opponent. In many cases rivalry starts out as competition with the primary purpose being the achievement of the goal—to win the game or the championship. However, it may end up as rivalry when the interaction becomes more personal. Rivalry has some of the attributes of other social interacting forces. Like conflict it is not a continuing process as much as competition. Like competition it can occur between individuals, individuals and groups, and groups. However, it is more likely to occur between individuals. Like cooperation it is governed by rules and codes of conduct and is generally carried on with the idea of fun and sports. However, rivalry frequently reverts to conflict.

Accommodation

Conflict can lead to another process known as *accommodation*. Accommodation is the altering of interaction between individuals and groups in order to avoid or reduce conflicts and to promote a type of coexistence. Since conflict must be resolved in some manner or overcome if confrontation is not to end in disintegration of the social processes, some way out must be found. Accommodation can be achieved by a number of processes leading to adjustment in overcoming conflict and resolving complete misunderstanding. It is a form of cooperation but in resolving conflict, it does not go as far as cooperation. Cooperation is more positive and through its processes, differences are submerged and common purposes are achieved. In accommodation, the differences are never entirely resolved nor are common purposes often achieved. It is sort of a negative form of cooperation and placed near the middle of the social continuum. The basic issue or issues are not settled and they may remain as latent problems which may break out again at some future time. However, due to the processes of accommodation the groups are able to function together and coexist, although they can't agree on the basic issue or the ultimate answer. America today is a pluralistic society in which diversity is not only present but in some cases encouraged. Differences in race, religion and creed can be accommodated and hopefully assimilation may eventually take place. Processes of accommodation are compromise, subordination, mediation, arbitration, toleration, and truce.

Compromise is prompted when neither competitor wishes to pay the price of further conflict and some mutual concessions are made. *Subordination* usually results when one group recognizes the strength or superiority of the other and chooses to submit to the demands of that group because it seems to have no rewarding alternative at that time. *Mediation* is an outgrowth of a stalemate when a third party is brought into the picture to serve as an adviser for a settlement. In this case, however, neither side is under any obligation to abide by the advice of the third party or the mediator's recommendation. *Arbitration* is similar to mediation except both parties agree to accept the decision of the arbiter. *Toleration* occurs when domination is out of the question and yet compromise cannot be effected. In this case, the differences continue to exist but are ignored or endured. *Truce* comes about when both parties seem unable or unwilling to continue the conflict. The fight is suspended by agreement, sometimes for a specified period of time. It generally settles nothing but may lead to some process which will.

Cooperation

Fifth, if interaction is to be achieved and integration of the group is to be successful, there must be *cooperation*. Cooperation is a type of social interaction where individuals or groups work together to achieve a common goal or purpose. Cooperation, too, is a part of original nature but probably is not as strong as competition since competition comes first in the growth and developmental process and takes longer to modify. However, both are a part of original nature and both can be modified by forces in the social environment. Cooperation is not the antithesis of competition, however, because they both can be a part of the same situation. For example, two teams compete with each other for the same goal—to win the championship—but cooperation is always present since the rules of the game must be obeyed, the decision of the officials respected, and the codes of sportsmanship upheld. In fact, no group could exist without cooperation in some form. It is probably true that cooperation must be present if competition is to be at its most stimulating best. Thus, competition and cooperation have a symbiotic relationship where each one benefits the other in some way (8–84).

Assimilation

Last, for complete socialization to take place there must be assimilation. Therefore, assimilation is the ultimate in cooperation but generally the process requires a long period of time to become effective. There has been much conflict in the racial issues and this has been followed by accommodation. In the final analysis the process of assimilation must gradually become operative. It is a process which leads to the establishment of homogeneity of groups. It is the highest level of interaction where each group takes on some of the traits and characteristics of the other, and cooperation is at its best. Assimilation connotes harmonious relationships and is a two-way process. The first level would merely be a first step and include only the acceptance by one group of the behavioral patterns of the other through contact. This level is called *acculturation*. The next level denotes thorough integration into all social systems and is known as *social integration*. The third level is *amalgamation* which is inclusive of social integration plus also biological integration through intermarriage.

In the final analysis, interaction is the key to socialization. Groups expect a certain type of behavior from their members. This behavior has been previously determined by the group generally in accordance with the customs, mores and laws of the cultural milieu and these, in a way, become the expectations of the group. When these group expectations are threatened through deviation from its norms of behavioral patterns by certain individuals or subgroups, pressures are brought to bear on the deviates.

These pressures are exercised by the group in order to maintain control. In fact these pressures are social controls. Such controls are generally in the form of sanctions, and sanctions are rewards and punishments. They are developed and applied by members of a society itself to encourage adherence to normative behavior (6–161). Positive sanctions are applied when the individual is motivated to conform through rewards such as recognition, acceptance, privileges, praise, money, fame or status. However, if he insists on nonconformity and causes conflict, he may be punished through negative sanctions such as lack of acceptance or recognition, scolding, sarcasm, ridicule, force, gossip, and rejection. In some cases the negative sanctions may carry as far as expulsion, dismissal, ostracism, or even death. Thus, such social controls vary from the informal type to the more formal type relating to law and order (1–287). However, if the individual has aspirations which are not acceptable to his society at the time, but through dedication, initiative and hard work he finally achieves them, the expectations of his group might be changed and the cultural patterns shifted hopefully for the improvement of the total group but not necessarily. Therefore, through the process of interaction, the individual is socialized but at the same time it is possible for the society itself to be changed. Another unit in this chapter will contend with the concept of social change.

In the processes of socialization through interaction, all of the social processes or group factors may be used along with the various types of group pressure. These pressures are brought to bear in many ways as a group attempts to socialize one or many of its individuals (1–280). Both negative and positive sanctions in the form of either rewards or punishments are employed.

Physical education through its program of sports and athletics utilizes all of these processes of interaction (8–123).

CULTURE

Man is not born as a social being, but becomes one as he takes on the qualities and characteristics known as human traits. Under the influence of the social and cultural environments accented principally by interaction with other individuals, the original nature of man becomes human nature. Original nature is animal-like until the processes of socialization become operant. It is for this reason that socialization was presented first in this chapter because before one can possess culture, he must be exposed to the processes of socialization. Social man is a product of his heredity and his environment. The environment in which he finds himself immersed is characterized by his culture—a culture which he has invented and must transmit to new generations. His social behavior in a sense is his heritage because he is born into a particular culture and his behavior from that point on is inexorably guided and in most cases dictated by the rules, codes and laws of that culture, and by the boundaries that have been set by its customs, mores and folkways. He has no more choice in the kind of cultural heritage into which he is born than he has in his biological heritage. However, it must be pointed out once again that culture is learned. Man cannot exist outside this culture. He must participate and share in it either in a negative or positive way.

Culture may be defined as a mosaic comprising the whole of man's learned and expected activities including ideas, knowledge, beliefs, laws, morals, traditions, art, customs, and habits as well as invented physical things like tools and buildings. Culture differs from social organization in that culture represents transmittable behavior patterns of living —norms and standards—whereas social organization deals with the concrete behavior of the people themselves. A society, too, differs from a culture. Perhaps this statement would serve to explain the difference. A society can function only because of certain codes of conduct which it formulates for itself. These formulated codes and rules become the culture of that society. Thus, a society and a culture are mutually dependent on each other. Culture is acquired behavior and is entirely the product of social invention, dependent on learning and communication for its transmission and maintenance. Culture and society are interrelated and interdependent. One cannot exist without the other. While culture deals with ideas, concepts and things as norms, it is the people in society who create them and in turn who are shaped by them once they have been created.

Thus, man has the ability to create his own culture but at the same time he becomes a product of that culture. He also has the responsibility to transmit it to succeeding generations. Society generally provides for this transmission of its culture through institutions of the home, school and the church. Historically the family has been the basic and most efficient unit to transmit cultural heritage. However, as a result of many developments the family has entrusted many of these historic duties elsewhere and is apparently about to abdicate others. In a modern technological and "suburbanized" society, the school has become the formal institution where culture is taught and learned. Education as a tool institution has the responsibility not only to transmit the cultural heritage of the past, but also to assist the individual in adjusting to its varied requirements and at the same time trying to improve on those requirements for the benefit of present and future generations. Since culture is learned behavior, it is modifiable and may therefore be changed. Culture is not always spread by the formal educational system, however. Much of our cultural heritage is transmitted through other processes of transmission which operate in many ways as people interact and react to each other. The church has played a prominent role in the past and the state is assuming more and more of the functions. There is a relationship here between transmission of culture and social change, and in America during the twentieth century this rate of transfer has been greatly accelerated.

Also, it must be pointed out that the forms of culture are both *materialistic* and *nonmaterialistic*. In addition to the ideas and the laws, mores and traditions which are concepts that govern behavior, there are myriads of tangible things created by man which are a part of his culture and which make up the materialistic forms. In more advanced technological culture, such material things as autos, television, radio, stadiums, golf carts, jet planes, and spacecrafts have great impact on the way men behave.

The nonmaterialistic forms of culture encompass the learnings of man which are used to direct behavior. These are divided into two categories of individual *norms* and *institutions*. Norms are standards of behavior and represent the average of a social group. They are the "rules" of the game of living and they provide the criteria for judging behavior (1–28). They are made up of knowledge, beliefs and values and are embodied in the *folkways*, *mores* and *laws*.

Folkways are commonly expected ways of acting in a society and include behavior such as courtesy, etiquette, modes of dress, and any custom that is common to the group. These can be changed, but practice has shown that they are relatively permanent and change very slowly over a long period of time. While they do influence behavior, they do not carry sanctions, and violations of these customs is met with an attitude not of general acceptance but at least of tolerance. Recently the long hair and beards worn by men are an example.

Mores, too, are expected ways of behavior in a society but they might be termed higher level customs or traditions. They have more force than folkways. They are usually accompanied by sanction and are strictly enforced because they encompass behavior which has been shown by experience over long periods of time to be necessary for the good of the group. Mores are a product of history, and one generation of society learns to profit by the experiences of a previous one. Such behavior is adopted out of expediency when it is shown that the needs and desires of the group can better be served by abandoning the old in favor of the new.

Laws have more force than either the folkways or the mores although they arise out of custom, tradition and mores which they codify and enforce. Laws have the connotation of the moral, and society expects them to be followed as it sets the necessary boundaries of the requirements and provides for means of enforcement through strict sanctions. Thus, the character of a culture is governed by a hierarchy of norms called folkways, mores and laws. It is true that these norms are frequently violated, but in general the expectations of society embodied in them are internalized in members who appear to want to conform. Conformity could be due to the sanctions imposed by others, however.

Social institutions are clusters of norms rather than individual norms, characterized by formalized relationships which permit no deviancy beyond certain points. These center around some basic function or need of society, and they have developed over long periods of time as evolving processes. Examples of these social structures are family, government, language, recreation, economic system, and education. However, one must not, for example, confuse "the family" as a social group with "the family" as an institution. They are different (1–91). In the first instance it is a primary social group, while in the second place it is a set of behavioral patterns.

Certain aspects of culture are frequently subjected to cultural lag which will be explained in the unit on social change. Along this same line is another interesting social phenomenon. Just as man vestigially retains some of his useless biological manifestations, he also maintains many vestigial social practices in his culture which have no excuse for being other than custom and tradition and the fact that they once served some useful purpose. Many folkways today are in this category, although many are not since these still retain their functional significance.

Culture has been fragmented into structural components for better understanding and identification. The smallest unit of culture which can be identified is called a *cultural* trait. When there is a combination of related traits, there is a *cultural complex*. When cultural complexes are related into larger configurations, they become *cultural patterns* (1–91).

The role of physical education must be understood in terms of a particular culture. Dr. J. F. Williams once said that every experience of the individual has social significance (9–139). If this is true, then physical education with its games, sports and dance provides an important cultural force. Games and sports are accepted as part of the cultural patterns in not only America but in all cultures. Little study has been made concerning cross-cultural patterns of play and games. While it is known and recognized that a society's sports and

play as well as their dance are as different from those of other societies as their customs, traditions and folkways, are there perhaps some universal patterns in movement that could be identified? The participant in play will always express himself in terms of the sanctions and customs laid down by his own culture. However, it would be interesting to learn the extent that fundamental skills are genetically controlled and to what extent they are culturally controlled.

Physical education with its play, games, sports and dance provides an important cultural force. In addition to the fact that the attitude and urge for play are universal qualities, it seems that games and sports in the United States have developed into a cult of success and prestige. America is truly a sports-oriented culture when the president of the country gets involved in sports either as a political move or to serve his own ego. But aside from these, all of these manifestations involve movement and when movement is integrated with play, self-expression and fitness, it has important implications in understanding man's behavioral design and also in helping to make his adjustments more easily to his cultural surroundings. Perhaps there is no other facet of society where the ideas of sanctions and role playing are as vivid and impressionable as in physical education. Thus, games, sports and dance have a part to play in shaping culture, but in turn are shaped by it. Language as a media of communication has been considered a most important facet of cultural identification and transmission. More recent trends in physical education would expound the idea that movement has always been a most important aspect of communication, and thus has cultural significance in this light as an important facet of socialization. Movement speaks its own language sometimes more loudly than words.

PERSONALITY

When man is exposed to his cultural environment, a process of socialization takes place. The impact that socialization has on the individual results in *personality* with special reference to social values since personality is made up of values. However, the facts of heredity must again be taken into consideration. First, of course, man is born into a cultural heritage already waiting to engulf him into its many facets. The heritage of the cultural, while it sometimes resists change, is subject to modification either by the group or by the individual's impact on the group. Second, man also has an inheritance of biological traits, organic drives and needs, and a psychological capacity for learning and behavior. Obviously these have their effect upon emotions, thoughts, and behavior. Personality is a product of both biological heredity and cultural environment. However, there is not sufficient evidence to state the parameters of each. The forces of the cultural environment do shape and modify human personality but they can do so only within the ranges set by heredity. Man's biological inheritance is a fixed condition, and it does play a role in personality development as it unfolds with the processes of maturation. Morphological factors play a role, also, in personality. Sheldon (7–9) has tried to show a relationship between temperament and body type. Culture, however, is not a part of one's biologic heritage as personality is. The cultural part of man's entity must be safeguarded by his social organization so that his personality may have a chance of being molded in ways according to norms set up in that culture. However, man has no instincts for his behavioral patterns. In personality development he takes on the way of behaving in his culture through the self-concept and through identification with others. These "others" may come from his peer groups or reference groups. A *peer group* is made up of individuals who are the same age and many times of the same sex, while the *reference group* is either a group or several individuals who are on the outside and who serve as models for value formation.

One's personality can never be viewed as something static. Rather it is dynamic because the society which nurtures it is dynamic, because one's interaction with new people, new ideas and new things is dynamic, and because even one's own whims of inner self vary from day to day. As socialization proceeds, the personality changes and is shaped. Ulrich defines personality as "the sum of a person's values and attitudes plus all his traits, and that this sum is always a dynamic organization." (8–32) It is the job of physical education to stress through its socialization processes these values and attitudes in physical education activities which come within its province and then to help generalize them to all areas of life. It is because of this reason that sports, exercise and dance should be looked upon as educational forces and not economical, commercial or entertainment.

Personality comes into focus by the process of socialization, already discussed. Obviously, this process operates differently with each person within the framework of an heredity that is also somewhat different. This interaction produces individual qualities that make one person different from all other persons. Personalities will differ in accordance with the type of culture which nurtures them. Each culture tends to have its own norms for patterns of behavior although there will be great differences within this frame of reference. Within a culture itself personalities will vary greatly because of hereditary factors on the one hand and the opportunity or privilege of participating in that cultural milieu on the other. In a sense most cultures run the gamut in opportunities and privileges. The personality that any one person has both reflects his culture and in another sense governs it. Personality is affected by levels of culture according to such aspects as wealth, family status and position, occupation, trade, profession, and even sex and age. Bertrand has suggested that the four important determinants of personality are: biological inheritance, geographic environment, social environment, and cultural environment (1–65).

The role one person plays in a group not only reflects personality but also affects it. Because man has the power to think and can communicate his ideas, and because he is gregarious, he interacts and reacts to others and learns. Thus, man's heredity is shaped by his social experience and socialization occurs for the individual and at the same time culture may be shaped or reshaped for the group. Each person plays a role in the socialization process as he interacts first with his parents and family, and later with teachers and peer groups. His personality is such that it seems natural for him constantly to seek acceptance in some or all of the above groups. If he receives full acceptance, his personality grows and develops toward his potential. However, if acceptance is lacking, personality may become dwarfed and even in some cases disorganized where the individual becomes a deviant and a burden to society. A well-adjusted personality is indicative of competence in a culture. An individual with such adjustment would be one who satisfies his own personal levels of aspirations within the parameters of the expectations of society.

If personality is shaped and molded in a sense by one's environment and society entrusts educational systems and schools with the responsibility of transmitting its social heritage as well as all knowledge which it holds valuable, it is important that the schools accept their role in personality development. The overall aim of the school in the socialization process should be to teach the ways of society in order to enable the individuals to become participating members of it, and to teach not only the acceptance of its standards and requirements which have been shown by experience to be valid, but also why these standards and values are valid. It has been said that personality is as personality does. In other words, personality can only be viewed and understood through behavior. Physical education has long been considered as one of the aspects of education where personality can be developed. It is rich in opportunities for such matters as role playing, interaction, leadership, and adherence to rules and standards—all so vital in personality development.

SOCIAL GROUPS

If the professional student in physical education is to understand the place of physical education in social development, he should know something about social structure and the cultural environment. He should be familiar with the nature of social groups—how they are constituted and how they function. In the evolutionary processes, the social aspect of man started to develop only when he began to live and interact with other men in groups. Perhaps these first experiences in group interaction spread over countless centuries, stemmed not so much from an inner drive of gregariousness as from an outward need to band together in combating the forces of a hostile environment. As man evolved, however, there is no doubt that his inescapable need to relate with others developed as a part of his nature as it evolved out of an expediency on his part in handling his environment. Man now lives in groups and operates in groups because he has not only learned that such groups are necessary for survival, but that through association rather than individualistic existence he is more effective and can achieve a higher level of excellence in his personal and group tasks.

A group can range in size from two people, a dyad, where the organizational structure is simple, to a large group with X number of people with a highly complex organization. Ulrich defines a social group as "two or more persons who interact with one another over a more or less appreciable and continual period; who are mutually aware of each other as members of the group; who are able to communicate effectively with each other by some acceptable means; and who have established a definite interpersonal structure which enables them to share a common purpose." (8–43)

In all social groups there must be interaction; the function of interaction is to achieve a common goal. The extent to which the group can function effectively in carrying out this common purpose depends on a number of elements of the social system. The size and homogeneity of the group is important. In every instance in all societies age, sex, family, place of residence, and voluntary association are the foundations of the social groups. The more complex the society, the more proliferation of interests and purposes, and therefore the more numerous the groups established in order to meet the needs of the problems brought on by increased complexity. Also, communication among members of the group is essential for interaction to occur.

Other essential facets of the social system operating to make the group function are role playing, status positions, stratification, and leadership. Every group has positions of status and offers opportunity for role playing. Basically, all social groups have a form of social stratification. It seems to be universal (1–163). The larger society needs *stratification* in order to exist and carry out its function. In all societies there is a division of labor related to stratification. *Status* is not an individual but a position among a hierarchy of positions in a social group. It is abstract and as a position may have no occupant. It is a bundle of norms since each position carries with it certain obligations, responsibilities, rights and privileges (6–179). The status one occupies in society or in a group is come by in one of two ways (1–29). It may be *ascribed status* whereby one is born into a status position or comes into it after birth without any effort on one's part. For example, race, sex, national group, wealth, and social position. The second way is through *achieved status* whereby status positions come to one through effort and choice. For example, one's profession, career, athletics, religion and the like. It is interesting that social position and wealth—two of the most prized status positions in America—may be either ascribed or achieved through effort. A high status carries with it prestige and sometimes in addition, power and wealth.

There is always opportunity in a democratic society or any open society for what is known as *social mobility*. This is a process whereby one moves up or down in a vertical manner from one status to another. To move up the scale of social status is an indication of success and achievement as well as prestige, among other things. It might even lead to power, wealth and social position. Social stratification is related to a society's value system. It is through a society's emphasis on certain values that opportunity is provided individuals to move from one status or social position to another. Universal ways of moving up are: through occupation improvement, economic success, individual achievement and power (1–188). Depending on the type of society and its values, there are other less often used ways of moving such as through art, acting, athletics, the military and the like. In America today prowess in athletics provides one of the best means of social mobility. This may or may not be a commentary on our value system.

Another element of the social system which is related to group interaction and especially to status is *roles*. A role is a pattern of behavior which is expected of the individual who occupies a particular status (1–29). Roles usually impose a responsibility on the role player, and sanctions are employed to enforce the obligations. The reward for playing one's role is esteem and honor (6–180). One may perform a role well and gain a measure of esteem. However, if the related status position is not high, the role player does not gain the prestige of society. Role playing involves interaction with other role players and can result in either processes of association or disassociation. Thus, role playing becomes an important element of the social processes.

Another element involves *leadership* since every group must have both leaders and followers (3–44) (also, see Chapter 5). Leadership is closely related to status positions and role playing. One boy becomes the quarterback (status position). This status position requires certain patterns of behavior. In carrying out this behavior the boy becomes a role player. The particular role he plays offers him an opportunity for leadership.

Social groups may be classified into a number of categories, but perhaps the most meaningful classification to the student are the categories of *primary* and *secondary* groups. Primary groups are based on such intimate association as the family, play groups, neighborhood gangs, friendship circles, fraternities, and all peer groups (6). A primary group seems to have a natural place in the order of a society where face-to-face cooperative interaction is evident. It does not have to be established or created; it is already there as a basic part of the cultural milieu since it is an essential facet of that culture. These groups tend to be intimate, informal and personal. They insist upon conformity to group standards and frequently resist change.

The *secondary* groups tend to be more formal and less intimate than primary groups and more impersonal in their relationships. They are directly an innovation of society and are subsidized by it. They are formed by voluntary association and include groups which are concerned with religion, economics, politics, education, and recreation. The chief characteristics of the secondary group are voluntary participation, a well defined goal, challenging activity, and frequent lack of sanction and stability. In most affluent societies today the secondary groups are gradually but surely taking over many of the functions once performed by primary groups. It is not so much that the secondary groups have usurped these functions as it is the primary groups have abdicated their right and in many cases responsibility. For example, sex education, once a function of the home, now is becoming a responsibility of the schools. It is not so much that the schools want this responsibility, but rather that the home has failed to meet its obligations adequately, and since society needs sex education in order to function more effectively in the new era, the schools seemingly must step into the breach. However, it is sometimes interesting to note how the primary groups, once they have relinquished a function, still want to tell the secondary groups how to perform it.

Thus, all groups have certain commonalities. Individual members of groups have assigned status in the group hierarchy from low to high. Also, each individual plays a role in his group depending on the character of the group, his opportunity, his status, and his role playing ability. Within the group some form of leadership is required. In fact leadership is a continuum which extends from deviation, through followership, to leadership of the highest level. It is difficult or impossible for a group to achieve its purposes if assigned status is not accepted, if roles are not played, if leadership is lacking, and if there is lack of communication.

SOCIAL CHANGE

Historically there has always been some type of change in social order either of an evolutionary nature, a basic change, or what sociologists call a cultural drift. *Social change* has been defined by Bertrand as "a continuous process which is manifested in alterations in social relations." (1–18) All societies with the exception of a few primitive stultified ones are dynamic in nature to varying degrees, and their culture is constantly changing. Since culture is learned behavior, it becomes modifiable. Of course some societies are more prone to change than others. Social change is a pluralistic process since in most cases the process of change cannot be laid to any one cause but to a multiplicity of factors. However, since culture is learned behavior and since behavior is always variable, change is inevitable.

Communication is a basic part of culture and of social change. In fact, it is the key to cultural transmission. Without communication there can be no transmission of culture from one society to another or from one generation to the next, and, thus no social change. Communication may be a first hand face-to-face thing or indirect through writing and other means. However, transmission of culture alone is no guarantee of social change. There must be some modification of cultural content or addition of new elements if social change is to occur through transmission.

This modification or addition is accomplished through the processes of *invention* and *diffusion* (1–123). Invention is construed to mean not only the creation or discovery of things but also ideas. In other words, it consists either of material or nonmaterial culture. Invention or discovery of either some new idea or thing is dependent partly on the intellectual potential in a society but also on the demand or the need for the new. Also, it is rare that something entirely new is ever created which is totally unrelated to old ideas and technology. Therefore, the store of existing knowledge and technology is conducive to the new since there is more opportunity to take known elements and combine them in establishing new relationships.

Diffusion, as opposed to the discovery of the new, is the spread of already existing cultural content or items from one society to another. It is a part of socialization and through it, culture can be transmitted between individuals, groups, and even nations. Material culture including technological processes is more readily transmitted than the nonmaterial involving ideas and abstract concepts. Sports and athletics are among the more important means of cultural diffusion. In the process of diffusion, each society selects the cultural traits it adopts, and most societies borrow more than they invent. Both individuals and groups often take a traditionalist's approach and resist change. Other individuals and groups place a high priority on change and cultural advancement; plans are made to implement its occurrence by innovation, invention, creativity, and manipulation.

In America today, as well as throughout the world, there is a state of rapid social change. This includes not only new concepts and interpretation about old ideas and beliefs, but also tremendous technological advances. In most advanced countries new technology and ideology are being introduced at an accelerating pace. Through invention new culture is acquired and through diffusion it is spread either directly or indirectly. Directly it is transmitted through face-to-face contacts while indirectly through such means of communication as writing, films, art and the like. Sports and games seem to provide a means of transmission and promote change through cultural diffusion.

Between the time that innovation and invention occur and when they actually cause social change, there may be a time lag of varying length, known as a *cultural lag*. It is characterized by an unevenness when one aspect, trait or pattern in a culture falls behind another or perhaps several. In education alone it is estimated that 25 years elapse between discovery of the new and its acceptance and application in general practice (5–2). In the field of technology, change is occurring so rapidly that social institutions have difficulty in catching up. Technology is always ahead of its use and adaptation. Much of the conflict that exists in today's society is due to cultural lag and resistance to change. This lag and conflict growing out of resistance is frequently fostered by a status quo group philosophy that tries to keep things as they are. The resistance may be led by vested interests and even by established institutions which stand to lose their sanctioning authority if change takes place, or it could be fostered by those who are more comfortable in the safety of the status quo. In general, however, cultural lag is temporary. Such a gap will tend to widen unless educational institutions

and other pertinent agencies keep up with the times and perform their functions in relation to new needs and demands. There is sometimes an element present in professions and particularly education where old cultural traits, complexes and patterns are held onto long after their function has become defunct.

There are many examples of cultural lag in physical education. One of the most serious is the status of an amateur in athletics today. Practice is no longer in accord with old beliefs, and as yet these beliefs have not changed to be compatible. Many instances of cultural lag in physical education are due to separate body-mind concept which has not kept pace with the findings of either science or philosophy.

Physical education has a stake in social change. It not only is affected by social change but it has also become an effector of change. The emerging concept that movement becomes a key process in the integration of man will not overlook the social as a part of man's entity. Thus, through movement— games, sports, dance and gymnastics— physical education can exercise control both for the good of the group and the individual.

SOCIAL VALUES

Socialization is a process by which the human personality is developed. The components of personality are *values*. When these values apply to behavior of of people, they are known as *social values*. Social values have been defined by Green as "a relatively enduring awareness plus emotion regarding an object, idea, or person." (4–143) In practice they are feelings about what is good or bad, or what should be and should not be. The big question today in education as well as physical education is how do these values become part of personality and character as a result of the processes of socialization. Also another question might be: what is the significance of these values to the individual and society once they become part of social behavior?

Culture has its own values and every society has some criterion or ideal of what constitutes a "good person," and a set of rewards and punishments to help mold men in that image. As was pointed out earlier, these values must be transmitted to groups and individuals in that culture through the process of socialization and enculturation. Social values are shared by many people as a part of that culture. Values are related to beliefs because they are frequently derived from beliefs. However, while a value is an emotional awareness, a belief is a conviction that something is factually true. It may not be based on scientific fact, but if it is considered a fact to the one who holds it, it is still a belief for him. Values, like personality which they structure, lie along a continuum. This area of attitudes, ideals and feeling is never a dichotomy where black and white, good and bad prevail. It is more than likely checked, plaid or shades of gray. In general, values range along a continuum from negative to positive. Thus, social values must be distinguished from ethical and moral values since the latter are always positive and in the upper quartile of what is considered good and right.

Sociologists recognize three levels of social values in personality as follows: *abstract sentiments, moral norms* and *self* (4–143). *Abstract sentiments* are used as a basis for decision-making not only by the individual but the group. They govern behavior, and while no one can deny the importance of these as concepts, the sentiments any one person holds are not always consistent.

They frequently lead to rationalization and in many cases one's sentiments contradict each other. An example of an abstract sentiment is "good sportsmanship." Also, an example of contradiction in sentiments is the mouthing of the sentiment of good sportsmanship while one still harbors a strong feeling of segregation. It seems to be a human trait that normal people can live with such contradictions.

Moral norms are standards which are used to judge the actual behavior of people. They serve as reference or anchor points for further interaction in social relationships. They are at a higher level than abstract sentiments and have more force in directing behavior although in most cases they are justified in relation to those same sentiments. They are more pressing because they encompass demands from the society for specific behavior. These norms are revealed in the folkways, mores and laws of a society. There are similar inconsistencies in these that one finds in sentiments. Such conflicts are accommodated within one's self by simply having two sets of values and a bit of evading the issue by rationalization.

The *self* is the third level of values and perhaps the most significant. The self of course is a product of social experience. Individual behavior is inexorably related to the norms of group expectancy. One's idea of self is never completely dependent on group expectation, however (1–179). Rather, it is uniquely an individual matter as one views himself mirrored in the moral and ethical expectations of his group. It is one's conception of himself in terms of his group's expectations of behavior. Thus, self-concept becomes a major goal for everyone as they strive for self-importance through adherence to group moral and ethical standards. However, without group interpretation or evaluation of these expected standards or norms, the individual could not achieve this conception of self. Also, there must be some feedback from others by which one measures the validity of his concept of self. If this feedback is negative, one then may be forced to change the conception he has of self. Also, it must be pointed out that not just any other people's judgment is accepted in self-awareness. It generally has to be someone or some group with status and prestige at least in the eyes of the one being socialized. For youngsters this generally implies someone from his peer or reference groups. It may be the coach, or the parent, or the teacher from the reference group or someone of status in the peer group.

IMPLICATIONS OF SOCIOLOGY FOR PHYSICAL EDUCATION

Physical education is involved with movement through games, sports, dance, and other related activities. These all involve play in some manner and play is a cultural universal along with language, moral codes and costume. It is as old as culture and while some have proposed theories, scholars can find no known reason for its existence except it is there. However, as Ulrich points out, while human mobility has traditionally been viewed in its biological context, it must also be identified and interpreted in ways other than biological aspects (8–1). Movement has implications for man's mental and psychological, but equally important, his sociological existence. It was pointed out in Chapter 1 that man learns to move but also moves to learn. The implication here is clear. Movement becomes an important means of concomitant and associated learnings. When man moves in the realm of sports, games and dance, something else happens to him physically, but also socially and mentally. Since much of human movement occurs in groups, or since much of it is done in a setting that has social implication and overtones, movement plays an important part in man becoming socialized man.

This chapter has been concerned with the social bases for physical education. While it has been briefly touched upon that these basic concepts of sociology have a relationship with movement, this relationship has not been specifically spelled out. Sociopsychological values will be discussed in Chapter 14. Perhaps more should be said here concerning the place of physical education activity as social processes. Sports and games are a part of basic human behavior and are among the most effective means of socialization of man. They are related to culture since they not only reflect culture but help to structure and shape it. They play an important part in the development of personality and the self. They provide dynamic social groups such as the team and play group. These groups seem ideal for the face-to-face interaction which is needed in the processes of socialization. They provide a media for cultural invention and diffusion and for social change. They make important contributions in the development of a system of values.

A little closer look at these areas shows the important role played by each in the social matrix of physical education. Each of these is related to the matrix and all are related to each other as they become operative as part of the social processes. For example, physical education is vitally interested in social groups —the team, the class, the peer play group, the intramural homeroom, the opponents among others. It is in these groups, however, that the individual is exposed to most of the social processes which eventually lead to socialization and social maturity. It is in these groups that he is assimilated and socialized. In a sense, particularly in childhood, they help him to identify real life situations because sports and games are mini-societies within themselves where most of the social processes function. Games and sports are probably more representative of society than any other aspect of education. Ulrich says games are a microcosm of society (8–118). Social groups expect members to behave in special ways. So does society. Each game or sport has its rules and boundaries and a code of conduct for the participant, and these clearly distinguish right from wrong. These play groups expect the behavior of their members to conform to the norms of the group. They are almost always accompanied by sanctions which are direct, immediate and easily understood by all members— the deviate as well as the conformer. They furnish means of socialization whereby the individual learns cooperation, competition, accommodation to resolve conflict, respect for authority, and discipline. The individual quickly learns the value of these concepts through experience in games. He plays the game for his own personal satisfaction. However, if he is to get this satisfaction, he must be competitive within the framework of the rules, he must be cooperative within the framework of competition, he must help to resolve issues of conflict which may arise, and he must learn to respect officials and authority by virtue of their status. He recognizes the importance of discipline if game situations are to afford him the most satisfaction. He, therefore, endorses its sanctions. If, however, he fails to measure up in any of these areas, the sanctions of his group are quick to catch up with his deviate behavior. On the other hand, the rewards of positive sanctions tend to serve as reinforcers for socially accepted behavior. Thus, positive sanctions, rewarding adherence to the sociocultural directives, and negative sanctions punishing those who violate prescribed norms become vital socializing factors.

These experiences and learnings in physical education games and sports are highly specific and apply to the smaller society of games only. They must, however, be generalized into the larger area of life. While it is probable that an adult will show the same codes of ethical and moral conduct in life that he showed in games as a youth, this has not been shown through scientific evidence as yet. It is sufficient to say at this point that it becomes the job of education and its leadership to teach for transfer so that the positive social learnings in sports and games will be generalized into similar life situations.

As sports, games and their functional integrity have a value placed on them in our culture, the team, the class, the homeroom, the club, and the playground group, when they are used as educational media they become most important means of developing social behavior approved by custom, folkways and mores of society. This is true because they have their own customs, folkways and mores which are similar to those of society. Also, they furnish wonderful media for such socializing factors as role playing, accepting of status positions, assuming leadership responsibilities, cooperating, competing and accommodating to issues. In a physical education group as well as an informal play group an individual will play many roles and accept the requirements and sanctions of many status positions, and be placed in positions where leadership must be exercised. Are these not replicas of real life? Through these media youth can be socialized not only as individuals but as participating members of the school, the home, the church, the local community, the state, and the nation provided that the behavior learned in games is generalized into the larger arena of life. Thus, games offer a potential for moral and ethical behavior and a most valuable media for personality development. One of the values of society is fairness, and the rules and codes surrounding games emphasize this concept. It is from these moral and ethical concepts that sportsmanship grew.

In addition to having an impact on

the social individual, games have an influence on the sociocultural processes themselves. In fact, games not only reflect sociocultural patterns but they have been instrumental in helping to structure them. The games and sports which are participated in by a society and the status those games occupy in its culture in a great degree reflect the system of values of that society. In America today our games and sports reflect those things we value. They emphasize the aspects that appear to have a high priority in our value system. For example, they emphasize equality. There is no place in our society today where a person is less subject to social stratification than in sports. His social mobility is dependent purely on his ability as shown by his achievement and performance on the field and not by virtue of his ascribed status. A person is selected to a position on the team on the basis of his ability and only ability limits his opportunity. Games emphasize independence. Most games permit the performer a chance to exercise free choice and independence within the framework of the plans laid down by the rules and the leadership of the group. Some coaches even still permit the quarterback to call the plays or give him the right to change them at the line of scrimmage. Games emphasize aggressiveness. Probably sports are the only area today where socially approved conflict is openly permissible in America. Man's biological heritage has been one of aggression and games, and sports can provide a socially approved outlet. Games emphasize leadership. When status is accepted and roles are played in games and sports there are abundant opportunities for leaders to emerge. Games reflect another American value—worth and dignity of the individual. In good programs of physical education there is room for all individuals where each one is treated as an individual and his unique personality is respected in the context of the larger group. There is dignity for everyone in a well-taught class of physical education —where the star, the average, and the duffer can each add to his own self-image. Sports emphasize fair play. Since fair play is a prescribed norm of society, it becomes a value high on the priority list. While it is frequently disregarded, it carries sanctions not only of the game groups themselves but also of the larger society.

Play and games have a close relationship to personality. Research shows what has long been suspected, that man's personality can be influenced through his movement. By the same token, the type of activity he chooses to participate in is influenced greatly by his unique personality. Socialization processes through games and sports are education's best way of helping the child identify his self-image and formulate his ideal-self. In a sense this identification and discovery process structures personality.

REFERENCES

1. Bertrand, Alvin L.: *Basic Sociology: An Introduction to Theory and Method.* New York, Appleton-Century-Crofts, 1967.
2. Broom, Leonard, and Philip Selznick: *Sociology.* New York, Harper and Row, 1963.
3. Cratty, Bryant J.: *Social Dimensions of Physical Activity.* Englewood Cliffs, N. J., Prentice-Hall, Inc., 1967.
4. Green, Arnold W.: *Sociology: An Analysis of Life in Modern Society.* New York, McGraw-Hill Book Company, Inc., 1964.
5. Rogers, E. M.: *Diffusion of Innovation.* New York, Free Press, 1962.
6. Ross, H. Laurence: *Prospectives on the Social Order.* New York, McGraw-Hill Book Company, Inc., 1963.
7. Sheldon, W. H. *et al.*: *The Varieties of Human Physique.* New York, Hafner Publishing Company, 1940.
8. Ulrich, Celeste: *The Social Matrix of Physical Education.* Englewood Cliffs, N. J. Prentice-Hall, Inc., 1968.
9. Williams, Jesse F.: *The Principles of Physical Education.* Philadelphia, W. B. Saunders Company, 1964.

Chapter 13

Anthropological Bases

INTRODUCTION

Man and his movements can only be understood when they have been revealed and studied in all their dimensions. Movement can be understood through biology, physiology, psychology, sociology, history and anthropology. Each of these disciplines provides a new dimension for obtaining greater knowledge and understanding about man and the dilemmas he is currently facing. Each of these disciplines in a sense furnishes a part of the multifaceted mosaic which makes up the wholeness of man.

If man is to be understood fully, it will be necessary to look not only at his present but also his past. This study of man and his past is a function of anthropology. The term *anthropology* comes from the Greek words *anthropos* meaning man and *logia* meaning study. Therefore anthropology is the study of man. It might well be called the science of man because the field is very broad in scope and includes anything which impinges on man. While other disciplines study different aspects of man, anthropology studies him as a unified whole. A fundamental premise of the discipline

is that no facet can be understood apart from the whole. In a day of fragmentation and proliferation it might well be that anthropology can be the one science that can keep the perspective of man's entity. Also, since it is concerned with man as a whole, it carries with it the corollary that the whole cannot be accurately perceived without an understanding of the parts. Thus, the work of anthropology cuts across many areas and is highly diversified. However, ultimately these diversified parts are always viewed in relation to the whole which in one sense brings a measure of unity to the discipline.

Since man cannot be separated from the culture which he has invented and now nurtures, culture, too, becomes a concern of the anthropologist. Thus, the discipline is limited only by man and his culture which he himself has founded. Man and culture are inexorably related, and one cannot be separated from the other. Therefore anthropology falls naturally into two main branches based on these two aspects: *physical anthropology* and *cultural anthropology*.

Physical anthropology is a study of the biological nature of man where emphasis is placed on his physical structure, his organic nature, and his physiology and anatomy. One point of emphasis here is the importance of this aspect in terms of time. Man is first of all a biological being and only secondarily has he become a social being with a culture.

Physical anthropologists study their field through four primary media—through fossils, through modern primates, through modern primitive people like the Australian Aborigines and through modern man and his cultures. They study man in different ways, and these ways form subdivisions of their discipline and become specialties. Perhaps the most important approach is through human evolution. Another approach is primatology where the anatomy and behavior of the apes are studied for information providing insights into man's biological nature. Still another field is somatology where man's physique and structure are studied for relationships with personality and behavior (see Chapter 9 "Biological Bases" under Somatotypes). Other special areas are: race, growth, and demography and anthropometry which cut across several specialties.

Cultural anthropology is concerned with culture which is man's learned behavioral characteristics as a part of society. It concerns all behavior and beliefs which are learned and shared with others in his social group and involves such matters as religion, political groups, social groups, language, economics, technology, and art. Both physical and cultural anthropology are divided into many subdivisions, and each of them becomes a specialty within itself.

Why should the professional physical educator become more conversant with anthropology? First, if for no other reason, it adds a new dimension to the biological sciences which now appear to be the most basic of foundation disciplines on which physical education

rests. For this reason this chapter might well have been placed in Part III, Section B in this book along with the biological bases. But this is not enough reason within itself. Since man cannot be separated from his culture, and can never be fully understood except in relation to it, this aspect must, too, be added as another dimension of man's wholeness. It is for this reason this chapter has been placed in Part III, Section C along with the social bases. Malina has pointed out that physical and cultural anthropology can have no clear cut line of demarcation drawn between them (1–147). They are so interdependent and interwoven that they bear an inextricable relationship with each other. Man produces his culture but at the same time he becomes a product of the culture he produced.

However, neither man nor his culture are of a short-lived nature. As Hoebel expresses it, they have a past, exist in the present, and will influence the future (5–12). What they are at the present time is a product of this past. What they will become in the future will be a product of that past, plus the impinging forces of the present and the new forces awaiting them in the future. Thus, it would appear that modern man, *Homo sapiens*, cannot be fully understood nor can his future be predicted and planned for effectively without some knowledge of the past. This knowledge and understanding can be found only through a study of evolution both cultural and physical. Since the two took place simultaneously and in a sense one became a product of the other, they cannot be completely separated. Thus the physical educators need to understand the unity of man in relation to the new dimensions provided by anthropology.

There are some important differences in biological and cultural inheritance. Culture is not passed on through heredity but must be learned from scratch by each individual in each new generation through enculturation; whereas biological inheritance is passed on by the genes through heredity. Also, there are differences in culture and society. In the evolutionary processes of man, while secondary in origin to society, culture has played a more important role than society. Society is more affected and shaped by culture than culture is by society.

BIOLOGICAL EVOLUTION

Reference has already been made to the "permanence of man's nature" in Chapter 1 as one of the five concepts which are most basic to the essentiality for physical education. This concept springs from man's nature, the result of his evolution. A study of evolution will make abundantly evident the changes which took place in the millions of years which were required for the evolutionary processes to be operative in order to culminate in the final emergence of man in the form he is known today. From the one cell organism, the processes of evolution over countless ages gradually were operative, and the appearing of the first muscular tissue was the catalyst which brought one era into focus after another until prehistoric man finally emerged.

Thus, knowledge of the origin of man as a human being with human behavior has great import. In addition to satisfying scientific curiosity, it could be a way to understand man more fully and to help solve some of the problems brought on by the dilemmas growing out of a complex, technological society. According to anthropologists, since man has spent all but an infinitesimal amount of his time in a prehistoric society, to understand how he developed as a species during this long and indistinct era shrouded in the mist and the mystery of bygone ages would help in meeting some

of the problems brought on by the dramatic changes in his environment in the last few centuries, especially in the technological twentieth century. If it were possible to reconstruct accurately the emergence of man out of the mists of the past, a clearer understanding might be had of the growth and development of the young child as he in some sense recapitulates the history of the race. However, to trace the making of a modern man is not easy. The remains out of which scientists must reconstruct man's past are fragmentary. Many gaps in knowledge can frequently lead only to conjecture and speculation, and one might add controversy in all too many instances.

From the earlier primates to *Homo sapiens* the evolutionary processes covered millions of years in prehistory. In fact history as opposed to prehistory is ordinarily recognized as beginning with the invention of writing, and this occurred only about 5000 year ago. On the time-scale of human evolution spanning millions of years, these 5000 years are but a small segment on the scale of infinity. Between man's earliest prehistoric primate ancestors and the earliest human there are missing gaps in knowledge spanning many millions of years. It is known, however, that primates experienced approximately 70,000,000 years of evolution as an order (5–106). Anthropologists are now seeking answers to these gaps in knowledge. Inevitably this leads to speculation and the search for the missing links. However, it is now recognized that there is no one missing link but innumerable ones as man and present simians have many common ancestral predecessors (5–106). In this process it is not probable that *Homo sapiens* emerged with human behavior over a short time span, but rather the process was a subtle one somewhat compared to the transition from darkness to daylight, covering perhaps hundreds of thousands of years. Even then that point may depend partly on one's definition of what constitutes "human." During this long process of transition from prehuman to human species or perhaps afterwards, the missing links, the many ancestral predecessors, from which man and his primate cousins rose have become extinct. Only time will reveal if traces of their existence in the form of fossils locked in the rock formations of the Cenozoic era can be found and identified. *Homo sapiens* probably evolved around 100,000 years ago. It was at this time that he seemed to have acquired enough intelligence to control his environment to a degree and to shape his future through culture.

Science has done much to unravel the mysteries of man's origin. Perhaps the most significant contributions have been made by the various branches of anthropology; much of this has been done in the last few decades. Since man is a primate, this chapter will deal very briefly with the origin of the making of a man from his primate ancestry. This involves evolution. However, evolution itself does not begin with man's living origin. It begins with inorganic matter which comprises the materials that make up the universe first and, second the earth. Hoebel points out that there are levels of evolutionary processes spread over billions of years starting with inorganic matter (5–17). Much later the inorganic evolved into the organic in a dramatic new kind of order, and a new level in kind was reached. Much later still, during the organic evolution the psycho-organic dimension was added whereby some forms of life developed a nervous system. This, too, was a dramatic change in kind. The most recent level is the psychocultural-organic where man began the invention of his own culture (5–17). This level was made possible by language because without communication, anything more

than an incipient culture is impossible. Language led to thinking man with a memory, and memory led to creativity and imagination. The evolution of thinking man was paralleled by an elaboration of his movements into more adaptive behavior so he could create and invent not only new behavior but also other more material forms of his culture. Thus, through biological evolution man gained the ability to build his culture, but in turn he became a product of that culture.

From the beginning of the universe until the birth of the earth is estimated in terms of cosmic time from four to six billion years. Geologic time began with the birth of the earth probably about 4,500,000,000 years ago. The earth is thought to have been created from solar materials breaking away from the sun, and all of this original material consisted of chemicals (13–13). Therefore, since all plant and animal life was created from earth materials, all life is composed of these chemicals. After approximately a half billion years of lifelessness, these chemicals in some mysterious way combined to form proteins and create a new order—life! (13–14). The first known animal life was the protozoa, and from this point on biological priorities have been established along with the physio-chemical laws in order to continue life. The protozoa evolved into the metazoa, multicellular organisms in which specialization of function came into existence. These formed the basis for the invertebrates—worms, snails, jellyfishes, and squids. Much later the chordate and vertebrate era led to the evolution of the fishes followed by the amphibians, the reptiles and the mammals in that order.

A timetable for the appearance of these various organisms has been prepared by geologists from the fossils found in the various levels of rock formation (5–115). Geologic time is divided into *eras* following violent changes in the earth. Within an eras there are *epochs* which are also representative of lesser disturbance in the earth's conditions. The five geologic eras are: Azoic, Proterozoic, Paleozoic, Mesozoic, and Cenozoic. There was no life during the Azoic period. The protozoa first came into being during the Proterozoic age and since that time not only the earth but all living matter has been undergoing consistent change as evolution relentlessly produced more complex and more heterogeneous life. This era began between 1,500,000,000 and 2,000,000,000 years ago. The Paleozoic era began about 500,000,000 years ago and was characterized by the invertebrates. The Mesozoic era dates back 200,000,000 years and was the period during which the fishes, amphibians, reptiles, and mammals developed. The last of the five eras was Cenozoic which occurred about 70,000,000 years ago and marks the time during which the primate evolution took place (13–21).

Within the Cenozoic era, there are six epochs: the Paleocene, the Eocene, the Oligocene, the Miocene, the Pliocene, and the Pleistocene. The last three of these are the most crucial in the emergence of man's antecedents because the primate evolution took place during these epochs. However, the Pleistocene, the last of the epochs, was the time when man himself finally emerged out of the mist of the past (13–46).

The anthropologist is prone to bring order to his discipline through classification. However, there are still some inconsistencies among scholars in nomenclature. In hierarchial terms, both Titiev and Hoebel have presented the following classification of man: man belongs to the upright species, *sapiens;* the genus, man (*Homo*); subfamily, anthropoids; family, hominids; superfamily, hominoids; order, primates; *group,* Eutheria (which means the fetus is nourished directly from the mother's bloodstream); class, mammal; subphylum, vertebrate; phylum, chordate; subkingdom, metazoa; and kingdom, animal (13–114) (5–100). This hierarchy is presented at this point in order to show man's relationship to the primates and emphasize that while he may be a sociocultural creature, he is still a biological animal in the final analysis.

The earliest primate was the *prosimia*, a small monkey-like mammal, and characteristic of the Eocene epoch which lasted from about 60 to 40 million years ago. These small animals furnished the ancestral stock for anthropoids and later, during Oligocene led to the early hominoids from which all men and apes descended. It was during the next epoch, the Miocene lasting some 20 million years, that the immediate hominoid antecedents of man evolved. The next epoch, the Pliocene, 12,000,000 to 14,000,000 years ago, led to a still more advanced hominoid. The last epoch, the Pleistocene, while closest to man in terms of time, is still somewhat a lost chapter in prehistory. There is a 10,000,000 year gap between the last fossil discovered during the Pliocene epoch and the arrival on the time-scale of *Homo erectus*, earliest variety of man. This is a period of missing links which still remain part of the secrets of the past until discovered at some time in the future if ever. *Homo erectus* was followed by a long slow process of Stone Age development which spanned more than a million years. During this time, however, man's mental processes were slowly developing and finally caught up with his physical development. At this point about 500,000 years ago man arrived at that place on the time-scale when he became known as *Homo sapiens*, intelligent man. At a later time—some 100,000 years ago—*Homo sapiens sapiens*, modern man, appeared.

Slow as the process was in man, the animal, becoming man, the human, the wonder is that it could happen at all. How could it all take place? While the transition took millions of years, it was a continuous unbroken process which came about in response to environmental influences acting together with biological processes. This interaction eventually led to the differentiation of man from other forms of life and his emergence as *Homo sapiens*, intelligent man. The processes leading to differentiation were Darwin's law of *natural selection and adaptation*, the law of genetic variation in cellular reproduction (*mutation*), *genetic drift*, and migration with *population mixture* (5–123).

In genetics there are two processes that operate to insure continuity of life but at the same time they hold part of the key to the gradual processes of change. If evolution is to take place even over long periods of time, there must be change in genetic structure. These two processes are *mitosis* and *meiosis*.

Mitosis is considered the basis of organic life and insures heredity stability. It is the repeated process of reproduction of cells through cell division whereby each half contains the same genetic material. In man each of the cells, with one exception, produces twenty-three pairs of chromosomes; and in cellular division each chromosome duplicates itself in the trillions of cells that comprise the human body. In the embryonic state, and later during the postnatal period, cell division is the key to growth and development. As each cell grows and divides, mitosis produces a replica of each pair of chromosomes in the two new cells. The exceptions are the sex cells called *gametocytes*.

Sex cells are subject to the process of *meiosis*. When the male and female gametes are united through fertilization, the fusion produces a *zygote*. Meiosis

insures that this zygote will receive only one chromosome from each pair instead of the two. At some point a reduction division must occur. Each sex cell has half the number of chromosomes—both male and female sex cells. This resulted from a reduction division in their formation. In mitosis $2 \times 2/2 = 2$, but in meiosis $2/2 + 2/2 = 2$. Chance dictates which of two parental chromosomes will pass to a particular sex cell, the zygote or fertilization nucleus being an entirely new recombination of genetic factors. This means the resulting offspring is unique. The process of meiosis offers a multitude of possibilities for variability. Thus, meiosis provides for continuity since only genes from the two parents can be transmitted, but it also presents the factor of variability because in the *combination* of chromosomes the new offspring will vary from each parent in many respects. Thus, meiosis is part of the key to evolutionary change through recombination of genes.

The chromosomes which are found in each of the myriad of cells can be further divided into units called *genes*. Genes are the real basis of heredity since they establish the genotype of the resulting offspring. The number of genes within each chromosome varies from a few hundred to several thousand. Genes are made up of DNA (deoxyribonucleic acid) (see Chapter 9, Biological Bases, for further discussion). DNA is the true determiner of specific traits in heredity. Point mutations (gene changes), combinations, recombinations, linkage and other associations of chromosomes provide variations (4–29).

Since both of these processes, mitosis and meiosis, tend toward continuity, and thus a type of genetic equilibrium, there must be some other factors leading to variation and adaptation that brought about gradual changes in biological structure over the millions of years between the protozoa, the prosimia, and

Homo sapiens. The most important factors in this process of upsetting the status quo biologically speaking are: *mutation*, and *natural selection*. The other factors of *genetic drift* and migration with *population mixture* are of less importance.

Mutation as explained in genetics is involved in the transmission of traits from the parent to offspring when there is variation in the process. These variations would occur when there are alterations in the DNA code which affects the growth of the cell—changes in genes (5-122). When these variations take place often enough to become stabilized and can be passed on as inherited characteristics, they are mutations. While these mutations come about through chance, if they are repeated regularly and often enough, they will eventually change heredity if the group that receives the new genes has a higher survival rate than groups that do not possess them (6-61).

Natural selection concerns the influence of environment on genetic variability so that the fittest survive. In a state of original nature, it seems to work in an automatic way. Genetically speaking, if individuals vary from the general population and if they reproduce and survive more often than the nonvariants, then they have adapted more readily to environmental conditions. This acts on genetic variability to eventually produce *differential reproduction.* Just as a new species is selected in, the old species which could adapt less efficiently to the environment is selected out. It is because of natural selection that missing links in man's ancestry have lost out. As environments changed, sometimes dramatically, all organisms were forced to make adjustments. If those with mutations could adapt and survive better than those without mutations, genetic change resulted in differential reproduction. These missing links have become extinct and have slowly been eliminated through natural selection as they failed to meet the demands of the new environment. By the same token, new and more complex organisms took their place, organisms which could adapt more effectively to the new environment. Therefore, a stable environment is not as conducive to genetic change as an unstable one. A changing environment producing new conditions lays the foundation for genetic change by increasing the influence of natural selection because the organism is forced to adapt or become extinct. Any one evolutionary change is followed by other changes in a sort of feedback cycle which has the effect of accelerating the whole process (5-124).

Thus, man is a product of both the forces from his environment and the forces of his nature interacting together to make him a more complex and variable being. Genetic variation and adaptation to specific environment through natural selection are the keys to persistent evolution that has occurred to place all anthropoids and hominoids on the scale of primates. Different species occurred when the two processes mentioned above produced such genetic differences that interbreeding became impossible (5-126). *Speciation* occurred to man and his primate cousins. Man and these hominoid relatives such as the gorilla, the gibbon, the orangutan and the chimpanzee all radiated originally from a common ancestor, or perhaps it would be more correct to say ancestors, now lost in the mysteries of the Miocene epoch (5-126). According to their genetic legacy, however, they each reached a point through speciation where their social and sexual behaviors were modified to such an extent that they could remain apart from the mainstream of their origin. Thus, *Homo sapiens* is not a direct offspring of the apes as is sometime the common belief and he did not pass through an evolutionary process where he at one time possessed the characteristics of present apes (5–106). The apes, too, have evolved into what they are today from what they were like when they shared a common ancestry with man.

This change in man's genetic heritage is a long slow process, and as far as all practical purposes are concerned will never be dramatic enough in one generation or even dozens of generations to be noticeable. In summary, man's biological evolution is still an ongoing process although no significant changes have occurred during the last 30,000 years (9–413). It has been and still is a result of an interaction of genetic recombination, mutation, natural selection, mixing populations and random drift. The raw material for evolution is genetic substance, and the basis for it is mutations which have a favorable effect and are multiplied through natural selection. This process is a slow one, however. It takes millions of years to develop a new species and hundreds of thousands of years to produce a new race.

In the processes of evolution and change, environmental influences cannot be underrated. When environments changed, the animal had two choices for survival and throughout evolution the most fundamental of all animal activities are survival and reproduction of their kind. The animal could either adapt to the change, or move to a new environment with the old characteristics. If he could do neither, he became extinct. If, however, he could adjust successfully to the environment through biological changes, he survived and the adjustment changes became a part of his biological nature and were transmitted genetically to new generations through sexual reproduction.

On the other hand primitive man as well as modern man has three possibilities for survival. He can adjust biolog-

ically; he can flee and escape the new environmental changes; or he can modify his culture in order to accommodate the changes. In the last several thousand years man has adjusted to this environment through his culture rather than his biology. This may account for the fact that there have been no perceptible changes in man's biological evolution in the last 30,000 years. A classic example of adapting to new environments through culture has been the moon walks and journeys through outer space by man. By nature he is not equipped to survive, but through his elaborate culture, he can. Thus, there are three possible courses for animal life. If there is failure to adjust, extinction results. If the environment remains stable or if there is adjustment to a changing environment through culture, there is little or no physical change. If the organism has been successful biologically in adapting to the new environment, there is evolutionary change with physical specialization. It is of interest to observe the result of genetic change. Genes which would have been selected out of the population formerly now thrive and even multiply in a highly artificial environment. For example, the diabetic can now live normally with insulin treatments where he would have been eliminated by natural selection in primitive times.

It should be of some interest to the physical education professional student to know how different races developed from *Homo sapiens* without creating new species or subspecies. First, all humans inhabiting the earth today have a biological commonality with more like characteristics than they have unlike. This places them in the mainstream of *Homo sapiens* since interbreeding is possible. However, since the advent of *Homo sapiens* with his rapidly expanding culture leading to more and more intellectual power, the earth has been populated with his species and other species of hominids, and missing links have either been overcome, absorbed, or in some manner, been selected out of the world's population. From this original population of the earth by *Homo sapiens*, races have developed as slight differences came about due to isolation and the inevitable roll of the genetic dice of mutation. The focal point for racial differentiation is geographical with an accompanying intrabreeding population. This tends to produce such differences which are noted between the races, the Mongolians in Asia, the Negro in Africa and the light-complexioned Nordic in northern Europe. There are some biological rules which partly explain these racial differences and perhaps the most important are climatic and heat retention and loss. However, many of the identifiable racial differences are unaccounted for. As man's culture grows more complex, as population increases, and there is greater social interaction due to the increased mobility between subgroups, racial distinctions will grow less evident. Hopefully, this might lead to less aggression among racial and national groups.

It might be informative to the professional student in physical education to perceive some of the important changes that occurred in man's hominoid ancestry which had great implication for man not only physiologically but also psychologically and sociologically. Also, these changes have implication today in education in understanding man's behavior and particularly his movements. Of course there were many subtle changes which took place during this 10,000,000 year period as well as these more major modifications. This long period has become a lost chapter in the history of man's emergence, and it can only be conjectured what took place and when. However, there are three decisive or crucial stages of change in the morpho-

logical makeup of hominoids which paved the way for *Homo sapien's* arrival on the scene (4–295).

The first of these was the critical modification of the chest-shoulder-forearm complex which was necessary for adaptation to brachiation (hanging and swinging by the forearms in trees) (5–136). Several implications stem from this dramatic change. The front paws became prehensile making extensive grasping possible with the opposability of the thumb to the fingers. This change enabled the primate to live in the trees and to move about there. The use of the forearms for something more than locomotion was no doubt accompanied by some new pathways in the brain centers. Also, the hanging in a vertical position as in brachiation laid the foundation in the visceral system for adaptation to the bipedal upright position. A further impact was an accompanying higher degree of flexion in the forearm.

The second drastic change involved the modification of the pelvis and lower limb complex for the upright stance and bipedal locomotion (5–137). This dramatic occurrence happened sometime between one and two million years ago, but what led to the primate first standing upright can only be speculation. Perhaps it grew out of brachiation and when the hominoid landed on the ground he was already in the upright position and remained that way; or perhaps it may have developed as a means of stalking his foe or prey as he stood to peer out over the tall grasses. It is known that when he came down from the trees, the grasslands became his habitat and that in the Pleistocene epoch, he became a meat eater and hence, a hunter. However, the greatest impact of the upright posture was the freeing of the forearms for use in defense, particularly of the exposed viscera, and for manipulatory acts. It is probable that the law of natural selection favored those who could protect themselves best. There is sound evidence now indicating that this significant change from the quadruped to the biped position ultimately led to the development of the brain and the eventual emergence of man. With the upright position, the primates could use their eyes more effectively and this together with the improved hand-eye mechanism and speech in man probably forced the third significant change.

This third crucial change involved the modification of the jaw-face-cranium complex. It might be conjectured once again that one of these dramatic changes led to another. However, it is conceded the first two may have evolved together, while it is known the third one came much later in time. In any event the jaws, dentition and snout became reduced in size; the eyes moved forward and into closed sockets where stereoscopic vision arose; and the skull became balanced in a vertical position over the spinal column. However, the most significant change was the increase in the size of the cranial cavity in order to provide for the ever-enlarging brain. As the brain area expanded, the size of the cranium increased from 750 cc to 1500 cc (5–149).

CULTURAL EVOLUTION

While most of this chapter has been concerned with physical anthropology and particularly evolution, the student must not forget the importance of culture and cultural evolution as a part of man's total evolution. While man's physical order started with the primate evolution approximately 70,000,000 years ago, it can only be conjectured when his cultural evolution began. In terms of "what happened," some say it was when man became a tool user and began to speak a language. Also, tool making plays a role in his early cultural development since tool making is more advanced than tool using. In terms of "when it happened," the answer could be any time between one-half million and two million years ago. In one sense it makes very little difference because only the last few thousand of these years carried beyond the "Old Stone" age (12–49). In any event cultural evolution followed man's biological, but the biological could not have reached its present state without the benefit of interaction with the cultural. Man's mind has evolved in a highly special way through feedback of his cultural inheritance and somewhere along the way there became a built-in faculty in man for culture; it is this facet which has become his most distinctive feature (4–32). Perhaps at the base of this need for culture is the natural tendency of the species to explore and investigate. Speech and language made possible the accumulation of culture and no doubt aided in such human abilities as thinking, memory, imagination, creativity, and invention. Thus, man's biological evolution reached the point where he could initiate his cultural evolution, and from that point on the two interacting together in a snowballing type of process ultimately resulted in the emergence of rational man. It could well be that man's own evolution has given him the power to direct and control not only his future cultural evolution but to some extent his biological. However, it must be admitted that this power is a two-edged sword. The same culture that created music, art and space travel also invented the atomic and hydrogen bombs which could lead to man's extinction.

Man's biological evolution has been decelerating and there have been no substantial changes in man's genetic heritage the last 30,000 years (9–413). Such changes in the environmental conditions which would normally call for mutation and natural selection have been met in another way. Man has adapted to his environmental changes through his culture. In fact Holmes has said that man's evolution shows that instead of adapting to a given environment, his cultural heritage represents a conquest over it (6). Culture provides a quicker and easier way of adaptation to change than genetic change. However, it must be kept in mind that man can adapt to his environment only within the ranges or limits of his biological constitution. Man in general, however, is relatively an unspecialized animal physically. Biological adaptation to environmental change results in physical specialization due to genetic mutation. Ross suggests that one of the disadvantages of physical specialization is its irreversibility (11–47). Once it occurs, the organism is stuck with it from that point on and becomes a pawn to its environment. Thus, when a radical change occurs again in the environment, the highly specialized organism fails to make new adjustments and becomes extinct. The fact that man can now adjust to such conditions through his culture rather than biological specialization means that he is no longer subject to the genetic gamble where sudden drastic changes in environmental conditions would lead to extinction with a second dramatic change. Thus, man has been successful in sculpturing his environment to meet his needs through his culture and there no longer seems to be great need in man for biological specialization. The freeing of the hands for manipulation and other exploratory movements has freed man from further biological evolution. However, Ross points out that it is not the hands alone which make man unique (11–49). Rather it is a complex of the hands, stereoscopic vision, and intelligence working in combination which has led men down the road to cultural independence and freed him from the necessity of further biological specialization.

It is interesting to note the difference in biological and cultural heritage. While there is universal biological similarity, man's cultural heritage is marked by great diversity. It has been said that biologically all men are brothers but culturally they are as different as their customs, traditions, mores, and technological advancement make them. Man inherits his biological characteristics from his parents, and from the time of conception on, he has no choice in alternatives and can never modify his biological heritage. There may come a time when this may become possible through genetic manipulation by scientists. On the other hand man cannot acquire culture until after he is born, and while he may be limited in some degree by the culture into which he is born, culture is learned and potentially man can take on any culture to which he is exposed within the limits set by his biological heritage.

Some other facts are becoming evident. The forerunner of *Homo sapiens* goes back much farther in prehistory than was thought until recently. Some current findings take man's ancestry back some 40,000,000 years and the evidence seems to indicate this is still not the beginning. While the mechanisms of biological evolution are known such as mutation, natural selection, and the like, man's present could be better understood if it were known just when, in what sequence, and under what circumstances the major changes occurred in his morphology and behavior. Since this behavior evolved toward the social and a culture, it would be important if this could be re-enacted. It is conjectured that man's first rise to a higher level socially than his primate ancestors started because of a need for survival. Survival involved, in a basic way, food, safety from attack and the reproduction of the species. At some point along the way, and what triggered this giant step is not known, man's ancestors found they could operate more effectively in small groups as they searched for food and fought for survival. Hence, cooperative behavior was engendered and out of interaction between individuals there apparently grew an increased intelligence and even the origin of language. All of these added up to culture. Language furnished one of the greatest strides upward in the cultural evolution of man because language marks one of the most distinctive features of man over animal. Language enhanced the cultural evolution of man because it provided the means of communication necessary to facilitate interaction. Culture would not be possible without language. Language and symbolism are major characteristics of all cultures (5–31). It is thought by anthropologists that as far back as a million years ago man had acquired sufficient intelligence to speak a language along with using simple tools, and that man's cultural evolution began when he became a tool user. Thus, as biological evolution progressed, man reached a level where he achieved the ability to produce his own culture and in turn he became a product of this culture.

Cooperative behavior had other implications for culture. It brought a type of diversification and specialization of work. This level led to significant biological and psychological changes as well as sociological. Cooperative behavior along with language and improved hand-eye coordination through tool using stimulated the thinking process which in turn enhanced mental functions leading over many thousands of years to an increase in the size of the brain with a corresponding increase in cranial capacity. This increase in the size of the head brought about changes in the female whose pelvis broadened in order to accommodate the birth of the larger headed infant. As the mental processes grew in power leading to a larger and more efficient brain, the infant's dependency period lasted longer thereby bringing about more diversification and specialization in man's behavior with the female being committed to infant care. These physiological changes themselves brought about changes in social behavior because they placed the female at a disadvantage in hunting activities and this, together with the long dependency period of the offspring forced her to remain at home to man lighter activities. It is further conjectured that these conditions brought into focus for the first time the pair-bond relationship which is now the basis for the home, marriage and family groups, and that this whole process triggered sexual dimorphism—pronounced differences between the male and female. It is speculated that these did not occur in sequence but together over a long period of time with minute progress and change in one followed by minute change in others.

IMPLICATION OF ANTHROPOLOGY FOR THE PHYSICAL EDUCATOR

A study of anthropology right now probably raises more questions in the mind of the physical educator than it answers in regard to his special field of movement. While the study of man and his culture and their evolutions have opened some new vistas in understanding man both in his diversity and his unity, knowledge of human movement—its role in man's past, his present, and his future—presents a tremendous challenge for the future. The physical education researchers and theorists can never meet this challenge alone. It must become a multidisciplinary approach where the psychologists, sociologists, biologists, physiologists, anthropologists, and medical doctors among others must share roles.

Perhaps one important reason for the physical education professional student to study the origin of man and his culture is to better understand man's problems today—not only his social and behavioral ones but also his physiological and psychological ones as well. As man evolved, he moved from a state where his survival depended entirely upon hereditary abilities to one where, due to his growing intellectual powers and remarkably movable body, he could adjust to new conditions through innovation, invention and creativity. He traded his instincts for the capacity to learn and think. No other living creature has such powers to adapt and make adjustments not only through his biological capacities but also his culture. Yet man is inextricably tied to his prehistoric past in a biological relationship. The wellsprings of his social behavior are deeply rooted in the wilderness of bygone ages; what is called his social evolution may be more biological than social. Historically, his social development and social organization as well as his physiological make-up and psychological awareness were aimed at survival in a wild hostile environment of predators and calamities—where he had to kill or be killed, or fight or take flight. Genetically controlled changes had to take place at this stage in his basic behavior or he would not have remained in the mainstream of evolution. In spite of man's great adjustment powers it could be that the time in which he had tried to civilize and socialize himself in a rapidly expanding technological world is much too short a period on the time-scale for his social evolution to become operative. If in the order of things his social evolution is tied too closely with his biological, change in his behavior would come about chiefly through the processes of genetics and natural selection, and these are operative only over long periods of time. In this event, since man does not have a long period of time to adapt as a species, he

faces a crisis. He must adapt rapidly or run the risk of extinction. He must recognize the fact that his basic biological behavior in many areas including reproduction, care of the young, eating habits, exercise, aggressions and the like will not change perceptively in the near future. Since they won't change, man must structure his culture and redesign his civilization so that he can live with his fundamental and basic urges which are probably more animal-like than he cares to admit. A best seller written by a biologist calls man the "naked ape" and implies that man must recognize himself for what he is—and that is basically an animal—if he is to survive in the culture he has invented. Since he can't change this genetic heritage, he must recognize it for what it is and then try, through use of his intellect, to make his biological inheritance work in the confines of his sociocultural heritage.

It is interesting to note that all of man's predecessors—the missing links between himself and present-day primates—are extinct. In time these species failed to adjust to physical and social environments and were selected out. If man is to avoid a similar fate, he must shift his behavior pattern that is still reminiscent of a prehistoric world to one that can meet the rapidly accelerated social changes that are taking place today and will continue to take place in the future as the pace will be even more accelerated. Man's whole history has pointed to the fact that, because he is intelligent man, he can always adjust although in the sociocultural arena sometimes less than perfectly. However, his adjustments in the past have been made over long periods of time and his powers to adapt have never been challenged to the extent that they are now being challenged by unprecedented changes over relatively small amounts of time.

This same biological-cultural evolution interacting together to build this potential means of species extermination has not been able thus far to overcome man's original animal tendencies of aggression. There was a time and a place for primitive man and his earlier primate ancestors to be aggressive. As these ancestors evolved it became necessary to develop aggression in order to maintain their social hierarchy (sometimes referred to as "pecking order"), their territorial rights, and the sanctity of their pair-bond relationship. Thus, biological evolution led to certain physiological changes which enabled the ancestor to become more aggressive and to be better prepared to fight or in some cases to take flight if it meant survival.

The interaction of the biological and the sociocultural has been pointed out previously in this chapter. Perhaps there is no better example of this interaction in the evolutionary processes than what happens to man under great stress of anger, fear and other strong emotions. These tensions and stresses are deeply rooted in the wilderness of bygone ages. They are a part of man's biological heritage and while he may try to mask these under the veneer of his culture, they are still there. In times of stress, historically the adrenal glands according to a pattern spanning millions of years, dump large quantities of chemicals in the bloodstream. These chemicals act on the body systems, especially the cardiovascular, respiratory and muscular systems. Physiologically, this process mobilizes the body for immediate and forceful action by drawing on the body's reserves. These products provide for instant animal energy in vigorous and sometimes violent muscle contraction above ordinary needs. The prehistoric environment called for this "alarm reaction" for either fight or flight and thus the fat products were energized in either a fight for one's life or a flight for it. In

modern times under stress the same physiological processes occur but with a few exceptions no such violent action results, and the fats remain in the bloodstream making one more susceptible to degenerative diseases. Civilization has enabled man to control his impulses for vigorous action through his cultural tools but not his emotions and behavior through his social self. He must learn to control these emotions which trigger the "make ready for fight or flight," state, or he must find some socially acceptable substitute for the fight or flight state which will consume the lethal products in his bloodstream. This would appear to be a matter of daily exercise vigorous enough to clear the system. A body that is fit with a strong heart and circulatory system is able to cope with this "alarm reaction" more effectively than an untrained system (see Chapter 10).

Man's biological evolution can never be entirely divorced from the sociocultural evolution. While culture and social evolution followed in the wake of the biological evolution by millions of years, they are still very much in evidence as ongoing processes. In the meantime perhaps man's biological evolution, while academically still an ongoing process, will vary little, if any, the next few thousand years (9–413). Beginning with the one-cell organism, evolution ran its course through the various stages—fishes, amphibians, reptiles, mammals, primates, and *Homo sapiens*. As life scaled higher and higher on the evolutionary ladder, the one central feature which initiated the whole process in the beginning and which kept the wheels turning inexorably and in an unrelenting manner was movement. Development of the muscular system through vigorous exercise was the key to the organism's total development in this upward struggle from lower to higher forms of life. It would be unwise and even foolish to ignore the lessons which come to man from a study of evolution. Such study reveals that man's growth, development and maintenance must depend upon movement. In his struggle upward in a hostile and slowly changing environment, physical activity was his primary means of survival. The demands of his environment literally kicked him into activity. He had little choice. It became probably the most important part of his heritage in a world of danger and constant battle to survive. Thus, man's biological and cultural legacy is an active one. It is incumbent on the professional student in physical education to know this heritage and understand its meaning in relation to man's welfare.

Another problem facing man concerning implications of his evolution is his inadequate adaptation to the upright bipedal posture (13–85). This weakness has been referred to in Chapter 9, Biological Bases, and will not be discussed further here except to point out that physical educators must be aware of these weaknesses growing out of evolutionary inadequacies and know how they can be prevented and ameliorated. One implication would seem to emphasize programs in physical education designed to strengthen the trunk and abdominal muscles which are related to maintaining verticality. The evidence would seem to indicate that man is several thousand years away from effective adaptation to his upright bipedal position (2–17).

There is a biogenic law which implies that ontogeny recapitulates phylogeny. This would mean that in the process of growth and development the young would have to repeat the history of their race by growing through the various stages of evolutionary change. This law has perhaps been too loosely interpreted by some uncritical scientist and some rather extravagant claims have

been made regarding it. However, there is sufficient evidence to indicate some degree of truth in the concept. It is known that the human embryo does develop in stages similar to the history of the development of his species (5–104). The child's embryonic morphological development is not only similar to apes until the later stages but also to other species further down the scale of phylogeny. Also, there is present in adult man certain vestigial parts like the coccyx. Embryology provides many such evidences of vestiges of structure which once performed important functions in man's ancestors but which now either have no function or a different one. In the future, research must help to provide new light on these and similar areas. The relationship of the hands and movement in general to the evolution of social and intellectual development of modern man offer further opportunity for study. Does the law of ontogeny recapitulate phylogeny after birth as Delacato stresses in his concept of neurological organization? (3) Also, the controversy concerning generality and specificity of movement skills could be partially cleared up if the extent to which the fundamental skills are genetically based and controlled could be determined.

A multitude of other questions stem from this area of study. Perhaps the one which is most important to the physical educator concerns the relative proportion of time needed to meet man's physical and intellectual needs. Underlying this question is one equally imposing. Does the present emphasis on intellectual abilities as opposed to physical abilities in meeting the demands of a modern technological society have implications for human evolution? Is there a possibility in the future that man can become more specialized in his physical structure and brain capacity in order to meet the needs of a future cybernetic world vastly different from anything imagined up to now? Can man's nature change with regard to the processes in his body which mobilize for the flight or fight state? Can man's biological nature complete its adjustments to verticality and reduce the present functional problems associated with it? Does the fact that youth today are taller, heavier and perhaps stronger than at any other time in evolution presage a trend toward gigantism? On the other hand, since man's environment no longer requires strength, size and brute force, would not a smaller more compact human body be more effective in meeting future demands? And perhaps the most important question of all: can man's cultural evolution working through his social behavior move fast enough in the future to protect man from himself? Can man's natural tendencies of aggression be curbed in time to save him from exterminating himself through the many ways at his disposal?

It is time to take stock of ourselves in this area of human values. When one person holds the key in his hand to all life on this planet—when, on his signal, the world could be converted into a holocaust of radiation from which culture has found no escape and biology has not had enough time for adaptation, the importance of social adaptation is crucial.

Another question must soon be answered by society in general, but scientists in particular. To what extent can genetic manipulation be sanctioned? Just as science has redesigned man's cultural environment, the time is not too far off when it will not only have the resources to redesign man himself but probably the power. Who will assume the moral obligations and responsibilities which accompany the consequences of such actions? The potential of such possibilities is staggering to the mind. In the hands of the unscrupulous, it offers a terrible possibility. Even in the hands of those who assume moral responsibility, it may be an area that offers choices depending on the nature of values, and in a pluralistic world these values will vary greatly. Aside from the moral issue, are the chances that genetic evolutionists would take in disturbing the fine balance of man which has taken millions of years to materialize worth the risk? Man is already the number one wonder of the earth.

REFERENCES

1. Brown, Roscoe C., and Bryant J. Cratty: *New Perspectives of Man in Action.* Englewood Cliffs, N. J., Prentice-Hall, Inc., 1969.
2. Cratty, Bryant, J.: *Movement Behavior and Motor Learning,* 2nd Ed. Philadelphia, Lea & Febiger, 1969.
3. Delacato, Carl H.: *The Diagnosis and Treatment of Speech and Reading Problems.* Springfield, Ill., Charles C Thomas, 1963.
4. Fried, Morton H.: *Readings in Anthropology.* New York, Thomas Y. Crowell Company, 1968.
5. Hoebel, E. A.: *Anthropology: The Study of Man.* New York, McGraw-Hill Book Company, 1966.
6. Holmes, Lowell D.: *Anthropology: An Introduction.* New York, The Ronald Press Company, 1965.
7. Hammond, Peter B.: *Cultural and Social Anthropology.* New York, Macmillan Company, 1964.
8. Jokl, Ernst: *Medical Sociology and Cultural Anthropology of Sports and Physical Education.* Springfield, Ill., Charles C Thomas, 1964.
9. Korn, Noel, and Fred Thompson: *Human Evolution: Readings in Physical Anthropology.* New York, Holt, Rinehart & Winston, Inc., 1967.
10. Rapport, Samuel, and Helen Wright: *Anthropology.* New York, New York University Press, 1967.
11. Ross, H. Laurence: *Perspectives on the Social Order.* New York, McGraw-Hill Book Company, 1963.
12. Shapiro, Harry L.: *Man, Culture, and Society.* New York, Oxford University Press, 1956.
13. Titiev, Mischa: *The Science of Man: An Introduction to Anthropology.* New York, Holt, Rinehart & Winston, 1954.

Chapter 14

Sociopsychological Values

INTRODUCTION

The idea was presented in Chapter 1 that perhaps the sociopsychological factors as a part of the unity mosaic will be the most important aspect of all in the years ahead if man is to survive as a species. If this thesis is accepted, there must be new emphasis or perhaps re-emphasis on human values. Perhaps this need arises not so much from the regression of present human values and eroding of behavioral norms but from the results of conditions growing out of the vast changes of the cultural environment. The problem lies not so much in change but in the magnitude of the changes over such a short time span. The technological world is changing so rapidly, and social institutions are responding so slowly that a vast cultural lag has been created. Thus, man's value system, his human relations area, has not kept pace with his materialistic culture.

Admittedly in some instances the moral fabric of society has weakened, and some current human behavior is no better now perhaps than in the time of Christ. There are still many social and moral problems characterizing man's activities. Historically, in many areas of behavior, however, one can point to remarkable improvements which have taken place in human thought, conduct and values. These changes have come about through trial and error learning and behavior. They developed slowly inch by inch through accumulation of human experience over the centuries with many slow advances followed by retrogressions to further progress along the social continuum. Minute progress in one attitude leading to similar progress in others has led to a much higher level of human behavior over the centuries. This is an important point because if this thesis of gradual improvement is accepted, then mankind presumably can do something about his social and cultural evolution if given enough time and sufficient insight.

In retrospect, while looking back through history one can trace the positive changes in human values regarding such matters as slavery, witchcraft, punishment of crime, mental illness, mental retardation, racial discrimination and others. On the reverse side of the coin, however, it is all too easy to point out the other side of the picture—the prevalence of violence, crime, prejudice, discrimination, dissension, graft, corruption, selfishness, greed, and emphasis on the material matters in man's modern culture. While these negative aspects are taking place at one end of the social scale, it would be a mistake to forget what is going on at the more positive end of the continuum. Unfortunately, modern news media with instant feedback are all too prone to emphasize the sensationalism of crisis, disaster and crime of the vocal minority at the expense of the lesser sensationalism of the good, the true and the beautiful from the too often silent majority. Under the impact of new knowledge and understanding, values for the most part around the world have changed for the better. People in general are perhaps more tolerant, more compassionate and more cooperative now than at any other age in history.

The establishment of values, or for that matter the identification of the true values, in present-day world characterized as it is by technology, space exploration, explosion of population and knowledge, overcrowding of space, inner city problems, and both air and land pollution is a most complex undertaking. Change brought on by technology and phenomenal growth in population and knowledge is almost of a runaway nature and is altering social and cultural conditions at a whirlwind pace. In some cases change has been the catalyst in eroding social values while creating controversy and lack of certainty in others.

Values can no longer be categorized into the social, moral, economic, and political. The true values that people display in a society—the ones they practice and not the ones they preach or ostentatiously adhere to—are a mosaic of all these. It does not seem logical that one can establish a set of values in his private life or his religious life and a different set for his economic or polit-

ical life. Is it possible, for example, for an individual to have a genuine moral value of honesty in his private life and then be dishonest in business or politics? Therefore, this chapter will deal with values per se and will make no attempt to categorize them into economic, political and social.

At the present time all values and beliefs—as well as all absolutes—seem to be targets for re-appraisal and re-examination. The scientific movement has all too well inculcated in man the urge to question and inquire. This intellectual inquiry is a desirable trait and certainly is near the center of a democratic society where democratic principles are predicated not only on the worth and dignity of the individual but also on his right to speak freely, to question and to exercise his choice within the wider parameters of the social good. This yearning for freedom of choice and the right to determine one's own destiny is not new. It is a part of the American tradition and a heritage of this nation's rise to prominence as a world power. The whole idea of protest did not start at Greensboro, North Carolina in 1960 with the first "sit-ins." Historians will recall a little gathering called the "Boston Tea Party." So it is inevitable that values come under scrutiny. Youth particularly is questioning the "Establishment." Some minority groups are questioning the whole social structure. Traditional human values are on trial as seldom before in history. They are not only being questioned and tested but in some cases discarded or restructured. However painful it may be to the traditionalist, this social revolution is not all bad; it has in it the potential of serving as a harbinger of better things to come. However, good education should teach that dissent can be constructive, but that the wrong in the status quo should be criticized only as long as the good can also be acknowledged.

Society has always been forced to protect itself from the anarchist and those with warped values or entirely without values. All too frequently some of those elements in society today would sweep all values aside without having anything constructive to offer in their place. It is, therefore, necessary for a society to have established values if it is to function effectively. Societies are predicated on the values they establish for their own welfare and the good of their members. In fact, all societies must place restrictions on that behavior which conflicts with their goals and purposes. Without such values and subsequent sanctions, anarchy would take over or the social fabric would erode and the society fail. History is replete with examples of civilizations which rose because they established high level value systems only to suffer erosion at some later date and eventually their decline and fall. Historically, there seems to be some relationship between the physical fitness of a nation and its moral fitness.

There are fundamental values today which must be preserved if life is to have meaning in the whirlwind of social turmoil and technological change. However, to say values are fundamental is not the same thing as absolute. Values are not absolute and may change and probably will change in a pluralistic society. In today's world it seems to be a cliché but also a truth that the only certainty is change, and no part of man and his culture is immune.

One of the basic needs of American society today in this area of values is to narrow the gap between what man says his values are and how his behavior actually reflects these values. If the youth today, the ones who are the most perceptive, who have empathy and who show concern, have a legitimate reason for their protests, demonstrations and dissension to call attention to injustice and rigidity of the "Establishment," it

is partly because they see this discrepancy between what man's value system dictates in the way of norms and the way he actually behaves. Many youths who attack the "Establishment" have repudiated the values of adults—that is, the verbally expressed values which are all too often not translated into consistent behavior. In turn, these young people find their own values which will have meaning and relevance for them. The question of relevance will become a vital one in the next decade. Youth's greatest needs in this quest for values and relevance are strong consistent models from the adult world. Just as in politics, there is a great need for the prophet in education who can speak for and lead the youth of America. The cult of youth has become a part of the fabric of American culture, but is in need of some mature understanding, communication and empathy from models in the schools with whom it can identify. When this identification and subsequent interaction can occur in a positive way, there will be reforms not only in education but also in the area of social justice. Education must help to provide values for youth today and meaning for life so they will be at least fairly well equipped for the mysterious world of tomorrow. Since change is so rapid and great, this world cannot be predicted, but there must be a value system even though this system must be flexible and adaptable instead of absolute.

ROLE OF EDUCATION IN HUMAN VALUES

This problem of value along with others of a social nature, places education in the mainstream of social involvement. Education is undergirded with values and as an institution has become the most important secondary social group concerned with the responsibility of guiding social change and transmitting social expectations. Psychologists are now in agreement that sociopsychological traits are influenced to a greater degree in the home by parents and other home influences than anywhere else. This is true because these traits develop early in life before the child enters school. In general, children should get their standards and values from the home, but when the home fails to teach these, the schools must step into the breach.

In order to combat deleterious home environments, schools will have to experiment with more creative and imaginative programs. Education as an institution and a process must assume its role in socialization processes. Some of the things the schools will need to know and must eventually try to do are not yet fully known in this area of intangibles. However, it will be the job of society in the next quarter century to seek answers to these unknowns so that gaps in knowledge may be filled in concerning what effects educational processes have on such social processes as personality development, values, social change, socialization, and self-image. Some things concerning these aspects are known but admittedly there is much controversy about other facets. In some areas there are only theoretical approaches which in most cases become mere speculation. Therefore, this chapter may raise more questions than it answers. However, an attempt will be made to set up a theoretical framework based on research and best held opinion at this time and hopefully the professional student in physical education will be able to have a clearer picture of the social matrix and the role that he and his other colleagues in education must pursue if the emotional and social goal mentioned in Chapter 3 is to be realized in some degree.

However, the die is cast. The problem of ethical and moral values in a changing culture might well become education's greatest challenge in the future. It does seem necessary for society to scrutinize its values and to work toward change if some of these values appear to have become too rigid, outmoded or obsolete in the course of rapid changes.

The school must assume more of a leadership role as an effector of changes in values although historically its role has been one of followership where culture and social order are reflected rather than constructed. The most important question will be this: Once these values have been accepted as the norms of a democratic society, how can they be made to function from one generation to the next? One characteristic of a value is that from generation to generation it must constantly be interpreted and promoted. Values are not passed on in the genes through heredity; they must be learned by each new generation. The role education must play in this process of human values—their formation, justification and adjudication—must become more clearly defined in the future. This will not be resolved by any one discipline or group but rather there must be an interdisciplinary approach with a concerted effort by all.

Since the school's primary role is to preserve and pass on the cultural and social heritage of a society, it is well to remember also that the hub of that heritage in America is a democracy. Education and society will have to strike a balance between authority and a type of control which might appear on the surface as over permissiveness. If democracy is to function, there must always be the opportunity to question, weigh choices and make decisions (18–4). This free choice of behavior always carries with it a personal responsibility. This relates to a sense of independence, involving freedom of choice and action. This is the fundamental difference between a democracy and all other forms of government. Independent behavior must become a goal of education but it must be achieved in a frame of reference of the norms established for the welfare and good of the larger society.

In some manner youth of today must learn that their culture is their means for survival—not only individual but racial as well. In addition to many other facets this culture provides ways of behavior for the society of which they are a part. If this society is to achieve success in group living, there must be values (standards of rightness and wrongness) and behavior in accordance with some social controls in the forms of sanctions to make the values work. Each society must provide the necessary sanctions for its own welfare. Perhaps the ultimate answer in the years ahead is to emphasize the positive sanctions: rewards for those who comply. However, the nonconformist must be made aware of the negative sanctions and that they will be carried out in a society ultimately either in a formal or informal way whether he accepts such sanctions as a part of his value system or not. Man, by nature, has a built-in capacity or urge to find meaning in life. Hoebel points out that the humanities are called "humanities" because they search for that which provides for psychological commitment to life and society (11–31). Therefore, by nature, man is humane and he values.

The purpose of this chapter is to look more closely at social practices and the cultural expectations and examine them in the light of how physical education might contribute most in the development of human values.

THE NATURE OF VALUES

The term value has been referred to repeatedly in the introductory phase of this chapter. What are values? Arsenian says that operationally speaking, *values* have to do with preference (2–20). This preference motivates an individual to action, and it initiates behavior. It apparently is something which has worth and esteem for its own sake, and it has characteristics that make it desirable and worth striving for. The most important thing in education as an agency in society's perpetuation is for there to be a value system which is meaningful and relevant enough for societal norms to function. These values will make the real difference in man and not his knowledge, his skill or his fitness. These values must not be beyond the scope of man's capacity as a group to behave accordingly. There has always been something unrealistic as well as immoral about the hypocrisy of Victorian moral standards.

The developing individual's responsibility in a culture to these values is twofold. First, he must learn what these cultural expectations are—he must know what is considered good. There must not be too wide a gap between a society's expectations and its behavior as a whole. Second, the educationally functional citizen in today's democratic society needs to become a more independent self-actualizing person (18–78). To be such a person would mean that he would be aware of the expectations and norms of his culture, or in other words what is considered good, but he would, as he approaches social maturity, be free to make his own moral judgments independently, based not on the sanctions of society but rather on his own evaluation and examination of the values and the consequences of his behavior regarding them (18–81). It would further imply that he would assume full responsibility for the consequences of his behavior. Perhaps this is a too idealistic approach to values and moral behavior. Perhaps some would contend that it tends to oversimplify. There is no intent to oversimplify one of the most complex and difficult-to-study parts of man's whole. As it is a part of the whole and because it does have impact on all of the wholeness, no simplification is possible. With respect to the idealistic approach, perhaps in these times of great social upheaval and emotional stresses a little idealism would help to clarify purposes and establish goals as well as some practical methods of implementation. However, this chapter does not take the evangelistic approach.

Basically all men have the desire and the urge to strive for the "good life." It seems to be an inherent part of man to seek an ultimate meaning in life. However, the "good life" will mean many things to many individuals within even one subculture, because mankind is characterized by diversity rather than similarity. No two individuals will have the same experience because each is separate and unique. However, man is separated from beast by his rationality and being a rational being means he values. Rational thinking, self-actualizing man must find a purpose for his life. He may call this purpose, as an end result, "the good life" or by any other name. He finds himself born and nurtured in a culture already existing with its complex of values. He gradually becomes a part of that culture through a process of enculturation or socialization by both his primary and secondary social groups. He can conform to the expectations of his group because of his fears of its negative sanctions, or he can conform because of his need to maintain his self-image through its rewards to those who comply, its positive sanctions. Most persons possibly fall into one of these two categories; their behavior is generally considered as conventional behavior.

For those who are in the upper quartile of rational behaving man, however, there is more to life's purposes and to one's choice of behavior. They may view the "good life" in different ways but they do believe in the "good life" which has the commonality of being on the positive side of the value continuum and in some way involves the welfare of mankind (18–156). It is through these goals of what constitutes the "good life" that these individuals become independent self-actualizing persons. It is with reference to this knowledge of what is good as shown by education and culture operating around this concept of the "good life," that there can become such independent self-actualizing citizens—who not only establish systems of values within the frame of reference of society's, but also make moral choices regarding them and then assume responsibility for the consequences of behavior. Rich states that each individual brings something with him to these situations of moral choice such as past experience, goals, relevant facts, inculcated social values, and a set of principles. On the basis of these, he makes his choice (18–106). His resultant behavior may not always be the same as conventional behavior but it will have been founded on his moral independence and not on the sanctions of his fellow men. Rich sums up the independent self-actualizing person as one who has bridged the gap between knowing the good and doing good (18–116). When he disagrees with authority of the "Establishment," he makes his disagreement known to the proper authorities and then sets about attempting to effect changes which he believes desirable not only for himself but for the welfare of the larger society. He does this within the parameters of law and order.

It would seem, then, that the problem of society and a major goal of education is how to develop this authentic, independent self-actualizing citizen. In general, the task will involve guiding and leading the individual from one stage in social development to another where values are at first externally imposed to one where values become internalized, and decisions concerning values are based on free choice of the individual. Maybe this concept of the independent individual is not feasible within the parameters of present educational processes. However, maybe it could well become the most far-reaching aim of education. While some knowledgeable individuals contend that the development of self-actualizing citizens is possible, they say the schools do not have enough time or qualified personnel to do it.

However, the concept, if applied, could be a great force in society. In the past when moral and ethical values became the expectations of society, perhaps the basic motivation for compliance was furnished by society itself through its sanctions. In a modern democratic society, where values can be questioned intelligently and where choices can be made also with the intelligent understanding and responsibility for consequences, perhaps moral behavior rests on much sounder grounds. When moral decisions are based on choices resulting from the independent self-actualizing citizen rather than a fear of sanctions of society, the epitome of human values may be approaching.

What are the values that should come within the province of education and physical education? For the physical educator this answer should be easy. The values he should be most concerned with in the social matrix are those he gives lip service to in his goals—his aims, objectives and outcomes. Since social learnings, like skills, are highly specific to the situation, he must first identify the specific kinds of behavior inherent in his activities, teach them and then he must teach for transfer from the sports and game situation to life's larger arena.

HOW VALUES GROW AND CHANGE FOR THE INDIVIDUAL

In addition to having some concept of values, it is important for the teacher and coach to know something about the social nature of the individual and his capacity for socialization and learning values. The formation of values in the individual is a changing and dynamic process. Value systems grow, change and are re-structured at varying rates of speed (3–55). In some instances they continue to grow for a lifetime. In others, social maturity or social rigidity comes at an early age. Because of heredity interacting with the forces of the environment, no two people are alike, although they do have many similarities. In spite of their dissimilarities each one follows a pattern of growth in social concepts which is similar from birth to adulthood. Peck and Havighurst have presented a conceptual framework for this growth pattern (16). They recognize that social growth follows along a continuum of ascent on a scale and individuals cannot be categorically classed into types. However, as moral and social maturity is approached, these dominant characteristics come into focus as types in spite of individual deviations. Also, in practice, any given individual might display qualities of more than one type.

The first type is the *amoral* and characterizes the stage of infancy. Infants are motivated to behave entirely by self-gratification. This is the animal stage in need of modification in order to meet the expectancy of society. Unfortunately some adults have never grown past this stage in sociopsychological and moral development as they have become fixated at an infantile level because they have never learned to accept sanctions. If they are hostile, they generally become criminals; but if they are not, they are still irresponsible and undependable.

The second stage is the *expedient* type,

characteristic of early childhood. As the infant grows into early childhood, he becomes an "expediency" character. His ethical and moral values are based entirely on external sanctions where he is punished for wrong and rewarded for right behavior. Honesty is the best policy only to the extent that acts of honesty are rewarded and acts of dishonesty bring negative sanctions. This is the self-centered type who must always have external sanctions to motivate his moral behavior. He will tend to "get by" with anything where he won't be caught. He conforms to social norms in the short-run only because he can achieve long-run advantages. When the teacher isn't around, he does as he pleases to gratify his own self-centered ego.

The third stage is known as the *conforming* type. As the child reaches middle childhood, his conscience has awakened to the extent that he wants to abide by the rules and codes laid down by his primary groups. He becomes "rules" conscious, although at times he may help set the rule in his peer group. His actions are on a higher level than the expediency type because he is motivated to abide by rules by some internalized force rather than external sanctions of rewards and punishment. Unlike the expediency character, he will not attempt to "get by" with anything if it is outside the rules of his group. However, he is governed not by the morality of his choice but by a crude conscience in not wanting to break a rule. He is governed largely by the sanctions of his group regarding how he "should" act according to these rules.

The fourth type is the *irrational-conscientious* type and is characteristic of later childhood. At this level the conscience concept has advanced a bit farther. The child has his own internal standards concerning right and wrong and he will not compromise them

because if he does, he suffers guilt feelings. An act is right or wrong not because of its effect on others but because of preconceived principles of right and wrong, good or bad. He is really not concerned with the consequences of his behavior on other people as much as he is in upholding his own set of rigid standards. The essence of his behavior is not to compromise his moral code as he understands it even if it be a narrow blind type of internal control.

The fifth and highest level of behavioral types is the *rational-altruistic*. As the child matures into adolescence and young adulthood, ideally at least, he should be approaching this highest level of social and moral development. This is the level where he gages his actions not only on the moral principles he has learned but also on how his behavior will affect others. This great concern for the effect of his action on others is altruism at its best. This individual's whole value system is a hierarchy of patterns of attitudes, appreciations and ideals which he will have attempted to actualize in all his behavior—personal, social, economic, and political. His public and private values are consistent. He does the morally right thing because he wants to and not because it is the thing to do. Naturally this highest level is an ideal and it is a difficult goal for anyone to achieve completely.

Another approach in the socialization process of the child has been presented by Piaget (15–3). He first introduces the idea that all morality consists of a system of rules and the essence of all morality is to be found in the respect which a person acquires for these rules. He recognizes there is a scale of increasing ascendancy somewhat similar to the framework presented by Peck and Havighurst in the preceding paragraphs. Piaget's approach was to classify the child's socialization into stages based on his *practice* and *consciousness* of rules.

In the practice of rules the first stage, which is simply *motor and individual* in nature, usually runs from birth to around age two. Rules, if they can be called that, are primarily ritualized schemes which grow out of neuromuscular development.

The second stage called *egocentric* runs from age three to approximately six years. Here the child knows the rules to the extent that he can imitate them, but he practices them in accordance with his own fantasy. He either plays by himself or if he plays with others, he doesn't try to win in the sense the older child would consider winning. He holds rules sacred and does not condone transgression. In a sense he plays on his own where he is the player, the referee and the spectator.

The third stage runs from approximately seven to ten years of age and Piaget calls this stage *cooperation*. The player no longer plays to himself but attempts to win. He shows more concern for mutual control of the game and unification of the rules. However, he is still vague concerning his ideas of the rules, and he frequently simplifies and invents for his own purposes.

The fourth stage starts around the age of eleven and is called the *codification of rules*. Here the child knows the rules which by now have a high level of agreement in his society. He is now not only capable but is also anxious to discuss rules and the principles on which they are based. To him rules are not sacred but are codes that have been formed by mutual consent and can be changed the same way. However, once agreed upon, rules must be observed and obeyed. Thus, rules become a part of the personality structure of each child and as he tends to internalize them into patterns of behavior, these practices and attitudes more closely resemble the adult.

According to Piaget the child's consciousness of rules does not quite follow the same pattern of progression as his practice. In the child's consciousness of rules there are three stages. The first stage runs to about the middle of the *egocentric* stage and is characterized by rules which are not coercive or obligatory. The second stage runs to about the middle of the *cooperative* stage, characterized by a regard for rules as sacred, untouchable and eternal. To change the rules would be a major transgression. The third stage covers the last of *cooperation* and the whole of the *codification of rules* stage. The child looks on rules as laws derived from mutual consent which can be altered in the same manner.

IMPLICATION OF THE VALUES GROWTH FRAMEWORK

If the above framework is applied to the problem of value development, several things become eminent immediately. First, there is a plan for social just as there is for physical and mental growth. While the concept is more controversial and the boundaries less clearly defined, there is an inherent readiness for certain types of social behavior at certain age levels. Second, these stages are characterized by the child moving from a role of dependency and lack of responsibility to one of independency and responsibility. These developmental stages might help the teacher and coach to understand behavior and perhaps to analyze needs. They might even see that certain expected behavior could be either above or below the developmental level of their students. This would seem to imply the need for determining specific outcomes of behavior for the various developmental levels. Three, since social development is a continuous type process, there is no point where the student would suddenly pass from a dependent, sanctioned-motivated person to an independent self-actualizing altruistic person. Social development takes time, much more time than skills, knowledge and fitness. The process must by necessity be a gradual one spread over a number of years. However, the point is there must be practice by the student in activities which would lead him down the road to social maturity. Just as physical and intellectual growth are most rapid in the first decade of life, so is the sociopsychological. The implication is to train them early, but still be understanding within the social continuum framework.

Thus, it would seem if the goal of the self-actualizing person is to be achieved, there must be opportunities along the social development continuum for the child to "try his wings." Since there is no point where he suddenly passes from a morally irresponsible person to a responsible one, it would seem to indicate that the process is a gradual one and can be assisted by giving the student more opportunities to exercise choices and make judgments within the parameters that have been set by his society. This is not the same thing as a permissive society. A permissive society overlooks the social framework where emphasis must be placed on principles of conduct and discipline. Some think that many present-day troubles in the younger generation are due to two things: the breakdown in the home and cultural environment of the disadvantaged youth, and the over-permissiveness afforded the advantaged one. It is always dangerous to dichotomize, and there evidently are other facets to the problem. The important matter in the value field is for the student to know what the principles and standards are; then as he grows and develops along the social continuum to be provided with the opportunities to practice them in an environment which could nurture the beginning of the self-actualizing citizen.

It would seem that one's system of values would be a lifelong process. Certainly there is no evidence other than speculation that growth in values stops at any given age. It does seem from investigation, however, that as the individual advances in age, it becomes more difficult to influence or change the deeper aspects of character. This is not to be construed as an indication that character cannot be changed in the older child, but indicates that the time and effort for substantial changes might be beyond the current capabilities of the schools. However, values do change in the older high school and college student, but for them to change requires a most stimulating and personalized environment. The college years find the student at the height of his physical and intellectual vigor and a characteristic of this age is the search for identity and meaning. This quest inexorably leads to the formulation of values. To aid the student in his quest there should be good models in the form of leadership and a more formalized approach. Education has been so committed to the teaching of knowledge and technical competence, that the teaching of values as such has gotten lost.

The examination of values should occupy a more important place in the educational process. More time should be devoted to the development of the student's self-image and self-identification, and the student should be regarded as having the capacity to make choices. Too often the student feels he has not been accepted as a person and the "Establishment" has no faith in him to choose wisely and assume responsibility. It would be essential that the self-concept idea be emphasized, that the student be confronted with value issues, that he be permitted to make some of his choices, and that he come in contact with leadership which possesses these values. Nixon and Jewett (14–136) suggest that education must become more personalized if value training is to succeed.

ETHICAL AND MORAL VALUES

At this point the professional student knows that individual character and personality are structured by social experience and not by biological inheritance. He further knows that as a result of social interaction, the values of the student including his attitudes, appreciations and his ideals can be markedly influenced by some type of education. He also knows the part played by the learning climate of the environment. Therefore, the type of society in which interaction takes place is highly significant. While the individual cannot inherit his values through his genes like he does his body type or his potential for speech, because of his psychological and biological potential, he can learn.

His learning takes place through experience where he interacts—observes, imitates, participates, experiments, communicates, and conceptualizes. The experience in which he is involved is carried on in the culture which he inherited, which already has established values in terms of the expectations for group behavior. This behavior has become accepted as being right and good for the group as it evolved over long periods of time. In fact it is speculated that moral and ethical standards evolved out of the survival value of altruistic behavior which grew out of the prolongation of childhood and the necessity for consolidation of the family. Thus, as man evolved, his conscience concerning right and wrong seems to have evolved with him.

Every society imposes controls over the behavior which conflicts with the major purposes and values of its culture. Thus, moral and ethical behavior is that which promotes the general welfare of the group. The Ten Commandments were based on this concept. All such ethical and moral values have been established in terms of a hierarchy of dominance which is based on their relative strength. Some values are more significant and take precedence over other values which are more subordinate. The more dominant ones are embodied in the mores and laws of the social system. It is these values which must be learned by the individual and taught by society. Many of the ethical and moral values necessary to become a good person and lead the "good life" in a democratic society come from Judeo-Christian ethics and they have not changed markedly. If one accepts this thesis, then these are the values which should become the aspirations of the individual today as they are the expectations of the larger social group. There is still nothing implied here, however, that these values cannot be questioned and evaluated. There are no absolutes in this area of intangibles. However, since history has shown that these have existed not only for the good of the individual but also for society, the rational individual would have to come up with some good evidence for abandoning them.

Ethical and moral values are developed through social interaction over long periods of time. The sentiments and ideals which now epitomize man's noblest moments are the accumulation of thousands of years and much trial and error behavior. Good leadership has been one of the keys to the process. Therefore, the individuals who play the various roles in man's social groups are important facets in the socialization process and the internalizing of moral and ethical codes. The coach, the teacher, the peer associates as well as other models from reference groups must be "right" for their roles. The coach and teacher must possess the values they hope to teach. The peer group has great impact because the young child as well as the teenager probably learns many of his values from his peers. Not only are the "role players" important but other facets of the socialization process are equally so including the physical environment. The values which are desirable to develop in the young must be a part of the mores and laws of their culture. The youth must first know what these values are and the reasons they have become important as guides for man's behavior. Then, through interaction within their groups and with individuals, they go through experiences which require expression of behavior involving these values. Interaction resulting in learning takes many forms; the student first learns and acts from authority through observation and imitation. He moves to moral behavior only when he can understand the rules. The best teacher here is one who not only teaches by precept but after setting the example, then provides learning experiences. So much of all learning for the young is a case of "monkey see, monkey do" process. However, social learning, like all learning, cannot be left to the chance of imitation through example, important as it may be. There must be some planned approach, hopefully followed by assessment of results.

Democracy is a moral system and its values, when based on logic and intellect, can lead to ethical behavior. Thus, ethical values are identified with democratic culture. Ethical and moral values are time-tested and time-honored in a society characterized by the democratic philosophy. To list even the most significant of these would be too time-consuming, as they are well known. A few examples are: honesty, truthfulness, generosity, fair play, justice, responsibility, dependability. While these concepts represent the intangibles of man's wholeness and would be hard to define, they also represent the bright banners which have elevated him to his present level of civilized man. They may be hard to assess but are easily recognized in behavior. Thus, within the social matrix which includes ethical and moral values as well as other social behavior covered by custom and tradition, there is this quality called citizenship. However, the quality of citizenship like the values of morality is no absolute. It will need to be re-evaluated, re-interpreted and promoted anew by each new generation.

HOW ETHICAL AND MORAL VALUES ARE TRANSMITTED

The crux of society is how these time-tested values may be transmitted to the best advantage. The sociologist points out that social change occurs through diffusion and invention. Since these values are held and sanctioned by society, they have to be transmitted in some manner and become a part of learned behavior. The problem of creating the best learning situation is significant. First, it must be pointed out that those interested in social change for both the individual and the group must understand the pertinent aspects of the socialization process. These social learnings are highly specific rather than general. However, it is possible that the learning of a specific value will transfer to larger patterns of behavior under certain conditions. The learning of a social attribute in one situation will not automatically carry over to other situations, but if the learner sees the relationship, the transfer can be made. These relationships may have to be emphasized by leadership in physical education. Since values are intangibles, they can be studied only through the ways they are expressed by behavior. One is as one does. Good sportsmanship can be revealed only through acts of displaying good sportsmanship.

Moral and ethical values are related to personality and character. While character has almost become an archaic term, it still means what it has always meant throughout history. It refers to one's system of principles or values and on the positive side embodies the moral and ethical standards just discussed. Just as values are not absolutes, neither is character. It no doubt varies in meaning to the extent that cultures vary. However, character is listed as one of the principles (objectives) in the Seven Cardinal Principles of Education (6). Therefore it is a function for the schools to develop. In fact it may be viewed as something more than an objective of education. All the other educational objectives should function around this goal. Like health, nothing else in education matters much if character is missing.

Over the decades schools have more or less sidetracked this central issue for knowledge and skills. They have done this without recognizing that knowledge and techniques without character can be fatal. In the modern world of the "bomb" and impending suicide by push-button technology, ethical behavior becomes a practical necessity. Yet the gulf between the knowledge that schools teach and the character that makes that knowledge worthwhile grows wider with time.

It must be clearly understood that man's moral codes live on in his culture and in his social groups, but for each individual they must be learned anew from scratch.

Through education in the home, the school, and other places where interaction takes place, the young must acquire in some measure the dignity and moral stature that their race has achieved. Thus, ethical and moral norms are cultural traits that must be transmitted to the new generations. There must be some mechanism for this process. In the introductory portion of Chapter 1 attention was called to the necessity for perpetuating the cultural and social heritage through the young. While it is fatal for societies to cling too closely to the past, it is equally fatal for them to ignore it. Therefore, society must, for the present, continue to use the mechanisms for perpetuating its culture and its norms which have been traditional in the past—the home, the school and the church. If these fail, some new systems must be invented.

Still these social groups have slipped in their responsibilities in the last few decades. The traits of personality and character which have become traditionally synonymous with the frontier and democratic spirit of America have been shaken to their very roots in the last few decades. Perhaps these responsible social groups have neither lived in the past nor abandoned it, but there is some evidence that they have failed to perpetuate in the new generations those moral and ethical traits of character that built America. With acknowledged exceptions on all sides, the evidences of this failure in some cases are all too clear. The behavior of American soldiers as prisoners during the Korean War can be cited as one example. The traditional traits and values which America had always held to be self-evident and important to the American way of life were ignored and these men began to behave in a selfish and un-American way. They did not show the courage, faith and sense of responsibility that is considered the American heritage and which was shown by their counterparts during World War II (13). Since these young men represented a cross-section of society, their behavior did not deviate too far from the norm.

There are other disintegrating forces which point toward a lack of respect for traditional human values and present a challenge to education. Among these are the increase in crime rate, low morality in youth regarding drugs and sex, emphasis on materialism, disintegration of the family and the home, violation of public confidence in many walks of life, and irresponsibility and dishonesty in politics, economics, education, and news media. Perhaps the time has come when both nations and individuals must look into their sense of values where moral and ethical principles are concerned. Perhaps the same complacency and emphasis on affluence and materialism that has been detrimental to physical fitness has carried over to the concomitant areas of social and moral fitness. It seems that too much prosperity, materialism and complacency may lead to both moral and physical unfitness. The deification of the mind at the expense of the body in educational institutions and the emphasis on materialism in our culture could lead to disaster.

PLACE OF PHYSICAL EDUCATION IN SOCIALIZATION AND VALUE FORMATION

If one accepts the levels of growth for personality and character development, as revealed by Peck and Havighurst (16) or stages of Piaget's (15), they should furnish the educator as well as the physical educator with some guides in establishing personality and character training needs. Situations must be created which are favorable to the learning of values or the changing or reorganization of values. Since value systems show their fastest rate of growth during the first few years after birth, the social and emotional climate of the home is of paramount importance. From birth to kindergarten, the home is the primary influence in developing values. However, as childhood years are reached, of secondary importance is the influence of educational institutions. Most societies look to the schools for imposing social control. Physical education must assume its share of responsibility in this matter. In fact, of all the school influences affecting the social area perhaps the most significant ones have to do with the games, sports and dance provided in the athletic and physical education programs. This is not a new or an original idea. The English have long felt they taught as much on the play field as in the classroom. It is said the Battle of Waterloo was won on the playing fields of Eton.

Physical education occupies a unique place in the order of social controls. The very heart and core of its program is play and movement. Both are characteristics of human behavior and both have become an integral part of the social matrix. Movement is generally defined in terms of the biological and psychological. However, beyond these parameters, it has great social implication. When it is combined with play, the two form one of the most potent educational media of our time for youth. Games and sports are representatives of society; in fact they might literally be called a mini-society, because most of the processes that operate in a society for socialization are present in the game situation. All aspects of socialization such as role playing, status, stratification, sanctions, boundaries, leadership, discipline, accommodation, competition and cooperation make the world of sports and games a fertile training ground for values (21–118).

In a time when both primary and secondary social groups are either relinquishing their sanctions or at least becoming more permissive, sports and games may become the last citadel where boundaries and rules are strictly enforced and respected. As society becomes more and more permissive in its controls, physical education, through its games, sports, and athletics offers a type of discipline that is needed to make a society function. No game can be carried on without rules and boundaries (21–39). When rules are violated and out-of-bounds lines infringed upon, sanctions are immediately inflicted. The individual and the group have learned to respect and endorse these sanctions because through past experience they have learned the game does not provide satisfaction unless these prevail. There must be discipline for the game to proceed in an enjoyable and expressive manner. Equally, there must be discipline in a society (21–119). Discipline is built over a period of time by experiencing discipline. Children learn this regimen by following rules and codes associated with the game. There is no other way. Rules and codes of conduct are as important in a society as they are in sports because everyone must follow rules in all areas of living for all of one's life. As the child moves up the social continuum, he needs rules to place limits on his actions. Such limits provide him with an environment which is not overly restricted but which offers a feeling of security and happiness. While these learnings in a game concerning rules are specific, somehow leadership must help the student to generalize them into life's larger arena. There is a connection between the rules and codes which a child learns and accepts in games and the values of sportsmanship. These sportsmanship values are related to the ethical and moral values he will live by in adult life.

The student learns in sports that he has a free choice. He can abide by rules, violate or ignore them. But he also learns very quickly the consequences of his breach of rules. He not only is denied the fullest enjoyment of the game because of his deviant behavior, but he frequently loses status with his peers and thereby brings about a lowering of his own self-image. The bully on the playground, while he may be the best performer, does not have status in the group that he would have otherwise. In addition to the rules of the game itself, there are socially acceptable codes of expressing oneself in a game with regard to one's emotions and aggressions. When unacceptable behavior is ex-

pressed, there is a type of sanction imposed by the group which serves as a feedback. This feedback influences the offender's self-image. Youth particularly uses his peer and reference groups as mirrors for his interpretation of himself.

Sports furnish the media along with strong and consistent models for sound character and personality development. However, there is still the feeling in physical education and sports that values can best be taught through example and association—that they are inevitable concomitants of play and participation. Values can be "caught" provided the teacher or leader possesses those values along with a charismatic type of leadership, and provided the setting is conducive. However, there is no guarantee that values will be "caught." Values are intangibles observed only through behavior, and behavior is a learned activity. If behavior is learned, it can be taught; if it can be taught, the values undergirding that behavior can also be influenced. In the same context, if behavior and its related values are learned, they are subject to the same laws, methods and theories which apply to other forms of learning. There are several social processes that play a part in value formation. These are:

Role playing is an important aspect of socialization processes. One of the responsibilities of the family first and the schools second is the assignment of role playing. Such roles are exclusive of those played in the child's peer play groups. The assigned roles are likely to relate somewhat to the social continuum framework described by Peck and Havighurst (16). At first the assigned roles tend to be dependent and subordinate but as the child grows and moves along the social development continuum toward maturity and hopefully toward the positive end of the scales, these roles may be expanded to more responsible and independent ones. This is the key to the development of the independent self-actualizing person. Assuming a role in any peer group carries with it a responsibility—a responsibility that is assigned by the nature of status position. This obligation is generally enforced by sanctions—either through recognition in status or lack of it. Ways of behaving are roles, and no experience can offer more opportunities for role playing than sports, games and other physical education (21–119). It is through role playing in these activities that the child can develop his own body-image, thereby adding to his self-image, which after all is the basis of a healthy personality. The child observes and then imitates the behavior of other role players as he develops his self-image. Role playing is highly related to status since the individual will frequently covet a role because it could very well lead to a higher status for him in the group. Particularly in childhood and youth, and in boys more than girls, social status is predicated more on performance in motor skills than any other one thing.

Historically, in addition to assigning roles in the social group, society has also assigned *status*. This is an important element in the socialization process because it is associated with self-image and self-esteem. One of the positive factors of sports in the socialization process is in the area of social status. Today our society is a sports-oriented one. This is true not only for youth but for adults also. There is a status related to participation in sports and status is gained through sports. Each sport or game offers status positions as a microcosm of society. The evidence is clear that proficiency in sports is a revered characteristic among youth and success in motor skills is related to social acceptance and prestige. This acceptance becomes one of the most dynamic factors in personality development. Evidence supports the thesis that average to good achievement in motor skills for all ages and both sexes is necessary for obtaining group status. Status in one's group is related not only to role playing but also to leadership. Probably there is no area today where one's status in the group is predicated on his ability alone as much as it is in the area of sports. Status, once attained, leads to different role playing and to higher levels of leadership. While roles and status may be assigned in the sports area in the beginning, each individual has the opportunity to change his role and raise his status according to his own unique abilities. Physical prowess has been shown to be important in gaining and improving status and can lead the way to higher leadership roles. Success or failure in meeting the expectations of peer group influences an individual's status with the group. In a physical education class it is the job of the teacher to build up success by modifying or manipulating the environment so that all can experience success as well as some failure.

Social *stratification* is another facet of the process of socialization. It, too, can affect personality and self-image as individuals are born and nurtured in a particular social stratum. They sometimes have wealth, prestige, influence, and opportunity in proportion to the level of class standing they inherit. Sports and games can provide an environment where there is less social stratification than anywhere else. However, sports can serve as the catalyst for social mobility, too, where one moves up in the strata continuum (21–71). New roles in sports based chiefly on ability but somewhat on leadership can create new status. Status leads to preferential treatment and this promotes stratification. The athlete is granted a degree of social mobility that may not be provided for the non-athlete. This is not a new thing in social mobility. It was a mark of the Greek and Roman empires.

Sports participation can lead to a better self-image on the part of the student and thereby enhance his self-esteem, self-control and sense of security. At the base of all these is the *body-image*. The child's emotions and behavior are reflected by and are largely related to the image he has of his own body, and if he is to achieve identity he must experience a feeling of being at home in his own body (2–29). The maintaining of a good body-image is not a constant thing once it is achieved, but continually has to be reinforced. In other words social learnings, like high level skill, are variables. In the learning process there must be constant feedback and reinforcement (8–10). Feedback is as important in social learnings as it is in skill learning. The child as well as the adult develops his self-image partly in terms of how he thinks other people view him. He sees himself mirrored in their eyes and this feedback either tends to flatter him if they approve or to depress him if he notes disapproval (21–33). Body-image is an important sociological concept as well as a psychological one. The attitude and appreciation one has toward his own body affects his behavior and ultimately his personality. During adolescence this body-image complex is an important factor for both boys and girls. The image one has for his own body will be reflected in his behavior and will dictate to a certain extent the type of physical education activity in which he will participate or whether he will voluntarily participate at all. One of the cruxes of education is to get teachers to understand this concept, to identify those who have poor body-image, to use empathy in their relations with these, and to help these students understand their own problems and to live reasonably happily with them. Since sports and physical activities are so meaningful to children and youth, and as they provide media where something can be done concerning body-image, the good teacher has a commitment to be concerned.

Cooperation and *competition* are two social processes that are highly related to the area of games and sports and value formation. In the last chapter on social bases these terms were discussed under the various processes of interaction leading to socialization. In fact they have become powerful forces in the socialization processes as well as motivators to learning in both intellectual and motor performance areas. In physical education's sports and games, the two processes should not be looked upon as diverse and antithetical and at the opposite ends of the social continuum. While it is true that competition seems the more basic of the two in terms of primitive drive and they represent different forms of behavior, they are both innate qualities and are interdependent. The sports and games area requires competition but also demands cooperation. Thus, to have competition is to include cooperation as a corollary.

Actually competition has several levels. An individual can compete against himself in terms of past performance or records; he can compete against established norms, or he can compete against an individual or team. While all of these may have some social implication and prove motivating to learning and performance, it is the competition with others with which this discussion is concerned. Cooperation becomes a necessity for competition to proceed effectively without reverting into rivalry or conflict. To compete with and against others requires various kinds of cooperation. One must work together in the most cooperative way with teammates if the most value is to be gotten from the game. He must cooperate with the

officials and even interact in a cooperative way with the opponents within the
framework of the game rules and codes.
The interaction of these various elements
makes sports and games one of the most
fertile fields for socialization.

Research shows that activities carried
on in the framework of competitive and
cooperative behavior is superior to a
no-incentive situation for learning (19–
255). Therefore, competition is good
for motivating and fostering incentive.
As long as it is carried on in the parameters of desirable cooperation and rivalry
is minimized and conflict is eliminated,
it becomes a valuable educational medium. Some contend that educational
athletics and sports can provide this
opportunity for socialization perhaps
better than any other aspect of the
school program. To maximize the
effectiveness of the student's cooperative behavior, the emphasis in education
must be placed on the achievement of
excellence in performance without reverting to rivalry and conflict which
place emphasis on winning at all cost
and degradation of the opponents. The
crux for the physical educator is to find
out how to use competition most effectively in establishing values without
either overemphasizing it or de-empha-
sizing it until it loses its value.

EFFECTS OF GAMES AND SPORTS IN VALUES

This much we do know in physical
education and athletics: teachers and
coaches have given a great deal of lip
service to their contribution in the social and moral value area through their
sports and games, yet they have done
very little in evaluating the product or
the process. In most cases teachers and
coaches operate under the assumption
that social and psychologic improvement are natural outcomes of the physical education process. Few coaches
and teachers can present supporting

evidence when they are pressed to do so.
They are too prone to talk in generali-
ties and their claims sometimes border
on being platitudinous.

The unit just discussed concerning the
potential of sports and games for purposes of socialization and value formation sounds good and reasonable. Yet,
when one pursues the question a bit
farther and especially looks into the
mounting evidence shown in research,
the results hardly support the thesis
assumed in the previous paragraphs
that sports always develop desirable
values. Perhaps the dilemma lies not
so much in the innate potential of
sports, games and physical activities as
means of developing desirable behavior,
but rather in the way such activities
have been conducted. At the present
time, however, the evidence is not overwhelming and as usual controversy
arises. There is lack of research studies
in the area of sports and games and their
relation to social behavior. Perhaps the
reasons for this lack are that few physical educators have been qualified to do
sociological research, and most sociologists have by-passed the area of sports
and games for more prestigious areas.

At the present time there does seem
to be positive evidence that participation in sports and games—particularly
at the higher levels—does have an
effect on personality. Since values being
discussed in this chapter must be learned
within the larger frame of reference of
dynamic personality development, then
sports and games can affect character
development. However, there is no
guarantee that this effect is always
favorable. It could be unfavorable or
negative. In the past it was assumed,
or at least a great amount of lip service
was given to the idea, that such changes
were for the better. Current research
does not support this thesis. In fact,
while the data on such research are still
not conclusive, much of them now begin

to point to the fact that while personality and character traits do change through participation in sports, they are not always desirable changes. Much more research of a longitudinal nature must be done. This is needed because the sociopsychological factors, unlike the physical fitness and motor ability factors, change slowly and over a fairly long period of time.

While sports and games do have an impact on personality, it is also true that personality has an equally important impact on sports. Individuals tend to select the sports in which they want to participate in terms of their unique personality (19–318). Studies have been made to determine the relationship between success in sports and personality. Differences have been shown between successful athletes and the average. However, the differences do not explain which is causal to which. It could well be that people are successful in a particular sport because of their personality. On the other hand, it could be they have a particular type of personality because they have been successful. There does seem to be a relationship between success in sports and the maintaining of an ongoing interest in them. Maintaining interest in sports participation along with fitness are values in themselves and are among those that should be promoted.

One of the values related to sports and games is sportsmanship. While sportsmanship is still a highly controversial and nebulous term, meaning different things to different people and groups, in general most persons see in it these three aspects: fair play, modesty in victory and self-control in defeat. It is presumably a general quality, but when analyzed it breaks down into a number of traits such as honesty, fair play, self-control, and others. It is assumed again that these traits, once they are learned in the sports situation,

will transfer to life's activities. The ethical values learned and practiced in youth will probably be the same values used in later life for business, politics and professional relations but this has not been shown through research. "Does participation in sports as we know them in the schools and colleges today bring about improvement in sportsmanship?" While the jury is still out on this case and the evidence is still not overwhelming, findings of research now seem to indicate the reverse may be true. The older the individual and the higher the level of competence he possesses in sports, the progressively poorer he becomes in sportsmanship (19–318).

SOME ASPECTS OF TEACHING VALUES THROUGH SPORTS

Values are inherent to the culture to which one is born. As was previously stated, they are not biologically or psychologically inherited in any sense; they must be learned. They may be learned either indirectly by association and imitation or directly through teaching. If they are "caught," they must be caught from someone who possesses them and with whom the learner has identified—someone with charisma. If they are taught, they must be taught by someone in the role of a teacher or leader who must also possess the values and who teaches more effectively if he, too, possesses charisma.

The teaching of values is not too unlike the teaching of knowledge or skills. While the latter two aspects of man have usually been on a planned basis as part of the formal educational program, it seems that his value system has been left to chance—either relegated to some outside agency for development and transfer or left as a hoped for concomitant outcome of other educational processes. It is paradoxical that the perpetuation of culture and society must ultimately depend on the collective values of the collective individuals in that society. Yet the assignment of responsibility for inculcating these values is more or less left to chance—it could be the home, the school, the church, the Boy Scouts, other agencies, or even the street gangs. Still it must be made clear that no one agency or discipline has a monopoly in teaching values. Since education is the one social agency other than the home that deals with all children and youth, it must assume more of this responsibility. It may be that the nature of educational programs are such that they have a better opportunity than some other groups. However, the learning of human values must be a many-faceted approach. Values have a multidisciplinary connotation and all disciplines must share to some extent.

Many persons connected with education today, other than physical educators, are saying that physical education through its sports and games program has the best opportunity and the best environment to teach values along with the necessary self-image and self-concept. These values and the individual's self-concept are significantly related. If this thesis is accepted, then certain things must be attempted. There are three dimensions in the teaching of values in physical education. They are:

Classification of Objectives

The first dimension concerns the objectives commonly referred to in the affective domain of learning. While this value objective is already there and has been since the time of Hetherington (10), it must now be clarified more carefully and broken down into more specific outcomes for the various levels according to the social framework presented by Peck and Havighurst (16) in this chapter. The student does not learn general behavior initially; he learns specific behavior. These are the concomitant outcomes mentioned in Chapter 3.

If the professional student will refer back to the educational and physical educational objectives, he will find these values high on the list. *Ethical character* is listed as one of the seven major objectives of education, and the social and emotional objective as one of the four major objectives of physical education. Under this major objective in physical education can be listed uncountable social outcomes which are revealed through specific behavior. These are the substances which make up the social content.

Formal Plan for Teaching

There must be some formal plan to teach these values which are inherent in the physical education environment. This does not negate the use of the "teachable moment" when it arises, but like health instruction, the teachable moment merely supplements the more formalized approach. Also, it does not deny the fact that value learning can and does take place through imitation. Nixon and Jewett maintain, however, that a curriculum must include at least a minimum of these democratic moral values as a facet of the formal curriculum and that they be emphasized in both the curricular and the extracurricular programs. In this formal approach they recommend the following four avenues to inculcating values: (1) through subject content, (2) through individual counseling, (3) through environmental modification and (4) through utilization of rewards and punishments (14–136). Each of these is an approach to teaching values which has met with some success in the past but basically these approaches need to be put to scientific tests. Each is an approach and is not a method. There are many methods under each and the best methods for each must be discovered through exploration and experimentation. Regardless of which approach is used in teaching values, there are three principles which apply to all of them:

First, if the student is to learn values either in a formal or an informal setting, he must be aware of the right concepts concerning these values. He simply cannot learn and apply in practice what he does not know and does not understand. It is helpful if a great deal of this teaching concerning what is right and what is wrong has been done in the home.

Second, it is not enough for the student to know the value concepts inherent in the physical education processes and environment; he must be taught to live by these concepts. As he participates and interacts in his physical education class or intramural or varsity team, he grows in his value system. This is the crux of the whole problem. It is one thing to know what is right and good in the sports situation, but it is still another thing to do good.

Third, the next facet of this problem is transfer. In sports and games, which are mini-societies within themselves with their own codes, rules and behavioral norms, it is necessary to teach for the transfer of these specific values inherent in sports to more general values necessary in the larger society. Teaching for transfer is education's greatest challenge in the social arena. As the student grows and progresses along the social continuum toward maturity, he should be helped to generalize both his knowledge and his behavior concerning these values. As he gains insight into the codes, values and behavior, as he sees their relationships to life in general, to his own life and self-fulfillment, and to other people, he is becoming that independent self-actualizing person mentioned earlier. He not only knows the concept of the value he should play by, but he understands its reason for being and why it is necessary for him and for his social group. He will then be able to make his choice of behavior based on judgment according to criteria not only of his own culture but also his own unique self.

Methodology and Procedures of Value Training

The statement has been made in the unit just discussed that knowing the concept of the value was not enough; the student must be taught to live by that value. This involves the methods and procedures which must be used to inculcate values. While there has been much lip service given to this area for centuries, not much has been done in the way of scientific studies to see how values may best be taught. It is such an intangible area and there are so many variables which cloud the issue. Admittedly, it is one of the exploratory areas where the dynamic and innovative teacher will experiment with new ideas. It is an area that calls for scientific investigation in the future. However, this comment should be made. Value training is learning and there are already many methods and techniques being used successfully in other areas based on the learning process. This could be experimented with at this point by the teacher with dedication and commitment to this objective and new approaches might be discovered.

When the more formal plan of subject content approach is used, values and issues involving values may be taught directly through the lecture method, class discussion, panels, and through the group processes. These methods may insure that knowledge of the concepts is acquired but the practice of values, like the learning of skills, is not learned by talking about them. The concept is learned but the behavior representing that value must be "stamped in" in the laboratory of the gymnasium, playing field or what have you. There must be integration of all approaches to value training for best results. The student may learn the concept in the subject content approach but he can only put that concept to work in an action situation. It is here in the gym or on the field that the teacher-coach can modify the environment to bring these values into focus, can use sanctions of rewards and punishments, and ultimately do some individual counseling in the case of the habitual offenders. Thus, the methodology can be a multifaceted approach. In the final analysis the indirect "caught" approach cannot be entirely separated from the more direct "taught" approach. No doubt great weight is added to the direct approach if the conditions are right to make the indirect function.

Measurement of Value Status and Progress

The last step to be discussed concerns measuring status and progress in these areas. Over the years a great many different devices have been employed, but admittedly there needs to be improvement in this area. One's value system is the most intangible part of his wholeness and presents problems in evaluation. If inventories are used where the student answers the questions himself, reliabilities are low because the student does not always behave like he says he does. If observations and ratings are used, they are time-consuming, highly subjective and not too reliable. When such techniques are employed, the rater does not measure the values directly but the behavior reflecting those values. Just as a student does not always behave as he says he would on an inventory, neither does he always act the same way in similar situations. However, in schools today where the administrator has to become dollar conscious, evidence must be presented that learning and positive change are taking place if time and cost figure in the teaching. Techniques for assessment

of social learning must be improved and then implemented. So identifying, teaching and measuring values become the focal points of formal education. The same principles of learning apply to the learning of values as skills. When the learner receives knowledge of results, it has been shown through scientific studies (see Chapter 16) that he learns more rapidly. This knowledge of results can be obtained through some type of measurement. The child wants to know "How good am I?" in a skills test or a fitness test. Why not "How *good* am I?" on a social evaluation test or scale?

The Learning Climate

There are three more things which are near the heart of this matter. *First*, one teaches what one is. If the teacher-coach does not possess these values he is trying to inculcate in his students, he is not likely to succeed. This implies that more emphasis must be placed on these basic intangible qualities in the selection and recruitment of such personnel for training in the professional training institution. A coach and teacher truly lives in a glass house every day, not only in the classroom and on the play field, but in his private life. Since the world of youth is so motivated by sports and games, it follows that those associated with the conduct of such activities will play an influential role in the lives of their students. Youth will identify with the coach if they admire him. They will reflect his values as they imitate his behavior and actions. If he attempts to teach one set of values by precept in a formal value training program but practices another set in his example, he negates the formal teaching aspect because his actions speak much more forcefully than his words in the sub-society with which he is relating. Also, his lack of consistency may lose him his role as a model and his ability to communicate with his students. In this case his influence on values is largely negative. It is this inconsistency, this difference between values that are preached and values practiced that causes youth to lose faith in the society of their elders.

Second, sports and games, when they are used as media for teaching values, must be educational and cannot be overemphasized for purposes of entertainment. Athletics and sports, in most instances, lose their value to education when wholesome competition is supplanted by rivalry and ultimately by conflict. Admittedly, one of the values of sports competition is the struggle and the challenge of competition. The participant is presumed to grow in character traits as a result of the competition. However, one of the problems facing the coach and teacher is how to motivate players to struggle and excel without forcing them into a form of rivalry where degradation of the opponent and winning at all cost become the primary issues. In athletics and sports for both colleges and schools the primary goals should be purely educational and not entertainment. When entertainment becomes the main goal, healthy competition more than likely goes by the wayside as interaction turns into rivalry and ultimately may result in conflict. When sports are carried on in an environment marked by conflict, few real educational values accrue from the "values" standpoint, and few positive educational objectives are achieved. Competition does not have to become conflict and commercial in the schools, but to avoid them, the objective of sports must remain essentially education oriented. This can be controlled by the good teacher in the physical education class. It can be handled equally well in the intramural program with adequate supervision. However, in interschool athletics, where the potential is greater because of the highly dramatic

nature of the climate, it is becoming more difficult to keep competition in its proper perspective.

It must be recognized, however, that sports are a basic part of American culture, and they seem to be demanded by society to fulfill a basic need of man. Since America is a sports-oriented culture, professional athletics are here to stay and perhaps "big time" athletics in colleges and universities. However, the point must be made here that there is a difference between sports for entertainment and commercial purposes and the types of sports which are pure and simple education as taught in the physical education class. Entertainment athletics may develop a type of discipline and provide the usual opportunities for role playing, status and leadership. However, they have little worth in the area of value training. Such social and moral values that have been discussed in this chapter are not even remotely a sought-after objective in professional or entertainment athletics. If they are developed at all, it would be due to mere chance. If such values are important to education and to society, they cannot be left to chance. Entertainment athletics have a commodity to sell—winning—and their success is based entirely on this "success" criterion. The cult of success took over man's work a long time ago. Now it has taken over his games. Winning is more important than playing, and playing seems to have value only in victory. The success criterion downgrades the loser and heaps accolades on the winner. Sportsmanship is an archaic term. The fact that ethical and moral values of youth and also institutions may be prostituted and values compromised is now tacitly sanctioned by society where sports are concerned. The important thing is to win and draw a big crowd, and that end justifies the means. This pressure to win at all cost has paralleled the eroding of moral and ethical values. Sports and athletics for all could be a force for stiffening our moral fiber and ethical codes and thereby help in establishing the basic stability needed to adjust to the vast social and environmental changes taking place. However, values in sports just don't happen. Values in sports are learned and like most learnings in education, they must be planned for in the educational processes. When they are planned for under the direction of good leadership, they can be attained, but it won't be easy. When all a coaching staff's efforts are directed toward winning, it is true there is no time left for value training. The coach who bluntly stated that he didn't have time to teach character is being honest and pragmatic. He has learned that character is not one of the criteria by which he is judged by a sports oriented culture. His salary, his prestige and his job are dependent not on the amount of character he teaches but on the number of games he wins. For this reason the interschool athletic program is not likely to offer much of a vehicle for character building in the near future.

Still, a *third concern* is apparent. The teaching of values faces the same roadblock that teaching knowledge and skill in physical education has always experienced. Classes are too large and time allotment is too little. Value teaching is not easy; it must be spread over time and it must be accompanied by face-to-face, one-on-one relationships where instruction can be individualized and personalized. When classes are overly large, the de-personalizing effect can provide a negative influence on value training.

Therefore, it seems apparent that values can be influenced but only under certain circumstances. There is need for a formalized plan for teaching. There must be a high level of leadership.

The class load and time allotment must be reasonable and adequate. And last, the program of games and sports, the medium for teaching values, must be carried on in an educational setting.

REFERENCES

1. AAHPER: *Developing Democratic Human Relations.* Washington, D.C., AAHPER, 1951.
2. AAHPER: *Values in Sports.* Washington, D.C., AAHPER, 1963.
3. Arsenian, Seth: Development of Values with Special Reference to College Years. *Values in Sports,* Report of a National Joint Conference of the Division for Girls and Women's Sports and the Division of Men's Athletics. Washington, D.C., AAHPER, 1963.
4. Bertrand, Alvin L.: *Basic Sociology: An Introduction to Theory and Method.* New York, Appleton-Century-Crofts, 1967.
5. Bucher, Charles A.: *Foundations of Physical Education.* St. Louis, C. V. Mosby Company, 1968.
6. Commission of the Reorganization of Education: *Cardinal Principles of Secondary Education.* Department of Interior, Bureau of Education. Bulletin No. 35, 1918. Washington, D.C., United States Printing Office, 1938.
7. Cowell, Charles C., and L. France Wellman: *Philosophy and Principles of Physical Education.* Englewood Cliffs, N. J., Prentice-Hall, Inc., 1963.
8. Cratty, Bryant J.: *Social Dimensions of Physical Activity.* Englewood Cliffs, N. J., Prentice-Hall, Inc., 1967.
9. Green, A. W.: *Sociology: An Analysis of Life in Modern Society,* 4th Ed. New York, McGraw-Hill Book Company, 1964.
10. Hetherington, Clark W.: *School Program in Physical Education.* New York, World Book Company, 1922.
11. Hoebel, E. Adamson: *Anthropology: The Study of Man.* New York, McGraw-Hill Book Company, 1966.
12. Luchen, G.: The Interdependence of Sports and Culture. Unpublished study presented to the National Meeting of the American Association of Health, Physical Education and Recreation in Las Vegas, 1967.
13. Mayer, William E.: Communist Indoctrination. Reprint of Speech, Director of Mental Health, State of Hawaii.

14. Nixon, John E., and Ann E. Jewett: *Physical Education Curriculum*. New York, The Ronald Press, 1964.

15. Piaget, Jean: *The Moral Judgment of the Child*. Glencoe, Ill., The Free Press, 1948.

16. Peck, R. F., R. J. Havighurst, et al.: *The Psychology of Character Development*. New York, John Wiley & Sons, 1960.

17. Raths, L. E., Merrill Marmin, and S. B. Simon: *Values and Teaching*. Columbus, Ohio, Charles E. Merrill Publishing Company, 1966.

18. Rich, John Martin: *Education and Human Values*. Reading, Mass., Addison-Wesley Publishing Company, 1968.

19. Singer, Robert N.: *Motor Learning and Human Performance*. New York, The Macmillan Company, 1968.

20. Sanborn, Marion Alice, and Betty G. Hartman: *Issues in Physical Education*, 2nd Ed. Philadelphia, Lea & Febiger, 1970.

21. Ulrich, Celeste: *The Social Matrix of Physical Education*. Englewood Cliffs, N. J., Prentice-Hall, Inc., 1968.

22. Williams, Jesse F.: *The Principles of Physical Education*. Philadelphia, W. B. Saunders Company, 1965.

PART III

Scientific Bases and Principles

SECTION D
Psychological Bases

Chapter 15

Psychological Principles

INTRODUCTION

In Chapter 1, *learning* was defined as a change, a modification or an adjustment in the behavior of an individual as a result of experience. The change is relatively permanent in nature and the experience is reinforced practice as opposed to maturation or other causative factors of change such as fatigue, motivation, and changes in the stimulus situation (21–2). This change is progressive in nature but not necessarily improvement, nor is it always intentional as it covers the whole gamut of human behavior. It involves experiences in the mental, social and physical domains and thereby concerns changes and modifications not only in knowledge concepts and motor skills, but also social values and behavioral attitudes and appreciations. The psychology of learning is concerned with how these changes take place and in general does not differentiate between so-called intellectual skills and simple motor skill learning. Learning theory and laws are assumed by some to apply equally to all areas, motor as well as academic, verbalization and social interaction. However, it may seem that motor learning would appear to be different due to the variety and complexity of responses.

At this point *learning* should be distinguished from performance. The main differentiating element is that performance can be observed. Measuring changes in performance is the method used to determine how much learning has taken place. However, while performance is based on learning, it is also influenced by other variables such as motivation, reinforcement, and fatigue. Therefore, it is difficult to be certain how much of the change in performance is due to learning and how much is due to one or more of the other variables.

The professional student should know that perhaps man's greatest asset is his capacity to adapt his behavior to widely diverse conditions. In order to survive in a diversified environment and adapt to constantly changing situations, he has had to develop a multitude of basic intellectual, social and movement skills. To understand the learning and performance of these skills, it is necessary to have a frame of reference within which man's abilities can be studied. His performance depends upon his ability to sense first, followed by the processing, storing and transmitting of the information which is sensed. Sensation, perception, memory, response followed by feedback are the basic components of learning.

This knowledge comes chiefly from a study of psychology, although other disciplines are now making some contribution. Historically, psychology was defined as the science of the mind. In fact, the derivation of the term is the two Greek words *psyche* meaning mind and *logos* meaning science. However, a more modern definition defines it as the science of behavior. Thus, psychology includes a study of man's mind and its functions along with his behavior. The goals of education are transmitted through the learning process. For a teacher to understand this learning process, he must know about the theories and laws governing learning and the factors and conditions which promote it. The basis for acquiring motor skills are these general principles of learning. As far as it is possible with existing knowledge, the teacher should understand neurological organization and the relationship between the mind and the muscles. The understanding of motor learning and performance, however, is dependent in part on physiology, anatomy, sociology, anthropology, and kinesiology as well as psychology.

The purpose of this chapter is not to provide the student with a deep discourse on psychology. It would be well, however, for the professional student in physical education to take courses in general psychology as well as adolescent and child psychology, and in motor learning. Meanwhile, this chapter does try to impart to the student that information which has been systematized and verified into principles and laws, relevant to understanding education and teaching its activities. Learning theories provide the guidelines that help to make teaching and learning more effective.

Inasmuch as there still remains a multitude of mysteries in the structure, operation, and function of the mind, there can be no absolutes. All theories are in a state of formulation and none holds the answers to all kinds of learning. Theories, as well as commonly recognized concepts, assumptions, and hypotheses are still open to question and this invites controversy. However, theories are an attempt to organize research data into meaningful and unifying systems, but verification in psychology is difficult. The researcher cannot delve into a mind with a scalpel or make a window showing all where he could observe openly how learning takes place. In the study of the human mind and its behavior, however, he can take the child into a clinical situation and research his theories and hypotheses in terms of the child's responses. His attempt at verification can then be made in terms of his interpretation of the data he gathers from behavior. While it is the job of the scientist to interpret his data, the theorist formulates theories. Facts are the bases of theories and theories offer a vehicle for more research followed by new hypotheses and formulation of new theory.

Some of the newer theories and hypotheses offer wonderful opportunities for understanding the human mind and the reactions and responses exhibited. In this study of the mind, psychology has moved closer to many of the answers to the mysteries of the human mind, and the scientific process has replaced the chart of the phrenologist. Yet so complicated is its mechanism and so delicate is its physiology that man may never completely grasp how his mind really functions.

In the past, in order to simplify learning and to reduce it to its bare essentials the psychologists have used animals in their research. This technique alone has led to controversy. While it is relatively simple to reduce learning to simplest terms for an animal that is basically governed by instinct, learning can never be a simple matter in man because of his rational powers. Even in the study of human performance, scientists have traditionally sought to explain complex behavior through simpler ones. Many, especially those who hold to cognitive theories, believe this oversimplification leads to further misunderstanding. Also, most learning psychologists have presented laws and principles of learning but not their application.

In formal education, learning is considered to be an outcome of instruction based on well defined and structured curricula, though it can go on at any time or place. Since learning can take place only as a result of one's own efforts, education takes place constantly whenever one uses his initiative. It is the sum of changes in the individual brought on by experience. Getman has said that everything a child knows he must learn and even learn how to learn (8–16). This is education in its broadest sense. When movement serves as a basis for learning, this is physical education. Not all behavioral changes are learning, however. As has been previously pointed out, if changes in behavior develop through a patterned sequence, and if practice and training do not materially affect them, then *maturation* is most likely the causative factor. While maturation does not cause learning, it does make learning possible. However, in most motor learning, especially in the young, changes and modifications in behavior are a result of a complex interaction of both learning and maturation. Also, if the holistic concept is to be considered, it seems important that the physical educator learn as much as he can about how social and mental learnings occur as concomitants to motor learning.

In keeping with this holistic concept,

however, learning as such cannot be categorized as either physical or mental —but as a continuum along a linear scale where at one end of the scale it is more physical than cognitive and at the other more cognitive than physical (14–4). Therefore, all learning involves both to different degrees. Thus, perceptual motor learning has become a new dimension in education where in many sources perception and movement are considered as one (11), (19). Also, the new idea of concept development through movement has now permeated the area of research and practice for both the psychologist and the educator (9). This idea of movement as a process of integration and mentioned as one of the five concepts on which the need for increased emphasis on physical education is based was stressed at some length in the introductory Chapter 1. It will also be touched upon in this chapter. In learning, particularly in the young, the setting generally takes place in a world characterized by movement. In fact the child's world may well be a movement world, since at this early age learning proceeds more efficiently in a concrete situation than in an abstract one. This takes the professional student into new areas where the terms proprioception, feedback, neurological organization, and body-image will become an important aspect of professional training.

THEORIES OF LEARNING

Since there are many contradictions in this field, there are many theories and laws. Presumably a law is the result of a hierarchy of principles and values which have become accepted as immutable. In the case of laws in psychology, however, this is not necessarily true because even the so-called "Laws of Learning" expounded by Thorndike are no longer accepted as absolutes (20). It will be the intention of the author in this chapter to present the principles and theories that have been generalized from interpretation of scientific data. While admittedly these are controversial areas and there are no universal truths as such in learning psychology, these concepts are generally accepted until new scientific evidence to the contrary comes into being.

Learning theory is based on theoretical assumptions which try to explain such phenomena as memory, reinforcement, satisfaction, transfer and the like. While there are numerous theories and theorists in the field of learning psychology, it is perhaps best to start at some point of reference where there is some general agreement. Perhaps about the only commonality is the fact that learning consists of some kind of a relationship between a stimulus and a response. In some theories there are no intervening variables between the S–R (stimulus–response), while in others there are intervening factors. Also, in all learning, reinforcement always seems present in some of its many forms. Therefore, mere contiguity of the S–R may be sufficient for learning but reinforcement probably always accompanies learning even if it is sometimes a self-administered type (14–6). Such reinforcement could be anything that increases the chances for the right response. Furthermore, from the pragmatic point of view, the physical educator has learned that regardless of the nature of this connectedness, or relatedness, or process of integration between the stimulus and the response, learning in movement skills can take place most effectively through movement itself, and this movement must involve motivated repetitious practice of the skill with a meaningful purpose.

These learning theories vary greatly. It could be they are basically different because they place emphasis on different aspects of behavior. Those who hold to this view would take an eclectic position toward them and incorporate all important theories into one all-encompassing theory (17–278), (16).

Traditionally there are two basic types of theories of psychology which relate to learning in physical education. These theories try to explain learning and at the same time attempt to predict behavior in its simplest form. They have some commonalities but are uniquely different. However, in spite of their differences, they have withstood the test of time. There have been other theories and modifications and extensions of these two but in general they give the traditional basis for learning. The first of these types of theories can be categorized as S–R (stimulus–response) learning where there are no complicated elements between the stimulus and the response. The two most well known are the *bond* theory and the *conditioning* theory. Together they are frequently referred to as *"connectionist"* theories. The second category encompasses the cognitive types. The *cognitive* approach views learning as having intervening variables between the S–R and these factors have cognitive connotations. Such theories involve generally going beyond what is given so that the learner views the S–R not as isolated specific stimulus–response factors but as representations of generalizations into general categories. More recent theories have somewhat lessened the difference between these two views and a more balanced approach now suggests that both be considered.

Bond Theory

One of the oldest theories in terms of time is the *bond theory*, sometimes called the *trial-and-error theory*. It refers to that learning which takes place as a result of repetition of the act. Through repetition which is a sort of trial and error procedure, or a random selection of behavior patterns, the errors are gradually eliminated and the correct response established. In this process of building the correct response, motivation becomes a prominent factor and Thorndike's so-called laws of exercise, readiness and effect are operative. The error type responses are eliminated because they are not reinforced. They do not bring satisfaction or reward to the learner. However, the correct type responses tend to be repeated because they are reinforced in some manner and are stamped in. This reinforcement may be an intrinsic type of thing such as a feeling of satisfaction after achievement or success, or it could be extrinsic such as rewards. This theory can account perhaps for some kind of learning but does not have the answer to all questions.

Association Theory

A second theory of learning is the *association theory* sometimes referred to as the *conditioning theory*. The classic example of conditioning psychology is Pavlov's work with dogs in establishing a transfer or an *association* between an original stimulus and a new stimulus to elicit the same desired response. The sight of the food was the original or unconditioned stimulus (US), the ringing of the bell was the new stimulus or the conditioned stimulus (CS), the flow of saliva after the bell was the conditioned response (CR). Thus, there is a transfer from the unconditioned response to the conditioned response. Learning occurs whenever a new response is associated with a stimulus situation or where there is the ability to elicit a response by transfer from one stimulus to another. When applied to physical education this theory explains learning as a process of conditioning. Thus, there is an association established between the CS and the US or UR (21–19). The learner reacts in the way he does because he

associates this reaction with a specific stimulus or stimuli, and this has been followed by some reward or reinforcement. In physical education this reinforcement can be accomplished in several ways, but perhaps the most important outside of the inward feeling of satisfaction accruing from the proprioceptors of the learner or his pride in personal achievement, is through the use of verbal encouragement and compliments by the teacher. Thus, in this theory, reinforcement in the form of feedback is control for transfer to take place. Leadership becomes a dominant factor in the learning process because it is the leader who sets up the transfer situation, furnishes the goals, motivates the learner toward greater effort, and finally reinforces his responses through some type of extrinsic feedback.

The work of Pavlov is an example of *classical conditioning*. This form of learning involves one stimulus followed by a single response. It can explain simple forms of learning and is generally regarded as the basic form of true learning as opposed to behavior based on instinct.

A second type of association learning is called *instrumental learning*. In this case a stimulus is followed by several possible alternate responses and the learner must choose from among them. In this type of learning, goals are set and any response from among the alternatives which leads to achievement of these goals is rewarded and will subsequently be selected over other alternate responses. This type of learning can account for more variability in learning than classical conditioning.

Another form of conditioning learning which allows for even more flexibility in behavior is known as *"operant conditioning"* as applied by Skinner (18). As contrasted with classical and instrumental conditioning where the learner's freedom to respond to a stimulus is limited, operant conditioning permits the subject not only complete freedom of choice in responses from alternates but also a choice of when he is to respond. The researcher then exercises control over behavior by reinforcement of the desired response when it does occur. Thus, operant conditioning is more concerned with consequences of acts than stimuli. In this manner, the researcher can in a sense shape behavior. Modern educational techniques have made use of this shaping concept with the teaching machine idea and programmed instruction.

However, learning seems to be much broader than any of these types of conditioning since they do not seem to have the ability to account for all learning situations. In fact all connectionist approaches to learning are rather mechanistic. However, they do have the advantage of predicting behavioral outcomes, and they are looked upon as models to the fundamental and basic nature of all learning.

Gestalt Theory

Another theory of psychology which has had great impact on education in general and physical education in particular is the *Gestalt theory* sometimes referred to as the *holistic* or *insight theory*. This theory refutes the idea of trial and error or that learning is accidental as a result of random selection. Rather, it is the result of the learner seeing relationships, similarities and differences and as he puts all things together as a whole, gains insight in learning (14–8). The psychologists say the learner "goes beyond what is given." This means he can generalize from either the stimulus or response (14–35). For physical education this theory implies that the learner must have a goal to achieve. As he repeatedly attempts to achieve this goal, he tries to understand the activity as a whole. As he works

continually toward the goal, he is not just repeating his previous attempts but rather he evaluates past performance and reorganizes his approach in each trial in terms of his past behavior. He sees the act as a whole, he tries to increase his understanding of this whole, and as he practices toward this total response, each succeeding trial is different from the last. When he at last puts the parts together as a whole, this whole becomes more than the sum of its parts (15–38). He uses past performance toward a hierarchy of responses. He may even try out mentally some different alternatives in responses before he attempts them overtly. Eventually the learner sees the true relationships and achieves insight so that he is able to accomplish that which he perceives. Thus, in a sense the learner's progress is affected by his perception of relationships. Insight involves cognition and problem solving. This makes the Gestalt theory less mechanistic and drill oriented than the S–R theory types.

Information Theory

A new approach to learning and perhaps a more fashionable theory today is the *information theory*. This approach to learning seems especially adapted to physical learnings, based on the hypothesis that the human brain and nervous system are analogous to the man-made electronic computer. In addition to information theory it has been called by various other titles such as *cybernetics* and *feedback* theories. The information theory hypothesizes that the complex human nervous system is made up of *input*, a *transmission system*, a *central data processor* or *integration* system including short- and long-term *memory*, an *output* system and *feedback*. The human system works in this manner. The input represents the data gathered by the organism itself through the senses of sight, hearing, touch, taste, smell, kinesthesis and balance. The transmission system represents the nerve pathways to the central nervous system. The central data processor represents the integrative areas within the central nervous system which evaluates and synthesizes the input, the output is some kind of overt response as a result of the input, and feedback is a process of feeding errors back into the input system.

This theory is based on the idea that all of man's activities are goal directed; successful performance toward that end can help to further direct and sustain that behavior. In fact, this theory not only encompasses motor learning but motor performance of all types along with physiological processes and social learnings. Activity is interpreted as a closed loop behavior involving a feedback-controlled process. It views behavior as being controlled and even to some extent generated by its own response. In its simplest form, feedback is information which arises as a result of an organisms's own action. As a feedback-controlled process, some of its advocates say that it negates all other learning theories of the S–R type which view behavior in terms of a series of discrete stimulus–response units (19). In other words, learning a motor skill is viewed as a continuous closed-circuit interaction between movement and the sensory effect generated by that movement. This view states that learning is not a result of strengthening of association, conditioning or reinforcement. It contends the stimulus–response theories do not give answers to questions raised by recent research.

Rather, this theory claims that learning is a result of improved integration of responses in an integration system by means of feedback of the closed loop control. Learning can proceed only when there is awareness of error information through this feedback. Both stimulus information and response movement are continuously involved in skills since much of the relevant information coming into the central nervous system as sensory input is a result of stimuli from previous response or responses through feedback (3–2).

Gardner describes feedback as a self-regulating mechanism composed of three parts (7). First, there is a *detector* or an *input* mechanism to receive the stimulus and pass on a signal concerning the stimulus to a *controller*. Second, this *controller* evaluates the input information with reference to a *standard* or *norm* and, if it is necessary, signals an *output* mechanism. Third, this *effector* or *output* mechanism makes adjustments which have been indicated to correct the deviation from the norm or the *error* from the standard. The simplest machine analogy is the home furnace unit with its controlling thermostat. That part of the thermostat which is sensitive to heat waves is the detector or the receptor of the energy forces of the heat. Thus, *input* is existing room temperature. This stimulus information is passed on to a control device which has previously been set at perhaps 72 degrees. Thus, 72 degrees is the *standard* or *norm*. If there is deviation from this standard by more or less than a given margin, an effector mechanism signals and the furnace either starts or stops as the case may be. Thus, furnace activity is *output*. Through this self-regulatory technique, temperature can be kept at a fairly constant level. The key is *feedback* which in this case is the difference between the original input and the norm. This process is sometimes referred to as a *servomechanism*.

In motor learning as well as motor performance, this feedback mechanism is a most important process. The three parts of the home heating circuit connected by electrical wiring are duplicated in a sense in the human machine and it can be identified in all movements.

First, the input mechanisms or the detecting devices are the senses. Second, the control devices are centers in the nervous system. Third, the output mechanism or the effectors are the muscles which cause movement. Just as heat regulating mechanisms are connected by wires, these human mechanisms are connected by a complex of nerves to carry signals.

The computer is even more complex than the home heating unit. However, the basic principles are the same. There is an input read into the computer which gives the machine the information needed for evaluation and comparison. When this information has been integrated for purposes of evaluation and comparison with some predetermined program, the comparison is either favorable, "yes" or unfavorable, "no." If the answer is "yes" the equilibrium or objective is achieved and the answer is printed. If, however, the answer is "no," there is a feedback of this error information as a new input in an effort to obtain a "yes" answer.

There is every indication that many commonalities exist between the computer and the mind in processing information. One analogy concerns the ability of both to store programs for future use. When a movement pattern is first established in the nerve centers, it becomes a stored program along with its built-in self-regulatory feedback mechanism. This movement pattern can be re-activated by an input stimulus. In most instances, this is a conscious stimulus from the cortical level after which the movement continues under the control of the feedback operations in much the same manner as it was stored in the memory bank during the process of learning. Some aspects of this control continue at the subconscious level, but some visual and kinesthetic aspects of the action may be monitored at the conscious level and subsequently

followed by correction and adjustment (7).

However, learning and feedback are not as simple as the heat-regulating system or the computer. Complex as these mechanisms may be, they can be explained by scientists, but the total process of learning cannot be fully explained. Learning is dynamic and is one of the most significant aspects of life. No one has ever yet fathomed its deepest mysteries. No one knows how the processes of integration work in the nervous system to organize and synthesize the sensory input. It is known, however, that skill learning takes place because of information coming into the nervous system. For this reason they are called information processing skills (6–5).

This information can be of a highly complex nature and the nerve cells, as a part of this complex, are each highly related but at the same time highly specialized. While the machine or the computer in response to input may have to evaluate and determine the amount of error within a given range of the reference, the nervous system's job is infinitely more complex as it processes and orders input according to importance, relevance or urgency, and in relation to a stored reference or goal, and then makes evaluations as a lead up to overt response followed by the feedback operations. There are many forms of energy impinging on the sense organs including heat, light, and pressure. These energies stimulate the sense receptors and cause input patterns. In turn, these input patterns are coded and transmitted to the central nervous system. Kephart has theorized that this central area corresponds to the controller in the computer and is a projection area in the cortical region (11). Here a process of integration operates to organize these many patterns into a single overall response pattern of overt behavior. At the same time the integrative process is operating to synthesize the current input pattern, its work is further complicated by having to relate this input pattern to past patterns which have been stored in the cortex through memory as a result of past experience. This summation of current and past patterns results in an elaborated pattern where both past and present play a part.

PERCEPTUAL–MOTOR LEARNING

Another approach to motor learning and performance, although it is not necessarily a new one, is the linking of *perceptual* ability with motor performance. Proponents in this area claim that perception and movement are but two sides of the same coin, and that they cannot be separated in the learning process (11), (19). Thus, perceptual motor learning has become a new dimension in learning theory and has many implications for physical education. However, until recently most of the work in this interesting and exciting area has been done outside of physical education by psychologists, optometrists, and special education people among others.

Perception itself may be defined as "the total pattern arising from many sensations and results in a meaning which is more than the sum of its parts" (3–24). In other words a percept is an entity idea formed by interpretation of the information identified from the senses. In most cases there is probably an interdependence of the different senses as these percepts are formed. Since the senses are involved, some people refer to this area of study as *sensory-motor* or *sensori-motor* or unhyphenated *sensorimotor*. However, by any other name, they all have similar meaning. *Perceptual-motor* refers to the ability of the individual to receive, identify, interpret, and react properly to a multitude of stimuli impinging on him from the outside and from within himself. Of course those stimuli from the outside come from the senses of sight, hearing, touch, taste, and smell, while those from within come from the kinesthetic or proprioceptive sense. *Motor learning* is the integration of movements into a pattern for a purpose as a result of training procedures or environmental conditions (12).

The uniqueness of perceptual-motor learning is the fact that the emphasis is now placed on the sensations or cues which influence performance and the interpretation of these sensations as well as the motor act or output which not only precedes but also succeeds them. In other words, the input-output processes cannot be separated and are inextricably related as they occur in a closed loop system controlled by feedback. It is obvious by now that these new ideas in the area of perceptual-motor development are based primarily on the *information* or *cybernetics theory* involving feedback with the receiving of stimuli (the input), the overt response (the output), the integration system (the control) and memory (the storage system). Much of the early work in this area has been done by psychologists and special education people who directed their efforts at dysfunctioning youngsters with special learning difficulties. A great deal of study and research has been done with regard to the relationship of perceptual-motor learning and the ability to read in the slow learner. One of the questions still to be answered satisfactorily is this: Do these perceptual-motor development programs which are now directed chiefly at the handicapped and slow learner have any implication for the total school enrollment?

In general most studies have taken a similar tack. However, it might be added that their generalizations are sometimes broader and their concepts encompass a great deal more than a program for the atypical. Through observation and study these workers have concluded that there are stages in the development of the child which are triggered by movement. During early childhood there seems to be a strong relationship between the intellectual, neurological and physical processes. Perceptual motor experience may lead to better perceptual awareness and in turn perceptual awareness can lead to better neurological organization and hence intellectual achievement. If this thesis is true that motor experience is basic to the development of intellectual powers of the child, its importance becomes a bit staggering. It would mean that sensori-motor development could lead to subsequent symbolic operations and the thinking process.

Several studies in the area of remedial work where readiness for school achievement was gained through a corrective program in selected motor learning activities will be briefly discussed at this point. These studies and their programs attempt to show that this perceptual-motor learning is basic to all learning and to all the processes of the mind—that no learning is all physical or all mental but is a continuum along a linear scale where at one end it is more physical than mental and at the other end the reverse is true (14–4). The literature describing this research is concerned with such words as motor learning, feedback, laterality, dominance, directionality, neurological organization, and body-image. Perhaps these need to be defined so that the student may have a basis for common understanding.

1. *Perceptual-motor* refers to the ability of the individual to receive, interpret and react properly to a multitude of stimuli impinging on him from the outside and from within himself. Of course those from the outside include stimuli to the senses of sight, hearing, touch, taste, and smell while those from the inside come from our kinesthetic or proprioceptive sense.

2. *Motor learning* is the integration of movements into a pattern for a purpose as a result of training procedures or environmental conditions (12).

3. *Feedback* is the self-regulatory process whereby a standard or norm is achieved through a continued readjustment.

4. *Dominance* is the theory that one side of the body is the leading side over the other.

5. *Laterality* is an internal awareness of the two sides of the body and their differences, and it can be learned only through movement.

6. *Directionality* is a projection outside the body of the laterality which was developed inside the body and thus depends first on the development of laterality.

7. *Body-image* is the impression one has of his own body as he uses it as a point of reference for all external information—it becomes the point of origin for all space relationships and objects.

8. *Neurological organization* is the logical development of the mental processes to recapitulate the phylogenetic neural development of man.

With these points as a frame of reference, an examination will be made of some of the recent research in the field of perceptual-motor learning. Two of the pioneer researchers receiving the most headlines are Delacato and Kephart. They are similar in their theories but differ in approach. Delacato developed the theory that the answer to normal neurological organization is lateral dominance (5). He states that confused lateral dominance causes confusion in the learning process and can be corrected by retraining neural patterns. He has researched his theory that the individual should be completely dominant on one side of the body—eye, hand and foot dominance. Where dominance is incomplete, lack of neurological development exists. In his research he accomplishes neurological reorganization by reverting the subject to infancy and his first movement stages, as a part of ontology. Delacato trains for dominance by forcing it. He forces it through establishing proper sleeping position and then through progressing through crawling, creeping and cross-patterned walking. He has experienced some dramatic success in solving reading and speech problems through his regimen of physical movements. However, he is criticized by many scientists for his failure to verify his theory of neurological organization and to show that motor activities train the central nervous system. More research is needed to verify why these children do respond to his training program, and physical educators should be working with special education people in this search.

Kephart agrees with Delacato that laterality is important but that it is achieved in a different way (11). Rather than forcing dominance, he would achieve it through motor activities. He contends that perceptual-motor training enhances normal kinesthetic development, and this development in turn sharpens internal awareness and establishes internal laterality and outside directionality.

Kephart believes that many youth of today are "kinesthetically deprived." They are reared in a limited environment without the freedom to develop the necessary refinement in tactual, kinesthetic and visual skills. They should have more freedom to develop the perceptual-motor processes which are necessary for concept formation, for learning and for thinking. He believes that perceptual-motor training improves classroom learning through the amelioration of postural tensions, through development of laterality and in general

through sharpening perceptual awareness. Kephart contends that the individual must be able to distinguish between the left and right side of his body, and this of course is laterality. When this internal awareness is projected outside the body, directionality occurs. Impinging stimuli have no meaning unless the child can establish laterality both inside and outside his body and become a normal space-oriented individual. Without this internal and external awareness of sidedness which adds up to good body-image, the perceptual processes will not develop normally and the child becomes a slow learner. The child does not read well because he cannot for example distinguish between a "b" and a "d" nor can he speak well for the same reason since his perceptual processes are disoriented space-wise. Thus, the child whose motor, tactile and hand-eye coordination skills are not properly developed will have difficulty reading because he cannot distinguish between letters nor move his eyes from left to right. He has difficulty in writing because for the same reasons he has not developed bilateral skills. Kephart's assumptions and research seem more tenable to physical educators than do those of Delacato, but they too need further study and refinement.

While Delacato's school of thinking is based on lateral dominance and the Kephart theory is based on laterality followed by normal kinesthetic development, another group of researchers claim both are guilty of oversimplification. This group contends there is no one factor which is the key or magic formula for learning. They try to study normal learning in the light of what has happened to those who fail to learn as they are unable to meet the demands of society. These are children who are categorized as having "special learning disabilities." Some of these failures are mentally retarded either through heredity or injury, and some have emotional problems, but many others appear normal since they do have native intelligence and are not emotionally disturbed. However, they still fail to meet the demands of education.

A typical study in this area has been done by Barsch and his associates (1). This research study is embodied in what is called "A Movigenic Curriculum," based on the physiologic approach to education. This simply means that the individual learns through the machinery of his own body and that through movement, the mechanism can be trained to operate more effectively. The theory behind this research is that the learner is a space-oriented individual with a physiologic makeup, and he is designed to move through educational space by processing perceptual information. If his basic training has been adequate, his perceptual processes function normally and he meets the demands of education. If he fails to meet the demands, it may not be because he lacks the intelligence or that he has emotional problems, but because his tactual and kinesthetic skills need further development and organization and his visual and auditory processes need refinement. This process of development, organization and refinement takes place through the movigenic curriculum which borrows its concepts from the fields of psychology, education, and physical education, along with numerous other disciplines. Principles from these varied fields are synthesized into a number of constructs which provide a theoretical framework for study and out of this study 12 dimensions emerged. The unique movigenic curriculum was developed from these 12 dimensions.

These dimensions are: (and one is struck with their identity with a physical education specialized area) muscular strength, dynamic balance, spatial awareness, and body awareness grouped

under a heading of POSTURAL–TRANSPORT ORIENTATION: tactual dynamics, kinesthesia, auditory dynamics and visual dynamics grouped under the heading PERCEPTO–COGNITIVE MODES, and bilaterality, rhythmic, flexibility, and motor planning grouped under DEGREES OF FREEDOM. Significant success was experienced with experimental groups over a two-year span.

Karl Smith and his associates have done much research in this field of motion and perception along with feedback (19). First, Smith has hypothesized that the primary organizational factor of response is space-centered where the integrative processes of the nervous system act to detect differences in input. His theory is called the *neurogeometric theory* where the internuncial cells as a part of the integration system act as differential detectors to respond to differences in input. This neurogeometric mechanism serves as a system to control the individual's response through continuous movement regulated by feedback. Thus, there is input, integration, output, and feedback with feedback acting as a servomechanism and the key to learning.

The basis for Smith's research has been the adaptation of closed-circuit television and video-tape recordings in order to study time and space displacement of feedback. It has been results from Smith's work in displacement of feedback which seem to substantiate his hypothesis (19). If Smith's postulations are true, a new era may be eminent in dealing with learning. Feedback as a cybernetic theory of behavior seems to negate older theories of learning such as association, conditioning and reinforcement. Smith states that learning is not a result of strengthening of associations nor does the stimulus-response theory hold up in the light of his research with displacement. This research shows that learning is a result of the improved integration of responses in the integration system by means of feedback of the closed-loop control. Learning can proceed only when there is awareness of error through feedback, and performance in general can proceed only when there are differences in input.

Smith's theory with respect to feedback does not end with movement learning. He suggests another frontier concerns the social factor and feedback. Traditional psychology theory looks on social learning and behavior as verbalization, motivation, attitude, and perception. In the cybernetic theory social behavior is looked upon as motor as well, and thus is regulated by the same type of closed-loop system with feedback, where one person reacts to another by regulating movement-produced sensory stimuli received from the other. Most forms of physical education activity require social behavior and, thus, are a feedback-controlled process of interaction (4–11).

CONCEPT DEVELOPMENT THROUGH MOVEMENT

Another dimension of learning that is related to motor skills and learning is the development of verbal concepts through movement skills. This is not the same approach as the one just discussed under perceptual-motor learning although related. They differ in purposes and objectives more than in procedures and process. In the perceptual-motor learning areas expounded by Kephart, Getman and many others, perceptual-motor activities were the media used to develop perceptual awareness—kinesthetic, visual, auditory, and tactile perception. It was assumed that an enhanced perceptual awareness could lead to improvement in the classroom. The concept development through movement is concerned directly with how movement activities are employed to

help the early school child learn skills and concepts in the verbal areas of mathematics, language, science, social studies, and reading. Humphrey has been the leading researcher in this area and has written widely concerning his work (9), (10).

This approach is based on the theory that the elementary children are essentially movement-oriented, and even their verbal learning will take place more readily when pleasurable motor activity is the teaching medium. Humphrey points out that all verbal and motor learning particularly at the elementary age level are not mutually exclusive types of learning but are on a continuum from verbal to motor with none being entirely verbal or motor (10). Motor learning is always accompanied by a certain amount of verbalization and by the same token, verbal learning is always accompanied by some motor components at least at minimum levels.

Humphrey's research shows that elementary age children definitely improve more significantly in the concepts of math, language, social studies, science, and reading when these subjects are presented in conjunction with physical education activities (10).

Some children may learn verbal concepts more effectively in these movement programs involving game skills because their age level is characterized as a movement world anyway where they are more used to dealing with concrete situations as opposed to abstract ones. Humphrey hypothesized that the desirable concepts are learned more readily because of motivation, feedback and reinforcement (10). All three of these concepts are described at some length in this and the next chapter so will not be elaborated further here. It is not suggested that this type of program be carried on during the regular physical education class. Rather it should become a part of the particular subject matter time allotment and become just another method of teaching verbal concepts.

MOVEMENT EXPLORATION

Another approach to physical education which is related to perceptual motor learning is *movement exploration.* This approach on the surface is more from the methodology standpoint but the idea behind the method is much more basic. While the remedial perceptual-motor learning programs have chiefly been designed for the atypical dysfunctioning student, movement exploration is for everyone. However, the basis of movement exploration is not too unlike the perceptual-motor learning program. The idea is to provide a rich and varied movement environment for the student in order to help him progress to the various stages of readiness. While the objectives of movement exploration are the same as those for physical education listed in Chapter 3, skills, fitness, knowledges and attitudes, the approach to those goals is not typical or traditional. The objectives are achieved through the creative process where each student in the group works separately but they all work toward solving the same movement problem but each in his unique way. Presumably, the creative approach to movement, where the child is forced to think out his movement skills in answer to the problem, will enable him to arrive at appropriate levels of readiness where he can become an achiever.

In general, movement exploration programs are aimed at the primary and intermediate grade levels and designed partly as a remedial program for those who may be deficient in basic motor skills. However, the goals are not primarily remedial but educational for all. Because the emphasis is on creativity and problem solving, there are no failures and all children experience at least some success. While there are no standards of performance in motor skill improvement, there is an opportunity for the youngster to develop his fundamental movements. When this has been done, he has the necessary background in motor behavior to progress on to more complex activities of games and sports. Since all children enjoy moving, and since movement exploration provides them with the spirit of fun and adventure in an atmosphere of creativity, participation is always a time of excitement and response followed by a building of a success constellation in each child. Perhaps one of the salient values is the fact that children may act out their thought processes. This process of developing a meaningful progression of motor skills to which concepts may be related by the child is a step toward showing causal relationship between the motor and the intellectual. Also, even beyond these parameters of the mental and physical are the social outcomes. All children need social reinforcement for normal healthy development. Movement exploration provides an avenue of social approval since everyone succeeds and no one ever fails completely. Success tends to develop a better body-image, carrying over to self-image and even into better performance in the classroom. Cratty has suggested that a "failure syndrome" on the playfield tends to be generalized in the classroom (2).

LAWS OF LEARNING

Perhaps this is the point to discuss the laws of learning. Traditionally when laws are mentioned in learning psychology, thought immediately turns to Thorndike's three laws (20). These laws have been modified and extended in current studies but still have implication for learning. His laws of learning include *readiness, exercise* and *effect.*

Readiness

The law of *readiness* is closely associated with the law of effect because it has a relationship with ends sought. It states that learning for the individual proceeds much more rapidly and efficiently if the individual is ready to learn. Readiness implies that sufficient maturation has taken place and that a mental set has been accomplished by a feeling of need and an intention to do something about it. Naturally, when a person is ready to learn, the act will be accompanied by some feeling of satisfaction. By the same token, if that person has not reached the point of readiness, he has no goals and no intention, and the learning act will in all probability be accompanied by a feeling of annoyance and dissatisfaction. Readiness keys attitude because it implies intent and goals, and attitude keys learning because it furnishes motive and drive. Oxendine states that readiness has now been extended to include interaction of maturation, prerequisite learning and motivation (15–27).

Exercise

A second law of learning is the law of *exercise*. This law simply states what another principle of learning claims. The individual learns by doing. This process is concerned with the repetition of the act over and over again, and through repetition the connection between the stimulus and the response becomes stronger and more efficient. While this is not the same as the law of use and disuse as expounded in physiology, it is similar to the extent that they both are a process and lead to strengthening. In the case of the law of exercise, learning is enhanced whereas in the case of the law of use and disuse, muscular strength and fitness are improved and the muscle grows and develops in both size and efficiency or weakens or atrophies through disuse.

The intelligent coach or teacher is fully aware that mere repetition or practice alone will not result automatically in better performance. There must be purpose and meaning accompanying the repetition if efficient learning is to occur. This of course involves goals and knowledge of results. Mere repetition without the knowledge of goals where skills are concerned results in the duffer performance usually.

Effect

The third law is the law of *effect*. This law states that one tends to learn that which is satisfying as opposed to annoying. This implies that the repetition referred to in the law of exercise must be reinforced by some feeling of well-being or satisfaction if it is to be repeated again. Otherwise the learner tends to try some other response in his attempt to gain the satisfaction he seeks through practice. According to Thorndike satisfaction enhances learning to a greater extent than annoyance.

In a sense these laws, when applied to learning skills in physical education state that the student must either be ready to learn the particular act through the process of maturation, or that he must be made "ready" through the efforts of the teacher. They further imply that the learning process is a "doing" process where the act must be repeated over and over again before one can become proficient. This process of doing proceeds toward the point of efficiency much more rapidly if the learner experiences satisfaction and this feeling of satisfaction can be experienced only when a reasonable amount of success has been achieved. Therefore, success or satisfaction provides the reinforcement that is needed for the correct response to be repeated. In the early part of the learning process goals must not be set too high or out of reach since the probability of attaining them will be remote and hence the learner may become discouraged. This could account for the reason many persons never get beyond the duffer or dub class in any sport. Goals should therefore be set according to the maturation levels of the students.

Where does the physical educator stand with respect to these laws, hypotheses or theories? Which seems best for what type of learning? How can he best achieve the purposes he hopes to achieve through his teaching and coaching? Granted that it is important for the educated professional to know about these theories and how they are similar and different, the matter of theory can really be left up to the research psychologists. The empirical results are essentially the same regardless of their theoretical framework. In practice, the teacher will proceed about the same regardless of the theory. First, each theory emphasizes that learning is a doing phenomenon. Therefore, practice precedes learning. Second, each theory recognizes that practice alone is not sufficient—it must be meaningful practice. Third, along with practice there must be some kind of reinforcement either of an intrinsic or an extrinsic nature. Most of the conditions and factors affecting learning which will be discussed in this chapter and the following one on motor learning are valid regardless of the theory to which one holds.

However, the field of learning is opening to some new approaches in the way learning theory is viewed. It would seem that the trend is not to find one all-encompassing theory which would apply to all kinds of learning. A possible approach to this problem is *functionalism* or an *eclectic* point of view (15–44), (16). In essence the eclectic approach states that different learning theories are needed to explain all the different types or kinds of learning. In this "functionalism" approach, advocates would concentrate their attention on the functional

principles of learning rather than the theories themselves. Physical education skills have not been studied to any appreciable degree by researchers or theorists in psychology. However, it would appear that motor learning would fit into the framework of the new cybernetic theory or feedback theory better than any others. A great deal of initial work has been done in this area and several motor learning theories have evolved. In fact, it is just possible that the eclectic view may become necessary in motor learning, too, where one theory would not explain the different categories of motor learning. It is possible that different categories of motor learning will require different theories of learning according to Singer (16).

CONDITIONS AFFECTING LEARNING

Motivation

An important aspect of learning and performance is *motivation*. In fact, neither will proceed in an effective manner without it. Oxendine states that motivation creates needs within the person and these needs cause him to seek specific goals in order to satisfy them (15–172). Motivation is an internal condition which may be triggered either from within the learner himself or by something or somebody on the outside. Thus, motivation gives rise to needs, and the needs in turn give rise to drives. These drives are directed in behavior which will tend to satisfy the needs and return the individual to a state of homeostasis. Homeostasis is a process of maintaining the physiological and psychological balance. The intensity of the need along with the drive dictates the level of motivation. This level of motivation is probably the most important essential in progressive learning and high level performance. It forces the learner to establish goals and then try to achieve them.

However, there is one question concerning motivation that the teacher must answer. How much motivation or how high a level of motivation is conducive to the best learning? This is a difficult question because like so many other areas in learning theory and principles it depends somewhat on the personality of the learner, the behavior goal which has been set and the learning environment. To generalize, however, it can be said that excessive motivation can be less effective than moderate.

Reinforcement

Regardless of the theory of learning to which one holds, one commonality always present is *reinforcement*. This is one of the most important aspects of the learning process because it seems to be the key to bridging the gap between a stimulus and the desired response. The striking feature of man is that he does not always have to be reinforced from outside because he has the faculty to reinforce himself (14–6). Reinforcement is frequently considered synonymous with rewards and punishments. However, this is not quite true. Some rewards and punishments do lead to reinforcement but others may have no effect on learning. In general, reinforcement is similar to Thorndike's law of effect which in essence says that when a modifiable connection between a stimulus and a response is accompanied by a feeling of satisfaction, that response tends to be repeated when the stimulus is given, and if it is accompanied by a feeling of annoyance, it tends not to be repeated (20). Thus, reinforcement is any condition following a response which increases the probability of that response being repeated at a later time when a similar stimulus is presented. A positive reinforcer would be some feeling of satisfaction or a satisfaction of some drive or need, whereas a negative reinforcer would be some form of punishment or some annoyance which one would not want repeated.

Most of the conditions affecting learning are related in some manner. For example, in reinforcement, if motivation is present, one of the important keys to learning is knowledge of results. This knowledge of results includes the concept of feedback which has been discussed already. Since feedback is the key to the "information theory" of learning, this self-knowledge is important. It is one of the best means of reinforcement since it provides the learner with a knowledge of results and an awareness of his progress. This knowledge of results can come through self-knowledge from either visual or proprioceptive feedback or it can come from external sources such as the teacher, coach, peers, or in some cases the teaching machine.

Timing is an important factor in reinforcement. Research has shown that immediate reinforcement is more effective than delayed and that while continual reinforcement is somewhat effective, random reinforcement is more so (15–66). Delayed reinforcement may be an impairment to some learning. Certainly if reinforcement is delayed too long, it loses its effectiveness as an incentive (14–9). Also, in complicated learning tasks where a successful response may come only after a long period of time and gradual improvement, reinforcement can be given for *successive approximations* (14–14). Since skill learning is goal-directed, then a successful approach toward the goal is reinforced and can serve to sustain effort as the learner achieves minor successes toward his goal. If reinforcement is a necessary condition for learning to take place, this situation would have to exist in learning complicated motor skills because the learning of a complicated motor skill is a gradual and sequential process with slight amounts of increments toward the successful goal (15–59). Therefore, ultimate success would be shaped in a sense through reinforcement of successive approximations.

The psychologist Skinner believes that man's behavior can be entirely controlled and shaped through reinforcement and to the extent that it can be manipulated, it can be predicted (18). This could be a dangerous philosophy of education in the wrong hands. The whole idea of the teaching machine, however, is based on this concept. The teaching machine will no doubt play a greater role in education in the future. It has many advantages. It permits each student to be personally involved, to work at his own pace, to be provided with immediate reinforcement, and to be provided with individualized instruction. Such programmed instruction in physical education offers possibilities but does present problems in complicated skills. It is difficult to break these patterns down into graded steps and even more difficult to provide instant accurate feedback.

When rewards and punishment are used as reinforcement for learning, they generally fall into the categories of praise for the desired response or criticism for the undesired behavior. They both are effective but the more positive approach is generally conceded to be best because it provides the student with the correct response. The negative approach of criticizing the wrong response does not tell the student what the correct response is.

Memory and Retention

There are many new theories in psychology now as a result of the wealth of research carried on in recent years. One has to do with *memory* or *retention* and specifically with the chemistry of learning. It might be pointed out here that man's power to reason is dependent on memory. Because he has the capacity to remember and the power to use past experience to foresee the future and judge alternatives and weigh consequences and to exercise behavior based on these, he is separated from animals. In the process of evolution it may be seen how, as progress was made along the scale of living species toward more intricate behavior, animal nature guided by instincts and blind drives gave way to the dawn of "reason." Not that memory does not exist to a limited degree in some animals but the power to reason as a result of memory is elevated in man—this power to think things out in the mind as opposed to mere action as a result of trial-and-error type learning.

One reasonable theory regarding memory categorizes it into two stages. The first stage, dealing with immediate short-term span, consists of a physiological mechanism which works after every experience to set up a short-lived electrochemical process. If there is no interference, and if there is attention, this process triggers a second stage. The assumption here is that the second stage is a chemical process in nature and this forms the basis for long-term memory process. There seems to be a possible relationship between memory and an increase in RNA (ribonucleic acid), a genetic substance in each brain cell sometimes called the memory molecule. Also, more recent theories relate it to the presence in the cell of DNA (deoxyribonucleic acid) which is a more stable molecule than RNA and is present in the human nervous system by the hundreds of thousands of molecules. If the present stage is interrupted before it has a chance to culminate in the second stage, long-term memory fails to materialize (3–66). Therefore, one of the causes of forgetting is interference. Something else occurs before long-term memory can set. Thus, if information is to be preserved in memory following stimuli and subsequent processing in the integration system, there should be a period of time given for the learner to focus his attention on it. Short-term memory lasts only about one moment without attention (3–66). The smaller the amount of information presented the subject and the longer it is rehearsed, the more likely it will be retained in long-term memory. Also, if the material is meaningful and tightly structured and organized, it will lend itself to recall more successfully. However, one never remembers all he learns and at the same time it appears that forgetting is never complete. Even though one can't recall an experience of long ago, it has a way of coming back into consciousness at times.

Transfer of Training

Learning and insight bring up the question of transfer of training. Obviously, if learning is to be most useful to the learner, there must be some transfer from one situation to another. In fact this is what education and teaching are all about. The old view of transfer of training came from the theory of formal discipline where learning was looked upon as general and learning experience in one situation would influence performance and learning in another. Faculties of the mind existed as separate entities and could be developed through training. The schools were looked upon as institutions to bring about transfer and it was assumed that what was learned in traditional subjects would transfer to other unrelated abilities and faculties. Greek and Latin provided for the mental training that would transfer to any life situation. Modern psychology, however, refutes this theory. Evidence now indicates that learning is highly specific. Transfer may occur but it will occur only in situations which are alike or similar and the greater the degree of similarity, the greater the transfer. Even in this case transfer is not

automatic. The learner must perceive and be aware of the similarities. The more meaningful the learning situation, and the more perceptive and intelligent the learner, the more likely that transfer will take place. In research it has been a problem to define exactly what is meant by similarity. Since no two stimuli patterns can ever be identical, any given movement pattern can never be repeated. Thus, similarity in stimuli could mean the extent to which the ones in question could elicit the same response. For this reason no two movements can ever be identical and response patterns are never operable in exactly the same way twice.

Transfer can take place when there are similar elements or when the learner can generalize principles. It is obvious why goals and purposes are important aspects of learning since the similar elements or generalizations may be inherent in these. Readiness and motivation must be present to provide an appropriate "set." Leadership is important, also, since good teaching would teach for transfer and is always alert and sensitive to transfer possibilities. Methods of teaching and learning as procedures are important aspects of transfer. It is the job of the teacher to see that learning situations are meaningful and to point out the possibilities of transfer. In order to help the students to generalize he can lead them to discover the relatedness and make the transfer themselves. New responses may be learned more readily because of certain habits from previous learning and these the students may be helped to discover. Since a basic purpose of education is transfer, fundamental and basic behavior should be overlearned since overlearning enhances transfer.

Just as there are likenesses and recurrent uses in patterns of motor responses, so are there similarities in social learnings. However, generalizations from a specific situation in a social relationship to one of a more general nature is subject to the same limitation as mentioned above for motor learnings and verbal learnings.

REFERENCES

1. Barsch, R. H.: *A Movigenic Curriculum.* Bulletin No. 25, Bureau for the Handicapped. Wisconsin, State Department of Public Instruction, 1965.
2. Cratty, Bryant J.: On the Threshold. Quest, Vol. VIII, May, 1967, pp. 7–14.
3. Cratty, Bryant J.: *Movement Behavior and Motor Learning,* 2nd ed. Philadelphia, Lea & Febiger, 1969.
4. Cratty, Bryant J.: *Social Dimensions of Physical Activity.* Englewood Cliffs, N. J., Prentice-Hall, Inc., 1967.
5. Delacato, C. H.: *The Diagnosis and Treatment of Speech and Reading Problems.* Springfield, Ill., Charles C Thomas, 1963.
6. Fitts, Paul M., and Michael I. Posner: *Human Performance.* Belmont, Calif., Brooks/Cole Publishing Company, 1967.
7. Gardner, Elizabeth B.: The Neuromuscular Base of Human Movement: Feedback Mechanism. Journal of Health, Physical Education and Recreation, Vol. 36, No. 8, October, 1965, pp. 61–62.
8. Getman, G. N.: *How to Develop Your Child's Intelligence.* A Research Publication. Luverne, Minnesota, 1962.
9. Humphrey, James H.: *Child Learning through Elementary School Physical Education.* Dubuque, Iowa, Wm. C. Brown Co., 1966, Chapters 6–10.
10. Humphrey, James H.: Evaluation of Physical Education as a Learning Medium for Skill and Concept Development in the Various Subject Areas of the Elementary School Curriculum. Unpublished presentation, Measurement and Evaluation Section of the AAHPER, National Convention, Las Vegas, 1967.
11. Kephart, Newell: *The Slow Learner in the Classroom.* Columbus, Ohio, Charles E. Merrill Books, Inc., 1960.
12. Lawther, J. D.: Directing Motor Skill Learning. Quest, Vol. VI, May, 1966, pp. 68–76.
13. Lawther, J. D.: *The Learning of Physical Skills.* Englewood Cliffs, N. J., Prentice-Hall, Inc., 1968.
14. Manis, Melvin: *Cognitive Processes.* Belmont, Calif., Brooks/Cole Publishing Co., 1966.
15. Oxendine, J. B.: *Psychology of Motor Learning.* New York, Appleton-Century-Crofts, 1968.
16. Singer, Robert N.: Learning Theory as Applied to Physical Education. Proceedings Annual Meeting—National College Physical Education Association for Men, 69th. Dec., 1965, pp. 59–67.
17. Singer, Robert N.: *Motor Learning and Performance.* New York, The Macmillan Company, 1968.
18. Skinner, B. F.: *The Behavior of Organisms.* New York, Appleton-Century, 1938.
19. Smith, Karl U., and William M. Smith: *Perception and Motion, An Analysis of Space Structured Behavior.* Philadelphia, W. B. Saunders Company, 1962.
20. Thorndike, E. L.: *Human Learning.* New York, Johnson Reprint Corp., 1931.
21. Walker, Edward L.: *Conditioning and Instrumental Learning.* Belmont, Calif., Brooks/Cole Publishing Company, 1967.

Chapter 16

Foundations of Motor Learning

INTRODUCTION

The previous chapter dealt briefly with the theoretical bases of learning psychology. This chapter places emphasis on motor learning which in essence is learning psychology applied to the area of motor skills. By way of passing, at this time it might be well to point out once again that while *learning* and *performance* frequently are used to mean the same thing, they could be different. In many cases performance could be learning but it is not always. Learning denotes a change and unless there is some permanent modification of behavior, learning has not taken place. Performance may have occurred without any permanent modification.

Most traits that are commonly referred to as qualities of a physically educated person are learned traits. While it may be that some of them are influenced significantly by maturation and heredity and hence are inexorably related to man's nature, they are characteristically a part of his nurture and environment and as such become a product of learning. Since these traits are learned and outcomes of teaching, the coach and teacher of physical education should be interested in the learning process. The physical educator should know particularly about skill learning and the laws, theories and conditions about how it takes place. Among the facts from learning which he should know and on which he should attempt to build his philosophy are such aspects as motivation, reinforcement, practice, satisfaction, feedback, transfer along with many others. The principles derived from these become a significant force in program and methodology. There are many theories of learning in this area which seem to have implication for the teacher and coach and in order for the professional to have a frame of reference in which to work, he should be familiar with those theories and principles which have stood the test of time or which show promise for the future. When he has this knowledge, he can approach his teaching and coaching in a more scientific and objective manner. Through this more scientific and knowledgeable approach, the student may profit to the fullest extent from both the time and effort devoted to teaching and learning. With all the pressure now brought to bear on education by technology and social change, there is a demanding need for more efficiency in teaching.

The learning of a motor skill by its very nature must be a highly complex and complicated process. There are many variables. Because these skills are so complicated and because there are so many variables, motor learning may seem different from abstract learnings, and it may even be true that it is more complex. In any event, it seems expedient for the teacher of motor performance to have a theoretical and unified framework within which he makes his approach to learning and teaching. This theoretical approach must be consistent with his more practical approach. It has already been pointed out that no absolutes exist in learning theory. No ready-made answers are available. Existing theories are constantly being restudied and reshaped by researchers and theorists and new ones formulated in the light of new findings. Perhaps the most important consideration here is that the dynamic teacher does not revert into a complacent level of professionalism whereby he accepts the traditional as universals. On the contrary, he should view the traditional theories as a starting point but always should be open to new ideas and new ways of teaching. It is incumbent on the professional to be aware of new concepts and extensions in learning theory, especially new ways of applying them.

While there are few absolutes yet in the area of motor learning, there is at present a mounting field of evidence. So far much of this research is not readily adapted to the gym or classroom. The principles developed by research psychologists and theorists are difficult to apply. To evolve a theoretical design is not to apply it. Much is left to be done by the practitioner in physical education in the way of generalization and implementation. In the meantime it is still

somewhat dangerous to generalize in motor skills from principles which have been developed by psychologists who worked with animals or with humans performing fine motor skills. Perhaps no principle, theory or even practice should be based on the results of any one research study. A single study may be a well-designed project but still should not be generalized beyond its immediate interpretation and implication. The total field of research must be used and the perceptive pragmatic teacher must employ some common sense in his approach to motor learning with respect to generalizing from any research. Even when thorough studies have been made of the total field of research, it is sometimes difficult to generalize because the evidence may be so conflicting (17–325). However, the professional student and the practitioner in the field must try to build a frame of reference for his own use of learning theory but he must stay abreast of the times, keep an open mind and be aware of the pitfalls.

This chapter raises as many questions in the minds of its readers as it provides definite answers. Further, students should become conversant with the exciting new literature and research of motor learning.

MECHANISM FOR LEARNING THEORY

The mechanism for motor learning is a complex system made up of sense organs, nerves, nerve centers, and response organs. The basic unit and also the simplest is the *reflex arc*, which is the pathway of a simple reaction to a stimulus. More complex units are elaborations of this sometimes involving conscious responses at the cortical levels. While simple reflex arcs are unconscious responses, they are still related to physical education activities when such skills become automatic. The reflex arc is made up of five units. First, there are the specialized sensory nerve endings called receptors. These receptors are the five senses of sight, hearing, touch, taste and smell and proprioception. Second, there are transmitting lines called afferent neurons to carry the impulse from the receptors to the central nervous system. Third, there is the junction or plexus in the central nervous system where the afferent and efferent neurons join. Fourth, there are other transmitting lines to carry the impulse from the central nervous system to the effector organs called efferent neurons. Fifth, there are muscles responsible for the appropriate response called effectors.

Since most reflex actions are automatic, most are performed through spinal centers of the nervous system. When more complex movements and the cognition element are brought into the picture, higher orders of the system are involved.

CONDITIONS AFFECTING LEARNING

In learning motor skills there are vast individual differences found among members of any group normally distributed. These differences are due to such factors as previous experience, growth, development, maturation, present ability, innate capacity, and attitude toward physical activity among others. These crucial factors place limits not only on the present and ultimate level of performance for each individual but also on the efficiency and effectiveness of his learning. However, there are certain conditions and principles which are conducive to learning efficiency within the parameters of the factors listed above. These are important aspects of learning motor skills and performance. In the remainder of this chapter these aspects will be discussed. They seem to have one thing in common. They are all *conditions* which affect learning. In short, they are producers of learning changes. In the discussion of these factors which follow, note should be made

of the interrelationships which seem to exist among many of them. For example, feedback is a type of self-knowledge, reinforcement, and at the same time can be motivation. Motivation is related to goals and, in turn, goals are related to need. A great deal of space will be devoted to the concept of feedback because of the particular place it seems to occupy in skill learning and performance and its part in the fashionable new cybernetic or information learning theory.

Goals

For the individual who is learning skilled movement patterns there is an important cognitive phase which must be experienced first. This first essential for any learner in skill learning is to get a general idea in his mind of what he is to do. This becomes his set—his immediate *goal*. Thus, skilled behavior is goal-directed. In this goal he must have an idea of what he is supposed to do and how to do it. It becomes a sort of mental set with a gross framework idea of the task to be performed. This goal or gross framework may be furnished first by the teacher through brief verbal directions or explanations along with some visual cues including the use of demonstrations and visual aids. In some cases manual manipulation may be employed. However, the evidence shows that a trial-and-error period of practice almost immediately or at least some exploratory practice is necessary in formuation of goals and getting the gross idea. Research shows that establishing goals through verbal instruction is much more effective at more advanced levels. The rank beginner does not seem to have enough of a skill vocabulary yet and words have little meaning for him (8-63). He needs a brief demonstration or explanation, or manual guidance followed by the exploratory practice. In fact too much verbalization by the teacher in the early stages of motor learning is a definite handicap to the beginnner. Most teachers talk too much anyway.

When the learner has gotten the gross idea, or the general idea, it becomes a part of the stored program in his memory bank and there are perceptual cues and responses which set the norm or reference. Once this goal is established, the most important thing is uninterrupted "meaningful" practice. However, there are many ways to achieve the goal since muscle groups are employed in various ways to achieve the same goal. As the learner progresses in his learning, his goal will become clearer and more precise. Mental practice is more effective at this stage than at earlier stages. However, learning does not really occur until error information is received by the learner and error information can only come through the processes of feedback. Feedback in turn is initiated by movement or through the efforts of the instructor. In the early stages of learning, there may be no meaningful knowledge of results through feedback from within the learner. Thus, the knowledge of results must be given from without by the teacher in a diagnostic way in order to help shape the student's response toward the goal. In this manner the learner will adjust to his goal, which is the ultimately desired total skill, within a frame of reference of his own individuality. While good form should be encouraged, the student should be permitted some leeway due to his own unique body type and physical structure. The goal should become clearer with experience but the good teacher or coach does not teach for complete uniformity. He does attempt, however, to eliminate major errors from these early goals. At the beginning stages the attention should be focused on the total goal and the "whole method" of approach should be used. In more advanced levels the whole can

be broken into parts for polishing although there is evidence that the skilled performer still conceptualizes the whole even when he is practicing the parts.

Feedback

In order for the physical educator to understand motor learning and performance, it is necessary that he know the basis of the "feedback" principle. This concept has already been discussed at some length in Chapter 15. Feedback is a commonly used term in today's highly technical and advanced scientific world. In industry it is viewed as a self-regulatory process by which a standard or norm is achieved through continued readjustment. In motor learning and performance it is viewed as a cycle initiated by movement caused by muscle action.

Feedback is essential for the performance of neuromuscular skills, and it contributes both consciously and subconsciously to the management and control of all movements. In general, movements have been categorized into the following three types: postural, transport and manipulative (19–6). All athletic, gymnastic and dance skills are superimposed over the first two of these. However, they are generally taken for granted since much of the sensations that serve as feedback for posture, for example, is at the subconscious level. Some of the feedback for transport movement is at the subconscious level as well as those movements involving both posture and transport. However, some sensations do involve the cortical area of the brain and the self-knowledge obtained is at the conscious level. A great number of the experiences of the child as he moves in space and time, and as he becomes aware of objects and manipulates these objects is at the conscious level with impulses coming chiefly from vision and the proprioceptors. When these impulses come from muscles associated with manipulative movements, the higher centers are involved particularly during the learning period.

Coaches and teachers of physical education have always used the principle of feedback in their coaching and teaching. Until recently they have done so without knowing much about its processes and characteristics. Feedback may be better understood if it is broken down into categories and studied more closely. Feedback can be divided into two general categories or types: *intrinsic* and *augmented* (15), (3–28).

Intrinsic feedback is furnished by something inherent in the action itself, or is a natural consequence of the action itself. The second type is *extrinsic* or *augmented* feedback and is information furnished by some outside source which is about the movement but which is external to it. Augmented feedback is generally provided by the teacher or coach in the learning situation. Both intrinsic and augmented feedback can serve as sources of *knowledge* for goal setting, *motivation* and *reinforcement*.

Intrinsic feedback can be divided into two classes based on the modes of receiving it (15). The first category involves the five senses of sight, hearing, touch, taste, and smell and is called *external* because the stimulus creating the impulse in these sense organs comes from outside the body. For example, light waves stimulate the receptors of the eyes. In this external category, *visual feedback* is the most important and is used in the coordination of muscles at the voluntary level. In the case of motor learning this type of feedback is not always necessary to the performance of skills. For example, blind people learn to play golf, wrestle and swim. Steinhaus has said that our muscles see more than our eyes (21). This is partly true because the constant flow of stimuli from the kinesthetic re-ceptors enables the individual to sense his body positions at all times.

The second category is called *internal* because the organs involved are stimulated from within through the individual's own movements. They are the kinesthetic senses with receptors located in the joints, tendons and muscles and certain specialized ones in the inner ear. In this second category *kinesthetic sense* is the most important, and it does seem essential to all coordinated movements. This sense has from time to time been called *kinesthesia* or *proprioception*, which is Latin for *self-knowledge*. It gives the individual the "feel" or the "touch," or an awareness of his body in space. Kinesthetic sense is located in sense organs of the joints and muscles and is like any sense organ since it can be stimulated and a nerve impulse created. This stimulus might be pressure, tension, weight, vibration, or stretch caused by the contraction and relaxation of muscles. This movement energizes the sense organs and produces impulses which give rise to sensations of "feel" or "awareness." These sensations provide self-knowledge. If the feel is right or if the movement approximates the reference stored in the nerve centers, there is the connotation that the sensation is pleasant and satisfying. If the "feel" is not right, the feedback processes facilitate adjustments needed to make the movement more consistent with the desired goal by reporting the error information. When the athlete says, "I can't get the feel of it," it is his kinesthetic senses which furnish him with the error information. It is these sensations coming into the central nervous system which give rise to the integrative processes. It might be pointed out, however, that if movement has been learned wrong and becomes habituated, the good feel may be wrong. If, in attempting to correct the error, a new pattern is practiced, it will probably feel wrong although it may in truth be right, form-wise (14). These sensations followed by a synthesis of perception and conception of movement furnishes the information for feedback. In a sense, man's physical skills and performance are monitored by his own movements and through this process his ensuing actions are controlled and his errors eliminated through these stimuli which arise from within himself. This is the uniqueness of kinesthesia since its feedback mechanism is of the internal type while all the others mentioned are of the external type and belong in the external feedback category (21). Stimulation of these must come from outside the body, whereas the proprioceptors are stimulated from within the body through its own movement.

Probably an equally important classification concerns the time of arrival in the nerve centers of the information for feedback. On the one hand it is *concurrent* and on the other it is *terminal* (15). In the case of *concurrent*, the information is up-to-date, and comes to the performer immediately during or an instant after action. In the case of *terminal* information, there is a delay between the time of the movement and when the feedback information is available. In a skill like swimming, feedback is concurrent as the learner repeats the same movements over and over in a *serial* task as he moves through the water. He can get up-to-date information on his action patterns both visually and kinesthetically. He might get intrinsic feedback immediately if the strokes were slow enough for concurrent feedback to occur. However, in such a serial movement repeated over and over, feedback information from the previous response is processed and used to influence the present response and make adjustments (3–116). For a quick-action skill of a *discrete* type like a baseball swing, the proprioception time is too slow to cause

continuous self-regulatory control. Such movements are programmed and only augmented feedback from the teacher can affect the next act. The act of stopping the golf stroke on the backswing when something has gone wrong with the pattern is an example of concurrent feedback followed by conscious awareness and regulation. However, in a skill like the serve in tennis, information may be delayed in its arrival to the central nervous system. The student may know the shot failed, but does not yet know why. In this case, augmented feedback by the teacher-coach may take place with terminal information and influence the next movement. One may have to be told where his error is or shown on a film, Polaroid picture, or instant replay on television. Some skills are executed so rapidly that there is no time for concurrent feedback. When time limits feedback occurrence for a given skill, it is obvious that these movements are programmed and once they are started they continue with little or no adjustment.

In motor learning and performance the feedback cycle is initiated by movement caused by muscle action. In skilled behavior there is always much relevant information from stimuli arising from the same or a previous response. The information furnished by the movement of the muscles along with the many other sensory inputs from the environment is fed back into the nervous system by a pattern of nervous impulses. This input is compared with the given norm or the "set" stored in the controller and if there is a deviation from this reference, some type of adjustment follows (4). The adjustment made by the receptors or the output is intended to reduce the error between the given pattern of the norm and the actual movement pattern. Motor learning can proceed only when error information is fed back as input (17–290). Every act is dependent upon a comparison of feedback with input to determine either the approriateness of the previous act or a comparison of progress toward the desired goal stored in the memory system.

Of course for feedback to function in motor learning, the learner must have some idea of what he is to do and ways to do it. He must know his goal since skilled behavior is goal-directed (see unit on Goals). This feedback mechanism to some extent controls stimuli which come into the brain centers because the error information makes up a substantial part of the total stimulus pattern. Once the idea or goal is there, the next step is sustained practice. Thus, perception precedes movement in skill learning. However, it is obvious these initial movement goals are imperfect but the clearer they can become, the more quickly learning will take place. While the teacher does play an important role in the learning of motor skills since he manipulates the learning environment and reinforces learning, in the final analysis this role is a passive one. Movement learning must take place chiefly through movement and therefore the learner must play the leading role and become an active participant. However, the teacher can help the learner by giving him perceptual cues and by shaping his behavior through diagnostic feedback of results. Through verbal directions plus demonstrations, mechanical and manual guidance and the individual's own perceptive processes, the learner can obtain a clear picture of his goal and at least some method for achieving it through action. Through practice toward this goal—this reference or norm—the key to learning is feedback of error information. Through careful guidance on the part of the good teacher and through an awareness of the feedback process, the learner achieves the major correct responses before the incorrect or imperfect one has become habit.

Therefore, as Robb points out, feedback can be regulating, reinforcing and motivating (15).

As a child performs even a simple skill, much information comes into the nervous system through the modes of vision, audition, tactuality, and kinesthesis. This information involves many nerve cells, and the integrative mechanism operates to organize them into a pattern. Not only does this integrative process involve all the information from the input but also those past patterns residual in memory. A highly complex system of programming is needed to produce the necessary evaluations. After the processes of integration and synthesis have taken place and error information delineated, there is the output or response; some of the output is isolated and fed back into the loop for new input as feedback occurs. The feedback mechanism itself is equally as complex as the integrative processes since effectors may involve several levels in the central nervous system at both the conscious and subconscious levels and may influence movement in many sets of muscles. Thus, the basic components of skill are sensation, perception, memory and response followed by feedback.

For example, a basketball dribbling skill would bombard the organism with a multitude of sensory input. Also, there are sensations extraneous to the skill itself. All of these are carried to the controller and organized and integrated. The process of integration orders this total input according to importance, urgency and purpose. It is then synthesized with the stored experience in the cortex and comparisons made with the standard for the desired movements, namely, one's goal. Any resulting deviations from the desired pattern would be used as new input to help correct the errors revealed in the skill by the integrative process. It is as though the skill is monitored on the projection area in the central nervous system. The feedback as a result of this dribbling act would be a complicated process as the visual and kinesthetic sensations would come from many sources. The integrative system in new input would make adjustments in the muscles controlling the various parts of the body involved in the action including the legs, body, arms, neck, hands, and perhaps eyes.

In a golf swing the feedback situation is different. Once the golf swing is learned, it becomes an action pattern which is stored in the nervous system much as a program is stored in a computer. Since it is a discrete, quick action skill and performed too quickly for concurrent feedback, it is programmed and once started, proceeds under automatic control. Henry calls this his "memory drum" theory (5). It can be activated consciously at the cortical level, and then it can proceed under the direction of its programmed mechanism, in the main, with some monitoring at the cortical level in certain visual and proprioceptor cues. While there is no general pattern, all golfers have certain cues that are at the conscious awareness level but in the main their golf swing proceeds at the subconscious level, as it was stored in the learning process. The more experienced the golfer, the fewer cues are attended to.

Practice

Once goals or references have been set, the key to learning is *practice* followed by feedback. "Learn by doing" is an educational principle and skills are best learned through one's own responses. However, practice alone does not guarantee learning. Uninterrupted and meaningful practice of a skill is necessary if learning is to progress efficiently. Practice will not be meaningful unless the learner is motivated and has some knowledge of results of his practice.

There are a number of other factors which affect practice. Of course the nature of the skill itself along with the nature and skill level of the learner is most important. There are conditions in the learning situation and the methods of approach to teaching skills which are of concern to the teacher and coach.

For example, research indicates that learning takes place more rapidly under *distributed* practice sessions than *massed*. Massed practice may be explained by the following example. A teacher has allotted six hours of instruction time to teaching handball. In massed practice the teacher could spend two hours on each of three days. In distributed practice he could spend one-half hour for each of twelve days. While distributed practice seems better for rapidity in learning, Singer has shown that ultimate retention may be greater under massed practice (17–195). This point is somewhat controversial, however. Also, it has been shown through research that when a performer is well skilled and motivated, he might profit more through massed practice. This might lead one to generalize that perhaps a progressive type of increase in practice length to relate to the increase in skill level as well as aspiration level would be best. If the learner is a beginner, however, fatigue becomes a factor after a short time and sessions should be shortened. However, since the highly skilled performers are less susceptible to fatigue, their sessions could be longer. One other facet of importance is the nature of the activity to be learned. If it is interesting and meaningful, practice sessions could be of longer duration. Too long practice sessions, however, could result in poor performer attitude. Also, if the rest periods or distributed practices are spaced over too long a period, learning will be impaired. In any event during any practice session, short interspaced rest periods enhance learning (3–13).

Another facet of learning related to practice is *overlearning*. If a skill is to be retained over any period of time, it must be accompanied by additional practice. This additional amount of practice is called overlearning and means the amount beyond original learning. In the case of researchers in this area, original learning is judged by a success criterion which they have set and may be relative. There is a relationship between the amount of overlearning and the length of time a skill will remain in muscle memory. Therefore, overlearning is related to memory and retention because the best way *not* to forget a skill is to overlearn it through additional amounts of meaningful practice. The more complex the skill, the more overlearning is required. Thus, the amount of time devoted to overlearning is dependent on the nature of the skill and the purpose for which the learner will use it. Since motor skills are enjoyable and are leisure-oriented, they are probably overlearned to a greater extent than any other form of learning. Much additional practice is needed in order to make skills more automatic and adaptable to environmental conditions. This process is one of generalization where the performer will react automatically regardless of the cues. In most sports and games the skill must be made adaptable to a wide variety of conditions. For example, the golf ball has to be hit from all types of lies with all clubs. Generally, skills used in varsity sports require more overlearning than those for a gym class or for recreation. Too much overlearning is wasteful in time and prevents learning in other areas. The technique for such overlearning is *drill*. Overlearning leads to more successful performance and successful performance leads to an increase in standards of excellence. Theoretically one might contend that practice at higher levels of skill is not overlearning but

really the learning of refined techniques. This is purely academic since in any type of practice or repeating a skill, no two acts are the same. In a sense all overlearning could be polishing, refining and progressive learning of a skill.

In the practice of a skill there is the question of whether to emphasize *speed* or *accuracy* of the act. In the past, some methods of teaching would have students practice some skills at slower speeds than the game conditions would normally call for. Briefly summarized the research shows that skills should be performed in practice drills the way they are to be used in the whole situation later. Learning in an activity emphasizing speed which is learned at a slower pace is generally lost when put into the real situation. If speed and accuracy are important in the whole or game situation, both should be practiced at the same time in learning and drill work. However, Cratty (2–122) points out that highly complex and dangerous type skills should not emphasize speed in early learning stages.

Another factor that affects practice is *fatigue*. The traditional view is that fatigue does slow learning. However, some research shows that while performance does drop with the onset of fatigue, learning may still be progressing. Thus, true learning may not be affected as much by fatigue as was previously thought (17–122). This might indicate a review in the concept concerning the length of practice sessions.

Motivation

Another important factor of learning is motivation. In fact one's performance is always determined by motivation. Motivation is related to goals since one is motivated to action because he desires goals. Man rarely achieves past the goals or standards of excellence he sets for himself, and in most cases these goals or aspirations are set at levels well below what he is capable of achieving. Motivation can come from two sources: *internal* and *external*. External sources are materialistic and are provided by somebody on the outside. This is sometimes called *extrinsic* motivation and could be any kind of external incentive or reward or award. Incentives are frequently used such as praise, grades, prizes and the like. In fact our culture seems to encourage this type of motivation. Many times the individual is motivated to achieve higher levels of skill development because of social status or prestige in his peer group, praise from the coach, or adulation from the crowd or audience, and in some cases, money.

The other type of motivation is *internal* and comes from within the individual. This is *intrinsic* motivation and could be satisfaction, self-fulfillment or just plain joy of participating along with self-respect and pride in achievement. Most games and sports provide their own motives since in skill performance a great deal of the motivation comes from the consequences of the skilled movement itself (3–27). This provides feedback and motivation occurs when the learner receives periodic knowledge of his results and of his progress. This could be in the form of feedback from internal sources such as proprioceptive feedback or it could be a type of feedback of knowledge of results as judged by a success criterion such as hitting the target or goal. This type of feedback should follow immediately after the response if it is to be the most effective.

In intrinsic type of motivation, the activity goals and the rewards are related whereas in the extrinsic, the goals may be unrelated to the final reward. For example, in a well-grooved golf swing the intrinsic motivation is the good feeling or sensation one gets from the results—the feel of the hit along with the thrill of the soaring drive far down the middle of the fairway. Whereas, in the case of earning a grade in gymnastics, there may be no connection between this extrinsic type motivation and the stunt itself except the stunt becomes the means to an unrelated end. However, there is no scientific evidence yet to indicate which is superior in learning. Both can bring about improvement. Educationally speaking, however, it has been empirically thought that intrinsic type is best and coaches and teachers have worked toward this end. In practice, they both play a role. In the final analysis, however, the student is probably better motivated by those things which he is successful in doing. Therefore, the teacher and coach must manipulate the teaching environment in order to include everyone and to see that all have a fair chance for success at least part of the time. Mosston's idea of teaching for inclusion is based on sound psychology (12). Another point should be made concerning motivation in general. It is a transitory type quality which might vary from time to time with each individual depending on his hierarchy of values. One way for the teacher to keep motivation high is to introduce novelty and innovation in the learning situation frequently.

One other point should be made. The amount of motivation needed for best results varies with the individual but each individual has tolerance levels beyond which his performance declines. This indicates that the individual can be over-motivated or can put too much pressure on himself. No doubt the very nature of performance skills provides the basis for high level motivation because of their emotional arousal. Oxendine sums up motivation for motor performance in this way (13–189). Above average motivation is an aid to learning; high level motivation is advantageous for gross motor performance, but may interfere with fine motor coordinations. However, there are always exceptions to these generalizations.

Success and failure are related to motivation as well as to levels of aspirations. The more success one has, the higher he will set his goals and the more he will become motivated to achieve them. On the other hand the more one fails, the more likely his goals will be lowered as well as his interest and motivation. Therefore, it is not realistic to set goals too high and have too large a gap between an individual's level of aspiration and his capacity to achieve. There are exceptions, of course, where failure is concerned, and some individuals are motivated to extra effort because of failure. In this case there is probably a relationship between this individual's need for achievement and his aspiration level, along with the fact that in the past he had experienced reasonable success.

Mental Practice

Since all motor learning is perceptual, mental practice in general seems to improve learning and performance of skills. *Mental practice* is sometimes confused with mental imagery but they are not the same thing. *Mental imagery* is the retaining of images from previous performance and may, in fact, be a result of one's actions and not an image of the action itself. For example, the golfer, before he swings, gets a mental image of a long straight drive down the fairway, rather than a mental rehearsal of the pattern of the skill causal to that drive. Whereas in mental practice the performer will actually rehearse mentally or review his cues for his physical performance. He will concentrate on the movement and not its outcome such as direction, distance, or accuracy. Lawther suggests that mental imagery plays little part in skill learning (8–75).

Mental rehearsal or practice does enhance the learning of skills. No doubt the more highly skilled performer, when learning a new skill, will bring the cognitive processes into play by mentally rehearsing different alternatives before overt action.

Mental practice can occur just before performance, just after, or between performances where a quick mental review is made by the performer of his entire sequence of movements with appropriate attention to the proper cues. This situation is frequently seen in diving and gymnastic performances as well as some track and field events. Mental practice can be encouraged between performances when one is waiting his turn to perform or for that matter between one practice and the next. Sometimes mental practice takes the form of mental verbalization, and it may be self-verbalization where one talks to oneself. Much mental rehearsal produces muscular movement at below the observed level.

Mental practice seems more advantageous in the upper skill levels for both learning and performance. For the beginning level, however, mental practice is of little value until the performer has gotten some first-hand experience through some exploratory learning toward achieving his goal for the skill. When he has gotten the gross framework idea about how to perform, then has advanced to the point where he can recognize some cues, he too can profit by mental rehearsal. Thus, transfer of mental images can be made to overt motor learning and performance if there is enough prior preparation where the learner has gotten his goal or mental picture in mind. Such mental rehearsal seems to slow the effects of retroactive inhibition. Succinctly stated, mental practice is frequently a valuable supplement to physical practice of skills but should never be used in place of it.

It might even become a good reinforcer immediately following a near perfect performance. Athletes of superior ability frequently review, analyze and conceptualize both immediately before and after their performance. The purpose of one is for review, while the other is to reinforce the near perfect performance.

Retention and Memory

Memory is an important component of the learning process for skills. All skill performance including the simplest form requires some temporary storage of information (3–61). It is thought that cognitive or perceptual type memory may be different from memory involving skills and motor performance. Henry presents the idea that neuromotor memory may be a "memory storage drum phenomenon" which is similar in design to the digital computer (5). According to Henry's theory, only specific skill patterns can be stored. This storage is at the subconscious level and the once learned skill patterns are stored for future use, and can be initiated effortlessly by the appropriate signal at just above the unconscious level (4).

It is probable that motor learning is more resistive to forgetting than are other types of learning. However, the teacher should not only teach for learning but should keep in mind those conditions which also promote retention. While retention is not quite the problem in skill learning that it is in cognitive forms, several conditions apply. First, retention is improved when the materials to be learned are meaningful. Most motor skills do have meaning to the learner. Also, retention is improved when learning is a pleasant experience and when there has been an adequate amount of prior learning. Thus, the onus is on the teacher to make the learning situation pleasant and to see that the skills being taught are not beyond the capabilities of the student.

Progression in teaching is important. Retention is improved when external reinforcement is only partially administered. In fact Oxendine suggests that for maximum learning and retention, reinforcement be administered frequently in the early stages of learning but less frequently as the learner progresses along the continuum toward becoming a skilled performer (13–67). Also, retention of skills is naturally improved through overlearning. In this regard it might be added that the finer and more intricate parts of skill are forgotten sooner than the basic framework of that skill. Therefore, overlearning through practice is necessary to remain sharp. Overlearning is more likely to occur in a continuous type skill or serial type than in the discrete type because these are generally executed more often; for example, skating, swimming and riding a bicycle.

A phenomenon which is related to retention is *reminiscence*. In this case there is an increase in performance following a rest or vacation period. The subject goes through a learning and practice session. He is tested at the end. After a period of time has elapsed, he is tested again on the same skills and improvement is noted. This phenomenon has led farm boys to say they learned to skate in summer and swim in winter. Singer suggests that reminiscence might be explained because the rest intervals would enable the learner to forget incorrect responses possibly because they were not reinforced during performance (17–203).

Transfer

All learning is influenced by *transfer*— simple skills combine into more advanced skills; adaptation and progression take place. The broader the base of these basic fundamentals, the more likely there will be development in a wide variety of motor skills (13–87).

Also, the greater the amount of practice and overlearning on these prior skills, the more likely they are to transfer. The greater their resemblance to the new skill pattern, the better transfer will take place. Transfer of simple patterns to a hierarchy of skills is a process of generalization (8–68). Response generalization is particularly important because as skills become more highly generalized, man becomes more successful in meeting contingencies. He learns clusters of related responses to a particular stimulus, and the same stimulus might elicit any of these. Thus, the real bases for transfer are the long established patterns learned through incessant play of the child. These simple patterns are combined into more complex patterns and these, in turn, into new hierarchies, and the whole becomes more than the sum of its parts (8–6). It is because of the presence of these long-established patterns that some doubt is cast on Henry's "Memory Drum" theory (5). His research does not take into consideration the long progression leading to skill hierarchies.

In skill learning and performance there is just a limited number of skill patterns that make up man's abilities. Gardner suggests that there are perhaps only about two hundred of these (4). However, these patterns can be integrated into almost unlimited combinations. After many years of performing skills, the learning of a completely new skill would be unusual (3–19). For the already well-skilled person, research indicates that the learning of new skills would involve the efficient transfer of an existing habit pattern or patterns to the new pattern under certain conditions. Thus, transfer plays a role in skill learning where there is a continuous reorganization of new skills from old habit patterns. Unless these basic patterns are learned early in life, however, there is difficulty in learning the more complex

skill hierarchies later on when the child should be ready for them through maturation or in adult life. This is why many adults have never achieved a satisfactory level in leisure skills. In childhood these progressive patterns of skill are built on a basis of posture and transport controls, and in turn these transfer to higher levels in sports, dance, gymnastic and work skills. All this requires time which the child has but as he matures into the adult if the patterns are not learned already, they probably will never be.

The point should be made here that since transfer is merely the effect that practice in one skill will have in performing another, all transfer is not necessarily desirable. Transfer can be either *positive* or *negative*, or it can be *zero* or entirely neutral depending on the effect. The transfer referred to above is positive since it is assumed that its effect is favorable on the new pattern as it facilitates learning. The amount of positive transfer depends on the similarities of the elements, the amount of overlearning of the prior skill, the intelligence of the learner so he may get insight, and the assistance given by the teacher-coach. However, if the new response is practiced in a situation which in the past required a different response, the transfer will have an unfavorable effect on the new skill in question and will be negative. For example, while there may be some positive transfer between the strokes in tennis and badminton since they are both fundamental striking skills, there is also a negative transfer since the stroke in tennis is more of a straight arm hit whereas the badminton stroke is chiefly wrist action. If the new skill is totally unrelated to the prior skill, transfer will be neither positive nor negative, and no transfer will take place. For example, the striking skill of the tennis stroke would probably have no effect on a balancing skill on the beam. Also, if positive and negative are equal in their effects, zero transfer results.

A good rule to follow is, if the learner is to make a new response to an old stimulus, negative transfer results; while if the learner is to make an old response to a new stimulus, positive transfer is effected. Since new stimuli result in favorable transfer, the teacher should approach teaching with this in mind. In the badminton and tennis analogy above, the stimulus is the same—a racket—but the new stroke, the new response, is different from the old response. Hence, the transfer is negative. In fact, negative transfer will generally result when the tasks are moderately alike. For example, the golf swing and the baseball swing will generally result in negative transfer when going from the baseball swing to the golf stroke. Therefore, in order to help avoid negative transfer and encourage positive transfer in skill learning, the teacher-coach must teach for transfer (13–88). Even positive transfer may not occur through chance. The learner may not see the similarity or relatedness. Both positive and negative transfer can involve either *proactive* transfer or *retroactive*. In the case of the former it concerns the effect a present skill will have on learning a new one; whereas the latter concerns the effect learning a new skill will have on a previously learned one.

Motor skills seem to proceed according to two general principles—from the *general to the specific* and from the *specific to the general* (13–86). The key to which principle any given task falls under is probably inherent in the nature of the task. The principles are best explained by the following examples. The *general to the specific* is observed in the process of differentiation where movement is first a general gross motor activity but through practice and learning is individuated into a specific skill pattern

with perhaps some fine motor connotations. The whole gross motor pattern is presented, and as the learner practices this gross movement, it becomes more refined and specific. The *specific to the general* is noted when a simple skill is learned and then combined with other simple skills to form a more complex pattern. As the learner moves up the learning scale from the simple to the more complex, he works on transfer by first concentrating on the fundamentals as components of the whole. In turn these fundamentals are combined into more complex patterns, and in turn these are integrated with still others to form the skill hierarchy that characterizes the skilled man. These principles are operative in early life and are taking place at the same time so that *differentiation* and *integration* are concomitant.

The Learning Curve

Research indicates that while there may be limits to the levels man's skills may be improved, in reality these limits would be rarely approached due to a lack of motivation, the aging process and other conditions. Therefore, learning, if it were plotted on a graph in the form of a curve, would be a continuous progressive line until the upper limits of the skill were reached after long practice. A *learning curve* is a graphic illustration of performance on a particular learning situation. The graph is plotted with the performance on the vertical scale and the practice trials along the horizontal base. Curves will take different shapes depending on the learner, the nature of the learning material, and the nature of the conditions involved in learning.

However, learning might be interrupted showing a leveling off in the curve called a *plateau*. A plateau is a flattening out of the curve at some point due to a period of time when practice trials show no improvement in performance. A *plateau* has not been shown through research to be a constant characteristic of *learning* itself but rather shows a leveling off in *performance*. Such plateaus are generally a result of outside conditions such as poor motivation, lack of reinforcement, inadequate knowledge of results, fatigue, and loss of interest. Probably poor motivation is the basic reason. The usual procedure is for there to be a period of acceleration following the plateau and the curve continues its upward swing as shown by increased increments of performance. These periods of increments following a plateau could be due to the removal of the basic cause in the first place, or renewed motivation, better attitude and so on. However, while plateaus have not been shown through research to be a result of a hierarchy of sequential organization of skills, it is hypothetical that this could happen. Learning could stop for a time while several patterns of skill were being organized into a new hierarchy so that performance could shift from a lower to a higher level in the learning process.

Whole and Part Learning

Many studies have been done concerning *whole and part* learning. In defining these terms the whole method of learning is the performing of the skills or learning material each time in its entirety until learning has taken place. The part method is breaking the whole down into its component parts, learning each part separately, and then combining them into a finality of the proper sequence. Sometimes it is a bit difficult to differentiate between the two methods. For example, in the team sport of basketball, is dribbling a whole or a part?

Frequently these two methods are combined into the whole-part, the part-whole, the whole-part-whole, or the part-whole-part. The *part method* has two approaches. First, each part might be learned separately and then combined into the whole at the end of the sequence. Second, learning can be a *progressive-part type* whereby part one can be learned, followed by part two, followed by a combining of the two parts. Then, part three can be learned and combined with parts one and two, and so on. The *whole method* works best when it is applied to skills which are a tightly knit unit. The student views the skill as a whole and practices it as such. The *whole-part* method could be used for the activities whose parts would have no meaning until they had been experienced as a whole.

Which method is best? The research is not clear-cut but it would appear that those skills which are a tightly knit unit and possess a coherent entity lend themselves readily to the whole method approach. It would be meaningless to break the whole down into parts if the parts had no meaning within themselves. The most essential aspect of a skill is its wholeness in the way it will eventually be used. For more advanced skills which are not only difficult to perform but are also highly complex in nature and seem to be composed of sub-skills, the best approach is to break them down into those component parts and apply some form of the part method. However, it must be emphasized again that the parts should be unified wholes and have meaning within themselves. Also, this method must be used only with reference to the concept of the whole activity. Lawther suggests that even when the skilled performer is practicing a part, he sees it in relation to the total pattern (8–76).

Sometimes the parts to the whole can be learned through lead-up activities and games. Learning of parts, if they are units within themselves, lend themselves to more immediate success and improvement than the whole, and thus might provide more motivation and reinforcement through a success criterion and, thus, faster learning overall.

Elimination of Errors

It has been stated under feedback that learning takes place only through feedback of *errors*. This would seem to indicate that the learner must be permitted to make his own errors in the learning process. This could be true with respect to minor errors which tend to disappear as the learner practices and gets a clearer goal. However, it is a learning principle that major errors in skill performance should be corrected before they have time to become habits. In correcting errors the instructor must be aware of errors of omission as well as commission. Major errors in form, if allowed to persist, will eventually become deeply ingrained in the subconscious storage system. These errors then become a part of the automatic response of the performer. In order to offset their handicapping influence, they will usually be accompanied by adjustments of a compensatory nature. Thus, the major error produces slow learning and a low level performance while the compensatory act may lead to some low level success but never high level skill (8–60). These bad habit patterns are difficult to break once they have become grooved. They must first be identified, brought to the conscious awareness of the performer, corrected and then practiced as a part of a new automatic pattern (8–60). All coaches and teachers experience situations where students have learned inappropriate motor responses because they have met with some success in their use and even moderate amounts of reinforcement (13–66). This learning error is compounded even more when attempts to correct it through new patterns may meet with failure. This failure is nonreinforcement, and it follows that interest and intention for correction both grow

weaker. For example, the student who learns golf the wrong way without proper instruction until the swing pattern is deeply ingrained in his muscle memory. He has made some compensatory adjustments to achieve some low level success which in itself is reinforcement. When the pro attempts to correct his major errors by substituting a completely new pattern, the new pattern not only feels wrong, but it may meet with early failure. Hence there is no reinforcement or motivation and interest to improve decline.

Self-Analysis

Another important condition affecting learning is self-analysis. When the learner has advanced to the stage where he has a good idea or a "gross framework picture in his mind" of the way he should be performing a skill—in other words, his goal—he is more qualified to engage in self-analysis. He can do this first by reviewing his performance. His performance could be reviewed according to the feedback or self-knowledge he obtained from either visual or proprioceptive cues. In the early stages he would place more emphasis on visual cues but as he became more skilled, he would depend more on the proprioceptive cues. He could review his performance on film, photo, instant replay or mirror reflection. In any event, early learning of skills requires the learner to give attention to many cues but as learning progresses the cues grow fewer in number until in highly skilled performance the act becomes virtually automatic and almost like reflex action. Thus, self-analysis and self-criticism on the part of the student should be one of the teaching objectives of the good teacher. The students should become aware of the kinesthetic sensations accompanying good performance so they can correct wrong responses. As learning progresses to higher levels, self-analysis followed by self-evaluation is as much conducive to learning as criticism by the teacher. Self-analysis can result in self-evaluation. Also, along this same line but yet not quite the same, is the idea of letting students analyze each other and make evaluations.

Knowledge of Results

Since learning does not usually take place unless there is some way for the learner to receive knowledge of his effort, the coach or teacher must be sensitive to the techniques of how these needs can be met. In general this knowledge of results can come in one of several ways: (1) verbal communication from the instructor, (2) visual confirmation to the student of his success, failure or progress, (3) the sensation or feel of a completed task, and (4) audio-visual aids such as films, instant replay, graphs, and the like. Whether feedback is intrinsic or augmented there are several important aspects connected with learning and performance. In general a student will improve more rapidly if he gets specific and accurate knowledge about his performance in relation to his goals instead of such vague and general reinforcements as "good," "that's right" and the like. Also, it probably means more to him if he can get this self-knowledge first-hand from himself rather than from others in a second-hand way. Sometimes with regard to feedback the results are obvious—the stunt, act or skill failed—but the student does not know why. At this point the experienced teacher or coach can provide the feedback by connecting the failure with the student's error and hence provide the desirable self-knowledge. However, this knowledge of results should be immediate before the student has lost his kinesthetic awareness. The beginner in skill learning sometimes gets little feedback of his own since he does not yet have a goal in the form of the gross

framework. Thus, he must have the second-hand knowledge of results if he is to progress. It is good teaching at this point to reinforce what the student did that was good even if the overall goal failed. It is equally true, however, that best results are achieved when the learner gets both the negative as well as the positive reinforcement. In this same frame of reference, spaced knowledge of results is more effective than continual feedback if that feedback is coming from an outside or external source (13–66). In other words the teacher can verbalize too much in communicating to the student about results. However, continuous feedback of the visual or kinesthetic type fosters greater learning. Perhaps visual feedback is more effective during early stages of learning while kinesthetic is more effective during more advanced stages.

Readiness

Thorndike's law of *readiness* has been discussed in Chapter 15. In the learning of motor skill this law seems to apply very well. Basic patterns of movement must be learned before the next higher levels can be taught successfully. There is little information at what age levels various activities can be presented; however, it is thought that there is a *critical* period for acquiring these skills— an optimal period when they can best be learned. One thing is becoming evident. The child seems to be ready for learning some skills much sooner than was originally thought. Evidently there will be individual differences in the matter of readiness due to heredity, sex, maturation, and the richness of the previous environmental experience. The latter is related to motivation and prerequisite skills.

Readiness is greatly dependent on the quantity of these motor experiences in which a child has participated early in his life. Home environment and association with peer groups have an important influence on prerequisite motor activity. The average child spends countless hours at play building the simple skill patterns which form the foundation for more complex activities. These prerequisite skills along with maturation and motivation trigger readiness (13–135). If, however, these simple prerequisite skills are not developed when the child should normally be ready, he falls behind and becomes a special case and ends up the motor moron or certainly a low-skilled individual. This, too, carries over into adult life where it becomes a condition almost impossible to correct because of the time necessary to re-educate the learner, not to mention his frustration, embarrassment and discouragement which are always involved when he does make an effort.

Differentiation

Movement is divided into gross and fine motor skills in one type of classification. This may not be the dichotomy it implies because motor skills would seem to lie along a continuum with fine motor skills at one end and gross skills at the other (1–11). However, for the sake of expediency, this classification will be used to explain *differentiation*. It is an important process of learning motor skill to separate that new skill from its gross motor act of which it is a part, and place it under voluntary control. Lawther calls this process *"individuation"* (8–7). It is readily apparent that in the early stages of learning much of performance is of a gross body nature where many parts and their muscle groups are used. Much of the activity is wasted. The process of differentiation is instrumental in eliminating the unnecessary and excessive movements which are not needed in the achieving of the goal of the skilled performer. As unnecessary movements are eliminated, the act begins to approach what is known as "good form."

In general the learner moves from generalization to specialization.

Form

After differentiation is as good a place as any to discuss "form" in skills. Form has been defined by Singer as a method of expressing movement with a purpose (17–117). In sports and athletics there are usually acceptable models of good form. However, most authorities recognize that a given skill act for any individual will be unique due to the individual differences in body type, size, age, personality and prerequisite basic skills. Purposive skills toward a desired goal may be expressed in varied forms. However, good performance is rare if established mechanical principles are violated. Many styles of performance are sound if they are expressed within the confines of accepted mechanics of movement. For example, most professional golfers have unique styles in their stroke; yet there are certain basic fundamentals in which they are all alike. Goals or sets should not ignore good form. Singer points out that good form serves two purposes: (1) to provide for learning which will lead to efficiency in skill performance, expressing force, precision, poise and ease of movement, and (2) to provide for esthetic appeal (17–119). Some baseball players "look good" striking out. Just as in the case of most areas of motor learning, there are no absolutes in form. Through the years acceptable form in many skills has shifted as these skills have been remolded to conform to new ideas of coaching or knowledge of body mechanics. Two of the best examples are the shot put and high jump in track and field. However, while even good athletes differ in form, there are still fundamental aspects to which they all adhere and these are the crux of good teaching. Research is not conclusive on the effectiveness of teaching the mechanical and kinesiological principles. It might take too much time away from needed participation. However, more advanced learners could profit.

Directions

This point of giving directions has already been touched upon to a certain extent under goals, motivation, transfer, feedback, and knowledge of results. However, it seems to be important enough in skill learning to summarize into capsule form. Cratty (1–48) and Lockhart (9) have devoted some time not only to the temporal considerations but also to the type of sensory experiences involved with the directions. The type of sensory experiences include: (1) verbal directions, (2) visual guidance and (3) movement guidance or manual manipulation.

Under temporal categories Cratty has listed the following three time stages: (1) *Pre-performance* directions which would include a type of warm-up appropriate to the occasion, good goal setting including good body mechanical principles and a mental set. This stage can best be met by verbal directions and visual cues such as demonstrations or visual aids. (2) *Actual performance* directions would include those directions given by the instructor during the performance of the action itself. Some verbal directions accompanied by visual cues are used here. (3) The *task-completion* phase which is accomplished through visual feedback of knowledge of results. These stages tend to overlap. Of course the type of directions will tend to vary with the type of activity and the level of the learner.

Emotion and Skill

Since this text has expounded the unity concept from its beginning, it would be in keeping with this context to relate the emotional aspects of man with his ability to perform motor skills.

Skills provide one of the greatest sources for the arousal of emotions. They offer a laboratory for the teaching of social and moral values, since social and moral values are related to emotions (see Chapter 15). However, aside from contributions as a media for learning values, skills are very much related to emotions where levels of performance are concerned. While performance in skills can arouse emotions, emotions in turn can influence both learning of skills and their performance. Emotions are always a part of performance. The professional student can analyze this situation himself. He will find that emotions may be aroused by the activity itself, by something in the learning or teaching environment, or by the individual himself from within (17–93).

Once again it is not only a bit dangerous to generalize in this area but extremely difficult because emotions can have a favorable effect on the performer as well as an unfavorable one. In general where there is emotional arousal, there is stress. While stress is an internal phenomenon, it makes itself known to the observer in an overt way by producing tension in the muscular system. Stress has a bearing on the learning of skills. If the skills are simple, a reasonable amount of stress can have a favorable effect. However, if the skills are highly complex, stress has a disorganizing effect.

One way to influence the emotions through stress is by an audience. Naturally there are other stresses involved with skills in addition to those brought on by the presence of one or more persons observing. However, the amount of stress caused by an audience will vary with the size of the audience, the nature of the skill patterns, the personality of the performer, and the learning or performance situation. In general, the stress caused by an audience raises the tension level of the performer. However, as has been pointed out, this could be good or bad depending on a number of variables. If the activity to be performed before an audience is of an endurance type, performance should be improved (2–162). If the skills to be performed are simple, the effect would also be positive. If, however, the skills are highly complex, performance becomes more of an individual matter. In this more complex type situation, perhaps the majority of people have exceeded their tolerance level for stress and their performance tends to decline. On the other hand, some individuals respond to the challenge of an audience and the higher tension that it presents. Their performance is enhanced and the stress becomes a positive force for them. These individuals are those who seem to have a high need for recognition.

REFERENCES

1. Cratty, B. J.: *Movement Behavior and Motor Learning*, 2nd Ed. Philadelphia, Lea & Febiger, 1969.
2. Cratty, B. J.: *Psychology and Physical Activity.* Englewood Cliffs, N. J., Prentice-Hall, Inc., 1968.
3. Fitts, Paul M., and M. I. Posner: *Human Performance.* Belmont, Calif., Brooks/Cole Publishing Company, 1967.
4. Gardner, Elizabeth B.: The Neuromuscular Base of Human Movement: Feedback Mechanism. Journal of Health, Physical Education and Recreation, Vol. 36, No. 8, October, 1965, pp. 61–62.
5. Henry, Franklin M., and Donald E. Rogers: Increased Response for Complicated Movements and a Memory Drum Theory of Motor Reaction. Research Quarterly, Vol. 31, 1960, pp. 448–458.
6. Kephart, N. C.: *The Slow Learner in the Classroom.* Columbus, Ohio, Charles E. Merrill Books, Inc., 1960.
7. Lawther, J. D.: Directing Motor Skill Learning. Quest, Vol. VI, May, 1966, pp. 68–76.
8. Lawther J. D.: *The Learning of Physical Skills.* Englewood Cliffs, N. J., Prentice-Hall, Inc., 1968.
9. Lockhart, Ailene: Conditions of Effective Motor Learning. Journal of Health, Physical Education, and Recreation, Vol. 38, No. 2, February, 1967, pp. 36–39.
10. Lockhart, Ailene: Communicating with the Learner. Quest, Vol. VI, May, 1966, pp. 57–67.
11. Manis, Melvin.: *Cognitive Processes.* Belmont, Calif., Brooks/Cole Publishing Company, 1966.
12. Mosston, Muska: *Teaching Physical Education: From Command to Discovery.* Columbus, Ohio, Charles Merrill Books, Inc., 1966.
13. Oxendine, J. B.: *Psychology of Motor Learning.* New York, Appleton-Century-Crofts, 1968.
14. Pleasants, Frank: *Kinesthesis: That Uncertain Feeling.* Unpublished Study. Greensboro, N. C., University of North Carolina, 1969.
15. Robb M.: Feedback. Quest, Vol. VI, May, 1966, pp. 38–43.
16. Singer, R. N.: Learning Theory as Applied to Physical Education. *Proceedings,* National College Physical Education Association for Men, Published by American Association for Health, Physical Education and Recreation, 69th, December, 1965, pp. 59–67.
17. Singer, Robert N.: *Motor Learning and Human Performance.* New York, The Macmillan Company, 1968.
18. Smith, H. M.: *Introduction to Human Movement.* Reading, Mass., Addison-Wesley Publishing Company, 1968.
19. Smith, K. U., and W. M. Smith: *Perception and Motion.* Philadelphia, W. B. Saunders Company, 1962.
20. Smith, K. U.: Cybernetic Foundations of Physical Behavioral Science. Quest, Vol. VIII, May, 1967, pp. 26–80.
21. Steinhaus, Arthur H.: Your Muscles See More than Your Eyes. Journal of Health, Physical Education and Recreation, September, 1966, pp. 38–40.
22. Walker, E. L.: *Conditioning and Instrumental Learning.* Belmont, Calif., Brooks/Cole Publishing Company, 1967.

PART IV

Implications for Educational
Processes

Chapter 17

Principles of Curriculum Design in Physical Education

INTRODUCTION

A curriculum is defined from time to time in terms of experiences, courses or subject matter. For purposes of this chapter it will be interpreted to mean experiences in physical education activities arranged at various educational levels. Since this is a textbook concerning principles and foundations of physical education, it is not intended to furnish the physical education major student with a thorough background in curriculum development and design. However, few undergraduate professional training programs in physical education include courses in curriculum per se. Therefore, a course such as this book is planned for may be one of the few times the undergraduate will be exposed to the processes of curriculum construction. Since many of these students will no doubt go out into the schools of America immediately after graduation and perhaps even work for a number of years without further training, it seems logical that they have some acquaintance with development of the educational process.

Whether they have any training or not, they will find themselves in situations where curricular planning must be done and where curricular revision is an ongoing process. Therefore, this chapter and the next will attempt to set forth some of the principles of curriculum building along with its corollary of evaluation. The author is fully cognizant that these two chapters are not enough. However, the student has been exposed to the materials in the first sixteen chapters, and he should now be able to start crystallizing his thinking with reference to the concepts and principles he has learned. He can do this best by applying them to their more practical use in the curriculum. If these concepts and principles are to be dynamic and meaningful in his professional life, the student should have the opportunity of visualizing them in their more tangible setting—the school program of physical education and a part of the total educational process. However, since the student's background will still be limited in this curricular area, he is urged to consult with the sources listed at the end of this chapter for more depth and understanding.

In conceptualizing a curriculum design to meet the needs of K through 12 (kindergarten through grade 12) or for that matter through college, many of the principles and concepts emphasized in previous chapters will be taken into account. Basically, a curriculum rests on philosophy and the broad goals that have been formulated from philosophies are its reference points. It is the achievement of these broad goals through the curricular experiences that society is able to function and to survive.

The program is also related to professional personnel and their training. If there are to be new insights and new dimensions for a "new physical education" the full import of this tack must be reflected in the teacher preparation programs. A curriculum can be no better than the leadership which plans, organizes and implements it. If a curriculum is to be related to the needs of those to be educated as well as the needs of the larger social group, those needs have to be established. This task becomes one of the overriding challenges of the curriculum makers. Once these needs have been established, the next logical step is equally crucial. The needs must be met through the program of experiences presented in the curriculum.

The needs of the student to be educated are inherent in the fundamental parts of his wholeness interacting with each other and with the forces from his cultural milieu. Some of his most pressing needs are to be found as a result of his biological heritage, referred to in Chapters 9, 10, 11 and 13. These come from biology, physiology, anatomy, physical anthropology, and kinesiology. Another facet of his totality concerns the social needs as revealed in Chapters 12, 13 and 14. These needs arise out of the interaction of the individual with his cultural and social heritage and come from sociology and cultural anthropology. The psychological and intellectual aspects of the individual were discussed in Chapters 11, 15 and 16, and are revealed in psychology and motor learning. From all of these areas come needs arising out of the conflict of man with his environment, which has in it the potential for disintegration and biological weaknesses discussed in Chapter 9.

In addition to establishing the needs of the individual, the needs of society must also be assessed. The thesis was made in Chapter 1 that two of the primary purposes of education were the perpetuation of society through the individual being educated and the helping of that individual to make his adjustments to that society. There is no claim made at this point that one of these has priority over the other. Since both man's biological and social needs must be related to his cultural environment, neither can exist separate from it. However, a rapidly changing culture has a way of forcing priorities where both biological and social needs are concerned. If there is an urgency for new approaches in education and a "new physical education," it is chiefly because of a runaway culture that is changing so rapidly and cataclysmically. These changes are reflected in man's environment and his social organization, and they will force changes in the role of educational institutions. They have implications for his biological heritage as well as his social as they challenge curriculum makers in all areas of education. There is "new math" and "new science" and a new approach to teaching languages as a result of these cataclysmic events. It would seem that in the light of man's needs there must be a "new physical education."

Premier Nikita Khruschev in a way became our minister of education when the Russians put up the first Sputnik in

1957. Since that time there has been an educational revolution in progress in this country. There has not only been a shift in emphasis due to the new point of view, but a tremendous shift in content due to the knowledge explosion. The emphasis in the total educational curriculum has tilted toward strengthening and toughening the academic climate of the schools. Math and science have become areas with top priorities. Critics of education like Dr. Conant have had a great deal of influence in shaping educational thinking and direction, and, of course, educational curricula (8). However, the seeds for this change in emphasis had been sown long before and were being nurtured by such an explosion of knowledge and information that the educational world is still reeling under the impact. It took 1750 years from the time of Christ for man's accumulated knowledge to double. Then, it doubled again by 1900 after a 150-year period which spawned the Industrial Revolution. It doubled again by 1950 and then in a dramatic ten-year period, it doubled again by 1960. The last decade since 1960 has been even more fantastic. It has been said that if man is being choked to death biologically by the pollution growing out of the population explosion and technology, he may be in as much danger of being choked intellectually by the information growing out of the knowledge explosion. Thus, society has to be selective in terms of what shall be taught in the schools and to what degree it shall be taught.

In the future man will struggle in a mainstream of ideas and knowledges from which he must extract that information which will be most useful to him not only in his economic and social survival but also his biological. D. B. Van Dalen has said, "Society is saying: you must teach more in less time more effectively and at less cost per unit" (25). Physical education can be no exception to this mandate from society. The curriculum of physical education has a body of knowledge which is basic to health and fitness and to their importance in not only survival but also fine living. It has a core of activity skills and techniques. Just as there is competition for the ways man will spend his dollars in the future, so there is competition in society's schools for the ideas, knowledges, and skills that the students will learn and how and where they will spend their time in those schools. The physical education curriculum must justify its right to survive in the educational spectrum. It must justify the time that the student spends in the experiences which it provides. It must justify the space which it occupies in presenting these experiences. It must justify its share of the educational dollar as well, and it so happens that its laboratories are among the most expensive provided by the schools. School administrators are time- and dollar-conscious, and they will need sound proof of what is to be done with the student's time and the taxpayer's dollars that have been allotted them for the total educational process.

In the past, physical education curricula could be based on empiricism because there was nothing better in most cases. The time is now at hand, however, and will grow increasingly more so when the experiences presented in the program will need to be justified through scientific evidence. Man now lives in a science-oriented culture, and it is no longer tenable to base important decisions on tradition or guesswork if supporting evidence can be found. Research, while it frequently is slow reaching the grass roots in education, will more and more be the catalytic force which brings about change in physical education. In addition to being architects of curriculum, professional leaders must prove through scientific measurement and evaluation techniques that their architectural efforts achieve results in the educational spectrum. The proof of the pudding is in the eating. The worth of the curriculum is to be found in the changes it brings about in the knowledge and behavior of the students as revealed by measurements. Until these changes occur or are initiated, no curriculum exists. According to Cassidy it is just a written report which is meaningless (6–14).

In the past there have been many inadequate programs of physical education. Bucher suggests that there has been a lack of progression and sequential arrangement of subject matter and lack of orderly developmental patterns for teaching motor skills (5–257). There are too many programs which offer the same old activities to the same students year after year, and too many people who have taught or tried to teach too many activities for which they were not qualified or prepared to teach. Voltmer and Esslinger give three main reasons for inadequate programs: (1) inadequate time allotment, (2) inadequate facilities and (3) lack of sound methods of curriculum construction (26–96). In modern education, with the competition for the student's time and the taxpayer's dollars, it is difficult to see how the first two of these can be significantly upgraded until the last one shows dramatic improvement. To these reasons for inadequacy may be added one of mismanagement on the part of administrators in permitting overcrowded classes, no plan for homogeneous grouping, using untrained teachers, and overemphasizing the interschool program as it relegates the formal program to a catch-all. While the needs of the student and society keep changing, far too many school programs of physical education have not re-tooled and have not searched for re-emphasis and re-direction in their curriculum.

In retrospect the past has not proven too flattering to the professional where school curricula are concerned. It is interesting to analyze the different tacks which observed curricula have taken. Kozman, Cassidy and Jackson have categorized such programs in the past into the following types: "take it and like it," "take anything you like," "feeder for varsity teams" (14–94). To these can be added such other types as "throw out the ball," "muscle building," and "basketball in winter and softball in fall and spring." These are all self-explanatory and do provide some insight into the paucity of well-designed programs in the past.

Thus, there are forces which suggest that the curriculum in physical education must undergo a process of retooling, re-emphasis or re-direction and change in order to meet the new challenges, problems and situations growing out of socio-cultural changes. However, change should not be made just for the sake of change. Admittedly there are some facets of education and society that are dynamic and subject to rapid change. On the other hand some are relatively stable and fixed. There are still many of these aspects of the educational processes which are basic to any curriculum at any time. It is granted that there is an educational revolution in progress brought on by the advent of technology and the explosion of population and knowledge, and this revolution presages change. However, it would be a mistake not to turn back and take a long look at the past. Historically, the first real program of physical education indigenous to modern America was developed by Clark Hetherington (11). If the student could obtain access to this rather rare publication, "The School Program," he would be amazed to find how much of this original work of a man now recognized as the "Philosopher of Physical Education" still is fundamental and applicable to present-day use. Also, the "Curriculum in Sports" by Seward Staley still has a contribution to make to modern programs (21). His presentation of conduct and control objectives adds a different dimension to this aspect of program planning.

Another curriculum study which is no doubt the most extensive project of its kind ever undertaken in the field is "The Physical Education Curriculum (A National Program)" by LaPorte and more recently revised and edited by John M. Cooper (15). This project is mentioned here because it cuts across the past into the present and clearly indicates the point just made concerning the real worth of the past in planning curricula for the future. If there were such a thing, this might well be called a longitudinal curriculum study since it was begun in 1930 and has been under study and implementation ever since that time. It is the only truly national program in existence and it does make provision for most of the elements which are recommended for curriculum construction. Basically, it provides the framework for a national program but possesses the flexibility so that each local system can develop its own curriculum unique to its situation from the elements that are provided. While Dr. Cooper has effected some changes particularly at the elementary and secondary levels and other changes have been made along the way in other years, there is still a great deal of the original work which serves as a basis for the existing program. Perhaps the scorecard for evaluation has been employed more on state and national levels than any other instrument of its kind.

CURRICULUM DEFINED

In the introductory portion of this chapter a great many references have been made to the terms "curriculum" and "program." Perhaps the time is now at hand to define each of them into a somewhat clearer and more precise meaning. The derivation of the word curriculum is the Latin word *currere* meaning "to run." It was no doubt related to foot races and the track or the "course" over which they were run. A curriculum has been defined in various ways depending on the point of view of the definition maker.

Defined broadly, it could mean all the experiences the student has connected with school from the time he leaves home on the bus until he returns. More narrowly defined, it could mean the subject matter or activities which are to be taught in courses as a part of the formal school program. This could either be the total body of courses offered by the institution or those courses offered by a particular field of learning. In some cases it is considered a course of study for a subject or a school level—for example English course of study or the junior high school course of study. If the broader concept is accepted, then the word "extracurricular" would have no further use or meaning since all such activities are "experiences" and would be included in the broader concept of the curriculum. When this broader connotation is used, the so-called extracurricular activities are frequently referred to as "co-curricular" or "extended curricular" activities.

Perhaps a more acceptable definition would delineate between curricular and extracurricular. Such a *curriculum* is defined as "a systematic arrangement of experiences which are designed to achieve the objectives of a specific area of learning at several educational levels." Thus, the physical education curriculum would be a progressive series of activities consisting of sports, gymnastics, fitness activities, and dance at the junior high school level, or the senior high school level, or K-12 or all of these designed to achieve the objectives and outcomes discussed in Chapter 3.

Willgoose suggests that a curriculum is a body of experiences between one's objectives and methods of teaching (23–57). In some places the entire school experience is recognized as the curriculum while the experiences for a particular subject area are called a course of study. In many instances curriculum and program are used interchangeably. Whether it is curriculum or program, however, Cassidy points out that the "real" program or curriculum is not the blueprint set down on paper, but the one that effects changes in the students (6–14). Thus, the curriculum becomes the means to an end— that end being a physically educated student relative to age, sex and grade level. The ideal curriculum would be one that would alter the learning experiences of the students so that the majority of them might achieve most of the ends listed under the "physically educated student" shown on page 303.

When the narrower approach to curriculum is taken, and that has been the emphasis in this chapter, such enriching activity experiences as interscholastic athletics, intramurals, extramurals, and school recreation are excluded. Yet there should be a direct and primary relationship between these enriching extracurricular programs as they are integrated into a meaningful unified whole. Perhaps the two most important relationships and certainly most necessary ones are these. First, the extracurricular activities provide the necessary opportunities for a continued participation in the curricular activities, particularly the junior and senior high schools and college levels, and second, the curriculum provides opportunities for the teaching of the skills necessary to participate in the extracurricular.

However, from the standpoint of educational outcomes, the curriculum which encompasses the instructional program is the most important in meeting the needs of all the students. The pyramid shown in Figure 17–1 clearly shows these fundamental relationships

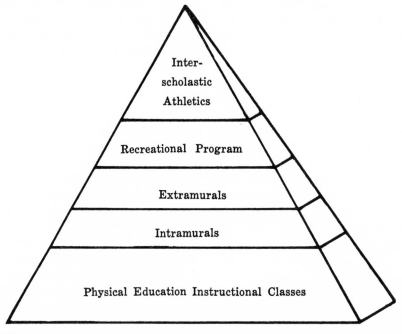

FIGURE 17–1.   Program Pyramid (Courtesy State Department of Public Instruction, North Carolina)

between the instructional program and the various extracurricular programs. The curricular forms the basis for all the extracurricular and is universal since it includes all the students. It does not exclude fun and enjoyment and participating but it is essentially an instruction program. It is generally required by law in most states although the requirements may not extend past the ninth grade in some. It provides the basis for the necessary skills which are used for participating in each of the other parts of the pyramid. All of these other facets above the base involve voluntary participation and a limited number of the total student group. Without these extended programs above the base of the pyramid, the school would offer few, if any, opportunities for competency above the novice level in its physical education experiences.

The interscholastic program is placed at the apex. It is the most highly organized, meets the needs of the most highly skilled students, requires the most time, costs the most money, and involves on the average about 5 to 10 per cent of the total students. The intramural, extramural and recreation programs offer laboratory opportunities in a wide variety of activities where competencies might be improved. It is hoped that these programs will involve all of the students but a more realistic figure might be 75 per cent.

CLEARING THE PATH FOR CURRICULUM DEVELOPMENT

There are always certain administrative and procedural matters which must be attended to prior to the actual start of curriculum planning. The procedures and techniques employed will vary to some extent depending on the purpose for which the curriculum will be used. For example, a curriculum may be developed for a single local school, a county or city system, an entire state,

and even a national plan (15). Regardless of the level of involvement, however, it is most commonly developed by a committee although it may be devised by a single teacher. Who are the persons most likely to share in the responsibility of working with a curriculum planning committee? There is a principle here of involving as many different people from as many groups as possible.

Cassidy has presented the idea of the "curriculum merry-go-round" which, among other things, indicates the people who might be involved on the study and planning committee (6-2). (See Figure 17–2.) Once again, of course the persons on the committee will vary with the level for which the curriculum is being developed. In general a committee will include teachers, parents, students, community leaders, administrative personnel, supervisors, consultants, and other school personnel who might have some area of interest, concern or speciality. The leadership in curriculum planning primarily resides in the administrative and supervisory staffs. The teacher, however, does play a key role because he is at the grass roots of the problem where he is cognizant of the needs and interests of the students as well as the local situation. Of course it is the teacher who must implement the curriculum once it is put into use. The role of the student should be an important one too, since he is the one for whom the processes are being planned. Since the democratic processes are recommended in curriculum construction, the student should have some share in shaping the curriculum. He should be given the opportunity to express his interests, and his likes and dislikes. The parents can make a significant contribution to curriculum planning by sharing in a two-way relationship where they provide information but also learn more clearly what the schools are attempting to accomplish.

FIGURE 17-2.   The Curriculum Merry-Go-Round*

The role the teacher plays, however, as well as all the other members of the committee is subject to many influences and pressures. Nixon and Jewett provide a list of these pressure groups at the national, state and local levels along with influences of colleges and universities (16–53). These agencies and groups include the National Education Association and all its many sub-groups, the American Association for Health, Physical Education and Recreation, the U. S. Office of Education, the President's Council on Physical Fitness and Sports, and the American Medical Association on a national scale. At the state level such groups include the State Department of Education, the Divisions of Health and Physical Education, the

State Board of Education, and the State Association of Health, Physical Education and Recreation. At the local levels there might be supervisors and consultants along with local boards of education. Colleges and universities have made great contributions to curriculum development in the schools by making trained personnel available as resource persons and consultants, and by offering courses in curriculum development along with exerting pressure and guidance through professional organizations. While the idea of pressure from outside the school has its distasteful overtones and connotations, it is a fact of life in a democracy that such groups do exist. Of course it has its credit side, too, even though it places limitations on the curriculum study groups. Most of these so-called pressure groups, while they may have axes to grind, make valu-

* Cassidy, Rosalind: *Curriculum Development in Physical Education*, 1954. Used by permission of Harper and Row Publishers, New York.

able contributions to curricular improvements. Consultants from the state department of education or from colleges or universities or from other school administrative units may be used effectively.

Regardless of level of involvement and the pressure groups working behind the scenes, the idea of the "curriculum merry-go-round" presented by Cassidy implies that there is room for many riders (those who work on the development committee) (6–25). However, the merry-go-round never stops even though some of the riders may drop off from time to time. A curriculum, like a philosophy, is always in a state of being built but is never completed. It becomes a continuous dynamic process with evaluation followed by revision followed by evaluation in a continuous ongoing cycle. The different facets involved in the curriculum rarely remain static. The needs, abilities and capacities of the students vary with change in cultural patterns. Facilities, budgets, and leadership are constantly being improved. Problems are constantly arising creating needs which the old curriculum does not meet. The old curriculum is evaluated in the light of its accomplishments and these changed facets, and is frequently found lacking. It follows that it must be continuously revised, rebuilt and improved.

The values of curriculum development are many. Obviously the primary purpose to be realized is effecting desirable changes in the student. However, there are other values which are concomitant to these. Those staff members who have worked at curriculum development and have shown a genuine interest in its construction are motivated to become better teachers. In the final analysis, it is not the curriculum but the quality of the leadership which brings about desirable changes. If curriculum study had no other reason for being, this value of effecting motivation and changed values in the teacher justify its existence. Also, it is only when the teacher plays an active and creative role in curriculum construction that he can be effective in the ongoing evaluation and revision.

STEPS IN CURRICULUM DEVELOPMENT

Once the committee has been constituted in the most democratic fashion possible, there are certain procedural considerations that must be carried out. The committee must be organized in the usual manner with a chairman and a secretary. If the committee is a large one, it can be divided into subcommittees with different areas of responsibility for part of the work. In a sense, every person on the staff should be involved either directly or indirectly. Each has a contribution to make in his speciality, and it is a fact of life that involvement makes for commitment. There are certain materials and information which must be made available to the committee for preliminary planning. The administrator who has probably initiated the study and who will be chiefly responsible for its continuation and finalization can save himself and the committee valuable time if certain data and materials are collected and made available to the study committee. This administrator will play a prominent role in the entire process. In fact, he is generally the catalyst that started the ball rolling in the first place. If other leadership is lacking, he should assume the role and through the democratic process exert the necessary influence to develop the best possible process.

The information which can be provided in advance should include such matters as the number of students now and the projected number, the socioeconomic backgrounds, the number of qualified faculty members who will be available for implementation of the new program, the amount and type of facilities, the financial support forthcoming, state rules and regulations, and the present philosophy of the school administration concerning physical education. An important facet of these initial steps would be a study of the existing curriculum—courses, activities, sequential arrangement, guides, source material and the like. Another preliminary step might involve ascertaining the interests of the students through a survey. In addition to these items, most of which can be obtained from local sources, there is an abundance of literature and materials on curriculum construction and revision which can be gotten from numerous sources including the pressure groups just referred to in previous paragraphs. Members of the committee must either be knowledgeable or become so in the learning process, growth and developmental needs of youth, needs of the community, state and nation, and what the experts recommend about curriculum development. In general, most of these materials will provide the basic information needed. There seem to be several well-defined steps or sequences which are to be followed. These steps leading to the evolving processes of the curriculum are given below.

Statement of Philosophy

The threads of this concept of the importance of philosophy runs throughout this book. All of man's practices and processes in education should be based on the scientific processes or philosophical judgments. Since philosophy is the source of man's aims, ideals and his direction, it must become an important aspect of educational planning. There are two facets concerning philosophy which must be considered: *social philosophy* and *educational philosophy*.

Social philosophy embodies those beliefs and concepts which are inherent in a democratic American way of life—the worth and dignity of the individual, equality of opportunity, individual re-

sponsibility, self-achievement, the importance of play in personality, the "doing" philosophy and the right to make mistakes. Physical education must become part and parcel to the larger society of which it is an integral segment. The practices and procedures of its program must be compatible with the dictates of society—not just society's minimum requirements but its ideals.

Also, the curriculum must be in harmony with acceptable *educational philosophy*. In Chapter 1 the student has learned that the primary purposes of education are to perpetuate the society and culture through the student, to improve upon that society, and to help the student to adjust to its norms and requirements and become a better citizen within the potential with which he is endowed. Therefore, educational philosophy represents the foundation upon which the curriculum is developed. Physical education must not be at odds with the purposes of general education. These purposes have been discussed rather fully in Chapter 3 under the aims and objectives of education. The Seven Cardinal Principles of Education (7) and the list proposed by the Educational Policies Commission (10) are examples from which the committee can draw. These objectives are derived from social and educational philosophy but they are also used to give direction to that philosophy and to help implement it. From a formulation of social and educational philosophy, it is only a step to the development of a physical education philosophy by the curriculum experts. This probably becomes the true starting point for the evolving curriculum since out of the philosophy established for physical education comes its aims and objectives.

Determining the Aims and Objectives

Philosophy is the source of all *direction, goals* and *purposes*. The goals of physical education have been delineated in Chapter 3 under *aims, objectives* and *outcomes.* A review of these goals encompassing a hierarchy of objectives will clearly reveal a concept that has been a consistent theme in this book. This concept is one of the basic ones presented in Chapter 1—the concept of the unitary aspect of the individual. If this holistic view is a basic assumption of both science and philosophy and if it is to govern educational philosophy and practice, it must become an important point of departure for a curriculum. When there is a summation of the goals discussed in Chapter 3, the whole of the individual is more than the sum of the parts as revealed by the objectives. It is the interrelationship that produces the organismic concept.

At the expense of some repetition, in Chapter 3 the goals of physical education were presented according to a hierarchy of aims, objectives, and outcomes. There is only one *aim* for a field of study—physical education— and it is remote and general in nature as it indicates the ultimate direction. An aim is relatively stable in nature and will change little even over a long period of time. *Objectives* are more immediate and specific, indicating steps or levels along the line of direction indicated by the aim. *Outcomes* are highly specific, generally stated in terms of the behavior of the student—attitudes, appreciations, skills, physical changes and knowledge revealed in the way the student behaves. These are the teachable specifics and can be measured. As they are achieved by the student, they are indicative of the attainment of the more general objectives (see Chapter 3 for further use).

The Physically Educated Person

When the aims and objectives of physical education are realized for any one individual, he is said to be "phys-

ically educated." The ultimate aim in physical education then would be *the physically educated* person. However, this individual could be a somewhat nebulous person without some clarification. The concept has been referred to in both Chapters 1 and 3 and the attributes of the physically educated person were discussed in a general way. A further study of this discussion will immediately raise the question of age level and its relation to the ultimate concept. Obviously it is not possible, for example, for the eighth grader to have achieved all the attributes of the adult physically educated individual. Therefore, it seems expedient to spell out these qualities in relation to the levels of age and maturity. The producing of the completely physically educated person would probably be rare. However, the perceptive physical educator would like to be able to observe if his time table toward this ideal is on schedule. If this idea is to be realized even in part there must be a continuity of experiences within the educational level and excellent articulation between levels. This striving individual simply cannot waste time in the useless repetition of activities year after year.

The National Conference on Fitness of Secondary School Youth in their report "Youth and Fitness" listed the attributes of a physically educated high school graduate (1–28). They are:

ATTITUDES:

1. Strong desire to be healthy.

2. Acceptance of the need to exercise daily to maintain physical fitness.

3. An awareness of the value of safety procedures in and on the water.

4. Appreciation of "change of pace" from work to recreational activities (an essential part of healthy living).

5. A desire to achieve a high degree of excellence in skills to enjoy participation.

6. Appreciation of one's strengths and limitations.

7. Acceptance of the concept of one's role as a member of a team.

8. Positive attitudes and desire for personal cleanliness and safe practices in physical activities.

9. Appreciation of wholesome intergroup relationships and respect for the rights of others.

10. Appreciation of the values in good sportsmanship and of its fullest application to total living.

11. Appreciation of the value of the creative aspects of correct body movements.

KNOWLEDGE:

1. Knowledge of what constitutes body mechanics (acceptable posture) and how this relates to good health.

2. Knowledge of the proper functioning of the body and of their responsibility to maintain personal fitness.

3. Knowledge of the rules of water safety (swimming, rescue, artificial respiration, boating, etc.).

4. Understanding of the nature and importance of physical fitness and knowledge of how to develop and maintain it throughout life.

5. Understanding of the rules, strategies, background, and values of sports and other physical activities.

6. Knowledge of proper selection and care of school and personal athletic equipment.

7. Understanding and appreciation of the role of physical education in the total education program.

8. Knowledge of the proper mechanics of sports and activities.

9. Understanding of the importance and role of physical fitness in successful academic achievement (sound mind, fit body).

10. Knowledges of the scientific and health reasons for proper hygiene and safety practices as applied in physical activities.

11. Understanding of one's physical capacities and limitations.

12. Knowledge enabling them to be intelligent spectators of the popular American sports.

13. The ability to distinguish between sound and unsound commercial health and exercise practices and programs.

SKILLS:

1. Ability to assume good posture and maintain it while sitting, standing, walking.

2. Development of skills in at least four seasonal team sports, the level of skill attained being such that there is enjoyment in participation.

3. Ability to swim well enough to feel at home in the water (involves mastery of the different strokes and survival skills).

4. Development in skills in at least four indoor and outdoor single or dual sports, the level of skill being such that there is enjoyment in participation.

5. Development of proper rhythmic response to music, including basic skills in folk, square, modern, and/or social dance.

6. Development of skill in one combative activity (boxing excluded) for boys, the level being such that there is enjoyment of participation.

7. Ability to apply skills in fundamental body movements—in running, throwing, jumping, lifting, carrying, etc.—to other physical activities.

8. Achievement of an adequate level of skill in self-testing activities such as track and field, calisthenics, tumbling, apparatus, etc.

9. Good habits of cleanliness, personal appearance, and safety practices in all physical activities.

Analyzing the Situation

The next step involved in curriculum construction and revision is a thorough analysis of the local situation or situations. The setting in which the new curriculum is to be implemented is of prime importance. While there are other aspects of the learning process which share in the total learning of students, the proper learning environment is one of the necessary attributes. The availability of equipment and facilities along with the other physical aspects which play a role in the total program must be anticipated. While a curriculum should not be developed based on the dearth of such physical requirements, the planning committee must be realistic on the other hand and not place the proposed program too far ahead of the existing facilities and proposed improvements. The development of a new curriculum or a thorough revision of the old one does offer a golden opportunity for expansion of facilities if the added expense can be justified. The new curriculum could be the catalyst to bring about significant improvements.

In addition to analyzing the equipment and facilities, the study group should learn about the entire environment in which the student lives and grows. Some knowledge should be had of the socioeconomic influences, inner city problems and possibilities for other out-of-school learning experiences.

Determining Student Needs

The next step is one of the most crucial in establishing the educational processes. It is concerned with the nature of the student as revealed by his biological, psychological, emotional and social needs. While all of these needs and characteristics obviously are not yet known, and this area is one of those in greatest need for further study, those which have been established do not have the attention in program planning and teaching that they merit. Establishing the students' needs is not the same thing as finding their interest. Needs are infinitely more complex than interests. The growth and development characteristics of the elementary, junior high school and senior high school student have been established in rather broad limits representing the norms which are most common to these groups. Since each particular student is unique, however, and develops at his own rate, there will be great variation within these three school levels and for that matter even

within one age level. Therefore the principle of individual differences must become an important factor in implementation once the program is planned.

While it may be that educators and physical educators know in general the adult behavior toward which education is directed, the child is no little adult. It is incumbent on those developing educational experiences to know the needs and characteristics that motivate his behavior at various age levels. When these needs, characteristics and behavioral modes are known, the curriculum planners are in a better position to fit the experiences to the student's needs. The following is a list of behavioral and special needs, and physical and growth characteristics of the children from preschool through adolescence (13).

A Developmental View of Children from Preschool through Adolescence:*

The Runabout (from two and one half years through four)

Physical Development

Motor skills unevenly developed—marked development in large muscle coordination, but small muscles and eye-hand coordination still not well developed.

Full set of temporary teeth by three years.

Gradually acquires ability to feed and dress himself with greater skill.

Rapid language development—from a few words to an average of 2000.

Change in sleep pattern—twelve hours needed at night with daytime naps gradually given up. But still needs rest period because children of this age fatigue easily.

Toilet habits established. Child usually takes care of his own needs by end of period.

Characteristic Behavior

Learning to understand his environment and to comply with many of its demands.

Often negativistic at beginning of period, but gradually becomes able to accept necessary limits and restraints. Wants adult approval.

Likes to be close to his mother, but his father is becoming increasingly important to him.

* Reprinted by permission: Text only from *See How They Grow* by Gladys Gardner Jenkins, Helen S. Schacter, and William W. Bauer. Copyright 1967 by Scott, Foresman and Company.

Likes to help around the house.

Imitative in language, manners, and habits.

Constantly active, but capable of longer stretches of quiet activity toward end of period.

Shows fatigue by being irritable or restless.

Gradually learning what is acceptable behavior and what is not.

Great curiosity. Asks countless questions.

Special Needs

Security of love and affection from parents.

Guidance and a pattern of behavior to follow.

Time, patience, understanding, and genuine interest from adults.

Simple, clear routines. Limited choices.

Opportunity to learn to give and take, to play cooperatively with other children.

Wider scope of activity. Limited freedom to move about and to move away from immediate home environment by end of period.

About Five

Physical Development

Period of slow growth. Body lengthens out and hands and feet grow larger. Girls usually about a year ahead of boys in physical development.

Good general motor control, though small muscles not so fully developed as large ones.

Sensory-motor equipment usually not ready for reading. Eye-hand coordination improving, but still poor. Apt to be far-sighted.

Activity level high.

Attention span still short, but increasing.

Little infantile articulation in speech.

Handedness established.

Characteristic Behavior

Stable—good balance between self-sufficiency and sociability.

Home-centered.

Beginning to be capable of self-criticism. Eager and able to carry some responsibility.

Noisy and vigorous, but activity has definite direction.

Purposeful and constructive—knows what he's going to draw before he draws it.

Uses language well, enjoys dramatic play.

Can wash, dress, eat, and go to the toilet by himself, but may need occasional help.

Individuality and lasting traits beginning to be apparent.

Interested in group activity.

Special Needs

Assurance that he is loved and valued.

Wise guidance.

Opportunity for plenty of activity, equipment for exercising large muscles.

Opportunity to do things for himself, freedom to use and develop his own powers.

Background training in group effort, in sharing, and in good work habits that he will need next year in first grade.

Opportunity to learn about his world by seeing and doing things.

Kindergarten experience if possible.

About Six

Physical Development

Growth proceeding more slowly, a lengthening out.

Large muscles better developed than small ones.

Eleven to twelve hours of sleep needed.

Eyes not yet mature, tendency toward far-sightedness.

Permanent teeth beginning to appear.

Heart in period of rapid growth.

High activity level—can stay still only for short periods.

Characteristic Behavior

Eager to learn, exuberant, restless, overactive, easily fatigued.

Self-assertive, aggressive, wants to be first, less cooperative than at five, keenly competitive, boastful.

Whole body involved in whatever he does.

Learns best through active participation.

Inconsistent in level of maturity evidenced— regresses when tired, often less mature at home than with outsiders.

Inept at activities using small muscles.

Relatively short periods of interest.

Has difficulty making decisions.

Group activities popular, boys' and girls' interests beginning to differ.

Much spontaneous dramatization.

Special Needs

Encouragement, ample praise, warmth, and great patience from adults.

Ample opportunity for activity of many kinds, especially for use of large muscles.

Wise supervision with minimum interference.

Friends—by end of period, a best friend.

Concrete learning situations and active, direct participation.

Some responsibilities, but without pressure and without being required to make complicated decisions or achieve rigidly set standards.

Help in developing acceptable manners and habits.

About Seven

Physical Development

Growth slow and steady.

Annual expected growth in height—two or three inches. In weight—three to six pounds.

Losing teeth. Most seven-year-olds have their six-year molars.

Better eye-hand coordination.

Better use of small muscles.

Eyes not yet ready for much close work.

Characteristic Behavior

Sensitive to feelings and attitudes of both other children and adults. Especially dependent on approval of adults.

Interests of boys and girls diverging. Less play together.

Full of energy but easily tired, restless and fidgety, often dreamy and absorbed.

Little abstract thinking. Learns best in concrete terms and when he can be active while learning.

Cautious and self-critical, anxious to do things well, likes to use hands.

Talkative, prone to exaggerate, may fight verbally instead of physically, competitive.

Enjoys songs, rhythms, fairy tales, myths, nature stories, comics, television, movies.

Able to assume some responsibility.

Concerned about right and wrong, but may take small things that are not his.

Rudimentary understanding of time and monetary values.

Special Needs

The right combination of independence and encouraging support.

Chances for active participation in learning situations with concrete objects.

Adult help in adjusting to the rougher ways of the playground without becoming too crude or rough.

Warm, encouraging, friendly relationships with adults.

Acceptance at own level of development.

About Eight

Physical Development

Growth still slow and steady—arms lengthening, hands growing.

Eyes ready for both near and far vision. Near-sightedness may develop this year.

Permanent teeth continuing to appear.

Large muscles still developing. Small muscles better developed, too. Manipulative skills are increasing.

Attention span getting longer.

Poor posture may develop.

Characteristic Behavior

Often careless, noisy, argumentative, but also alert, friendly, interested in people.

More dependent on his mother again, less so on his teacher. Sensitive to criticism.

New awareness of individual differences.

Eager, more enthusiastic than cautious. Higher accident rate.

Gangs beginning. Best friends of same sex.

Allegiance to other children instead of to an adult in case of conflict.

Greater capacity for self-evaluation.

Much spontaneous dramatization, ready for simple classroom dramatics.

Understanding of time and of use of money.

Responsive to group activities, both spontaneous and adult-supervised.

Fond of team games, comics, television, movies, adventure stories, collections.

Special Needs

Praise and encouragement from adults.

Reminders of his responsibilities.

Wise guidance and channeling of his interests and enthusiasms, rather than domination or unreasonable standards.

A best friend.

Experience of belonging to peer group—opportunity to identify with others of same age and sex.

Adult-supervised groups and planned after-school activities.

Exercise of both large and small muscles.

About Nine or Ten

Physical Development

Slow, steady growth continues—girls forge further ahead. Some children reach the plateau preceding the preadolescent growth spurt.

Lungs as well as digestive and circulatory systems almost mature. Heart especially subject to strain.

Teeth may need straightening. First and second bicuspids appearing.

Eye-hand coordination good. Ready for crafts and shop work.

Eyes almost adult size. Ready for close work with less strain.

Characteristic Behavior

Decisive, responsible, dependable, reasonable, strong sense of right and wrong.

Individual differences distinct; abilities now apparent.

Capable of prolonged interest. Often makes plans and goes ahead on his own.

Gangs strong, of short duration and changing membership. Limited to one sex.

Perfectionistic—wants to do well, but loses interest if discouraged or pressured.

Interested less in fairy tales and fantasy, more in his community and country and in other countries and peoples.

Loyal to his country and proud of it.

Spends a great deal of time in talk and discussion. Often outspoken and critical of adults, although still dependent on adult approval.

Frequently argues over fairness in games.

Special Needs

Active rough and tumble play.

Friends and membership in a group.

Training in skills, but without pressure.

Books of many kinds, depending on individual reading level and interest.

Reasonable explanations without talking down.

Definite responsibility.

Frank answers to his questions about coming physiological changes.

The Preadolescent

Physical Development

A "resting period," followed by a period of rapid growth in height and then growth in weight. This usually starts sometime between 9 and 13. Boys may mature as much as two years later than girls.

Girls usually taller and heavier than boys.

Reproductive organs maturing. Secondary sex characteristics developing.

Rapid muscular growth.

Uneven growth of different parts of the body.

Enormous but often capricious appetite.

Characteristic Behavior

Wide range of individual differences in maturity level.

Gangs continue, though loyalty to the gang stronger in boys than in girls.

Interest in team games, pets, television, radio, movies, comics. Marked interest differences between boys and girls.

Teasing and seeming antagonism between boys' and girls' groups.

Awkwardness, restlessness and laziness common as result of rapid and uneven growth.

Opinion of own group beginning to be valued more highly than that of adults.

Often becomes overcritical, changeable, rebellious, uncooperative.

Self-conscious about physical changes.

Interested in earning money.

Special Needs

Understanding of the physical and emotional changes about to come.

Skillfully planned school and recreation programs to meet needs of those who are approaching puberty as well as those who are not.

Opportunities for greater independence and for carrying more responsibility without pressure.

Warm affection and sense of humor in adults. No nagging, condemnation, or talking down.

Sense of belonging, acceptance by peer group.

The Adolescent

Physical Development

Rapid weight gain at beginning of adolescence. Enormous appetite.

Sexual maturity, with accompanying physical and emotional changes. Girls are usually about two years ahead of boys.

Sometimes a period of glandular imbalance.

Skeletal growth completed, adult height reached, muscular coordination improved.

Heart growing rapidly at beginning of period.

Characteristic Behavior

Going to extremes, emotional instability with "know-it-all" attitude.

Return of habits of younger child—nail biting, tricks, impudence, day-dreaming.

High interest in philosophical, ethical, and religious problems. Search for ideals.

Preoccupation with acceptance by the social group. Fear of ridicule and of being unpopular. Oversensitiveness and self-pity.

Strong identification with an admired adult.

Assertion of independence from family as a step toward adulthood.

Responds well to group responsibility and group participation. Groups may form cliques.

High interest in physical attractiveness.

Girls usually more interested in boys than boys in girls, resulting from earlier maturing of the girls.

Special Needs

Acceptance by and conformity with others of own age.

Adequate understanding of sexual relationships and attitudes.

Kind, unobtrusive, adult guidance which does not threaten the adolescent's feeling of freedom.

Assurance of security. Adolescents seek both dependence and independence.

Opportunities to make decisions and to earn and save money.

Provision for constructive recreation. Some cause, idea, or issue to work for.

Selecting the Learning Experience

The remote, intermediate and immediate objectives of physical education indicate to the curriculum makers the ultimate direction the program is to take. The needs and characteristics of the students have been categorized into various grade levels. The next logical step is the translation of these needs into learning experiences which will achieve the listed objectives. The selecting of lear ing activities to meet the listed needs for each level probably becomes the most difficult task of the curriculum specialists, and these activities once selected become the very *heart* of the curriculum. There are so many activities from which to select. No student can participate and learn in all the experiences that are available in the areas of sports, games, gymnastics and dance. Some of these activities have more value in meeting the stated needs than others. If one should dichotomize, the activities would fall into those which are developmental in nature and those which are more recreational and have carry-over value.

Curriculum makers in general must make their selection of activities for the various levels based on the needs of students as revealed by certain criteria or principles of selection. In general these principles are based on physiological, psychological and sociological principles. Learning experiences to be selected cannot meet all the criteria and considerations but naturally those will have the greatest value which meet the greatest number of criteria. The following is a list of principles which have been used in the selection of learning experiences:

The principle of validity. The program of activities should be related to the objectives previously stated.

The principle of pupil interest. The activity should satisfy the immediate interest of the student.

The principle of functional utility. The activity should lead on to participation after school, and to further participation as carry-over interest in after-school years.

The principle of maturity. The activity must be within the range of the student's ability as revealed by age, sex and grade.

The principle of variety. The total activities offered must cover a wide variety of games, gymnastics and dance.

The principle of individual differences. There must be activities included in the program which will meet the needs of the exceptional students.

The principle of universality. The activity should be universally accepted and popular.

The principle of hygiene and safety. The activity should be hygienically acceptable and should not present too great a safety hazard.

The principle of relative worth. When choices have to be made between activities, the ones that contribute most in terms of the objectives and needs should be selected.

The principle of administrability. The activity must not make unreasonable demands of space, time, equipment, and leadership.

The principle of progression. The activity should lend itself to levels of learning so that progress is made from the simple to the complex.

The principle of socialization. The activity should provide for social interaction and concomitant learnings, leading to sociability, citizenship and character.

The principle of leadership. The activity should provide opportunities for the development of leadership.

The principle of continuity. The activities should lend themselves to sequential arrangement within each educational level and articulation between levels.

The principle of intensity. The activity should be selected, placed and enough time allotment provided so that it might be learned reasonably well by the student.

The principle of seasonality. The activity should be selected to meet the seasonal interest and drives of youth.

The principle of flexibility. The activities should provide for enough flexibility to take care of geographical and climatic conditions as well as local differences.

The principle of achievement. The activity must be related to the prior level of learning for the student so that he does not repeat the same activities and so that program continuity may proceed.

The principle of practicality. The activity must be selected in terms of time allotment, facilities, and capabilities of the teaching staff. In general, a curriculum should not be based on a dearth of facilities.

The principle of wholeness (totality). All activities selected for any given educational level should provide the experiences which should lead to a physically educated person for that level.

The activities from which curricular experiences are selected cover a wide scope, and they do not lend themselves to easy classification into categories. Any division into categories will always find some activities which do not seem to belong at all or some that could be placed in more than one category. However, classification of activities does serve a useful purpose. Due to the nature of various educational levels as well as the nature of each activity, it would seem feasible to use three different schemes of classification: one for the primary

grades, one for the elementary and one for junior-senior high schools and colleges. See Table 17–1 for a primary classification and Table 17–2 for elementary, and Table 17–3 for junior-senior high school levels.

Grade Placement and Time Allotment

After the activities have been selected, the next step consists of assigning them to the proper educational and grade levels with suggestions concerning time allotment. Because there is no standard amount of time allotment—it might vary anywhere from two to five days per week—the time allotment may be given in terms of percentages for the whole. No doubt much of this procedure of grade placement can be done in conjunction with the selection of the activity to be included. Perhaps this process of placement is the most difficult in curriculum planning. It is one thing for the committee to select volleyball as an activity because of its contribution to the principles of selection. However, it is another thing to decide at what

Table 17–1. Sample Program for the Primary Level (Grades 1–3)

1. Fundamental Movements 20%
    Locomotor: walking, running, skipping, galloping, whirling, swaying.
    Axial: swinging, sustaining, etc.

2. Rhythmic Activities: (Could be combined with locomotor activities if music accompaniment is used.) 20%
    Farmer in the Dell, Looby Loo, Mulberry Bush, Chimes of Dunkirk, Old Roger Is Dead, The Swing, Carrousel, Jolly Is the Miller, Oats, Peas, Beans, etc.

3. Games 30%
    Simple chasing games such as, Cat and Mice, Jack Be Nimble, Squirrel in Trees, Cat and Rat, Hound and Rabbit, Midnight, Lame Fox and Chickens, etc.
    Athletic games such as, boundary ball, dodge ball, hand polo, kick ball, bound ball.

4. Self-testing Activities 30%
    Duck walk, rabbit hop, human rocker, crab walk, forward roll, frog hand-stand, etc.

5. Relays (part of games and/or self-testing section)

TOTAL   100%

    Swimming should be offered here if a pool is available.

Courtesy John M. Cooper (Ed.): *The Physical Education Curriculum (A National Program).* Los Angeles, Calif., College Book Store, 1968.

grade level or levels volleyball will be taught. It is significantly important to find the appropriate level for the introduction of an activity. Critical learning periods need much more study by motor learning specialists. It is equally important to set the sequential progression.

It is at this point that the objectives of the program, the needs and characteristics of the students, and the principles for the selection of learning experiences are combined to determine grade placement and time allotment for the activities. Proper placement for grade or age level for each activity provides the gradual progression from the simple to the more complex in all areas of learning covered by the objectives— skills, fitness, knowledges, and values. This process is known as establishing the *sequence* of the curriculum.

It is entirely proper that some activities appear at more than one grade level or educational level. When this does occur, however, the activity should not be repeated on the elementary level again. When an activity does appear in

Table 17–2.   Sample Program for the Elementary Level (Grades 4–6)

1. Games 50%
    Athletic games
        Basketball type: captain ball, captain basketball, corner ball, line basketball, nine-
            court basketball, newcomb, six-court basketball, six hole basketball, quadruple
            dodge ball.
        Softball type: bombardment, bat ball, circle strike, end ball, fongo, hit pin baseball,
            long ball, one and two old cat, triangle ball, and work up.
        Soccer type: advancement, circle soccer, corner kick ball, field ball, kick ball, punt
            back, rotation soccer, simplified soccer, soccer dodge ball, and soccer keep away.
        Volleyball type: bound ball, feather ball, net ball, school-room volleyball, and
            sponge ball.
    Chasing games
        Bears and cattle, circle chase, gathering sticks, two and three deep, catch of fish, last
            man, pom pom pullaway, all stand, club snatch, cross tag, dare base, duck on a rock,
            prisoner's base, etc.

2. Rhythmic Activities 20%
        Broom dance, Dutch couple dance, Pop Goes the Weasel, Bleking, Virginia Reel,
        Sellengers Round, Ace of Diamonds, Gustaf's Skoal, Seven Jumps, Norwegian Moun-
        tain March, Lottie Is Dead, etc.

3. Self-Testing 30%
        Events: Batting for accuracy, base running, baseball throw for accuracy, basketball
            pass for accuracy—for-goal—for distance, pull up, push up, broad jump, high jump,
            soccer kick for goal—for distance, etc.
        Stunts: Head stand, forward roll, backward roll, cartwheel, heel click, wooden man,
            jump the stick, Indian wrestle, Eskimo roll, front foot flip, knee and toe wrestle,
            hand wrestle, knee spring, elephant walk, triple roll, etc.

4. Relays (Part of games and/or self testing sections)
        Arch ball relay, hopping relay, stunt relays, all-up Indian club relay, over and under
        relay, shuttle relay, stride ball relay, skin the snake relay, etc.

5. Inclement Weather Activities (Games that may be conducted in the classroom.)
                                                                        TOTAL   100%

Courtesy John M. Cooper (Ed.): *The Physical Education Curriculum (A National Program)*. Los Angeles, Calif., College Book Store, 1968.

Table 17–3. Suggested Program by Grades Based on Three Class Periods per Week

WARM-UP AND CONDITIONING ACTIVITIES—
EIGHT TO TEN MINUTES DAILY VARYING THE TYPE ACCORDING TO THE ACTIVITIES BEING STRESSED IN THE PLANNED PROGRAM

BASIC:

GRADE 7	Class Pds.	GRADE 8	Class Pds.	GRADE 9	Class Pds.	GRADE 10	Class Pds.	GRADE 11	Class Pds.	GRADE 12	Class Pds.
Orientation and testing	7	Orientation and testing	7	Orientation and testing	5	Orientation and testing	5	Orientation and testing	5	Orientation and testing	5
Basketball	12	Basketball	12	Basketball	12	Basketball	12	Apparatus	14	Apparatus	14
Soccer	10	Soccer	10	Soccer and/or speedball	10	Soccer and/or speedball	10	Golf	12	Golf	12
Softball	10	Softball	10	Softball	8	Touch football (boys)	10	Swimming and life saving*	12	Swimming and life saving*	12
Touch football (boys)	10	Touch football (boys)	10	Touch football (boys)	10	Volleyball	10	Tennis	12	Tennis	12
Volleyball	10	Volleyball	10	Volleyball	12	Apparatus	12				
Stunts, tumbling type games	10	Stunts, tumbling and beginning apparatus	10	Swimming*	10	Swimming and life saving*	10				
Stunts, tumbling and beginning apparatus	10	Swimming*	10	Track and field	10	Track and field	12				
Swimming*	10	Track and field	10	Tumbling and apparatus	12	Wrestling (boys)	10				
Track and field	10	Body mechanics (girls)	9	Wrestling (boys)	10	Square and social dance	8				
Body mechanics (girls)	9	Folk and square dance	10	Body mechanics (boys)	9	Modern dance	9				
Folk and square dance	12			Folk, square and social dance	9						

SELECTIVE:

GRADE 7	GRADE 8	GRADE 9	GRADE 10	GRADE 11	GRADE 12
Aerial dart	Aerial dart	Badminton	Archery	Archery	Archery
Box hockey	Badminton	Bowling	Badminton	Basketball	Basketball
Games of low organization	Box hockey	Deck tennis	Bowling	Badminton	Badminton
Shuffleboard	Games of low organization	Handball (boys)	Deck tennis	Bowling	Bowling
Table tennis	Horseshoes	Horseshoes	Field hockey (girls)	Field hockey (girls)	Field hockey (girls)
Tetherball	Shuffleboard	Paddle tennis	Handball (boys)	Handball (boys)	Handball (boys)
	Table tennis	Shuffleboard	Horseshoes	Touch football (boys)	Touch football (boys)
		Weight training (boys)	Paddle tennis	Track and field	Track and field
			Softball	Soccer and/or speedball	Soccer and/or speedball
			Weight training (boys)	Volleyball	Volleyball
				Weight training (boys)	Weight training (boys)
				Modern dance (girls)	Modern dance (girls)

*If swimming facilities are not available in the school or community the class periods allotted to swimming should be used for units in selective activities or the expansion of the basic activity units.

Courtesy of State Department of Public Instruction, North Carolina.

the curriculum more than once—this seems to be the rule rather than the exception in most schools—the activity should be presented and taught at levels of progression. Classes must progress in logical sequence and must not be subject to the insipid, monotonous repetition which has been so characteristic of some programs in the past. For example, the first time an activity is taught, it is presented on the *elementary* level, the second time on the *intermediate* level and the third time on the *advanced* level. If, in the judgment of the curriculum planners, an activity has a high rating in meeting the objectives of the program, the needs of the students and the principles of selection, it can be justified in the program a number of times, provided of course that it is taught at different levels of progression. It goes without saying that the activity should be complex enough to justify three levels of progression. It is conceivable that some activities such as dance, gymnastics and aquatics might be included on five levels with the lowest level being *"fundamental"* and the highest *"enrichment."* These two levels would, of course, encompass the other three levels just mentioned—elementary, intermediate, and advanced.

When activities are presented in sequence for proper progression from one grade level to another, the program has continuity. When they are presented so that there is progression from one educational level to another, the program has articulation. Continuity and articulation are the products of a vertical curriculum which conceivably could run upward from kindergarten through college. There is merit to this orderly arrangement inasmuch as it provides for the integration of the necessary learning experiences to achieve the objectives of a physically educated student.

Another type of curriculum which should be mentioned at this time is the horizontal curriculum. It is more of a pupil-centered approach to learning. In this approach the focus is on the pupil rather than on the subject matter. Pupil experiences are centered on large core areas involving several subject matter fields and each subject makes its contribution to the unified experience in its unique way. There is probably more evidence of this type in the elementary school. Where there is an attempt to involve physical education in the "correlation" or "integration" type curricula, it has generally been at the primary or upper elementary levels. The work of Humphrey which was referred to in Chapter 16 provides ideas on how to integrate play and other physical activities with academic fields (12). Of course, it is possible to combine the vertical and the horizontal approach.

Development of the Curriculum Guide

If the curriculum is to function effectively, there must be a summation of all the work of a committee into a curriculum guide, sometimes called a course of study. The guide includes the social and educational philosophy stated briefly, the aim and objectives, the activities listed in sequential arrangement to show progression from one level to the next, methods of teaching and techniques, graded outcomes for each activity at all levels, sources and techniques of evaluation. The published guide can then be used by the teacher as a reference for planning and conducting a comprehensive program which has a definite progression of skills and competencies from grade to grade. The curriculum guide provides the suggested framework or skeleton for the program, and it is left up to the staff to fill in the structure or the meat of the program.

There may be a different guide for each educational level such as primary, elementary and secondary. The best approach is for the guide to carry from kindergarten through grade 12, although smaller guides are easier to handle by teachers. A recognized disadvantage of the curriculum guide is that once published, it is not revised frequently enough. Therefore, while a curriculum is dynamic and changing, a guide is static and lacks flexibility. Perhaps the answer lies in more frequent revisions since the advantages of a guide far outweigh the disadvantages. Perhaps another answer might be a loose leaf publication where new material can be added and old discarded. Also, it can be assumed that good teachers can adapt new ideas and techniques to old guides as a matter of expediency until the revision is published.

The curriculum should provide a yearly plan of activities. Such a plan is shown in Table 17–3 for grades 7–12. This particular yearly program is part of the North Carolina state curriculum guide. It provides for uniformity while maintaining a certain amount of flexibility to meet local conditions and to provide for individual needs (17). To implement this approach so that it will have both scope and sequence, the activities have been dichotomized into *basic* and *selective* categories. The basic part of the program is the one required for every student at any given grade level although time is left at each level for some participation in selected activities. The selective activities are slanted toward carry-over interest. They would be offered only when time, facilities and leadership are available. In studying the chart one will note the junior high school program is predominately basic in nature with only a limited number of selected activities which are offered to give the student the opportunity to explore. The senior high school, however, includes more selective activities as progression takes place. This is in keeping with the principle of electives. There is a recommended time allotment for each

of the basic activities which is based on three periods per week, with 108 days per year.

When the yearly program of activities has been delineated by grade level, the next step in preparation is the development of a unit plan for each of the activities. This plan would consist of a breakdown by days in the total time allotment and the order of presentation of the basic skills for the particular activity. Table 17–4 shows an example of the unit plan (17).

The next step is the daily lesson plan, probably the one most likely to be omitted. It is one, however, that is needed for good teaching. For the inexperienced teacher, it becomes a necessity. Even the experienced teacher must have such a plan in his mind if good teaching is to occur. A lesson plan should include the following (17):

Objectives to be accomplished by the end of the class period

The organization for each activity to make maximum use of all available space and equipment

A record of activities taught in each lesson to aid in planning lessons to follow

Time for review and skill drills if needed

Alternate activities in case of inclement weather or other situations requiring a change of plans

It should be obvious to the student by now that the elementary program is different from the junior and senior high school programs. There is also a difference between grades 1–3 and grades 4–6. Sample curricular experiences are shown for the primary grades in Table 17–1 and for the upper elementary grades in Table 17–2. The student may furthermore note the difference between these two tables and Table 17–3. However, Nixon and Jewett maintain that the core of these elementary programs should focus on movement exploration (16–110) (see Chapter 15).

Table 17–4. Suggested Unit Planning of Instruction for Ninth Grade Soccer*

1st Day	2nd Day	3rd Day	4th Day
Conditioning activity	Conditioning activity	Conditioning activity	Conditioning activity
Review description of the game of soccer	Review skills taught in eighth grade	Review dribbling and passing skills	Review trapping skills
rules	Demonstrate kicking skills:	Demonstrate trapping:	Demonstrate heading skills:
positions	dribbling	legs	side of head
responsibilities of player	passing	heel	heading under ball
general team strategy	Squad practice on kicking skills	stomach	Demonstration of tackling skills:
Relays	Relays	Squad practice trapping	front
		Modified team play	side
			hook
			Squad practice of skills

5th Day	6th Day	7th Day	8th Day
Warm-up activity	Warm-up activity	Warm-up activity	Warm-up activity
Review all skills taught	Review offensive and defensive team play	Team play	Practice basic skills
Work on team play offensive attack defensive tactics	Team play		Team play
Modified team play			

9th Day	10th Day		
Warm-up activity	Warm-up activity		
Knowledge test	Skills test		
Team play	Team play		

* This table is intended to illustrate the various factors involved in planning a complete unit of instruction in a given activity. It is suggestive rather than prescriptive. It is essential that the unit lend itself to modification in order to meet apparent needs. The amount of time given to the teaching of the basic skills will vary from class to class. The total time provided for a given unit should be generally adhered to so that all of the various activities, originally planned for, may receive their proper emphasis.

Courtesy of State Department of Public Instruction, North Carolina.

Evaluation of the Curriculum

The last step involved in the curriculum building cycle or the "merry-go-round" is continuous ongoing *evaluation*. The curriculum is a dynamic instrument and, in the light of changes brought on by many forces and influences, is in a constant state of restudy, revision and being rebuilt. The basis for the orderly but ongoing improvement is evaluation. Every school should provide for some permanent ongoing evaluation and the necessary machinery to keep the cycle turning. This might be the original committee with new riders from time to time. In any event, all staff members must have the opportunity to communicate and relate with the committee. In small staffs, there is no problem. The entire staff becomes the committee.

The process of evaluation will be covered in some detail in the next chapter (Chapter 18) and will only be summarized at this point in relation to the curriculum. Since the curriculum is a democratic process, so are its parts.

Therefore, evaluation should take place in a democratic manner with all staff members involved and any other school personnel who can shed light on the matter. Just as staff members are a part of the need assessment and the design, they must be involved in the evaluation stages. The student still has a role to play here, also, and should be represented as a rider on the merry-go-round for his role in evaluation.

Evaluation can be both a formal and informal type. It can measure the process directly through evaluative criteria being applied directly to the program including rating scales, score cards and inventories. It can measure the process indirectly through the student with the many type tests which will be discussed in the next chapter. If the latter tack is taken, this product, the student, should reflect the quality of the program. A good program should produce a quality student moving toward the ideal of a physically educated person. Regardless of the approach, however, the ultimate purpose of measurement and appraisal is to determine the extent that objectives are achieved. The learning experiences should reflect the objectives, and both should be reflected in the student if the curriculum is a good one under proper leadership.

ADMINISTRATIVE AND ORGANIZATIONAL PROBLEMS FOR IMPLEMENTATION

While *time allotment* and *scheduling* are administrative matters, it is highly related to the curriculum. The usual physical education time allotment for the junior and senior high school is three days per week for a 45–60 minute period. In the elementary school the time allotment is usually a 20–30 minute period meeting daily. Scheduling is reasonably simple in this type school. However, many present schools have moved to a *"flexible scheduling"* system, sometimes referred to as *modular sched-*

uling. This new pattern generally involves fewer periods but of varying lengths. Scheduling may be set up based on a module of time, for example, 20 to 30 minutes. The flexibility comes in when on given days the module of time can be doubled or tripled in size. Generally a class will not meet on a daily basis but will meet two or three times per week for these various length periods. These varying length periods adapt themselves to new methods of teaching which are not possible under the traditional scheduling. In physical education the student will probably spend more time in class activity when he participates in the flexible periods. For example, a class might meet for a 50-minute period on Tuesday and a 100-minute period on Thursday. For the physical education student who spends a large amount of time dressing and showering, there would be a significant gain of approximately twenty minutes more of activity in the two-day flexible program over the traditional three-day program. Flexible scheduling has some other advantages. It can involve classes of varying sizes; classes from two or more instructors may be combined for special lectures, films or instruction.

The curriculum must recognize the importance of *co-education* as part of the program of activity. Co-recreation has now become a standard part of curricular implementation. Most activities other than contact sports are appropriate for both sexes and, with slight modification, these can be adapted to co-education activity. Some caution may be observed in initiating these programs where they have not existed before, but generally such participation with mixed groups has valuable social implication and at the same time is motivated by the natural interests of the students. Co-education classes may have a block of time allotted to them, for example, a three-week period, or they may meet regularly one day each week.

In actuality, the curriculum should provide the scope for three types of programs. With the medical exam as a basis, students are categorically divided into those who are physically able to meet the demands of the regular requirement and those who are not. Those who cannot meet the requirement should be placed in the *"adaptive program"* and a planned program be individualized for each student classified as an individual case. For those who have been given medical clearance, some means of further classification should be provided. Teaching proceeds more effectively and curriculum objectives are more nearly achieved when students are classified into *homogeneous ability groups* based on some type of classification scheme. Such classification would especially provide for the needs of those at the fundamental level and the enrichment level.

Also, at the beginning of the fourth grade there should be a different program for the *sexes*, of course, excluding that part of the program which lends itself to co-education activity. The differences between the sexes after grade three involving anatomical, physiological and psychological characteristics place girls at a disadvantage in participating with and against boys of similar age. Therefore, the sexes should be separated at that time and a different curricular experience provided for each based on their different needs and characteristics.

SOME NEW CONCEPTS AND THEIR IMPLICATIONS FOR CURRICULUM

It was suggested earlier in this chapter that the curriculum maker should not turn his back on the past because there is still much that is good and usable even in the first such program of modern times. However, it would be even more disastrous to ignore the present with its implications for the future. There are new concepts and developments in education and society today which have implications for the curriculum makers and cannot be denied. Some of these have to do with new techniques of teaching and others with organization and administration of the curriculum.

One of the most important of these is *movement education*. The student is now familiar with Chapters 15 and 16 on movement learning. He has learned that while one learns to move, he is also moving to learn. This is an exciting new field and curriculum makers must make use of its various approaches such as *movement exploration* and *concept development* through play, games and related activities. Movement exploration is adapted to the elementary level where its main purpose is to guide pupils in a progressive manner from teacher-directed activities to more child-directed experiences (see Chapter 15). In the concept development through play, Humphrey has shown how children learn concepts in academic areas more readily when they are combined with the movements of play (12).

Another new approach concerns the teaching of the *conceptual framework* or the *cognitive domain* which has now made its appearance for the first time (see *Knowledge and Understanding in Physical Education*) (2). A need for a recognized body of knowledge in physical education has long existed which defines its structure and explores its domain. In tne past a great deal of lip service was given to the "How's" and "Why's" of physical educatio without any common acceptance as to what constituted the concepts and subject matter. A start has now been made in this crucial area and in the years ahead as the knowledge explosion continues unabated, this area will be an important part of the learning experiences designed to meet student needs and must be included in a curriculum.

While the development of *fitness* is not a new concept, there is a new emphasis on it as a result of a number of things (see Chapter 10, Fitness). While Cooper's program on *aerobics* has not invaded the schools to any great extent, it has served as a catalyst to awaken the interest of the public to the need for fitness in the schools. Curriculum makers must assign activities to the program which will meet the fitness objective, serving the needs of the students now and in the future. The implication here, of course, is that the student must learn knowledges and understandings concerning fitness as well as the techniques and methods of gaining fitness so that the acquired attitudes and values will motivate him to self-discipline. This self-direction objective is an important one for the student. To meet the challenge of his complex culture, he will need to have achieved maximum motivation and self-direction if he is to live his life fully where fitness and health are concerned.

Programmed instruction has become a new dimension in teaching in many areas. This approach to learning has been made possible in the academic area through use of the teaching machine and the programmed textbook. The work of Skinner in psychology in *shaping behavior* (one act tending to lead into the next) probably spawned the idea (see Chapter 15) (20). The techniques and methodology of programmed instruction have not been used widely in physical education as yet. Nevertheless, they do offer new vistas. This approach enables the student to move toward mastery of a subject through a series of smaller steps arranged in orderly sequence. He masters one step before proceeding to the next one. He can proceed at his own rate and the process enables hin to receive individual

attention. Penman has developed a program at the college level which might be readily adapted to the secondary level (18). However, a program of motor skills and related activities does not lend itself as well to the programmed teaching methods as the academic areas where teaching machines can be used with immediate feedback of results for the learner. Most motor activities are somewhat weak in the immediate feedback that shows the right or wrong answers of the teaching machine.

Team teaching is a comparatively new approach in the physical education class although it has been employed in athletic coaching for years. Its purpose is to make use of competencies and specialities and thereby increase the quality of teaching. Team teaching at its best presents an integrated pattern of presenting curricular materials by several different staff members where there is cooperation in the planning, teaching and evaluation of a class. The role that each staff member plays on the team is related to all the other roles played by other staff members, and each is a significant part of the whole course. Team teaching does not mean that one staff member teaches swimming to a class for six weeks and then gives way to another instructor for a unit in volleyball instruction. The "team" must work as a unit and could be comprised of several people including experienced veterans, cadet teachers, practice teachers, teacher aides, and supervisors.

Teacher aides and differential staffing are innovations which will probably play a significant role in the future for physical education. With the explosion of population along with the burgeoning cost of education due to inflation and increased use of more sophisticated techniques there is an increased burden on the schools. This is accompanied by an emerging trend on the part of the public to resist increased school taxes. Also, there is a shortage of teachers in many fields related somewhat to the low morale of the teaching profession and its lack of prestige coupled with lack of opportunity for career advancement. One of the many possible innovations to help offset these constellations of problems is, of course, *differentiated staffing.* However, this approach to complicated educational problems has created controversy in spite of the fact that it does offer some answers to the achieving of some educational outcomes which would be too costly under present traditional staffing patterns. Such differentiated staffing would be a means to an end with the end being the increased learning of the student and the upgrading of the status of the teacher. Such staffing would require a major break with traditional methods of certification. Through study and research, the skills, knowledges, and competencies of teaching for a specific field would be categorized into levels and a reclassification of certification based on these categories be made. There are many tasks connected with the teaching of physical education that can be done by teacher aides. Many of them are tasks that do not require highly specialized training but do take time. The idea of training and employing individuals for these various levels of tasks or categories makes sense if it can improve teaching and increase learning to the student at little or no extra cost to the taxpayer. There is much work to be done in establishing these proposed hierarchial roles and seeing that their use is not abused in the name of economy.

One of the most drastic breaks with tradition has been the *nongraded school.* This innovation eliminates the traditional placement of students in school by grades. Pupil progress and promotion in the traditional sense has given way to a program of continuous progress where each pupil moves through the curriculum experiences at his own rate. While there are variations in system, the usual plan calls for four levels of education with three years in each. These correspond to the primary, elementary, junior high school and senior high school. Within each level, however, there are no grades as such; each student may move up the educational ladder at his own ability rate and aspiration level. Achievement tests are used for initial placement and there are frequent retests and evaluation sessions to enable the student to progress. It is obvious that the teaching machine and the team teaching concept would adapt themselves to the nongraded school approach. The physical education curriculum in the nongraded school needs much study and experimentation. Physical education will need to learn much more about student needs and characteristics and then how the sequential arrangement of their activities can become a "best fit" for student needs. For example, when is the best time to present tennis in the curriculum experience and what are the skills that need to be learned in moving from the fundamental to the more advanced levels? Also, how does physical education relate organic values and mental objectives with skill objectives in this approach?

The use of the *digital computer* has added new approaches to education. In the area of curriculum it has future implications for curriculum construction although that is still something for the future. However, in large systems with thousands of students and many courses with multiple sections, the computer can simplify scheduling practices. Flexible scheduling is particularly difficult to implement, but with the computer the necessary information can be fed into the computer as input and within a very short time a master schedule is made available along with an individual schedule for each student.

REFERENCES

1. AAHPER: *Youth and Fitness.* Report of the National Conference on Fitness of Secondary School Youth. Washington, D.C., AAHPER, 1959.
2. AAHPER: *Knowledge and Understanding in Physical Education.* Washington, D.C., AAHPER, 1969.
3. Bookwalter, Karl W., and Harold J. Vander-Zwaag: *Foundations and Principles of Physical Education.* Philadelphia, W. B. Saunders Company, 1969.
4. Bookwalter, Karl W.: *Physical Education in the Secondary Schools.* Washington, D.C., The Center for Applied Research in Education, Inc., 1964.
5. Bucher, Charles A.: *Administration of School and College Health and Physical Programs.* St. Louis, C. V. Mosby Company, 1967.
6. Cassidy, Rosalind: *Curriculum Development in Physical Education.* New York, Harper and Brothers, 1954.
7. Commission on the Reorganization of Education: *Cardinal Principles of Secondary Education.* Department of Interior, Bureau of Education, Bulletin No. 35, 1918. Washington, D.C., U. S. Printing Office, 1928.
8. Conant, James B.: *The American High School Today.* New York, McGraw-Hill Book Company, 1959.
9. Cowell, Charles C., and Helen W. Hazelton: *Curriculum Designs in Physical Education.* Englewood Cliffs, N. J., Prentice-Hall, Inc., 1955.
10. Educational Policies Commission: *The Purposes of Education in American Democracies.* Washington, D.C., National Education Association, 1938.
11. Hetherington, Clark W.: *School Program in Physical Education.* New York, World Book Company, 1905.
12. Humphrey, James H.: *Child Learning through Elementary School Physical Education.* Dubuque, Iowa, Wm. C. Brown Company, 1966.
13. Jenkins, Gladys G., Helen S. Schacter, and William W. Bauer: *These Are Your Children.* Glenview, Ill., Scott, Foresman Company, 1966.
14. Kozman, Hilda Clute, Rosalind Cassidy, and Chester O. Jackson: *Methods in Physical Education.* Dubuque, Iowa, Wm. C. Brown Company, 1967.
15. LaPorte, William Ralph: *The Physical Education Curriculum (A National Program).* Los Angeles, College Book Store, 1968.
16. Nixon, John E., and Ann E. Jewett: *Physical Education Curriculum.* New York, The Ronald Press Company, 1964.
17. North Carolina Public Schools: *Physical Education for the Public Schools of North Carolina.* Raleigh, N. C., State Department of Public Instruction, 1966.
18. Penman, Kenneth A.: *Physical Education for College Students.* St. Louis, C. V. Mosby Company, 1968.
19. Phi Delta Kappa: Curriculum for the 70's. *Phi Delta Kappan,* Vol. LI, No. 7, March, 1970.
20. Skinner, B. F.: *The Behavior of Organisms.* New York, Appleton-Century, 1938.
21. Staley, Seward C.: *Curriculum in Sports.* Philadelphia, W. B. Saunders Company, 1935.
22. Staley, Seward C.: *Sports Education.* New York, A. S. Barnes and Company, 1939.
23. Wilgoose, Carl E.: *The Curriculum in Physical Education.* Englewood Cliffs, Prentice-Hall, 1969.
24. Williams, Jesse Feiring: *The Principles of Physical Education.* Philadelphia, W. B. Saunders Company, 1959.
25. Van Dalen, D. B.: "Coping with Change." *California Association for Health, Physical Education and Recreation Journal,* May–June, 1966.
26. Voltmer, Edward F. and Arthur A. Esslinger: *The Organization and Administration of Physical Education.* New York, Appleton-Century-Crofts, 1967.

Chapter 18

Principles of Evaluation

INTRODUCTION

Evaluation is a term that can be applied to a wide area, and it has broad connotations. In a general way, evaluation is the art and science of judgment or appraisal applied according to preconceived criteria and standards in those criteria. Thus, it deals with judgments and appraisals and is related to criteria and standards.

In Chapter 1 the concept of education was presented as a dynamic ongoing cycle called the "Education Cycle," and evaluation was a distinct phase of that cycle (3–15). It will be recalled that the cycle starts with the establishment of values and the selection of goals, continues with the development of procedures or means to implement the goals, is related to techniques of teaching and methodology, and eventually culminates in judgment or appraisal of results. However, the education cycle does not stop at this point. In the light of data gathered from judgments, there is a review of the values and goals with possible restatement, a restudy and replanning of the procedures and methodology followed by another appraisal of

results, and the whole cycle is repeated again and again in a sequential pattern. Thus, the education cycle is a continuous dynamic circular pattern as shown in Figure 18–1 with evaluation being the final step before the cycle is repeated (3–15).

The figure does not describe the nature of this evaluation, however. Such evaluations are made with reference to the two most important elements of the school: (1) the student who is the *product* of educational procedures and (2) the *process* which includes all those means by which the product is educated.

Therefore the purposes of this chapter are twofold. First, since it follows immediately in the wake of the chapter on curriculum (process), it will be concerned with those principles of evaluation evolving out of the processes of physical education. Second, it will also be concerned with the principles involved in evaluating the product since one way to evaluate the process is through the product. Since the two elements cannot really be separated, there are basic principles which are inexorably related to both.

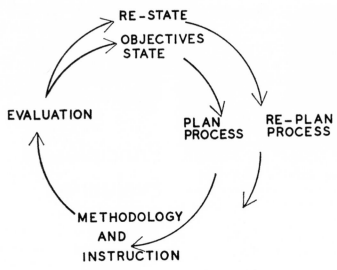

FIGURE 18–1.   The Education Cycle*

DEFINITION OF TERMS

The student should have a clear idea of the terminology in this area of measurement in physical education. When values have been established, when goals have been formulated, and when processes have been planned, it is incumbent on the physical educator to determine how nearly his objectives have been met, how effective his process, and how good is his ultimate value—his product.   This phase of the education cycle is concerned with *tests, measurements* and *evaluation.*   These are techniques used to estimate status, progress and worth in both the process and the product.   They are similar in meaning but they do not have the same connotation and should not be used interchangeably.   The following definitions are suggested:

Test—A technique of measurement and implies a response from the person or thing being measured.

* Barrow, H. M., and Rosemary McGee: *A Practical Approach to Measurement in Physical Education,* 1964.   Reprinted by permission of Lea & Febiger, Philadelphia.

Measurement—A technique of evaluation which makes use of procedures which are precise and objective, and which will result in quantitative data that can be expressed in numerical form.   Measurement may be applied to qualitative traits when its procedures and techniques are objectified (3–20).

Evaluation—Is a process of education which makes use of the techniques of measurements to obtain data either from the product or the process in either quantitative or qualitative form expressed in either objective or subjective manner to be used for comparison with predetermined criteria (3–20).

These definitions imply a hierarchy of terminology.   Evaluation is a process of education, measurement is a procedure of evaluation and a test is a tool of measurement.   Evaluation is broader in meaning than the other terms and its results are generally expressed in more qualitative terms.   Measurement is used as a procedure to obtain status and its results have little meaning until they are used in evaluation. However, when these status measurements are related with some preconceived criteria, evaluation occurs. These criteria run the gamut from a previous measurement to the aims and objectives of the field. Other criteria include norms, standards and expert opinion. Measurement answers the specific questions relative to quantity and quality but evaluation compares these answers with some of the criteria listed above and makes some appraisal regarding that quantity or quality. Measurement is fact finding and is terminal whereas evaluation is continuous and ongoing involving a follow-up with prescription for improvement. Thus, evaluation is a continuous process.

PRINCIPLES OF EVALUATION

Probably no area in education has been more controversial and has been more maligned in the past than the area of measurement and evaluation. There is always the inevitable controversy of how much testing shall be done or for that matter whether any at all shall be done. This question in a sense has little relevancy because in one way or another all educators and physical educators must make use of evaluation in some form. In its wider usage it includes making judgments, estimations and sometimes just plain guesses. It is a fact of life that every teacher must make these evaluations or estimations as he has to make judgments every day about almost everything with which he comes in contact — his students, program, methods of teaching, other people, and even himself. These evaluations may be formal or informal, and objective or subjective. They may even be made unconsciously. The least valid form of evaluation used is a hunch or a guess. The most valid form is the use of scientifically validated tests.

Therefore, the progressive physical educator will formulate a program of planned evaluation as a part of his total program. Just as the curriculum is an ongoing process, so is evaluation. Basic to this planned program is a philosophy of measurement involving guidelines or principles. These principles should provide the framework over which the individual professional will form his own basic beliefs regarding measurement and evaluation. The following principles are vitally important in this planned approach (3–24):

The Product of Physical Education Must Be Determined before Testing and Evaluation Can Become Effective

The product here is the value that has been established by one's philosophy. It is *the physically educated* person defined in Chapter 17 and referred to in Chapter 1. The ideal person becomes the ultimate value and furnishes the criteria for evaluation. This product is a mythical or hypothetical individual whom the school hopes will become the typical. Naturally, achievement levels for this mythical individual will vary with age and sex, and it is true that present standards are not available for all of the necessary levels. This will be a challenge for the future to more nearly pinpoint these levels of achievement for the various educational levels.

The Goals of Physical Education Must Be Defined

It is not enough to know the values which are sought in the product. In the education cycle there must be direction. Education has been defined in Chapter 1 as a change, a modification or an adjustment on the part of the student as a result of educational experience. Thus, if there is education, change is inescapable and if there is change, there must be some direction to that change. In order to insure the proper direction and that the qualities of the ideal physically educated person are achieved, there must be some points of reference. These points of reference are in the nature of goals and have been referred to in Chapter 3 as aims, objectives and outcomes. The procedures of evaluation are used to relate these goals to the values desired.

The Process of Physical Education Should Be Established and Related to the Selected Values and Goals

When the desired product has been conceptualized and the objectives have been established, the next logical step in the education cycle concerns implementation—the achieving of the physically educated person through the objectives. Implementation involves procedures, and when all the procedures are combined, they are called the *process*. Basically, the process includes staff, facilities, equipment, program, methods of instruction, supervision, and administration. These are the prescribed ways and means by which the product becomes physically educated. For each of these aspects of the process there should be acceptable educational criteria. Without these criteria and ancillary standards, it would not be possible to achieve the desired product, since the process is a means to an end—achieving of the physically educated product.

Both the Product and the Process Must Be Evaluated

When the product has been selected, when the goals have been formulated, and when the process has been planned, it becomes necessary to see how well the objectives have been met, how effective the process, and how good the product. This is the phase of the educational cycle that is concerned with tests, measurements and evaluation. These techniques are means to an end and not ends

within themselves. Their ultimate purpose is to determine the worth of the process and the value of the product. Basically, these measurements occur in two ways. They may be used to measure directly either the product or the process. *First*, they may be used to measure the product in order to determine his accomplishments in the hierarchy of objectives which were discussed in Chapter 3. These are: (1) organic development including fitness, (2) neuromuscular development including emphasis on sports, gymnastics and dance, (3) mental development including knowledges and understanding about sports, gymnastics, dance and the physiological "Why's" and "How's" of health and fitness and (4) social learnings and values involving sports with emphasis on sportsmanship. These objectives are measured by applying techniques to determine status, progress, growth, development, adjustment, and achievement.

Second, techniques may be used directly to measure the process of physical education. There are acceptable educational standards for the required program, the intramural program and the interschool program.

All Measurement Is Not Objective

One of the oldest principles in measurement is that all techniques will not give results that are objective. Much of the measurement in physical education does consist of tests which are objective and which render results in terms of inches, feet, times, and seconds. These are quantitative measures and are simple and, in most cases, subject to quick verification. However, there are many qualities and characteristics in physical education which are vitally important but which cannot be measured by objective techniques, and their results cannot be expressed in quantitative terms. Some of these are related to social man and his values. These are the intangibles of character and personality of the product—such qualities as dependability, sociability, courage, courtesy, sportsmanship, cooperation, leadership, citizenship, and the like. No one will deny that these traits exist and that perhaps they are far more important in living the "good life" than are some of the more tangible and objectively measured traits. The entire area of affective learnings involving values, attitudes, appreciations, and ideals falls into this category. Also, there are other facets of both the product and process which do not lend themselves to objective measurement. For example, skills in diving and gymnastics, the dance and qualitative aspects of program, methodology, and instruction. There is another well-known principle which gives some light at this point. It states that whatever exists, exists in amounts, and if it exists in amounts, it can be measured. Therefore, those traits and qualities which are important in physical education—both in the product and the process—can be measured. If they do not lend themselves to the use of objective techniques, there are subjective techniques which can be used or devised by the ingenious teacher. When this is done, however, the subjective techniques should be quantified as much as possible. Rating scales are one of the best ways to quantify results in measuring intangible factors.

Testing and Measurement Do Not Take the Place of Teaching

The basic function of the teacher is to teach and tests and measurements are merely techniques to help make that teaching more effective. While the majority of the teacher's time should be devoted to instruction, it is inevitable that some testing will be done. Testing will probably become a dynamic learning experience for the student. The trained teacher will organize testing as a part of the instructional program and will frequently be teaching while he is testing. When this is done, testing serves more than one purpose and the time devoted to it should never be considered as wasted. Testing then becomes an educational activity in itself like any other procedure of education. Some tests have "developmental value" for the student, and the administration of the test constitutes teaching in a direct sense. While there is no arbitrary rule in the matter of time allotment, it is generally conceded that testing should take no more than ten percent of instruction time. However, once again, if the tests serve in a multiple role as a teaching device and a measuring instrument, this percentage may be increased. In some instances, a test's results may be used for classification, partial grading, guidance and motivation while the test itself serves as a skill drill. In this context, good teaching involves testing, and in the same way most testing can be teaching.

Tests and Measurements Should Be Used for a Purpose

Testing for the sake of testing is wasteful of time and energy for both student and teacher. Therefore, testing must become a means to an end, and it must have a specific purpose or purposes. When measurement is applied to the product, its results can be used for such purposes as grading, classification, guidance, motivation, appraisal of knowledge, research, and program evaluation. When measurement is applied to the process, values may be reviewed, objectives restated, program revised, instruction improved, and methods changed. In all these uses except research, the results have been related to some predetermined criteria or standard and thus, evaluation has taken place. A follow-up to test results has been made.

Evaluation and Measurement Are Necessary for Advancement in Scientific Physical Education

It is axiomatic that in all fields of endeavor today progress is related to the development of sound measurement techniques and methods of evaluation. Medicine is one of the best examples where diagnosis, prescription and treatment were raised above the level of the medicine man and a guess, when such instruments as the thermometer and the electrocardiograph were invented for accurate measurements. However, it would be naive to assume that the field of measurement in physical education does not have shortcomings. Many tests and measures are valid and reliable instruments. On the other hand many are crude measures in the first place and are lacking in validities along with being too time-consuming for practical use. Also, it seems that undue emphasis may be placed on tests which can be scored objectively. Much research is still needed to develop valid and usable measurement procedures for the advancement of scientific physical education. However, in the meantime evaluations will continue to be made in those areas where measurement is weakest either on an incidental or perhaps even an unconscious basis.

Evaluation Must Be Conducted by Qualified Personnel

The point was made in the chapter on curriculum development that many different people should take part in program evaluation. This statement holds true equally well in other facets of measurement and evaluation. In the final analysis, however, it is the person who has the training in its procedures and practices who can carry the load and conduct an effective measurement and evaluation program. There are certain competencies concerned with knowledges and practices used to implement the principles just discussed. The trained professional should have the following competencies (3–28):

1. The teacher must know the availability of measurement instruments. This includes knowing what techniques are available and where the information for their effective use can be found.

2. The teacher must know how to evaluate and select the right test for the specific purpose.

3. The teacher must know how to administer tests so that data are valid and reliable, and so that time has not been wasted.

4. The teacher must know how to interpret test results to himself, the student, the parent, and the administrator.

5. The teacher must know the uses of test data both for the product and the process. He must know the precise purpose for which results are to be used before he can select his test.

6. The teacher must be able to construct measurement instruments of his own for both knowledge and physical performance tests as well as social ratings. This competency is necessary until the gaps are closed by research.

7. The teacher must have a knowledge of statistics if he is to interpret his test results effectively, establish his own local norms, or construct his own test.

8. The teacher must know how measurement relates to the total educational program so that he can visualize the relationship between his teaching and his evaluation, and how they both fit into the complex educational cycle. In this context, he must know what constitutes a good program and the criteria by which it will be judged.

USES OF MEASUREMENT RESULTS

One of the principles of evaluation was that the results of testing and measuring must be used for a purpose. Also, one of the competencies needed by the teacher was to know how to use such results. The primary use of a test is to determine *status*. If it is used again with the same group, it could show *progress* or *achievement*. If test results— either status or progress—are compared with predetermined criteria such as norms or standards, they show how the student or the program relates to other students or programs, or how they either could relate to goals or objectives. The ultimate purpose of a test, however, is to serve the needs of the student. The secondary uses of measurement vary with the product or the process.

Uses of Tests to Measure the Product

1. GRADING. Perhaps test scores are used more often for grading than for any other purpose. However, the student should not confuse the two. Grading may be an end of measurement but it is a means in education. While many techniques of measurement can be used for grading, measurement is far broader in scope than grading and more comprehensive. Grades are symbols of achievement, and they represent a teacher's evaluation of the student in terms of objectives and outcomes.

2. CLASSIFICATION. Classification is the placement of students in groups for a specific purpose. This purpose generally requires homogeneous grouping but on occasion heterogeneous grouping may best fit the situation. The classification or grouping is generally accomplished by the use of motor ability tests, fitness tests, sport skills tests, or some growth and development type scheme. The benefits and values derived from such grouping of students more than offsets the time devoted to testing. There are several steps in the implementation of a classification scheme. In logical order these steps are: medical examination, grade, sex, and ability. In survey type programs where activities change frequently, classification can best be im-

plemented by some general ability such as fitness, motor ability, strength, or age, weight and height. When the activities carry through a semester, classification is more effective through the sport skill test or rating for that sport.

3. GUIDANCE. One of the competencies of the teacher in testing was the interpretation of test results. While the teacher's role in interpretation is broader than guidance, guidance and counseling do become one of the primary uses of test results for the teacher. In fact for the trained teacher, the whole area of testing is inexorably related to guidance and counseling, and evaluation can become a key factor in motivation which enhances the climate for guidance. There are three different type tests which have been used for guidance in physical education.

Diagnostic Tests. These are designed to identify weaknesses, and as a general rule should be a comprehensive battery sampling for levels of innate or potential performance. Such tests should be the basis of the physical educator's program because they determine status; this status determines individual need. Need, in turn, is the starting point for individualizing the student's program. Perhaps some of the innovations mentioned under curriculum such as flexible scheduling, differential staffing and nongraded schools can help. When diagnostic tests are suitable they may be administered again to indicate progress.

It is highly motivating to the student and helpful for the instructor in counseling if the student's performance can be kept on a card with a profile of his performances. The profile indicates weaknesses and provides for counseling opportunities. The student sees where he stands compared with his peers, and most of all, it shows his improvement in a graphic way.

Prognostic Tests. These are designed to ascertain levels of innate or potential performance. These tests would involve the ultimate capacity and could presumably predict an individual's potential ability. While such tests would be highly desirable and useful in physical education, there are none which are sufficiently valid to be used at the present time. This is a fertile field for the researcher.

Proficiency Tests. These are designed to determine levels of performance needed to excuse students from a part of or all of a physical education requirement. In the future these type tests will be used more at the college level to pass students out of the general requirement and more at the junior and senior high schools as standards for promotion. In nongraded schools they could be used for progression from one proficiency level to another.

4. MOTIVATION. Practically all tests in physical education activity are of the self-testing type. The student has a built-in urge to test himself and is motivated to do so. He may test himself against norms for his peer group or against his own past performance. The important thing is that he show some progress. It is a principle of learning that students will learn more rapidly and be motivated to higher levels of performance when there is self-knowledge of results, or a feedback of results in the form of test scores (see Chapter 16). Actually, motivation and guidance are related because good guidance should lead to better motivation.

5. PROGRAM EVALUATION. The program or process of physical education can be measured in either one of two ways. It can be measured directly by applying techniques to the process itself, or it can be measured indirectly by applying techniques to its product, the student. Studies have shown that there is an inextricable relationship between the process and the product (4). This simply means that a good student is the result of a good process and by the same token a good process should be reflected by a good student. If students measure up to high standards on tests over sports skills, fitness, knowledges and social values, it may be assumed that there is a good process basic to these achievements.

6. RESEARCH. Most testing of the product is done primarily to serve the needs of the student in a direct manner for the reasons given in the first four of these uses. However, the product is frequently tested for purposes of research. The use of test data for research may be incidental to their uses for other purposes such as grading, classification or guidance. On the contrary, the data may be collected and used primarily for research. In this case, testing is still being done to serve the needs of the student in an indirect manner. When such testing is done, the researcher sets up research designs seeking answers to questions which could lead to new approaches, new methods and different programs. If the research results enhance the program, testing still serves the needs of the students. Frequently, it is the teacher who is the researcher, and this can be a stimulus to professional growth. More often, however, such research testing is done by someone other than the teacher. Since research is time-consuming and requires some interest and aptitude, many teachers feel they can't spare the time, or they don't feel qualified.

Uses of Tests to Measure the Process

It was pointed out in the last unit that the process could be measured indirectly through the student or directly by applying measurement techniques directly to the entire process or to facets of it. This unit will be concerned with this direct approach in discussing uses.

1. FOR PROGRAM EVALUATION. The program here actually refers to the curriculum—the sequential arrangement

of activities for all levels. The purposes of evaluation are multiple but the basic aim is to see how well the curriculum is meeting the objectives which were established for it. This is an ongoing study starting immediately with the initiation of the curriculum and continues as long as it is in use. The procedures of evaluation are varied and many, and the individuals involved in using them encompass all the staff members.

2. IMPROVEMENT IN METHODOLOGY. The purpose of this approach to evaluation of the process is to look not at the program itself, but at the various methods of implementing it. Usually there is no right way or method of instruction, but many. However, some teachers work better in particular situations than others. Evaluation helps in identification of the best methods. Methodology, like curriculum, is not static; it is constantly changing as new techniques and new approaches to teaching are tried out. New methods need to be evaluated and compared with the old.

3. IMPROVEMENT OF THE TEACHER. The first approach to process evaluation placed emphasis on the curriculum, the second on the implementation of the curriculum through methodology, and the third approach is teacher evaluation. Teacher evaluation basically can be dichotomized into two categories with respect to uses: (1) for the improvement of the teacher and thereby instruction and (2) for sound administrative decisions affecting teachers such as salary, promotions, tenure, re-employment, placement, and transfers. This last category deals with merit, long a highly controversial and much studied aspect of educational processes. Regardless of which approach is used, however, the one overriding goal of such evaluation is improvement of teaching. There are many facets to such evaluations. It would seem that a logical sequence of steps would start with self-evaluation by the teacher, evaluation of the teacher by one or more evaluators, review and discussion between the teacher and the evaluator, and, of course, hopefully the follow-up where emphasis is on self-correction. If the merit system is in use, there must always be a procedure for adjudication of disputes.

4. MOTIVATION. While the purpose of motivation alone may not be just cause for an evaluation of the processes of physical education, the in-service training value of such a study to staff members is incalculable. The knowledge concerning programs, methodology and self-knowledge through teacher evaluation not only makes the individual staff member a more informed person, but also a more committed and dedicated one. Also, the esprit de corps that can come from a self-study and replanning makes for a more integrated staff.

5. RESEARCH. Process evaluation is frequently carried out in the schools for purposes of research. Some projects can be limited to local city or county units but others are statewide or even national in scope. The best known such national project is the survey using the LaPorte's Health and Physical Education Score Card No. II (6). These were a series of studies directed by Karl Bookwalter (4). Data were collected from 26 states and national norms have been established on the score card as a result of the research.

6. GAIN ADMINISTRATIVE UNDERSTANDING AND SUPPORT. Frequently the physical educator needs to communicate with his administrator concerning his program or particularly proposed programs. If he needs support for these programs, he will need to be armed with objective data when he presents his case. If program objectives are to be achieved, the understanding and the support of the administrator are necessary. In today's schools there is competition within the school for both

money and time. The administrator will generally support those programs which can justify their worth by showing how they contribute to the desirable changes which education seeks in the lives of the students.

SELECTION OF TESTS

One of the competencies of testing for the teacher is knowing how to evaluate and select tests and measures. There are many tests available from which the teacher may choose. Therefore, it is essential that a good selection be made. In the first analysis the choice of a test will depend on the information desired by the teacher. If a test is to be efficient, it must be used with a specific purpose in mind. A test must measure with accuracy and honesty whatever it does measure and do so with efficiency. It is this honesty which is inherent in the purpose for which the test is used. Therefore, the teacher must have a knowledge of the selective criteria for tests and these criteria will enable him to choose the appropriate test for his specific purpose. Recognized criteria for selection may be classified into two categories: *Technical Standards* and *Practical Standards* (3–38).

Technical Standards

The technical standards are generally arrived at through statistics and will have been established during the original development of the test by the test maker, or at least prior to the time of publication and use. If these standards are not furnished by the test maker or if they are too low to meet acceptable standards, the test may be valueless for the purpose for which it was chosen, or at least it should be used with extreme reservation. The technical standards include the three little words of *validity*, *reliability* and *objectivity* (13). These standards for a test are generally expressed through a correlation coefficient.

Table 18–1.   Arbitrary Standards for Interpreting Correlation Coefficients*

Coefficients	Validity	Reliability and Objectivity
.95 to .99		excellent
.90 to .94		very good
.85 to .89	excellent	acceptable
.80 to .84	very good	acceptable
.75 to .79	acceptable	poor
.70 to .74	acceptable	poor
.65 to .69	questionable (except for very complex tests)	questionable (except for groups)
.60 to .64	questionable	questionable (except for groups)

* From Barrow, Harold, M., and Rosemary McGee: *A Practical Approach to Measurement in Physical Education.* Philadelphia, Lea & Febiger, 1964.

Table 18–1 shows some coefficients for the three criteria of validity, reliability and objectivity and some arbitrary standards. Another technical standard is *norms* (3–42).

1. VALIDITY. Validity is the *honesty* with which a test measures whatever it does measure. This is the most important of the selective criteria because if a test does not measure what it is purported to measure, the teacher cannot place confidence in test results. If a test is purported to be a measure of basketball skills but is so complex and demanding physically that fitness factors weigh heavily in the performance scores, it would be unfair to use the results to assign grades in basketball skills. Therefore, a test is valid only when it measures accurately whatever it is described as measuring. This is conclusive evidence that validity is inherent in the purpose of a test. There are numerous methods of establishing validity but they are too technical for discussion at

this point. However, in general, validity coefficients are found by the test maker comparing (relating, correlating) his test with a criterion. This criterion may be a previously validated test, composite scores, subjective ratings, and tournament standings.

2. RELIABILITY. If validity is the honesty with which a test measures whatever it does measure, reliability is the consistency with which it does it. If a test is reliable, similar results will be obtained when the test is repeated by the same group under the same conditions. This is called the test-retest method and it, too, can be found by correlating the results of the two administrations of the same tests to the same groups. Thus, reliability is inherent in the performance of the test.

3. OBJECTIVITY. Objectivity is related to the personal influence of the instructor in scoring. By definition it is the degree to which two or more scorers can obtain the same results. A correlation coefficient can be found by relating scores obtained by each instructor on the same testing period.

4. NORMS. Norms are averages and are generally in the form of scale scores used to convert raw scores to some more meaningful form. Most raw scores are meaningless and cannot be compared or added. Test results have meaning only when raw scores have been compared with norms and converted into more meaningful scores which can be compared and interpreted. The most common way for norms to appear is in the form of scale scores placed in scoring tables. The type of scale scores generally used are percentiles and some form of standard score such as T-score, Six-Sigma score, Stanines, Hull scale and C-scale. Percentiles are better understood and interpreted by teachers but such scores from different tests cannot be compared or added. The standard score has these advantages.

Practical Standards

It is important to be realistic in the selection of tests. A test may meet all of the technical standards in an acceptable manner but for many reasons may not be suitable because of practical considerations. Practical standards are more immediate than the technical ones and can be divided into two categories: *administrative considerations* and *developmental values*.

1. ADMINISTRATIVE CONSIDERATIONS. In selection of a test there are a number of administrative problems to be considered. These are concerned with the amount of supplies, equipment and facilities that are required. They are also concerned with the amount of time required to administer the test. It may be that too much of the students' or teacher's time is required. Leadership can be a problem in test administration. Are there enough qualified leaders available to administer the test effectively? Another consideration may be cost in money. Some tests are highly specialized and require expensive equipment. The utility of the test may be another consideration. Is there a quick and accurate way to convert the raw scores to more meaningful terms and then interpret the final results to the students? Can the data be used for more than one purpose—for example, classification, grading and guidance with a single test? Also, does the test produce disagreeable psychological and physiological reactions in the students? Any one of these administrative considerations might eliminate an otherwise highly desirable and valid test. It is logical to use the simplest to administer and least time-consuming test if it can meet the technical standards adequately.

2. DEVELOPMENTAL VALUES. While this consideration may not be as immediate as the administrative one, it could still have some weight in the selection of one test over another. Some tests in-

volve learning and, therefore, the teacher is teaching while he is testing thereby making better use of the allotted time. Also, some tests seem to be more challenging than others and as a result students are motivated to try harder not only on the test but in learning the skills or developing the qualities for which the test is a measure. Thus, tests promote learning and some are said to have developmental value. In general, most motor performance tests seem to fall into this category. It is probable that the social evaluation instrument could become a valuable learning medium under the right leadership.

ADMINISTRATION OF TESTS

One of the competencies mentioned earlier was knowing how to administer tests. This has been one of the weaknesses of professional people; it seems due to inadequate preparation in the techniques and recommended practices for administering tests. It is an essential facet of good teaching that after a test has been selected, it should be administered to the students in such manner that resulting scores will be valid and reliable and so that time has not been wasted. This kind of efficiency is a result of step-by-step planning and careful preparation on the part of the teacher and is based on sound knowledge of techniques and practices. One of the essential points in testing is the conservation of time. Unless careful planning is done, testing can take much more than its proportional share of the time allotment, or else, in order to prevent this, the overall testing program must be curtailed.

The knowledges, techniques and practices which will be needed in test administration can be used by the instructor to prepare a lesson plan or a procedural approach. These procedures for successful administration can be listed under the following three headings (3–52):

(1) *advanced preparation* such as deciding on the purpose or purposes of the test, selecting the appropriate test, assembling equipment and supplies, preparing facilities, preparing score cards, standardizing directions, developing organization and administration procedures, selecting class organization, selecting scoring procedures, orienting the students, and training the student leaders; (2) *duties during testing* include such facets as warm-up procedures, demonstration, explanation, scoring, safety, and encouragement to the laggard, and (3) *duties following testing* include converting raw scores to scale scores by means of scoring tables, interpreting results to the students and planning for the follow-up.

MEASUREMENT OF THE PRODUCT

Evaluation in general can be more easily understood if it is categorized into those measurements dealing with evaluating the *product* and those dealing with the *process*. The matter of the product will be dealt with first.

Among the principles of measurement which were discussed earlier are these two. Before evaluation can become effective, the ideal product must be determined. After the processes of physical education have been applied, the student must be evaluated in terms of the ideal. This evaluation takes place with respect to various facets of the student. While the concept of unity of the individual and his organismic entity is the consistent theme throughout this book, it might seem there is a departure from this concept as the individual is segmented for measurement. In evaluating the student, however, expediency dictates that he be divided into parts and the parts be measured separately. This part method of evaluation is an educationally sound procedure because it is learned from psychology that, while the student may be viewed as a whole, he must learn specifics. Therefore, it is these specifics which must be measured. However, this part method of evaluation is educationally sound only if the instructor fully comprehends the unity concept of the student and understands that, contrary to a well-known mathematical principle, the sum of the parts adds up to something more than the whole when human entities are at stake.

As the teacher looks perceptively at the parts of his students in relation to the whole after measurement, he should see something more than skills, fitness, knowledge and social behavior. While his knowledge of each of these facets will provide insights, it is not until they are welded together through a process of synthesis or integration that the whole is revealed and this whole—this personality with its accompanying self-image—is more than any summation of the parts that have been measured. This is a plea for the teacher always to be aware of the unique individual personality of each student as he interprets and follows up his test scores which have been collected from his students when they have been fragmented for educational purposes.

While the objectives take into account the unity concept, it is all too easy for the teacher to view the student and teach him entirely in terms of a physical being. Inherent in the objectives, however, are the areas of learning including knowledges, skills, fitness, and social and emotional patterns. These have been referred to by Staley as the controls of conduct (14). An individual's behavior, physically, mentally, and socially, depends on the extent to which these controls have been acquired. Learnings in the area of physical education are classified into psychomotor, cognitive and affective.

Psychomotor learnings involve movement in its varied forms and chiefly concern skills, dance and fitness activities.

Cognitive learnings concern the knowledges which surround sports, gymnastics, dance and fitness.

Affective learnings concern patterns of behavior as shown by the emotional and social self.

Thus, learning in physical education is a many-faceted thing. Broadly speaking, these traits or components which should be learned or acquired are included in the ultimate values which have been established for the physically educated person. The physically educated person is more than one educated in movement. Being physically educated involves this "whole" student and while learning comes primarily through movement in the form of sports, dance, fitness activities, and the like, it encompasses far more than skills and fitness. It involves the unified person and influences the total person. This unity concept operates in all physical education activities as the student learns and acquires specificities but his whole being is affected because these particulars are all interrelated. Therefore, when measurements are made by the instructor over these particulars, let him not forget to evaluate the student also as an entity. If skills served no other purpose than skills, there would be little excuse for them to occupy so much of the educational processes.

For purposes of this chapter the measurement of the product will be discussed under the three basic areas of learning in physical education.

Evaluating Psychomotor Learnings

The psychomotor learnings area basically encompasses the physical development or organic objectives along with the motor skill development objective. These areas cannot be discussed fully since the techniques of measurements do not come within the scope of an introductory and principle book. Some of the most used and recognized techniques for the various facets are listed below and if students seek more information regarding them, it can be found in the references at the end of the chapter.

1. FITNESS TESTS. Most fitness tests in physical education are actually motor fitness tests. There are many more tests than are mentioned here since only those tests are listed which are most frequently used.

> AAHPER Youth Fitness Test
> California Fitness Test
> Glover Physical Fitness Test for Primary Grades
> Harvard Step Test
> Indiana High School Fitness Test
> Indiana Motor Fitness Index
> Illinois Motor Fitness Tests
> Kraus-Weber Test of Muscular Fitness
> Motor Fitness Tests for Oregon Schools
> New York State Physical Fitness Tests
> North Carolina Fitness Test

2. CARDIOVASCULAR TESTS:

> Cooper's Aerobics Point System
> Cureton's All-Out Tread Mill Run
> Schneider Cardiovascular Test
> Tuttle Pulse Ratio Test

3. ANTHROPOMETRIC, BODY TYPE AND POSTURE TESTS:

> Meredith Physical Growth Record
> New York Posture Test
> Somatotype
> Wetzel Grid

4. STRENGTH:

> Cable Tension Strength Tests
> Larson Dynamic Strength Test
> Rogers Strength Test

5. GENERAL MOTOR ABILITY TESTS:

> Barrow Motor Ability Tests
> Brace Test of Motor Ability
> Carpenter Test of Motor Ability
> Cozens Test of General Athletic Ability
> Humiston Test of Motor Ability for Women
> Larson Test of Motor Ability for Men
> McCloy Test of Motor Ability
> Scott Test of Motor Ability for Women

6. MOTOR EDUCABILITY TESTS:

> Brace Motor Ability Test
> Carpenter Test of Motor Educability for Primary Grade Children

> Johnson's Test of Motor Educability
> Iowa Revision of the Brace Motor Ability Test

7. MOTOR CAPACITY TESTS:

> McCloy General Motor Capacity Test

8. SPORT SKILLS TESTS:

Numerous sport skills tests are described in the literature and there are still others the descriptions of which have not been published. The most ambitious project is the AAHPER Sports Skills Project which has developed or is developing sport skill batteries for the following activities: archery, badminton, baseball, basketball, bowling, football, golf, gymnastics, field hockey, softball, swimming, tennis, track and field, and volleyball. The batteries which have already been completed present acceptable standards in test criteria and have the further advantage of national norms. Other skill tests which may be found in the literature and which have been used widely are:

Archery:

Hyde Achievement Scale in Archery

Badminton:

French-Stalter Badminton Skill Tests
Lockhart-McPherson Badminton Test
French Short Serve Test (Badminton)

Basketball:

Leilich Basketball for Girls
Johnson Basketball Test (Men)
Knox Basketball Test (Men)
Lehsten Basketball Test for Men

Field Hockey:

Schmithals-French Field Hockey Tests
Friedel Field Hockey Test
Strait Rating Scale for Field Hockey

Golf:

Vanderhoof Golf Test
Brown Test of Golf

Handball:

Cornish Handball Test

Softball:

Fringer Softball Battery
New York State Softball Test
Repeated Throws (softball)

Soccer and Speedball:

McDonald Soccer Test
Schaufele Soccer Volleying Test

Smith Speedball Test
Warner Test for Soccer Skills

Swimming:

Cureton Swimming Tests
Hewitt Swimming Achievement Scales
Wilson Achievement Test for Intermediate
  Swimming

Table Tennis:

Mott-Lockhart Backboard Test

Tennis:

Broer-Miller Tennis Test
Dyer Tennis Test
Scott-French Revision of the Dyer Wallboard
  Test

Volleyball:

Brady Volleyball Test for Men
Russell-Lange Volleyball Test

Evaluating Cognitive Learnings

The point was made in discussing psychomotor learnings that being physically educated meant more than being educated in movement, and that all facets of the individual are interrelated. This is illustrated when a specific skills pattern is learned and there are knowledges associated with the activities that are acquired at the same time. Therefore, mental learnings will take place as a corollary to activities but those knowledges which are desirable should not be left to chance alone.

The knowledges that are most common in the areas of associated learnings growing out of sports, gymnastics, dance, and fitness activities are: rules, techniques, strategy, terminology, historical background, equipment and facilities, game codes and etiquette, and the values to the participant inherent in the activity. Most of this information seems necessary before satisfying and effective participation can be experienced in the activity. Also, there are certain other knowledges which would seem essential if the student is to achieve continuing and intelligent participation. These are the "why's" and the "how's" of physical education with emphasis on the importance of fitness, how one becomes fit and how to maintain fitness.

The generally accepted way of evaluating cognitive learnings is through written tests which may be either of the teacher-made type or the standardized type. A standardized test is constructed by experts who present supporting validities and reliabilities and frequently test norms. The teacher-made tests generally do not provide these supports, but they still can have great value at the local level in measuring what has been taught in the program. It is for this reason that the competency of developing one's own written tests has been emphasized so highly. With the new publication prepared under the direction of the AAHPER, *Knowledge and Understanding in Physical Education,* there are standardized achievement tests at three levels to measure achievement in the information (1). The tests were developed and norms were prepared by the Educational Testing Service of Princeton, N. J. These two projects have not only given a big lift to the area of cognitive learnings, but also to the body of knowledge for the field and its evaluation. There are many other standardized tests over sports from archery to volleyball. However, none except the tests of ETS have national norms. National norms add a new criterion to evaluation —a teacher can compare the performance of his students with the national sample. There are also many standardized health tests which are available for practically all educational levels.

Evaluating Affective Learnings

Movement activities involving sports, gymnastics, dance and fitness activities are inevitably accompanied by social and emotional learnings. A widespread idea in the field is that, since these learnings may be concomitant, they do not require planning or a specially designed program. By the same token, people who give only lip service to the social objectives, do little evaluation with respect to it. However, in being consistent once again with the unity concept and with the values that have been established for the physically educated student, the unity mosaic is not complete until the social value objective begins to receive a just share of attention in program planning, instruction and evaluation. The justification is simple.

When the student engages in any kind of movement experience, something happens to him physically, but something also happens to him mentally and socially. The emotional learnings include attitudes, appreciations and values. These social "happenings" are inevitably present and cannot be excluded from the movement learning experience (see Chapter 14 on Values). They are going to take place—good or bad—whether the instructor is aware of them or not. In order to insure that positive learnings may take place, there has to be a planned program and a method of instruction. It is interesting to note that while elaborate programs and methodology have been devised to develop skill, fitness and knowledges, no uniform approach has been made to the teaching of these emotional and social patterns except as they accrue as by-products of the environment. It is generally expected that these patterns of behavior are "caught" from identification models such as the teacher, coach or sports hero.

In being consistent with the principle of evaluation, there should be a definite place in the program for teaching values. This should not be too difficult since physical education is abundantly rich in opportunities for social experiences. Then, if these values are to be taught, as a part of the physical education program, measurement becomes necessary.

It would be misleading to imply that these traits can be measured by the same objective and scientific techniques which are used so freely in the areas of cognitive and psychomotor learnings. Objective techniques for this area are not readily available. The entire area is concerned with the human value aspects; these are personal, inconsistent and highly subjective. Such values can only be observed through behavior and behavior is inconsistent. Measurement becomes difficult because of the complexity of the factors and the subjectivity of the techniques. The various components in which the physical educator is interested are inexorably related to others and exist as factors within a complex of interrelationships with many other factors. This makes it difficult to isolate them completely, to identify and measure them as distinct factors. It is difficult to isolate an attitude and measure it without the influence of many other distracting factors. Thus, attitudes and values are not always consistent since they are influenced by other relationships. In other words, a student does not always respond or behave in the same way to the same social stimulus, nor does he always behave as he says he would behave.

It would be misleading to evaluate one's program in social values training through the response of students on social measures. It is impossible to tell how much may be due to other influences. Since the social objective is a shared one, it is possible that the good sportsmanship revealed on a sportsmanship test or rating, or in a game situation, is an outcome of a well-adjusted home, Sunday School or the YMCA or a recreation's little league baseball or a class in English. Physical education has no monopoly on social and moral training. However, physical education does have a unique opportunity to teach these values due to the informal laboratory situations of the gym and play-field, and the highly dramatic appeal of its subject matter. Since there is the opportunity, there should be the commitment.

Measurement instruments for evaluating social learnings fall into two categories: (1) those which call for the student to make the response himself and (2) those which call for a response about the student made by someone else (3–369). If the measurement process is to be most effective as a learning situation, the student should make the responses himself. In this way he becomes more aware of the values worthy of being attained in physical education. However, scales used by the teacher could be interpreted to the student and thus could serve a similar purpose. Perhaps the teacher with ingenuity could construct his own social evaluation scale in the form of a rating device. The ratings could be made objective and fairly accurate measurements be made in quantitative form.

The following instruments have been used to evaluate social learnings (3–369):

Action-Choice Tests for Competitive Sports Situations
Cowell Personal Distance Scale
Cowell's Outcomes of Sports: An Evaluation Check-Sheet
Cowell Social Adjustment Index
Blanchard Behavior Rating Card
Barrow Evaluation Score Card
Mercer Attitude Inventory
Kneer Attitude Inventory and Diagnostic Statements
Carr Attitude Inventory
McGee Scale to Measure Attitudes Toward Intensive Competition for High School Girls

EVALUATION OF THE PROCESS

Two principles of evaluation state that the educational processes must be established, and then they must be evaluated. These processes can be evaluated to some extent by measuring their product, and a positive relationship is shown between the quality of the process and the quality of the student (4). Studies show that achievement of students in the objectives of physical education is highly related to the school's attainment in acceptable standards. If students score high on tests of sport skills, fitness, knowledge, and attitude, it may be reasonable to expect that a good process of physical education is behind such achievement. Also, if the school's physical education process attains a high rank on rating scales or score cards pertaining to standards of physical education, it might be reasonable to expect its students to do well on achievement tests in sport skills, fitness and knowledges. This last statement implies that there are recognized standards for the process. Therefore, there may be times when an evaluation of the process directly would reveal more specific information than indirectly through the student. It seems expedient at times that the process be evaluated in a direct manner.

Just as the student is fragmented for measurement, so is the process. The process is made up of basic factors or components just as the product and these must be measured. They may all be measured together in a total evaluation of the entire process or they may be measured separately depending on the purposes. Larson has suggested a framework for total evaluation which includes the components of administration, leadership, facilities, equipment, activities, and participation (7–268). Just as the components of the product are inexorably related, so are the components of the process. For purposes of this chapter the following components of the process will be discussed with their implication for evaluation: curriculum, methodology, staff (teacher, administrator, etc.), and the total program.

The inevitable question always arises: "Who does the evaluating?" This depends on the nature of the component and the purposes for which the data will be used. Ultimately the primary purpose of any evaluation is the improvement of the process so that it will become more effective in producing the good product. When it is feasible, evaluation should be the self-appraisal type where the staff evaluates its own program or the teacher evaluates himself. This approach has merit because it becomes one of the best means of in-service training. However, there are times when the purposes of evaluation can best be met by evaluation from outside the staff. This outside interest might include the students, the parents and evaluation teams of experts.

Evaluation of the Staff (Teacher Evaluation)

Teacher evaluation is an old subject and the National Education Association states that more time and research money have gone into studies relating to it than any other facet of education. Historically, it has been a most controversial topic in education and has long been unpopular with most teachers. In general teacher evaluation serves two purposes: (1) for the improvement of instruction and (2) for sound administrative decisions affecting the teacher such as salary, promotion, tenure, re-employment, placement, and transfer. The latter use has been called "merit rating." This does not necessarily mean that the two purposes are dichotomous for even evaluation for the purpose of merit presumably could be an incentive toward improvement of teaching. Therefore, the one overriding goal of evaluation of teachers is improvement of teaching.

Time and space are too limited to dwell longer on merit ratings. However, it appears that the idea behind it is logical since it follows a democratic premise that all men should be paid what they are worth. It would get away from the sacred white cow— training and years of teaching experience—which has always dominated as an easy way out for administrators when salary and promotion are involved. Merit ratings have failed in the past because no adequate basis for a teacher's worth could be agreed upon, and there was no acceptable way of adequately and fairly judging and measuring the worth, if it could be established. The NEA recommends that efforts be made to develop teacher evaluation programs through identification of the following three things: (1) What are the factors that determine professional competencies? (2) What are the methods or techniques of evaluating these identified competencies? (3) What are the ways of recognizing professional competencies once they have been identified? (9).

Who evaluates teachers? In the past it has usually been done by administrators and supervisors with some participation by the teacher's peers and in a more limited sense by the student. While parents rarely share in a formal evaluation, they do make evaluations, and often evaluators are very much aware of parents' opinions. The most important person to share in evaluation, however, is the teacher being evaluated. Whether the teacher is being rated for merit or for the improvement of teaching, the most important educational value to accrue as a result of evaluation is his "improvement in teaching." If this is to occur, however, it can come about only through the teacher's own initiative. Ultimately there must be self-evaluation.

A suggested "How" of evaluation would include these steps: *First*, the initial planning must be a cooperative affair between the teachers and the administration at which time the criteria for the basis of evaluation are established—the characteristics of a good teacher. These may well vary according to the different disciplines. *Second*, the evaluation instrument can be designed. There are many possibilities here such as forms, check lists, rating scales, open narrative types and the like. *Third*, the evaluation itself must be made. A general principle to follow here is to take a positive approach whereby the teacher's strengths are highlighted rather than weaknesses. This does not mean that weaknesses can't be revealed, but experience has shown that the positive approach offsets the problem of low teacher morale which has characterized most of the evaluation programs in the past.

The evaluation itself should follow certain well-defined procedures. *First*, there is self-evaluation by the teacher on forms designed for that purpose. *Second*, there is evaluation of the teacher by one or more evaluators. *Third*, there is a review and discussion between the evaluated and the evaluators. *Fourth*, there should be a follow-up. Three more steps might be added at this point. *Fifth*, there should be a procedure for adjudication of disputed evaluations especially if some form of merit is involved. *Sixth*, there should be a continuous evaluation of the evaluating system with both teachers and administrators involved. *Seventh*, so there will be a two-way process, there should be an evaluation of the administration by the teachers.

Some of the methods which have been used are observations, conferences, comments from the parents, evaluation of students, record of students' achievements, and rating scales.

What are the specific factors that are usually covered in teacher evaluation? These vary of course and hardly fall into well-defined categories. However, for sake of expediency, they have been classified by McGee (8) into the following four categories: (1) *personal qualities*

such as character, poise, social amenities, grooming, sense of humor, health, vitality and the like, (2) *teaching performance* such as knowledge of subject matter and instructional skills, (3) *professional qualities* such as ethics, pride in the profession, desire for improvement, support of authorized policies and procedures, and willingness to take advantage of in-service training opportunities and (4) *relationship* with the students, parents, staff, administration, school, community and professional groups.

Evaluation of the Curriculum

The principle was emphasized in the last chapter that curriculum development is a continuous dynamic process. The first part of this chapter, in a philosophical approach to measurement, expressed the point that education, too, is an ongoing process in the form of a cycle starting with the formulation of objectives, continuing with the establishment of processes and determination of methodology, and ending in evaluation before the entire cycle is repeated. These two points of view imply that the curriculum should be constantly evaluated by all persons involved in any manner that could lead to its improvement. While there are formal techniques to evaluate the program as a part of the total process, perhaps the best approach is a more informal one taken by the staff as they review, discuss and appraise various curricular aspects in terms of how well they think original objectives have been met.

This review and evaluation should answer the question of how good is the curriculum which has been prescribed for the student. This area of restudy and evaluation is closely related to curriculum study and construction. In reviewing the existing curriculum, it seeks answers to such questions as: Is the program of activities varied and broad enough? Does it show progression and a sequential arrangement of learning experiences from one level to the next? Is it adapted to the age and sex needs of both boys and girls? Does it provide a balanced program of experiences? Is it flexible to meet the changing circumstances? Are the coeducational experiences adequate? Does it provide for the needs of the more gifted students? For the "fundamentals" or lowest group in motor skills? Are the needs of the handicapped being met through an adapted program?

In some situations the extracurricular activities are considered a part of the total school curricula. If this is the case, intramural and interschool programs should become a part of the evaluation too. There are instruments in the form of rating scales and check lists to evaluate the interschool program. The best known of these is "The Check List of School Athletics" by the Educational Policies Commission (5).

Evaluation of Methodology

It is difficult to separate the teacher from the teaching act just as it is difficult to separate them both from the curriculum. In a sense, then, this discussion of methodology cannot be separated entirely from the last two units on evaluation of the teacher and the curriculum. However, in a well-organized and -administered physical education program there are established ways of approach, instructional procedures and methods of doing things. These need to be reviewed, discussed and evaluated as does the curriculum. This component of the total process deals with the methods and materials staff members employ along with the equipment and facilities to make the curriculum work. It is concerned with the techniques of actually teaching the class, class management, class administrative details, demonstrations, explanations, and drill techniques. Also involved are the kinds of materials which are used as audio-visual aids, charts, models, chalk boards, bulletin boards, and textbooks and reference materials. Even the ways the product and the process are to be evaluated and the methods of administration of the selected tests and measures are a part of methodology.

Evaluation of the Total Process

Instead of evaluating the various aspects separately, there is an approach to the total process for measurement. Some purposes make it necessary to learn about the total situation. This includes not only the leadership, curriculum and methodology but also such facets as philosophy, the organization and administration aspects, equipment, outdoor and indoor facilities, intramurals, interschool athletics and participation, all of which involves time requirements and the uses made of time.

Numerous tools can be used for evaluating this total process. In general the devices which have been employed for the most part are check-lists and rating scales. In a rating scale, for example, the standards which have been included conform to those established by experts in physical education. The scale is constructed with categories so they can be checked to indicate the extent of compliance with the accepted standard. This may be just a plain "yes" or "no" or in some cases a third category of "U" added for undecided. In others, the categories may be a simple three-point scale or five-point scale. The points on the scale are usually defined to indicate the degree of compliance with the standard.

The purpose of most of these tools is to reveal weaknesses. When weak areas are revealed, attention can be given to ways and means of improvement. Therefore, the primary purpose of such evaluation is process improvement. In some cases evaluation is a step toward accreditation. These criteria tools are available at the elementary, the secondary and college levels. They are designed so that an individual, a staff or an evaluation team may apply them. Generally when a school seeks accreditation on the basis of an evaluation by a team of evaluators, the physical education staff is required to do a self-study and an evaluation. This self-evaluation is then used by the evaluators as a part of their total evaluation.

However, since evaluation is a constant ongoing process and as many people should share in it as possible, the rating scale or check-list is not the final answer. Another facet of evaluation is through the students. What the students think and how they view the total program can be found through rating scales and through interest questionnaires. The data, when obtained from these sources, should be used to supplement information from other facets of the evaluation processes. Student evaluation, although not always highly reliable and valid, does provide a more complete picture and has the added advantage of involving the student actively in evaluation and curriculum construction processes.

The following are some of the best known devices for assaying the total process of physical education:

1. LaPorte Health and Physical Education Score Card No. I (For elementary schools) (6).

2. LaPorte Health and Physical Education Score Card No. II (For secondary schools) (6).

3. The State of New York Check List for Physical Education (15).

4. Arkansas—A Physical Education Checklist for Secondary Schools (16).

5. Ohio Evaluative Criteria for Physical Education (12).

6. Physical Education for Girls—Evaluative Criteria. 1960 Edition. E–15 (10).

7. Physical Education for Boys—Evaluative Criteria. 1960 Edition. D–14 (11).

8. AAHPER School Community Fitness Inventory (2).

REFERENCES

1. AAHPER: *Knowledge and Understanding in Physical Education.* Washington, D.C., NEA, 1969.
2. AAHPER: *Your Community—School-Community Fitness Inventory.* National Education Association, 1959, pp. 14–28.
3. Barrow, Harold M., and Rosemary McGee: *A Practical Approach to Measurement in Physical Education.* Philadelphia, Lea & Febiger, 1964.
4. Bookwalter, Karl W.: A National Survey of Health and Physical Education for Boys in High School, 1950–54. *Professional Contributions.* American Academy of Physical Education, No. 4, 1955 pp. 1–11.
5. Educational Policies Commission: Checklist on School Athletics. *School Athletics.* Washington, D.C., National Education Association, 1954, pp. 88–97.
6. LaPorte, William Ralph: *The Physical Education Curriculum* (Edited by John M. Cooper). Los Angeles, Calif., College Book Store, 1968.
7. Larson, L. A., and R. D. Yocum: *Measurement and Evaluation in Physical, Health, and Recreation Education.* St. Louis, C. V. Mosby Company, 1951.
8. McGee, Rosemary: Methods of Evaluating Teachers. Proceedings: 36th Annual Convention, Southern District, AAHPER, Memphis, Tenn. February, 1969.
9. National Education Association: Merit Provisions in Teachers' Salary Schedules, 1967–68. NEA Research Memo, NEA Research Division, Washington, D.C.
10. National Study of Secondary School Evaluation: *Evaluative Criteria—Physical Education for Girls,* 1960 Edition. Washington, D.C.
11. National Study of Secondary School Evaluation: *Evaluative Criteria—Physical Education for Boys,* 1960 Edition, Washington, D.C.
12. Ohio Association for Health, Physical Education and Recreation: *Evaluative Criteria for Physical Education.* (Approved by State Department of Education.) Columbus, Ohio, 1957.
13. Phillips, Marjorie, and Karl W. Bookwalter: Three Little Words. The Physical Educator, Vol. 5, March, 1948, p. 21.

14. Staley, Seward C.: *Curriculum in Sports.* Philadelphia, W. B. Saunders Company, 1935.

15. State of New York: *Check List for Physical Education.* Albany, Division of Health and Physical Education, State Education Department, New York.

16. State of Arkansas: *A Physical Education Check List for Secondary Schools.* Little Rock, Arkansas, Division of Instructional Services, State Education Department, 1957, pp. 28–34.

Index